Mrs a. m. High

DISCARDED

B. a. H.
Christmas 1958

University of Winnipeg, 515 Portage Ave., Winnipeg, MB. R3B 2E9 Canada

DISCARDED

GEORGINA HOGARTH
and the Dickens Circle

GEORGINA HOGARTH, c. 1905
Photograph by Charlotte Roche
By courtesy of Henry Charles Dickens, O.B.E.

PR
4586
A4
1957

GEORGINA HOGARTH

and the Dickens Circle

ARTHUR A. ADRIAN

LONDON
OXFORD UNIVERSITY PRESS
NEW YORK   TORONTO
1957

Oxford University Press, Amen House, London E.C.4

GLASGOW   NEW YORK   TORONTO   MELBOURNE   WELLINGTON
BOMBAY   CALCUTTA   MADRAS   KARACHI
CAPE TOWN   IBADAN   NAIROBI   ACCRA   SINGAPORE

© Oxford University Press, 1957

PRINTED IN GREAT BRITAIN

'She is the active spirit
of the house, and the children
dote upon her.'

Letter of Charles Dickens

To the memory of

FINLEY M. K. FOSTER

who introduced me to Dickensian studies

Preface

I N spite of her long and close association with Dickens, his children, and his friends, Georgina Hogarth has hitherto inspired no biography. It is curious that she should have been neglected when other women whose association with the novelist was briefer and no more significant—notably Maria Beadnell and Ellen Ternan—have received book-length consideration. To be sure, as Dickens's sister-in-law and confidante she has of necessity been given some attention by his biographers, but frequently with negative results. If only a few of her detractors have accepted the unsavoury gossip aimed at her from irresponsible quarters, more have condemned her as a clever and ruthless schemer bent on usurping the position of her sister, Catherine Dickens. Where criticism of her has not advanced such unsupportable charges, she has usually emerged only as a shadowy figure or an enigma.

To such treatments there are, happily, exceptions, particularly the definitive biography of Dickens by Professor Edgar Johnson, which has appraised Miss Hogarth objectively. Understandably, however, the focus of that work has not permitted a detailed chronicle of her life as a member of Dickens's household from 1842 to 1870 nor any consideration whatever of her forty-seven years after the novelist's death.

Such emphasis has been the purpose of my study, which reviews her connection not only with Dickens himself but with his family circle and his friends. Though Part One covers what to most Dickensians must be familiar territory, especially since the appearance of Professor Johnson's comprehensive two-volume work, to ignore this material would be to ignore thirty-eight years of Miss Hogarth's life. While I have tried to summarize and condense wherever possible, I have not hesitated to introduce well-known details whenever they were needed to point up interpretations of character or prepare the reader for Miss Hogarth's association with Dickens's children and friends in the second half of the book. If this work seems to devote a disproportionate amount of space to Dickens and his family, it is because her relationship with them was not only the mainspring of her life, but also the chief justification for a biography of her.

In presenting this portrait of Georgina Hogarth, I have let the evidence speak for itself. Dickens's letters to her, both published

and unpublished; his recorded comments on her; her own considerable correspondence with close friends during the latter half of her
life, particularly with Mrs. James T. Fields; and the testimony of
family and others who knew her intimately—on such sources I have
relied heavily. But I have not ventured into a highly technical area
which should be reserved for professional psychologists. Though to
many readers the more elementary psychological implications of my
material will be obvious, as a layman I have eschewed the sort of
analysis which, in unskilled hands, could only have led to pseudo-
scientific conclusions.

Where quotations from unpublished sources have been introduced,
I have made every effort to render the originals accurately, but, for
the sake of clarity, have often taken the liberty of changing to semi-
colons or periods the dashes to whose use Miss Hogarth was addicted.
At times the transcription of her letters posed difficulties, for, by
her own admission, her hand was frequently almost illegible. For
consistency I have regularized the spelling of 'Georgy', 'Katey', and
'Mamie', which in the family letters are written at different periods
in two or three ways, often by the same person.

If the portrait that emerges from this study reveals a woman with
human shortcomings, it also presents a person of generous impulses,
strong loyalties, and great perceptiveness. Above all, it is the story
of unfaltering devotion to the genius of Dickens, a devotion by
which Georgina Hogarth justified her very existence.

A. A. A.

Cleveland, Ohio
January 1957.

Contents

List of Illustrations

Acknowledgements

WITHOUT much valuable aid given me during the past five years, this book could not have been written. From the earliest stages of my research to the completion of my final manuscript I have had the support of numerous persons and institutions. I take pleasure in acknowledging my gratitude to all of them.

To members of the Dickens family, first of all, I am deeply indebted for a generous endorsement of my undertaking. Mr. Henry Charles Dickens, O.B.E., has not only given me permission to quote from unpublished letters but has also shared with me his recollections of his Aunt Georgina and has provided me with the frontispiece of my book. Further choice details came from two of his sisters, Mrs. Elaine Waley and Mrs. Olive Shuckburgh. Still another Dickens descendant, the late Mrs. Sydney Whinney, recalled for me, with a vitality and enthusiasm that belied her eighty-four years, her association with 'Auntie'.

Indispensable to my work have been the rich collections of letters and documents in libraries and other institutions. In America I have had free access to manuscripts in the Henry E. Huntington Library and Art Gallery, the Pierpont Morgan Library, and the Berg Collection of the New York Public Library. To their officers and staffs I am considerably obligated, especially to Miss Mary Isabel Fry, Miss Phyllis Rigney, Dr. Herbert C. Schulz (Curator of Manuscripts), and Mr. Tyrus G. Harmsen (Cataloguer) of the Huntington; to Mr. Herbert Cahoon, Curator of Autograph Manuscripts at the Pierpont Morgan; and to Dr. John Gordan, Director of the Berg Collection, and his assistant, Miss Adelaide Smith. Also invaluable have been certain unpublished portions of Mrs. James T. Fields's diaries, owned by the Massachusetts Historical Society of Boston. I am grateful to the Society for permission to publish my findings and to Mr. Stephen T. Riley, Director of the Library, for checking numerous passages in my transcripts. To the William Andrews Clark Memorial Library of the University of California at Los Angeles I am also grateful for permission to quote from one of its letters.

In Great Britain I likewise had ready access to useful materials. To the Trustees of the Dickens House, London, I am indebted for permission to examine and reproduce extracts from its remarkable holdings. To Miss Doris Minards, its librarian, and to Mr. Leslie Staples, Editor of the *Dickensian*, I am especially grateful for a sincere interest in my work. They have directed me to valuable sources of information, answered numerous inquiries, and furnished some of my illustrations. I am further indebted to the Dean and Chapter of Westminster and to Mr. Lawrence E. Tanner, the Keeper of the Muniments of Westminster Abbey; to the Victoria and Albert Museum, especially to the Keeper of the Library, Mr. Arthur Wheen, and to Mr. G. W. Nash, Curator of the

Enthoven Theatre Collection; to the National Library of Scotland and particularly to Mr. J. S. Ritchie for his prompt and generous response to numerous inquiries; to Mr. W. A. Taylor, Borough of Saint Pancras Public Library, London; and to Eastgate House, Rochester.

Among the collections in private hands I have found extraordinarily valuable the large body of Ouvry Papers at 66 Lincoln's Inn Fields, London. To the owner, Sir Leslie Farrer, K.C.V.O., I am greatly indebted for the privilege of studying and transcribing some of this material, and for the many courtesies extended me at the offices of Farrer & Company. To Mr. William Miller of Brighton I am deeply grateful for putting at my disposal his wealth of holographs and other treasures, and for repeatedly drawing on his extensive knowledge of Dickensiana to answer my questions. Several others have given me permission to quote from letters in their possession: Lady Hermione Cobbold, Mrs. Mary Walker, and Mr. S. E. Budden. To Mr. A. J. Sluman of Henry Sotheran, Ltd., I am grateful for allowing me to examine and reproduce portions of a letter included in the valuable 'Dora Collection' of that firm.

Generous, too, has been the assistance given me by several Victorian scholars. Mr. K. J. Fielding has put me greatly in his debt by calling my attention to the Ouvry Papers and allowing me to utilize some of his discoveries. On his extensive publications I have drawn heavily, particularly for Chapter Five. From time to time, furthermore, he has sent me transcripts of significant documents. Information and helpful suggestions have come also from another well-informed Dickensian, Mr. W. J. Carlton. From the late Humphry House I received permission to use unpublished correspondence which will appear in the forthcoming edition of Dickens's letters. From his wife, Mrs. Madeline E. House, I have had transcripts of valuable manuscripts and helpful replies to queries. To Professor J. Lee Harlan I am indebted for copies of important Forster letters; and to Professor Gerald G. Grubb, for directing me to significant sources of information. Mrs. Kathleen Tillotson and Professor Clyde K. Hyder have put me heavily in their debt by reading my manuscript and suggesting improvements. To Professor Hyder I owe my final choice of title.

Still others have put their specialized knowledge and services at my disposal. Mrs. Lisa G. Puckle gave me some treasured letters written to her father, Sir Nevil Macready, by Georgina Hogarth; and called up many interesting memories. Similarly helpful was the information given me by Miss Gladys Storey, O.B.E., relative to her association with Kate Perugini, Dickens's second daughter. Generous responses to miscellaneous requests have come from Mrs. Gladys Reece; Mr. George Almond; Mr. Alec Robertson; Mr. Felix Aylmer; Major C. E. Pym, C.B.E., D.L.; Mr. B. Eldridge, Society for Army Research; Mr. H. A. Johnston, Public Record Office; Mr. Emerson Greenway, Director of the Free Library of Philadelphia; Miss Winifred A. Myers, of Myers and Company, Booksellers, London; and Miss Hebe Elsna. Mr. J. Jarman transcribed some letters in the Fitzgerald Collection, Eastgate House, for me; Professor Carl Woodring lent me photostats of two Georgina Hogarth letters; Professor James Austen let me use his microfilm of the Fields Papers; and Miss W. Stewart Burt, Gad's Hill Place, Kent, graciously conducted me through Dickens's last home.

For generous grants-in-aid of research I express heartfelt thanks to the American Philosophical Society, to the Henry E. Huntington Library and Art Gallery, and to the Modern Language Association of America.

I am grateful also to Western Reserve University for granting me sabbatical leave to work on my book, and to the staff of the University Library for many courtesies. To the Cleveland Public Library, and especially to Miss Marie Corrigan, Director of the Literature Division, I am indebted for long-time loans of indispensable materials.

My greatest indebtedness is to my wife, Vonna Hicks Adrian. Since the completion of my preliminary draft in the spring of 1955, she has laboured with me, subjecting my findings to rigorous scrutiny and working tirelessly on the revisions of my manuscript. There is hardly a paragraph of this book that does not bear her imprint. Quick to discern significant implications, she has repeatedly made me aware of interpretations that would otherwise have been lost to these pages. For time and help cheerfully given, at a sacrifice of her own creative writing activities, I am deeply grateful.

PART ONE

1835-1870

Chapter One

THE GENESIS OF AUNT GEORGY

It was an evening in early summer, two years before the young Victoria mounted the English throne. In Fulham Road, Chelsea, an indolent breeze floated the scent of nearby orchards into the drawing room where George Hogarth and his large family were tranquilly assembled.[1] Suddenly, though, their privacy was disrupted as, through one of the tall french windows opening on the garden, a sailor lad leaped into the room and danced a hornpipe to his own whistled accompaniment. Almost before the Hogarths realized what was happening he had scampered out again. After a brief interval the door opened and in came the suitor whom Catherine, the eldest daughter, had been expecting. It was Charles Dickens, a young newspaper reporter. Having disposed of the sailor uniform, borrowed for the performance, he betrayed no evidence of his recent impersonation, but shook hands decorously all around. The startled faces of the family proving too much, however, he broke into a hearty laugh.[2]

On no one did this prank leave a more vivid impression than on eight-year-old Georgina Hogarth, a blue-eyed child dressed—so the mode dictated—in a quaint counterpart of her older sister's frock: slim-waisted, with ballooning sleeves and long, wide skirts, beneath which peeped an inch or two of white pantaloon frills. Decades later, as an old lady in a beribboned cap, she was to delight her grandnieces and grandnephews with accounts of the sailor episode, the first bead in her cherished rosary of Dickens memories. For the child Georgina was destined to become the confidante of Charles Dickens—'the best and truest friend man ever had', he was to call her in his zenith years. But if he noticed the little girl now, it may have been only because her name touched a sentimental chord. While still in his teens, so tradition has it, he had admired and perhaps considered marrying one Georgina Ross, but her family, like Maria Beadnell's several years later, had not smiled on a young man of such slender means and undistinguished background.[3]

Who were the Hogarths with whom this theatrical young man was soon to ally himself? At this time they had been in London only a

year. Originally they had lived in Edinburgh. There, in that citadel
of the legal profession, George Hogarth, the father, had grown up
and been educated for the law. At the age of twenty-seven, his
apprenticeship finished, he had been admitted to the practice of Scots
law. Four years later, in 1814, he had married Georgina Thomson,
daughter of George Thomson, the amateur musician and publisher,
who is remembered today chiefly as the friend of Robert Burns.[4]

Because of the young wife's background and the husband's inclina-
tions the couple were part of a musical and literary environment
from the beginning of their marriage. When two years later
Hogarth's sister married James Ballantyne of the ill-fated publishing firm which bankrupted Sir Walter Scott, Hogarth became the
intimate of the novelist, as well as of J. G. Lockhart and others in the
intellectual aristocracy of Edinburgh. Soon he was Scott's valued
legal adviser, heavily relied upon when the publishing firm failed.[5]
Lockhart spoke of him as a 'gentleman . . . well known in the literary
world; especially by a History of Music, of which all who understand
that science speak highly.'[6]

Indeed, music, more than law, was Hogarth's forte. A violon-
cellist and composer, he had served as joint secretary for the first
Edinburgh Musical Festival in 1815. He also acquired a reputation
as a music critic with his pieces in the Edinburgh *Courant*.[7] As a
lawyer, though, he was less successful. By January of 1827, when
the Hogarths were expecting their eighth child, he had begun to
doubt whether the legal profession could be counted upon to support his family adequately. The new baby, who was given her
mother's name, arrived on 22nd January, three weeks after the
Hogmanay celebrations and three days before that other great Scottish occasion, the birthday of Robert Burns. At this time the
Hogarths were living at 2 Nelson Street, in the New Town, only a
short walk down the steep slope from Princes Street. Before little
Georgina was a year old, they moved to 19 Albany Street in the
immediate vicinity.[8] Nearby were the lodgings at 6 St. David Street,
where Scott, newly a widower, had stayed in 1826 during the darkest
months of his debt and sorrow. In the same neighbourhood were
houses occupied only a few years earlier by David Hume, Adam
Smith, and William Robertson.

But another change of scene was already imminent, for in 1830,
after subscribing himself Writer to the Signet for full twenty years,
Hogarth, then forty-seven, abandoned the law. Perhaps he had no
talent for advancing himself financially, or at any rate was unable
to do so without initial capital. His lack of funds and the keen competition from 'other members of a profession so much overstocked'

were the reasons he gave Scott in a letter announcing his decision
to relinquish law and 'do something for my family in another way'.[9]
The other way was to be the congenial path of journalism, for which
he had already demonstrated his fitness.

Having failed to find an editorship in London, in spite of the
recommendation solicited from Scott,[10] he became interested in
Halifax, in the West Riding of Yorkshire, attracted, perhaps, as
much by its musical festival as by the invitation of the local Conservative Party to found and edit a weekly newspaper there. When
Georgina was four, the family therefore left Edinburgh, then in its
golden age as the Athens of the North, and settled in the provincial
city. The following year, 1832, Hogarth launched the Halifax
Guardian, with the ambitious aim of returning a Conservative candidate in a red-hot radical town.[11] Since only two issues of the
Guardian preceded the election, the party's failure that year is not
surprising.[12] The next year, however, saw a Conservative victory.
At the ball celebrating this triumph, each lady received an exqui-
sitely bound copy of a literary annual, *The White Rose of York*,
edited by Hogarth. Dedicated 'To Her Most Gracious Majesty,
Adelaide, the Queen,' the silver-stamped purple volume, made up
largely of local contributions, reflected in its Preface the pride of the
editor in his newly adopted town and county, an attitude which
must have endeared him locally. He served the community still
further by helping to found the Halifax Orchestral Society and by
making his home a cultural centre, frequented by musical amateurs
of the district. His wife shared this musical interest, an inheritance
from her father, who had published the five-volume *Select Scottish
Airs*, a work which doubtless graced the Hogarth musical library.
Like his son-in-law, Thomson had been one of the directors of the
first Edinburgh Musical Festival.[13] To her children Mrs. Hogarth
must have told the story of how their Grandpapa Thomson had carried on a bulky four-year correspondence with Robert Burns, whom
he had commissioned to supply the words to a number of old Scottish
folk tunes, and she would hardly have neglected to point out to her
brood their distinguished grandfather's likeness by the great
Raeburn. Still another, by W. S. Watson, would one day hang in
the National Portrait Gallery in Edinburgh.[14]

That the Hogarths in Halifax, as in Edinburgh, were richer in culture and family pride than in worldly goods, may be gathered partly
from figures indicating the father's income as Georgina approached
her sixth birthday. A typical issue of the *Guardian*, that of 1
December 1832, brought in only £28 4s. 7d., out of which came all
production expenses.[15] What remained went for the week's support

of a large family. Obviously Hogarth needed to supplement these
earnings by other ventures. One such was the instruction of private
pupils, as announced in the Halifax *Guardian*:

To Parents and Guardians

*Mr. Hogarth begs leave to state, that during the holidays, he
proposes giving* PRIVATE LESSONS *in the* CLASSICS, MATHE-
MATICS, ARITHMETIC, BELLES LETTRES, *and the* PRACTICE
OF ENGLISH COMPOSITION, *either at his own house or at the
residence of the Pupil as may be found more convenient.
Mr. Hogarth's terms, &c, may be known by application to
him at his House, 8 Clare Place, Ward's End, Halifax,
4 December 1833.*[16]

Besides making himself available as a tutor, Hogarth compiled a
small geography and short histories of England and Rome. Designed
primarily for elementary classes, these sold at tenpence each and
were used in several of the smaller private schools of Halifax.[17] In
addition, he met a number of other publication commitments.

Early in 1834 came the move which brought three of his daughters
into the Dickens orbit. Following a disagreement with his proprietors, Hogarth resigned the editorship of the Halifax *Guardian* and
took his family to London, where he joined the staff of the *Morning
Chronicle* as music critic. Here he was to meet his future son-in-law,
Charles Dickens, the young journalist who was to write a series of
Street Sketches for this paper. When some months later an offshoot,
the *Evening Chronicle*, was projected, Hogarth, as the newly
appointed editor, asked the young author for a contribution to launch
the first issue. Dickens complied, welcoming the prospect of additional earnings.[18] Accordingly the first of his twenty *Sketches of
London*, signed 'Boz', appeared in the introductory number, exactly
one week before his twenty-third birthday. His weekly salary was
thereupon raised from five to seven guineas.

Soon his relations with Hogarth became quite cordial. With the
older journalist's help he was able to place his libretto, *The Village
Coquettes*, for which John Hullah had composed the music.[19] Before
long he was visiting the Hogarth home, where he was attracted to
Catherine, a buxom young lady whose heavy-lidded blue eyes gave
her an indolent look. With her cultivated manners, fresh colouring,
and voluptuous curves she was quite attractive, in spite of a noticeable lack of chin. The attachment became so compelling that, at the
time of the sailor prank, Dickens had temporarily taken lodgings just
around the corner from her house. It was his second serious affair,

an earlier one with the capricious Maria Beadnell having ended
abruptly in a lovers' quarrel. Between visits he sent Catherine
frequent notes, often through his younger brother Fred, who shared
his rooms. Presently 'Dearest Kate' or 'Katie' replaced the formal
'My dearest Catherine'. Sometimes he asked her to pay a morning
visit to his rooms, usually around ten-thirty or eleven, for his
reporting kept him out late at night. As for the proprieties, they
were satisfied by the presence of Mary, the next younger sister, a
great favourite of his. 'Will you indulge me by making breakfast for
me this morning?' he once asked Catherine. 'It will give me pleasure;
I hope will give you no trouble; and I am sure will be excellent practice for you against Christmas next.'[20] It was almost the cajoling
tone one might take with a child whose training must be achieved
by tactful reasoning and kindly persuasion.

Finally, with the consent of Catherine's parents, the couple
planned an early spring marriage. Dickens was proud of his
betrothed—proud, especially, of his alliance with gentlefolk of distinction. To his uncle, Thomas Barrow, he boasted that Catherine
was the daughter of 'one of the most eminent among the literati of
Edinburgh'.[21] In the early months of 1836, as the wedding day drew
near, he alternated between playful excitement and critical admoni-
tions. He sent his Katie '1000000000000 kisses'. She was his 'own
dearest Pig', his 'dearest Wig', his 'darling Tatie', his 'dear Mouse'.
'Here's another day off the fortnight. Hurrah!' he exclaimed in
March. But he showed little indulgence toward her petulant accusations when duty kept him away. Though he sometimes inquired
playfully whether she felt 'coss' with him, he also made it plain that
his work was exacting, that its success was necessary to their future,
and that her childish attitudes of suspicion and sulkiness 'in anyone
else would have annoyed me greatly'. Yet, significantly, he felt con-
strained to defend himself by a protest of 'working as a duty, and
not as a pleasure'.[22] Plainly, Catherine lacked sympathy with the
satisfactions of artistic creation, and could excuse her lover for preoccupation with literary activity only if it was presented as an
arduous duty. Therefore he wrote her only of the more prosy aspects
of his work: the daily schedule of composition, publishing contracts,
appointments. He discussed with her no ideas as such, nor did he
exhibit the sparkle that characterized his other correspondence. If
he saved this side of his nature for their tête-à-têtes, the letters give
no hint of it.

March found the Hogarths in the midst of modest wedding preparations, too simple to linger in the memory of little Georgina. On
Saturday, 2nd April, the marriage took place at St. Luke's Church,

Chelsea. Though Charles Kingsley's father was the rector here, it was a curate who read the vows. Writing of the event in after years Thomas Beard, the bridegroom's friend and best man, called it 'an altogether quiet bit of business. . . . To the best of my recollection, the only persons present beyond the members of the Dickens and Hogarth families were Macrone, the publisher of the *Sketches by Boz*, and myself.'[23] On Henry Burnett, Dickens's brother-in-law, the wedding made a similar impression. 'The breakfast was the quietest possible,' he recalled. 'A few common, pleasant things were said, healths were drunk with a few words said by either party—yet all things passed off very pleasantly, and all seemed happy, not the least so Dickens and his young girlish wife. She was a bright, pleasant bride, dressed in the simplest and neatest manner, and looked better perhaps than if she had been enabled to aim at something more.' Burnett described Catherine's father as 'a gentleman in feeling and education', one who 'would not have made any show if he had possessed the means'.[24]

In this last particular the Hogarths and the Dickenses were, perhaps, not strictly in accord. Still, the marriage had united two whose background had one significant point in common: lack of worldly substance. Both families had attempted to supplement their regular incomes by offering private instruction. As Catherine's father had advertised in the Halifax *Guardian* for pupils, so Charles's mother had once posted on her door a plaque announcing her intention of opening a school for small children. It is not known whether Hogarth was more successful than Mrs. John Dickens, who waited in vain for the first applicant. The fathers of both families were at times losers in the struggle against poverty. The story of John Dickens's imprisonment for debt is too well known to require repeating. Even after his three months in the Marshalsea in 1824, he was never free from financial embarrassment, but required constant assistance from Charles. Similarly Hogarth, after his Edinburgh failure, continued to have money troubles. In later years, according to one source, he wrote a friend from debtors' prison, remarking that Catherine's husband, though very kind, had been unable to help him in his present predicament.[25]

Of the events immediately preceding and following the wedding, Georgina was to retain few memories. Some delightful musical evenings with Dickens in attendance and her father as chief performer, an isolated incident or two during the courtship, and finally the arrival of the wedding morning—these were her recollections as she looked back in later years. She did not even witness the ceremony at the church, but stayed at home with her younger brother and sister, Edward and Helen, the twins whose birth in Halifax had brought to nine the number of Hogarth children then living—five sons and four daughters, another daughter having died in infancy.[26] However, she saw the couple leave on their honeymoon, which they spent in Chalk, a Kentish village not far from Chatham, where the bridegroom had lived during the happiest part of his childhood. And when Catherine and her husband returned to Chalk to celebrate their first anniversary, she visited them in the honeymoon cottage, run by a Mrs. Nash who let lodgings.[27]

Of Georgina herself little has been recorded from this childhood period. Whether she attended a private school, as did her older sisters in Halifax,[28] or whether her father taught her at home, is not known. Her later reputation as a woman of culture and taste indicates that her girlhood must have laid the foundation for the musical and intellectual attainments of her maturity. The Hogarth background would obviously have provided ample opportunity for her development.

For these years far more is known about Mary Hogarth, the gentle sister between Catherine and Georgina. Already fond of her during his courting days, Dickens had her join him and his bride when they went to housekeeping. He found her an 'amiable companion, sympathising with all my thoughts and feelings more than anyone I knew ever did or will. . . .'[29] Possibly her cheerful charms threw Catherine somewhat into the shade as the couple adjusted to the overcrowded rooms at Furnival's Inn, where Dickens had had his bachelor quarters. As his brother Fred was also a member of the household, the four of them doubtless managed with some difficulty. Surely the arrival of the first child, Charles Culliford Boz, on 6 January 1837, must have complicated matters enormously.

In April of 1837, however, having achieved sudden fame with The Pickwick Papers, Dickens considered his prospects bright enough to warrant a move to a three-story house at 48 Doughty Street, near Gray's Inn. But this pleasure in the new home was short lived, for the next month Mary Hogarth died. She had accompanied Catherine and him to the theatre one evening, apparently in the best of health and spirits. Taken ill upon her return, she died in his arms the following afternoon. 'Since our marriage she has been the peace and life of our home—the admired of all for her beauty and excellence— I could have better spared a much nearer relation or an older friend, for she has been to us what we can never replace, and has left a blank which no one who ever knew her can have the faintest hope of seeing supplied,' he wrote Mary's grandfather the day after her death.[30] From that time on he was to wear the ring he had slipped from her lifeless finger. That he should have felt the presence of an outsider necessary to complete his domestic happiness in the first year of his marriage suggests that something was even then lacking in the match.

Though Catherine suffered a miscarriage, brought on, her husband believed, by the agitation following Mary's death, she sensibly reconciled herself to the loss of her sister and in ten days' time, he reported to Tom Beard, was 'so calm and cheerful that I wonder to see her'.[31] Her mother, however, refused to be consoled, and was still nursing her gloom on the eve of the new year: 'I wrote to Mrs. Hogarth yesterday,' her son-in-law explained, '. . . imploring her, as strongly as I could, to think of the many remaining claims upon her affection and exertions, and not to give way to unavailing grief. Her answer came to-night, and she seems hurt at my doing so—protesting that in all useful respects she is the same as ever. Meant it for the best, and still hope I did right.'[32] The incident was a faint prelude to later discord between Dickens and his mother-in-law, whom he was never to address by any name less formal than Mrs. Hogarth.

In spite of sore grief Dickens, urged on by genius and domestic responsibilities, had entered upon a period of feverish literary productivity. Keeping pace were the additions to his family: Mary (Mamie) in March of 1838 and Katey in October of the following year. By the end of 1839, with his literary success assured, he confidently took his growing family to a more pretentious home, 1 Devonshire Terrace, Regent's Park. Here, to a large room furnished as a nursery, Georgina, now entering her teens, came to play with the children. Here, too, the novelist maintained the pace of his literary output. Nor did Catherine's own productivity lag behind, for in February of 1841 a fourth child, Walter Landor, arrived. With him Dickens initiated the practice of naming his sons after noted literary figures.

Early in 1842 there developed a situation which brought Georgina entirely within the Dickens orbit. For some months the novelist had craved a change of scene and a look at American institutions. So, on 4th January, accompanied by their maid, Anne Brown, he and Catherine sailed for Boston, having prudently let Devonshire Terrace and taken a small furnished house in nearby Osnaburgh Street for Fred Dickens and the four children, who were left in the care of friends, the noted actor William Macready and his wife.[33] During the Dickenses' absence Georgina saw much of her little nieces and nephews. They in turn grew so fond of her that they babbled constantly of 'Aunt Georgy' when their parents returned in June. The result was that Dickens invited her to become a regular member of the household at Devonshire Terrace, to fill the void left by her sister's death. She was fifteen now, almost the age Mary had been on joining the Doughty Street ménage. Thus began the long association between Georgina Hogarth and Charles Dickens, a tie which strengthened with each passing year, ending only with the novelist's death in 1870.

Chapter Two
A 'PAIR OF PETTICOATS'

THE Devonshire Terrace household contrasted sharply with the comfortably shabby one which Georgina had just left. At her father's home it had not been easy to stock the larder or keep the growing children in kilts and pinafores. But these and other burdens had been somewhat lightened by an easy-going attitude. If the butcher had been forced to wait for his money, if meals had been served at odd hours, if several weeks' dust had accumulated on floors and furniture, no one had seemed greatly upset. Her new home, on the contrary, was a model of elegance and order. In keeping with the social position Dickens was determined to establish, paintings, bric-à-brac, and furnishings of the latest fashion filled the rooms. Furthermore, the household was regulated by a martinet: Dickens's daily tour of inspection allowed no slovenly lapse in the care of his home, nor was prompt payment of tradesmen's bills ever neglected. Transferred to such an environment in the plastic period of adolescence, Georgina—intelligent, impressionable, and eager to please—began cultivating her lifelong habits of punctuality and attention to detail.

Not that she was deprived of relaxation, or even hilarity—far from it. There were frequent parties, picnics, and junketings. And there were the evenings at home when the sisters bent over their fancy needlework while the young father sent the children into a riot of giggles as he roared out 'The Loving Ballad of Lord Bateman' or the ludicrous ditty about Guy Fawkes and the Gunpowder Plot.[1] Among the listeners, his ear cocked attentively, sat the white spaniel, Timber. And there was another pet, a garrulous raven who, in Georgina's first summer at Devonshire Terrace, turned maniac, falling into periodic fits, throwing 'himself wildly on his back', and plucking 'his own feathers up, by the roots'. Topping, the groom, pronounced it a case of 'aggerwation', a diagnosis scorned by the 'medical gentleman'—none less than the attendant on Queen Victoria's birds.[2] Whatever the affliction, the raven survived to amuse the household for several more years.

Yes, it was an interesting establishment in which Georgina found herself. But more worthy of her attention than the engaging Timber or the raucous raven were the four children. To them she was as dear as their own mother, perhaps dearer, for Auntie never tired of playing with them. And when worn out after a full day of games and prattle, they were ready for bed, she prompted them as they knelt beside her to say the prayer their father had composed for them: 'Pray God who has made everything and is so kind and merciful to everything he has made: pray God to bless my dear Papa and Mama, brothers and sisters, and all my relations and friends: make me a good little child and let me never be naughty and tell a lie, which is a mean and shameful thing. Make me kind to my nurses and servants and to all beggars and poor people and let me never be cruel to any dumb creature, for if I am cruel to anything, even to a poor little fly, you, who are so good, will never love me: and pray God to bless and preserve us all this night and for ever, for the sake of Jesus Christ, our Lord. Amen.'[3]

Nor could Auntie consider her responsibilities ended when the youngsters were asleep. Should one of them wake screaming from a bad dream, she was there at once to drive the bogy away. During their waking hours she took on the duties of a nursery governess. Before the children were old enough to read for themselves, she read to them from their father's manuscript of *The Life of Our Lord*, written especially for them.[4] Then, as the time came, she taught each one to read and write before his formal schooling began.

Though Georgina spent much of her day with the little ones, she was, despite her youth, treated as an adult. Socially inexperienced as yet, but fully aware of her distinguished brother-in-law's position, she strove to make herself acceptable in a circle dominated by an aristocracy of talent and an exuberance of spirit, a combination which she came increasingly to admire. Prominent in this group was William Macready, whom she first saw in *Macbeth* and whose quiet yet terrifying portrayal in the dagger scene was so vivid that she shared the murderer's tortured mind and all but saw the dagger floating in air.[5]

All the Dickens circle seemed quick to recognize the charm of this responsive blue-eyed girl whose dainty nose was 'tip-tilted like a flower'. One, the painter Daniel Maclise, had her pose barefoot, water-jug on shoulder, looking down the rapids of the St. Knighton waterfall, a background which he had sketched in Cornwall. Entitled 'The Girl at the Waterfall', the painting was shown at the Royal Academy in 1843. Dickens was so eager to possess it, yet determined not to have Maclise sacrifice it as a gift, that he bought it under an assumed name.[6]

Before long Georgina was accompanying the Dickenses to all social affairs. If she was not included in an invitation, her brother-in-law speedily dispatched a note asking permission to bring her.[7] When guests called at Devonshire Terrace she helped receive them, for Dickens considered her a social asset. Once, however, during her first year in the household, the duties of hospitality subjected her to something of an ordeal. Having learned to hypnotize from the famous Dr. John Elliotson, Dickens could not resist giving a demonstration as a parlour trick. On this occasion he experimented with his sister-in-law and wife, both of whom, Macready observed, became violently hysterical. Invited to be the next victim, the actor resisted. 'I did not like it. . . . Reasoned myself out of it', he wrote in his diary.[8] But to Georgina and Catherine, Dickens's whim was law, and neither would have thought of reasoning herself out of compliance with his demands.

Of the sisters' sixteen-year association under Dickens's roof, the 1840's were the most harmonious period. Though domestic discord lurked even then, any thought of an open marital rift, with the subsequent estrangement between Georgina and Catherine, could hardly have occurred to either. Moreover, the rise in fortunes and honour was still novel enough to call forth thankful wonder. The two might well have said with the Psalmist, 'Thou hast set my feet in a large room'. In this atmosphere the younger became a worshipper of genius in general and, most of all, of the particular genius who had achieved this miracle.[9] Performing her daily devotions, she took on added perfections in the eyes of her deity. Clearly, both Dickens and Georgina cultivated their best traits for each other, each basking in the other's approval. And if the younger sister was the elder's superior in grace, personality, and abilities, she was likewise exalted, as Mary Hogarth had been, by the becoming cloud of reverential incense which hung about her. (*Reverence* and *veneration* were ever to be her words for the proper attitude of the world toward Dickens.) Such a situation must have been a trying one to Catherine, whether or not she openly resented it.

If the idol sometimes tottered on his pedestal, his worshipper was ready with the convenient philosophy: 'A man of genius ought not to be judged with the common herd of men.'[10] This she was to apply to his major transgressions as well as to mere venial faults, such as the extreme nervous irritability and moody outbursts which beset him when the fit of creation was upon him. How different his periods of literary production from those of her father!—a difference not only of major and minor. But, after all, how different the personalities of the two men! Carlyle said of Dickens in 1844, 'I . . . discern in the inner man of him a tone of real music. . . .'[11] But the music of Dickens's personality was that of a trumpet—strident and brassy at times, perhaps, but stirring, heart-lifting. In contrast George Hogarth gave forth the music of his own mild, genial violoncello.

For the sisters, life at Devonshire Terrace was no unbroken succession of social diversion. Always their activities were bound by those of the resident genius, who alternated between feverish slavery to creation and equally feverish liberation from it. In the fit of composition he was likely, he wrote Miss Angela Burdett Coutts (the heiress whose philanthropies he helped direct), 'to be so horribly cross and surly, that the boldest fly at my approach. . . .'[12] And there were the nerve-shattering days when he could not produce a line, however hard he tried. Such times occasionally culminated in a treat for the sisters. 'In a kind of despair,' he once confessed to his friend John Forster, 'I started off at half-past two with my pair of petticoats to Richmond; and dined there!! Oh what a lovely day it was in those parts. . . .'[13] Even when the writing flowed, Georgina, Catherine, and the two little girls might be invited to end the day with a drive in an open carriage to Hampstead Heath. Rambling about, picking wild flowers, watching Dickens and the children romp, his 'pair of petticoats' would note with relief that the tensions of authorship had disappeared. After a pause at Jack Straw's Castle for refreshments, they would all drive home.[14]

Late summer usually found the family, servants and all, retreating from oppressive London to Broadstairs, a fishing village on the south-east coast. There Georgina moved quite easily between the adult world and the shouting, active world of the youngsters. From the window near which he wrote in 1843, Dickens would watch the children 'throw up impossible fortifications' in the sand.[15] Sometimes they took thrilling donkey rides, with Auntie always in attendance.[16] Through the handsome pair of ivory binoculars, Georgina's recent gift to him, their father could follow their antics from afar.[17]

When the family returned to London that autumn, the neighbours could have observed in Catherine visible promise of a fifth child. But even earlier they might have conjectured. For, they chuckled among themselves, didn't Mrs. Dickens always take a walk religiously twice a day as soon as a new baby was expected?[18] The approaching birth was somewhat overshadowed, however, by the December publication of A Christmas Carol. Never had Georgina seen Dickens more excited by composition; he 'wept and laughed and wept again' over his manuscript pages. While she and Catherine slumbered, he 'walked about the black streets of London, fifteen and twenty miles many a night. . . .' Small wonder that he 'broke out like a madman' when it was done.[19]

The occasion called for a series of seasonal celebrations: 'Such dinings, such dancings, such conjurings, such blind-man's-buffings, such theatre-goings, such kissings-out of old years and kissings-in of new ones' as Georgina had not witnessed before.[20] The climax of the holiday merriment was the usual children's party on Twelfth Night, Charley's birthday, a revel to which not only juveniles but 'some children of a larger growth' were customarily invited.[21] Catherine was then hardly presentable to do the honours, but to Georgina it was a gay evening of games, magic lantern entertainment, and conjurer's tricks. So riotous was the celebration that the pet guinea-pig later expired, convinced, according to his master, that the conjuring had killed him, though 'he forgave his enemies, and died . . . believing in the whole Bench of Bishops'.[22]

Nine days after the party, Francis Jeffrey (Frank) was born. It was exactly eight months and five days after Dickens, congratulating a friend whose wife had just presented him with offspring, had confessed, 'I hope *my* missis won't do so never no more'.[23] But now, resigned, he summarized the infant's arrival: 'Nurses, wet and dry; apothecaries; mothers-in-laws [*sic*]; babies; with all the sweet (and chaste) delights of private life.'[24] Even a month later his somewhat satiric tone was not yet replaced by the fond rapture that invariably ensued as his children began to develop. 'Kate is all right again, and so . . . is the Baby', he remarked. 'But I decline (on principle) to look at the latter object.'[25] With the advent of this fifth child Aunt Georgy was needed more than ever.

Dickens now found himself increasingly drawn to his young sister-in-law, for she had all but taken the place of the seventeen-year-old Mary Hogarth. Georgina was also seventeen now, and of the same cheerful, helpful, adoring nature. Only a few months earlier, on the sixth anniversary of Mary's death, as he had been thinking of the past, there had arrived a note from Mrs. Hogarth, with a packet containing a portrait of Mary and a lock of her smooth dark hair. Thanking his mother-in-law for the keepsakes, he had written feelingly: 'I trace in many respects a strong resemblance between her mental features and Georgina's—so strange a one, at times, that when she and Kate and I are sitting together, I seem to think that what has happened is a melancholy dream from which I am just awakening. The perfect like of what she was, will never be again, but so much of her spirit shines out in this sister, that the old time comes back again at some seasons, and I can hardly separate it from the present.'[26]

*   *   *

In July of 1844 Georgina entered upon an enriching phase of her girlhood, a series of sojourns abroad. All agog she climbed into the miraculous second-hand carriage—'about the size of your library', Dickens had boasted to Forster[27]—which was to transport the entire family, plus four women servants, a courier, and Timber, to their destination on the Bay of Genoa. (The cost of a year's residence on the Continent, Dickens had estimated at half that of the same period in London, where his expenses had mounted ruinously.)[28] As the vast carriage lumbered south across France after the Channel crossing, Georgina savoured anew the fruits of her brother-in-law's resourcefulness and organization: from its numerous pockets and 'leathern cellars' he conjured up titbits to refresh the party; he devised amusements for the children; and with Roche, the efficient courier, he transformed primitive roadside lodgings into havens of comfort.[29]

There was need of the utmost in such ingenuity when the travellers finally rolled into the courtyard of the dilapidated pink villa in Albaro which was to be their home for the next three months. It was a 'stagnant old staggerer of a domain' with a stable 'so full of "vermin and swarmers",' Dickens wrote Forster, '. . . that I always expect to see the carriage going out bodily, with legions of industrious fleas harnessed to and drawing it off. . . .' Poor Timber, an immediate victim, had to be clipped in lion style, whereupon, humiliated by the transformation, he slunk about, 'turning round and round to look for himself'. Even then the fleas tormented him by colonizing in his mane.[30]

Georgina adjusted to life in Italy more happily than Timber. She could sit on the vine-covered terrace and watch the Alps dissolving into purple distance beyond the ever-changing blues of the Bay of Genoa. And she had all the new and delectable fruits of the region to enjoy—lemons, green figs, green almonds. For diversion she could play the piano which Dickens had installed after their arrival. Though her upstairs bower was, as always, near the nurseries, life was relaxed.[31] The younger children had their nurse, and the older ones could amuse themselves safely in the vineyard and garden.

At the end of September, when Dickens transferred his family to more livable quarters in Genoa, Georgina began life in a palace 'larger than Whitehall multiplied by four'.[32] Set among terraced gardens and fountains, the Palazzo Peschiere looked down on orange groves and, beyond the towers of the old city, a sweep of blue Mediterranean. But a rainy autumn, 'worse than any November English weather', dampened the scenery and her delight.[33] So did the rather boring guest, Mrs. Macready's sister, Susan Atkins, currently in their midst. Evidently Georgina and Catherine thought of packing her off to Rome or leaving her with the frescoed nymphs and satyrs and all the antique grandeur of the *palazzo* while they escaped to Milan on a sightseeing expedition. The occasion stands out in the annals as almost the only time Georgina ever displeased her brother-in-law. From Milan, to which he had already preceded them, he sent his wife a sharp reminder that Susan, in spite of her 'inanities', must be shown more courtesy, lest the valued friendship with the Macreadys lapse. Georgina in particular had grieved him with a 'glaringly foolish and unnecessary silliness', for her indiscreet messages to Forster had placed 'huge means of misrepresentation in very willing hands'. Even though the presence of Susan in Milan would be 'a positive grievance', she must be invited to join them. Should she have a prior opportunity to leave, properly escorted, for Rome, well and good; but she must in no circumstances be permitted to go in the custody of an utter stranger. This matter disposed of, Dickens, still in the mood for forestalling petticoat error, admonished his wife, 'Keep things in their places. I can't bear to picture them otherwise'.[34]

Presumably Susan departed without incident, for the sisters alone joined the head of the family in Milan, whence he left for a brief visit to London to try out his new Christmas book, *The Chimes*, in a pre-publication reading to a few friends. His first letter from England reported a triumph. 'If you had seen Macready last night,' he gloated to Catherine, 'undisguisedly sobbing and crying on the sofa as I read, you would have felt, as I did, what a thing it is to have power.'[35]

Just before her eighteenth birthday in January, Georgina was left in Genoa with the household staff and the children while Catherine went travelling with her husband. First, though, he had satisfied himself that Georgy could 'be perfectly happy for a fortnight or so in our stately palace with the children'; for he loved her 'too dearly', he protested, 'to think of any project which would involve her being uncomfortable for that space of time'.[36]

But early in February 'Dearest Georgy' received a plea from him, full of regrets that she had not come along to witness the Carnival in Rome. She must pack up and come south 'by the first boat'— or, 'if there be a good one a day or two before it', she noted with amusement, she was to 'come by that'. But first she must fulfil the commission 'to have the darlings' bonnets made at once' in the bright colours their father invariably favoured.[37]

On 9th February she arrived at the Victoria Hotel in Naples, bringing letters from England and news of 'the darlings'.[38] What she had expected in novelty and thrills—how could a trip with exuberant Charles provide anything else?—was more than fulfilled in the adventure of scaling Vesuvius. Months before, Dickens had planned that she should 'top and cap' all her former walks with him by clambering up to the very crater.[39] As the day approached, Catherine was also included in the party. Preparations were elaborate: twenty-two guides, an armed guard, and six saddle horses had to be engaged. The climbers started on horseback at four in the afternoon, hoping to see the sunset midway and the raging fire of the crater by dark. When the sightseers dismounted on reaching the snow, the sisters were transferred to litters and carried up a nearly perpendicular incline. They scarcely dared steal a downward glance at the fearful chasm behind them as their bearers worked cautiously up toward the lava rock. Entering the fiery regions as darkness fell, they gasped and choked from the 'smoke and sulphur bursting out of every chink and crevice. . . .' At last, nearing the summit, Georgina and Catherine, still game, finished the ascent on foot, stumbling into beds of cinders and ashes at every step. At the base of the crater they were horrified to see Dickens scramble on up for a look down 'into the flaming bowels of the mountain. . . .' Roche, 'tearing his hair like a madman' and predicting a fatal issue, did nothing to ease their terror. They could only wait for the daredevil to return singed but safe.[40]

The descent proved even more perilous. Supported by half a dozen men, the two women faltered down the narrow track gouged into the ice and snow. Suddenly Georgina, between Dickens and the head guide, froze to feel a jerk as the latter lost his footing and plunged down into the blackness, followed by a shrieking Italian boy and another guide carrying spare cloaks. Shaken, she and Catherine inched on, their garments in torn disarray. Not until midnight was their exhaustive ordeal ended. By then the head guide and the boy, both painfully injured, had been rescued; but the third victim— Dickens's cloak with him—was still missing next morning. 'My ladies are the wonder of Naples,' Dickens boasted, 'and everybody is open-mouthed.'[41]

Before returning to the Palazzo Peschiere and the children, Georgina underwent another memorable experience, Holy Week in Rome. This interval, in which she continually saw 'the poor old Pope' being carried 'about on men's shoulders like a gorgeous Guy Faux', served to imbue her with her brother-in-law's anti-Catholic sentiments. But she revelled in the Vatican's treasured Raphaels, Correggios, and Titians, which, Dickens admitted, were of such lofty beauty as to compensate for 'legions of whining friars and waxy holy families' encountered elsewhere.[42] Altogether, the whirl of sightseeing was a radiant adventure for her.

But for her sister it was a period of distress. Not that Catherine failed to find strange places and modes of life entrancing, but she was tormented by worry and jealousy. For Charles showed too much attention to Madame De la Rue, the English wife of a Swiss banker in Genoa. Actually, his frequent calls on these friends were prompted by an attempt to relieve Madame De la Rue, through hypnotism, of a nervous affliction and terrifying hallucinations.[43] But when, heightening the tension, the Genoese pair appeared in Rome and stayed at the Dickenses' hotel, Catherine was beside herself with anxiety and suspicion. As the two families travelled back to Genoa together, she brooded, aloof and silent. Embarrassed, Dickens tried to explain her behaviour as a nervous breakdown. In private he urged upon her the absurdity of her jealousy. But she remained so cold and distant that he was finally driven to make a 'painful declaration of [her] state of mind to his friends'.[44]

*   *   *

At last, in June, Catherine was relieved to see her household stowed away in the commodious carriage and bound for England, where by the end of the month they resumed domesticity in a Devonshire Terrace transformed by paint, new wallpaper, and ingenuity, all in accord with Dickens's detailed instructions sent on in April— plans in which his passive mate had taken small part.[45]

The ensuing summer was given over to double anticipation, for autumn was to bring not only a sixth heir—no novelty—but the first amateur theatrical performance under Dickens's direction. Georgina already knew what fascination the stage held for her brother-in-law: she had watched him playing half-seriously with young Charley's toy theatres, designing scenery, pasting, cutting out cardboard characters.[46] And now, in September, she saw him act the star role of Captain Bobadil in his own production of Jonson's *Every Man in His Humour*, given at Miss Kelly's Theatre, Dean Street, Soho.

In the convenient interval between this and the repeat performance at St. James's Theatre in November, Catherine was confined 'with what', her actor-husband announced, 'is usually called (I don't know why) a chopping Boy'. He had hoped for a girl. 'But never mind me,' he added with resignation.[47] The baby was christened Alfred D'Orsay Tennyson, both Tennyson and Count D'Orsay standing as godfathers. Before long he was nicknamed 'Skittles'.

(His brothers and sisters had their own ridiculous names: his immediate predecessor, two-year-old Frank, was 'Chickenstalker'; in
infancy Walter had been 'Young Skull'; auburn-haired Katey of the
fiery temper was 'Lucifer Box'; gentle Mamie was 'mild Glo'ster';
and Charley was 'Flaster Floby', a corruption of Master Toby.)[48]
As nursery governess Aunt Georgy saw her situation stretch forward
interminably.

By June of 1846, though, she was enjoying another lighthearted
expedition abroad. Because her sister, still nursing memories of the
De la Rue affair, was set against seeing Genoa again, Switzerland
became the family residence for the summer.[49] With the children,
two nurses, the other servants, and Timber settled in Lausanne,
Georgina and Catherine maintained their Neapolitan reputation for
hardihood by going forth on Alpine excursions, riding muleback
once with Dickens for *'ten hours at a stretch'* over the Col de Balme,
'a mountain pass not often crossed by ladies'.[50]

At the end of November they moved on to Paris, where they were
domiciled at 48 Rue de Courcelles, Faubourg St. Honoré, in a house
whose décor and arrangement Dickens pronounced 'most ridiculous
and preposterous'.[51] By then Catherine was over four months pregnant and possibly in no mood to relish the ludicrous. But Georgina
found Paris exhilarating, particularly the long rambles through the
streets with Dickens, whom she often made 'weak with laughter' by
her impersonations of various acquaintances.[52]

Among the Parisians she learned to know was Amelia Fillonneau,
a sister of Henry Austin, the husband of Dickens's sister Letitia.
Mme. Fillonneau had in her possession the manuscript of a farce
which Dickens had composed in youth for private performance by a
few of his relatives and friends, a circle of which she had been part.
But now, ashamed of what he regarded as juvenile rubbish, he made
a bargain with her, taking her keepsake in exchange for the manuscript of his newly composed Christmas book, *The Battle of Life.*
Thereupon he burned his youthful dramatic effort.[53] (Decades later
this exchange was to involve Georgina and Amelia Fillonneau in an
interesting manuscript transaction.)

Late in February the carefree atmosphere of Paris visits and
rambles ended for Georgina when she was left alone to supervise the
children and the servants. Catherine and Dickens had hurried back
to London to be with Charley, who had contracted scarlet fever at
King's College School and was being cared for by his Grandmother
Hogarth in Albany Street lodgings.[54] Devonshire Terrace being let,
Aunt Georgy could not follow with her charges until Dickens had
found temporary quarters for them. Meanwhile, though, she could

see to it that Mamie and Katey wrote to cheer Charley.[55] In the second week of March, Roche, still in Dickens's employ, came over from London to convoy the household back to Lodgings at 1 Chester Place, near the Hogarths.[56] There, to complicate matters further, Catherine, after a difficult labour,[57] was delivered of her seventh, Sydney Smith Haldimand, on 18th April. She was now well on the way to rivalling her mother, who had borne ten children.

Whatever the views of Georgina on her sister's fecundity, by the end of that same year, 1847, she must have had knowledge of an anticipated eighth child to whom she might one day teach the ABC's. For in December, left with the youngsters while Catherine accompanied Dickens to Scotland for the first anniversary of the Glasgow Athenaeum, she received a startling communication from her brother-in-law. After an elated account of his own part in the anniversary programme ('The Inimitable [his customary humorous reference to himself] did wonders') came the revelation: '*Kate didn't go!* having been taken ill on the railroad. . . .' The reason for her absence, he predicted, would out, 'like murder', for 'to hope to veil such a tremendous disgrace from the general intelligence is out of the question'.[58] Georgina was trusted to read between the lines: her sister's illness had been a miscarriage.[59]

When by April Catherine was again pregnant, a whirl of social engagements began; for, freed by the completion of *Dombey and Son*, Dickens, more and more restless, sought to lose himself in the theatre, banquets, and parties, a programme that invariably included Georgina. But always her role of social butterfly alternated with that of useful spinster aunt, that ubiquitous adjunct to so many Victorian households. As she was hence to do frequently whenever the family left home for an extended stay, she preceded Catherine and Charles to Broadstairs in July, taking her young charges with her and directing the servants as the premises were put in order.[60]

This summer Catherine was especially glad to leave London, having 'entreated' her husband, so he told Bulwer-Lytton, 'to bring her away from town and let her grumble "unbeknown" to all, but our old hoarse monster-friend, the sea here'. Still, though she found visiting—and, presumably, receiving visitors—'irksome', she and Georgina entertained a number of Dickens's friends before the return to London in October.[61] And in November, when Catherine must have been still less disposed to social exertion, she issued, at her husband's behest, an invitation for a small dinner to be given at Devonshire Terrace the second week of December while the Thomas Mittons, friends from Northampton, were in town. As the evening

was to be climaxed by the lengthy reading of Dickens's new Christmas book, *The Haunted Man,* dinner must be served promptly at
six o'clock, she wrote Miss Coutts.[62]

Thus, as their sixth year together under Dickens's roof was drawing to a close, the Hogarth sisters sat in the drawing-room, listening
to his performance. It merited whatever applause it received; for,
in perfecting his dramatic techniques, Dickens always took endless
pains, as if to ensure appeasement of the hunger for recognition, a
need fostered by his meagre early years. In the little group before
him that night he could not have found anyone who catered to his
craving more fervently, and sincerely, than Georgina.

Chapter Three
THE 'LITTLE HOUSEKEEPER'

As Georgina's twenty-second birthday drew near, the household was in an even madder whirl of January activity than usual. On the 3rd a group much larger than the December party gathered to dine and hear the reading of *The Haunted Man*. Next came the usual Twelfth Night gaieties, to which not only juveniles but Captain Marryat and other adults were invited.[1] On the 15th followed the birth of Henry Fielding (Harry), a healthy ' "moon-faced" monster' whose arrival was eased by chloroform, which Dickens had urged against the conservatism of Catherine's doctors.[2] The next day he accepted a dinner invitation from his Unitarian friend, the Reverend Edward Tagart, promising to bring 'the gentle Georgina', as Mrs. Dickens would be, 'according to the precedents, hardly presentable yet'.[3]

The confinement safely over, Devonshire Terrace settled down as Dickens began concentrating on his next novel, *David Copperfield*. An idealized portrayal of his own early years, it would dip into the shadowy past, the blackest depths of which Georgina was never to suspect in his lifetime. She little dreamed how much of himself he was confiding to this 'favourite child' among his books: the secrets of his bitterest disappointments, his early bouts with poverty, his first love frustrations. But as he recalled his youth to reconstruct in Dora the idealized image of his boyhood sweetheart, the coquettish Maria Beadnell, Georgina may have recognized unmistakable suggestions of Catherine as the delineation became a curious blend of past and present. For Dickens had long been aware of his wife's shortcomings. Like Dora, she exerted little control over the management of her household, having surrendered such responsibilities to more capable hands during her constant childbearing. Like Dora, furthermore, she did not share her husband's intellectual interests, his efforts at improving her mind resulting only in nervousness. Like David Copperfield, Dickens had to tell himself that 'there can be no disparity in marriage like unsuitability of mind and purpose'.[4]

Into the breach created by the growing incompatibility stepped Georgina Hogarth. Just as David depended on Agnes Wickfield for the qualities he missed in Dora, so Dickens turned to his sister-in-law for intellectual companionship, sympathetic understanding, and practical common sense. Far too perceptive not to recognize her sister's inadequacy as the wife of a distinguished novelist, Georgina tried to earn her keep by providing the well-ordered household her brother-in-law required to carry on his creative work. Observing this capable and meticulous young woman, he may have recalled at times the child who had spent a day with him and Catherine at their honeymoon cottage, may have asked himself, like David, 'And the little girl . . . , where is she?' In her stead was 'quite a woman' moving about the house—'my sweet sister, as I call her in my thoughts, my counsellor and friend, the better angel of the lives of all who come within her calm, good, self-denying influence. . . .'[5] In the years since Mary Hogarth's death Dickens had been confiding in Georgina. To her his 'heart turned naturally . . . and found its refuge and best friend'.[6] As Agnes Wickfield to David Copperfield, so was Georgina Hogarth to Charles Dickens—his right hand. And David's words of praise, words that unwittingly make a colourless paragon of Agnes, may have been the author's way of privately acknowledging his debt to his 'best friend'. But it is significant that David's admiration, though excessive, never convinces one that this was a lover's rapture. The whole tone of the Agnes episodes suggests Dickens's own lack of romantic ardour for Agnes Wickfield's prototype.

Georgina may have inspired still another capable, self-denying character in *David Copperfield*—Sophy, the fiancée of Traddles. For Sophy, too, assumes domestic responsibilities not her own, in which she acquits herself cheerfully and efficiently, and she is the fourth daughter in a family of ten, as was Georgina, if the Hogarth birth records are reliable.

It is noteworthy that Dickens's preoccupation with his indebtedness to his sister-in-law should have been reflected in these two portraits, even before he had passed the mid-point of his career. Depending upon her for the guidance of his children, looking to her for the practical management of a large household, and finding in her a stimulating companion, did he sometimes anticipate losing this indispensable young woman? He must have felt that she deserved a home and children of her own. But did he, perhaps, place the barrier of unreasonably high standards in the way of her marriage? Here again he may have used *Copperfield* as a vehicle for his own sentiments. 'But there is no one that I know of, who deserves to love *you*, Agnes,' says David. 'Some one of a nobler character, and more worthy altogether than any one I have ever seen here, must rise up, before I give *my* consent. In the time to come, I shall have a wary eye on all admirers; and shall exact a great deal from the

successful one. . . .'⁷ That Georgina needed no advice on appraising
any possible suitors is a reasonable assumption. Having lived with
Dickens since the age of fifteen, she had acquired his tastes and
sense of values. With his wife's mind already formed at the time of
their marriage, he had turned, perhaps unconsciously, to the more
rewarding prospect of moulding his impressionable sister-in-law. His
success with respect to her matrimonial ideals is borne out in his
statement to William de Cerjat, the Swiss friend with whom he had
become intimate in Lausanne. 'We have had no marriages or giving
in marriage here,' Dickens wrote him during the serial publication
of *Copperfield*. 'We might have had, but a certain young lady,
whom you know, is hard to please.'⁸

He should also have reflected that under his roof Georgina had
witnessed more than one deterrent to matrimony. Not only was there
her sister's distress, nervous as well as physical, during her frequent
pregnancies; still more discouraging must have been the husband's
deprecating tone toward his wife in 'that *uninteresting* condition',⁹
and his irritating acceptance of the resulting infant as superfluous—
the attitude that had prompted his half-jesting declaration of reluctance to look at Baby Frank.¹⁰ And there was the impatience of a
genius toward what he chose to term stupidity in his wife, an attitude that occasionally revealed itself to outsiders under a mask of
levity. 'It is more clear to me than ever,' Dickens had written to a
feminine acquaintance in 1842, 'that Kate is as near being a Donkey,
as one of that sex . . . *can* be.'¹¹ Yes, genius was difficult to live with,
but Georgina could scarcely be content now with less.

Moving in the aura of genius, she relished, as Catherine did not,
the contacts with such prominent literary persons as those who
gathered around the Dickens table one March evening in 1849. Of
all the social events at Devonshire Terrace perhaps none occasioned
a greater flurry of preparations than this dinner, at which appeared
Mrs. Gaskell, Sam Rogers, and Jane and Thomas Carlyle. To have
the latter accept an invitation was no mean triumph. Once before,
Dickens had tried to lure Carlyle to Devonshire Terrace, only to be
told that he and Jane were 'such a pair of poor silly creatures' that
they had to deny themselves 'with great reluctance' the 'pleasure of
dining out anywhere at present'.¹² But if the Dickenses had hoped
to dazzle their guests with lavish decorations and fashionable service,
they failed utterly to impress Jane Carlyle, who judged the event
with her usual acerbity. 'Such getting up of the steam is unbecoming
to a literary man,' she objected. 'The dinner was served up in the
new fashion—not placed on the table at all—but handed round—
only the dessert on the table and quantities of *artificial* flowers—but

such an overloaded dessert! pyramids of figs, raisins, oranges—ach!' She contrasted such profusion with the restraint shown in the decorations and service at one of Lady Ashburton's dinners: 'Just *four cowslips* in china pots—four silver shells containing sweets, and a silver filigree temple in the middle! but here the very candles rose each out of an artificial rose! Good God!'[13] Rogers had also carried away an unfavourable impression of the evening at Devonshire Terrace. There had been so much loud talk that the old man had heard only confused noises, though Jane suspected that his displeasure had arisen from not having had 'the talk to himself—in other words Mr. Carlyle was there, the greatest affliction that can befall Rogers at a dinner party'.[14]

The hint of vulgarity, the burgeoning vitality of Cockneydom that the mature Jane Carlyle had detected in the host and his table, very likely impressed the inexperienced Georgina as enviable exuberance and luxury. True, the setting may have been unlike anything her father would have sanctioned in his home, even had he been well-to-do, but Georgina had been away from the influence of that home for seven years now. Perhaps she discerned no trace of vulgarity in her hero; on the other hand, she may have been too far removed from snobbery to wince at it.

The lonely Thackeray, though, envious in spite of himself, commented sourly on the lusty appearance of the family when he glimpsed them that July on the pier at Ryde—'the great Dickens with his wife his children his Miss Hogarth all looking abominably coarse, vulgar and happy bound to Bonchurch where they have taken one of White's houses for the summer'.[15] But though the Isle of Wight and the Reverend James White's cottage promised a paradise—'cool, airy, private bathing, everything delicious',[16] within a few weeks the family was shepherded back to the mainland to finish the summer at a hotel in the familiar Broadstairs. Dickens had found the gentle island climate too enervating for his work schedule.

The following year the schedule became still more rigorous with the launching of *Household Words*, a weekly journal 'designed for the instruction and entertainment of all classes of readers'. Henceforth Dickens as editor would spend many hours at the headquarters of his periodical in Wellington Street. Of this publishing venture and W. H. Wills, its assistant editor, Georgina was to hear much in the years to come. In charge of production were Bradbury and Evans, who had replaced Chapman and Hall as Dickens's publishers, a change which was to have family repercussions later.

In July Georgina, with the help of the governess and nurses, again took charge of the children on their usual holiday in Broadstairs. Catherine, now awaiting her ninth child, stayed behind in the less riotous atmosphere of Devonshire Terrace, where her mother had come to be with her. There Dora Annie was born in August. In the meantime, whenever Dickens could escape his duties in London, he relaxed at Broadstairs and received guests there. All arrangements for their accommodation were turned over to Georgina. 'Write . . . to my little housekeeper Miss Hogarth,' he instructed Wills, 'and she will expect you.'[17] Now and then, unfortunately, these visitors brought vexations. There was the time, for instance, when Forster, in 'a tip top state of amiability', caused his host to complain: 'I think I never heard him *half so loud*(!) He really . . . so disordered me that by no process I could possibly try, could I get to sleep afterwards.' Finally Dickens was forced to pace about the house until five, having got Georgina up for company.[18]

During the Broadstairs holiday, Sydney, now three years old and his father's special pet, delighted his Aunt Georgy by his curious unchildlike habit of pausing in his play, cupping his tiny hands under his chin, and casting a faraway look over the ocean. At such times a film seemed to pass over his eyes, as if—Dickens laughingly suggested—he were entertaining a 'clear vision of futurity'. Subsequently Sydney was known as 'Ocean Spectre', rendered in baby talk as 'Hoshen Peck'.[19]

Soon after this seaside holiday Georgina was introduced to a great country house, Knebworth, Bulwer-Lytton's Hertfordshire estate, when Dickens accepted an invitation to bring an amateur troupe there to present *Every Man in His Humour* before a county audience. Knebworth, with its magnificent galleried banqueting hall the full height of the house, was an ideal place for a theatrical production. Here, surrounded by old leather, tapestries, armour, stained glass, colourful banners, and burnished plate,[20] Georgina might gratify whatever antiquarian and luxurious tastes she possessed. Lord Lytton himself she found a match for the grandeur of his estate. Lounging in his gorgeous Oriental robes and smoking chibouks,[21] this slender, hook-nosed dandy shared Dickens's love for the flamboyant and the dramatic. He shared, too, something of Dickens's creative talent and his vanity. These resemblances, combined with Lytton's cordial regard and admiration for her brother-in-law, were enough to charm the young guest. The man whom Carlyle described as '*tragic-gawky*', whom Henry F. Chorley considered a glossy, 'thoroughly *satin* character',[22] Georgina found magnetic. He in turn responded with gallant and lasting affection for this girl who was only half his age.

Assembling a cast for Lytton's dramatic festival, Dickens assigned
to Georgina the part of Mistress Bridget, whose wooing and marriage
climax the play. Addressed to her in the fourth act was an apropos
line to delight possibly all but Georgina herself: 'You are ripe for a
husband; and a minute's loss to such an occasion, is a great trespass
in a wise beauty'. The speech may have elicited some banter at
rehearsals, particularly if anyone suspected that Georgina was the
object of a growing romantic attachment on the part of Dickens's
painter friend, Augustus Egg, A.R.A., also a member of the cast.
Sensitive, rather small in stature and delicate in health, this talented
bachelor of thirty-four had the instincts and tastes of a gentleman.
Having inherited a comfortable fortune from his father, a London
gunmaker, he lived independent of his art, occupying his own attractive home, Ivy Cottage, in Bayswater.[23] But it was not he who
played the part of Georgy's stage lover on this occasion. Though he
was frequently to appear in Dickens's theatricals, it was invariably
in such minor roles as Cob, a water-bearer in the Jonson comedy.

To Catherine also went a minor role, that of Cob's wife Tib,
involving few speeches longer than 'What say you, sir?' But as the
production shaped up, poor Catherine, whose clumsiness had irritated Dickens as early as the American tour, fell through a stage
trap door at the London rehearsals and sprained her ankle. The
situation, if not the ankle, was eased when Mrs. Mark Lemon went
to Georgina to offer herself as a substitute. A few days later Dickens
assured Bulwer-Lytton that his 'unfortunate other half' would
nevertheless be in the audience, having planned to travel to Knebworth 'in the brougham, with her foot upon a T.'[24]

During October and the first half of November Georgina prepared
and rehearsed not only her role in *Every Man in His Humour*, which
continued for the three nights of the festival, but also two roles in
the farcical afterpieces: Constance in *Animal Magnetism* for the first
night and Miss Knibbs in *Turning the Tables* for the last two nights.
In Dickens's judgment she 'covered herself with glory' in her main
role of Mistress Bridget.[25]

In January she had a chance to appear again in *Animal Magnetism*, for Dickens, exultant over the recent triumph at Knebworth,
needed no urging to stage his amateur theatricals at Rockingham
Castle in Northampton, the seat of his friends the Honourable and
Mrs. Richard Watson. Catherine, her ankle healed, was cast as Lady
Clutterbuck in a short piece whose title, *Used Up*, made a wry com-
mentary on her own state. Dickens also appeared in this comedy,
opposite Mary Boyle, the sprightly niece of Mrs. Watson. Thence-
forth they were to address each other by their stage names: he would

always be her 'Joe', she his 'darling Mary'.[26] With Mary Boyle, seventeen years her senior, Georgina was to form a lifelong tie based on their shared idolatry of Dickens.

Though Catherine was ever fond of the theatre, she seems not to have entered happily into the group at Rockingham Castle—nor, perhaps, into that at Knebworth. On the brink of a nervous collapse and pathetically insecure as to her own charms, she may have resented the mock flirtation between her husband and the talented niece of her hostess. By March she was suffering from 'an alarming disposition of blood to the head, attended by giddiness and dimness of sight',[27] a disorder not entirely new to her and more mental than physical, her husband stated in letters to Dr. James Wilson of Great Malvern, to whose care she was entrusted. Anne Brown, her dependable maid, was sent to Malvern to 'take some cheerful cottage or house', Dickens assuming from the experience at Rockingham Castle that his wife would not adjust contentedly to the proffered lodging under Dr. Wilson's roof.[28] Georgina then accompanied her sister to the spa, where Catherine began the prescribed 'vigorous discipline of exercise, air, and cold water'.[29]

Their absence from London just then was unwelcome to both. For Georgina it meant interrupting a fascinating task just begun—that of amanuensis to Dickens, who was using his spare time to write *A Child's History of England*, dedicated to his own offspring in the hope that it might induce them 'by and by, to read with interest larger and better books upon the same subject'.[30] (From this work the children and their aunt must have absorbed the author's highly subjective notions of English monarchs: Henry VIII was a 'blot of blood and grease on the History of England'; James II had 'a remarkable partiality for the ugliest women in the country'; and the entire Stuart line was 'a public nuisance altogether.')[31] For Catherine the stay at Great Malvern meant leaving little Dora Annie, only seven months old and frail from birth.

Some four weeks later the Malvern sojourn was interrupted by upsetting news: Dora Annie, though not 'in the least pain' and appearing as if 'quietly asleep', had been stricken by grave illness—so stated a note from Dickens. Catherine was entreated to 'come home with perfect composure', remembering her duty to the rest of the children, even should she find on returning to London that the baby was dead.[32] Upon reaching Devonshire Terrace, she and Georgina learned that Dora Annie had died of convulsions in her nurse's arms the night before Dickens had chosen to break the news in this diluted form. Catherine bore the shock well and seemed quite resigned, though her nervous malady continued for some weeks.[33]

As the melancholy winter of 1851 brightened into spring, plans were afoot that would set Georgina in the more ample environment suited to Dickens's growing prestige. The expanding family needed a larger home than Devonshire Terrace, sublet now as their summer holiday began at Broadstairs. In September, when his twelve-year lease would expire, Dickens hoped to have a new dwelling ready for occupancy. After several unsuccessful attempts at house hunting he learned that his artist friend Frank Stone was vacating Tavistock House in the Russell Square vicinity. Following a thorough inspection of the place by his sister Letitia's husband, Henry Austin, Dickens bought the three-story building and immediately launched extensive alterations.

As late as October these 'convulsions of repairing' were still going on, while Georgina and the children waited at Broadstairs until the completion of a 'pigeon-hole or two into which they [might] creep'. By this time Catherine was back in London, occasionally inspecting the remodelling and, her husband quipped, 'gradually falling into fits of imbecility' and getting herself 'all over paint' as though she were 'somehow useful' in that condition.[34]

Georgina, banished with the children to Broadstairs, had seen little of Tavistock House while the transformation was in progress. But what she saw when she returned to London in November delighted her. Not even the garden had been overlooked, having been redesigned, drained, and stocked with flowers and shrubs. Some of these looked hauntingly familiar—as, indeed, they were; for Dickens had gone back to Devonshire Terrace with a gardener in September to see whether the shrubs could not be transplanted. 'I put them there,' he told Wills, 'and I don't want to leave them there.'[35] Such practicality and thrifty concern for his just rights were Dickensian qualities which Georgina took increasing note of and had already begun to cultivate in herself.

As she stepped into the entrance hall, newly extended to the rear of the house, there stood the marble bust executed from Maclise's portrait of Dickens in his twenties. (Just so Charles had looked while dancing the hornpipe in her father's drawing-room that summer evening in 1835.) Everywhere paintings, engravings, bas-reliefs, mirrors, new curtains, and carpets 'on a scale of awful splendour and magnitude' graced the house.[36]

Even the bathroom was a model of careful planning. As Dickens had specified in his detailed instructions to the architect, the water closet was partitioned from the rest of the room, for he could not have endured the 'enforced contemplation of the outside of that box' while taking his morning shower. As for the bath itself, he had devised a shower-tub combination, enclosed by 'light, cheerful-coloured water proof curtains'.[37]

Also bearing the original stamp of the owner was the study. The door leading from it had been ingeniously faced with simulated shelves and dummy bookbacks to give the impression of a continuous wall of books. For these pseudo-volumes Dickens had playfully devised such titles as *History of the Middling Ages*, *The Quarrelly Review*, *Jonah's Account of the Whale*, *King Henry the Eighth's Evidences of Christianity*, and (in twenty-one volumes) the *History of a Short Chancery Suit*.[38] The sumptuousness of this room led George Eliot to remark sarcastically: 'Splendid library, of course, with soft carpet, couches, etc., such as become a sympathizer with the suffering classes. How can we sufficiently pity the needy unless we know fully the blessings of plenty?'[39] It was here that Georgina resumed her secretarial role whenever Dickens was in the mood to relax from the arduous composition of *Bleak House* by pacing up and down the carpet, dictating *A Child's History of England*.

As she took up her residence at Tavistock House, it was in a position markedly different from her earlier one in those first days at Devonshire Terrace. Then she had been a mere girl, the children's playmate. Now she was a poised young woman of twenty-four. Already largely in charge of the household, she was unconsciously training for the years when she would generally be recognized as Dickens's hostess.

Perhaps it was fear of being superseded as mistress of her new home which led Catherine to assert her worth by publishing under the pseudonym of Lady Clutterbuck (borrowed from her role in *Used Up*) a slim octavo volume listing the menus once served at Devonshire Terrace and giving some of her favourite recipes. Entitled *What Shall We Have for Dinner?*, the little book in its blue and tan marbled covers appeared near the close of 1851 under the imprint of Bradbury and Evans, Dickens's own publishers. Was Catherine perhaps hoping to prove to her husband that she could be creative in her own right—aside from bearing children? Or had the strain of marital insecurity driven her for consolation to a preoccupation with menus and recipes? Or did she choose thus to remind Charles that he had once found pleasure in her domestic endeavours? Wistfully her preface declares that 'attention to the requirements of his [Sir Joseph Clutterbuck's] appetite secured me the possession of his esteem to the last'.

If the menus and recipes are any indication, Dickens's digestive powers were truly phenomenal, as doubtless were those of many

Victorians. Combinations of mashed and browned potatoes and macaroni, topped off with breads, rice pudding, and the ubiquitous toasted cheese, would daunt the hardiest glutton today. Though the title page states that the bills of fare are planned to serve from two to eighteen persons, in general a larger number of guests results merely in the addition of more dishes to an already staggering menu. The overladen meals were, of course, only in keeping with the heavy diet of the times. But some of the dinners assembled in the Clutter-buck opus strike the reader as odd for any period: for instance, one listing three separate broccoli dishes. Too, more than one of the 'receipts' could have led to culinary disaster. One wonders about the results achieved by the trusting amateur who followed implicitly the directions for rice blancmange: 'Boil rice in milk, put it into a mould, and let stand until cold'. No sweetening, no seasoning, no specified proportions! Perhaps Lady Clutterbuck was more adept at supervising such dishes than in recording the methods of prepara-tion. If not, it was well that her sister had taken over the practical side of the household.

If Dickens examined his wife's effort at authorship, his orderly soul must have been dismayed by the volume's slipshod organiza-tion. Though the bills of fare are arranged according to the months in which they are to be served, the recipes appended in a final section do not follow the order of the corresponding dishes in the menu section, nor do they follow any other logical scheme—entrées, sweets, sauces, and soups being jumbled together indiscriminately.

Having concluded her one publishing venture, Catherine returned to her familiar role. On 13 March 1852 Dickens announced to Wills: 'I am happy to say that Mrs. Dickens is just confined with a brilliant boy of unheard-of-dimensions'.[40] Writing to William Howitt six days later, he was less elated, doubting whether he had 'particularly wanted' the infant, but admitting the possibility 'that he is good for me in some point of view or other'.[41] The new boy, christened Edward Bulwer Lytton, was later nicknamed 'The Plornishghenter'. He was the tenth and last child. With him Catherine had tied her mother's record for fertility.

Once life at Tavistock House had resumed its normal routine, Dickens withdrew to his study and concentrated on *Bleak House*, the first number of which had gone to press shortly before the baby's arrival. As he had already done with Agnes Wickfield, so he again modelled a heroine on Georgina. Industry, self-sacrifice, and warm affection being the qualities which he repeatedly attributed to his sister-in-law, he bestowed them liberally on Esther Summerson. But, having chosen to make his heroine a compound of these virtues

D

and having at the same time chosen to make her the narrator of her own story, he was compelled, unwittingly, to create a prig who proclaims her own merits and records the good opinion in which others hold her, affecting all the while an irritating meekness in striving 'to be useful to some one in my small way'.[42] The high spirits, the natural lapses into indiscretion, the slight touch of malice in mimicking the idiosyncrasies of others—none of the human traits which made Georgina so amusing and congenial a companion were allowed to taint Esther's perfection.

Yet, if one discounts the note of false humility, Esther bears undoubted resemblances to her prototype. Like Georgina, she is the constant companion of those younger than she and assumes responsibility in moulding them. 'I . . . was very soon engaged in helping to instruct others,' she explains. 'I had plenty to do, which I was very fond of doing, because it made the dear girls fond of me. . . . They said I was so gentle. . . . I often thought of the resolution I had made on my birthday, to try to be industrious, contented, and true-hearted, and to do some good to some one, and win some love if I could.'[43] This attitude prompts Esther's guardian to declare that her life must not be devoted entirely to others, a sentiment which echoes Dickens's own as he half-guiltily deplored Georgina's dedication to his own family.

Like Georgina, Esther has a talent for home management. Identified throughout the novel with her little basket of housekeeping keys, she makes methodical notes on her slate about jams, pickles, preserves, bottles, glass, and china, and demonstrates her 'capacity for the administration of detail'.[44] Grateful to his 'little housekeeper' for providing him with the antithesis of the chaotic Jellyby ménage, Dickens might well have addressed her under cover of Skimpole's words to Esther: 'You appear to me to be the very touchstone of responsibility. When I see you . . . intent upon the perfect working of the whole little orderly system of which you are the centre, I feel inclined to say to myself—in fact I do say to myself, very often—*that's* responsibility!'[45]

Chapter Four

'THE SKELETON . . . IN THE CUPBOARD'

GEORGINA was proud of her nieces and nephews. The older children were maturing fast: Charley, now fifteen, was at Eton; Mamie, reserved and attractive, displayed considerable poise at fourteen; and vivid Katey, almost thirteen, had been enrolled at nearby Bedford College to cultivate her talent for art.[1] Of the younger contingent, only eight-year-old Frank, afflicted with a decided stammer, gave his elders anxiety. Every morning Aunt Georgy sent him to the study, where his father read him a passage from Shakespeare and made him repeat it many times, distinctly and slowly.[2]

The years that had seen the children developing had marked Timber, too. Now in his chimney-corner decline, he usually sat with his bowed forelegs wide apart and his venerable 'head apparently nailed by the left ear to the kitchen door'.[3] But no such placidity had overtaken his master. Georgina had observed the growing tension, the restless energy Charles poured into his work, travel, and even play. His amateur theatricals especially had cost him endless pains ever since his 1845 promise of 'merry rehearsals innumerable'.[4]

From that year, when Georgina had helped by taking over the billing of the actors for their share of expenses in the production at Miss Kelly's Theatre,[5] she had been involved in these frolics in various capacities. Whether she was mere spectator, musical accompanist, secretary in charge of invitations, or actress, she might also expect to be responsible for finding neighbourhood lodgings for an actor's family, or for keeping sufficient steak and 'an extra morsel of Fish' on hand for the diners that rehearsals brought to the Dickens table.[6]

On a few occasions she accompanied the amateurs on provincial tours. It had been delightful to find bouquets waiting for her and Catherine and the actresses of the troupe at the hotel in Manchester when *Every Man in His Humour* and *The Merry Wives of Windsor* had gone on tour in June of 1848. The air of expectancy and the generous applause there and at Leeds and Birmingham had been exhilarating.

Again in August of 1852 she and Catherine had accompanied the troupe and shared the gaieties when Lytton's *Not So Bad As We Seem* was touring to build up a fund for the Guild of Literature and Art. Whether or not the sisters knew it at the time, they were part of an uncomfortably jittery audience at Sunderland. The new hall had been rumoured unsafe, and Dickens had taken care to place them near an exit. The anxiety proved unjustified, but every round of applause with its vibrations had strained his nerves.[7]

Young Charley, who shared the family enthusiasm for the stage, began with his birthday that year an annual custom in which Aunt Georgy was ever to assist with gusto: the annual Twelfth Night theatricals in the schoolroom at Tavistock. Of these celebrations, none was more hilarious than the third, in 1854. The children and their friends, with Dickens as director and manager and composer of the incidental lyrics, acted a revised version of Fielding's *Tom Thumb*. The hit of the show was the author's namesake, Henry Fielding Dickens, not yet five, who toddled through the title role, piping the songs with Auntie's assistance.[8] 'Miss Hogarth will preside in the orchestra [at the piano],' announced the programme, handsomely printed in red, green, and gold.[9]

She was to provide the accompaniment again the following Twelfth Night when the young people presented Planché's *Fortunio and His Seven Gifted Servants*, in which Dickens himself and Mark Lemon, the children's fat 'Uncle Porpoise', took part. Lighthearted captions in bold type announced the cast, including Harry, 'who created so Powerful an Impression last year'; Katey, 'who declined the munificent offers of the Management last season'; and 'Mr. Plornishmaroontigoonter [Edward, not quite three], who has been kept out of bed at a vast expense'. Charley was billed as returned 'from his German engagements'. (He had been studying German in Leipzig in preparation for a mercantile career.) After the performance a supper, followed by Scottish reels and country dances, finished the evening.[10] At such revels Auntie loved watching her young nieces whirling about in their best sashes and white satin slippers, and she took care that shy little girl guests were not neglected. Years later Anne Thackeray still remembered how Mamie and Katey's Aunt Georgy had seen to it that she and her younger sister had dancing partners.[11]

The next Tavistock theatricals, in June 1855, promoted Georgina from 'the orchestra' to the stage. The play was *The Lighthouse*, a melodrama by Wilkie Collins, now one of Dickens's most intimate friends. Georgina played the shipwrecked Lady Grace, a secondary character. She was also cast in the farcical afterpiece, *Mr. Nightingale's Diary*, as Susan.[12] *The Lighthouse* commanded professional sets by Stanfield, including a seascape backdrop. Equally realistic were the sound effects for the first act: wind, rain, thunder (on sheets of iron)—all were there, and so were lightning flashes and blown sea spray (handfuls of salt thrown through the open window by Stanfield, stationed in the wings).[13]

In October of 1856 Georgina began rehearsing for another of Collins's melodramas, *The Frozen Deep*, designed to open as part of the next Twelfth Night celebration and to continue for three performances thereafter: 8th, 12th, and 14th of January. Every Monday and Friday evening, for ten weeks, the cast worked on the melodrama and the two comic afterpieces, *Animal Magnetism* and *Uncle John*. Georgina took a role in all three: Lucy Crayford, a minor part in the main play; Jacintha in *Animal Magnetism*; and Niece Hawk in *Uncle John*. December seemed 'one long rehearsal'. Dickens was everywhere, checking costumes and scenery, suggesting stage business, interpreting lines.[14] And everywhere, on stage and off, was Georgina. For, ever since Catherine's activities had been mainly reduced to childbearing, she had largely assumed the direction of the household staff. Rehearsals on the current scale complicated her domestic routine considerably, what with the stage carpentry, scene painting, and dressmaking going on, and actors and workingmen being boarded on the premises.[15]

At least a month before the performance Georgina was busy sending out invitations, approximately two hundred handwritten notes, many of them composed especially for the recipients. For example, her message to Sir Joseph and Lady Olliffe in Paris suggested that certainly they would not mind the short journey over to London, and added that two seats would be reserved for the night of their choice.[16]

To crown all her footlight appearances, Georgina played before the Queen the following July. In the months after the January theatricals Dickens had sunk into intermittent periods of moodiness. But now, conceiving the idea of repeating *The Frozen Deep* as a benefit for the widow of the journalist Douglas Jerrold, he could escape from the canyon of gloom by his customary route. Applied to for a subscription to the Jerrold fund, Her Majesty made it clear that, to forestall a deluge of similar appeals, she never patronized benefits for individuals. But she wished to see the play and asked Dickens to bring his troupe to Buckingham Palace. He thereupon insisted that, since his family had not been presented at court, he preferred not to take his ladies there 'in the quality of actresses'. Queen Victoria acknowledged the validity of his objections and accepted his invitation to a private presentation for herself and a court party on 4th

July at the Gallery of Illustration in Regent Street.[17] This was to be followed by public benefit performances on the 11th, 18th, and 25th.[18]

At the end of April Georgina plunged into rehearsals that continued throughout May and June. On the night of the dress rehearsal, when the actresses were 'a perfect blaze of colour', she initiated the costumes designed for her (with fond care, one may assume) by Augustus Egg, whose sketches for the garments of the entire cast had been followed so minutely that not a 'pocket-flap or a scrap of lace' but was executed 'to the quarter of an inch'. Katey, almost eighteen now, had supplemented the drawings by detailed written instructions to her dressmaker for a white silk creation to be worn with 'a very handsome lace tucker' and a voluminous red scarf in 'soft net, *not* spotted'.[19]

The command performance turned out happily, and Georgina was overjoyed to report that the Queen and her party 'made a most excellent audience; so far from being cold, as was expected, they cried and laughed and applauded and made as much demonstration as so small a party (they were not more than fifty) could do'.[20] Both Her Majesty and the Prince Consort had laughed at Augustus Egg's comic bit about seasickness. Since there had been some qualms over this scene, its reception as one of the hits of the afterpiece had come as a relief.[21]

As absorbing to Georgina as the theatricals, as necessary to Dickens in providing an escape from private tensions, were the public benefit readings from his own books, a venture begun early in 1854. The previous November she had received his bid to attend the première performances: 'I suppose you won't object to be taken to hear them?'[22] Between Christmas and the New Year, therefore, she and Catherine accompanied him to Birmingham, where he gave three readings of *A Christmas Carol* for the benefit of a new working-men's institute. He was so elated with the response, particularly from the third night working-class audience, that he felt as if he and they 'were all bodily going up into the clouds together'.[23] Thereafter *Carol* readings became an annual affair. Not alarmed as yet over such exhausting expenditures of energy, Georgina could feel a surge of unmixed pride in this new achievement.

*   *   *

Between 1853 and 1856 Georgina spent three summers and a winter in France with the family. By these further Continental sojourns Dickens was seeking to divert his mind from domestic friction and free his body from the strain of multiple exertions. These

University of Winnipeg, 515 Portage Ave., Winnipeg, MB. R3B 2E9 Canada

had so reduced his vitality by early June of 1853 that he succumbed easily to exposure in a chill hailstorm. While he convalesced and hatched plans for a change of scene, Georgina helped with his personal correspondence for a few days. Fervent was her relief when she could report that the patient, after being cupped, was pronounced by the doctor *'most decidedly* and *greatly better*, thank God!'[24]

The ensuing change of scene gave her a blissful summer—on the surface, at least—among the terraced rose gardens surrounding the hillside Château du Moulineaux in Boulogne.[25] She rejoiced in the exploratory tours and the bracing walks which soon rejuvenated Dickens. Only she—and Mary Boyle during a visit—could match his sustained speed.[26]

The following June she was again in Boulogne, living in a delightful house on the hilltop. A high point of her summer was the illumination of the town in honour of the Prince Consort's visit. On the appointed night she stationed herself at a front window—as did seventeen others of the household, including guests and servants—and waited for Dickens's dinner-bell signal. In one moment, as all their lights flared up simultaneously, the house became a sparkling beacon to be admired from miles away.[27]

In autumn of the following year Georgina was back in France again. (Her parents had been temporarily installed at Tavistock to keep house for Charley, now a clerk in Baring's Bank at £50 a year.)[28] While Catherine and the children waited at Boulogne, she went on to Paris to find a house for the family. It was a season when dwellings were scarce and rents exorbitant,[29] but with the help of Lady Olliffe, wife of the physician at the British Embassy, and after various bafflements, Georgina found quarters on two floors of 'a Doll's house' at 49 Avenue des Champs Elysées. Dickens, who joined her to complete the rental arrangements, cautiously wrote to prepare Catherine for the worst as well as the best features of the place.[30] The drawbacks of the ill-ventilated, neglected rooms (only 'larger than meat safes') had been apparent to Georgina on her first night's occupancy with Dickens and the servants. 'Oh it's dreadfully dirty,' she had complained to her brother-in-law, routed out by her restless prowling. 'I can't sleep for the smell of my room.' The next day he convinced the proprietors of his aversion to dirt and cajoled them into 'offering new carpets (accepted)' and 'embraces (not accepted). . . .'[31]

With the reunited family soon settled in the sweetened and refurbished abode, Georgina took up her old pastime of walking through the Paris streets with Dickens in all weathers. Mud-spattered to the eyebrows at times, she presented 'a turned-up nose . . . in the midst gina Hogarth and the Dickens Circle*

of splashes, . . . nothing more'.[32] If she shopped with him, it was to
find the name of 'Monsieur Dickin' well known to tradesmen
(through the current serialization of *Martin Chuzzlewit* in the
Moniteur). One day she had a chat with a man who had delivered
some vases to the family apartments. He declared himself a regular
reader of Monsieur Dickin, whose characters he found 'si spirituelle-
ment tournés!'—especially Mrs. Todgers: 'Ah! Qu'elle est drôle, et
précisément comme une dame que je connais à Calais!'[33]

At this time Alfred, Frank, and Sydney were attending an English
school in Boulogne. When eight-year-old Sydney had joined the
older two, his father had given the headmaster special instructions
not to put the boy 'back into strokes', as he had already 'learned
from his Aunt to write very well' and had even carried on 'a large
imaginary correspondence with scores of people'.[34]

The three boys being still in Boulogne the following June, the
Dickenses and Georgina came over to join them for the summer.
Walter, on holiday from Wimbledon, and the Boulogne boys all
brought away prizes from school. 'In honour of these achievements,'
wrote the proud father to Miss Coutts, 'we have made rejoicings with
five franc pieces, running matches, and cricket ditto.' But in spite
of vacation and scholastic glory, discipline was not relaxed. The
boys had to keep their bedrooms scrupulously neat and clean. 'Each
in his turn is appointed Keeper for the week,' explained Dickens,
'and I go out in solemn procession (Georgina and the Baby [Edward,
'Plorn']—as we call him—forming the rest of it) three times a day,
on a tour of inspection.'[35] Georgina, twenty-nine now and solidified
in the Dickens mould, needed no such expeditions to form her character and habits. Whatever taint of Hogarth carelessness she might
have been born with had been irretrievably dissipated.

For all an outsider could see, the Dickenses' life in Boulogne was
idyllic. The garden was pure enchantment: the sweet pea blossoms
swayed on seven-foot vines, the honeysuckle was a delicate cascade
of fragrance, roses and a hedge of giant geraniums almost hid the
house. Supplied by all this bloom, Mamie daily improved her talent
for flower arranging.[36] The younger children, too, seemed busy and
happy. Benign matrons, observing their devotion to their charming
aunt, might have beamed to reflect on her probable destiny with a
brood of her own.

Such thoughts had haunted her brother-in-law for some time now.
Three years earlier, when he had toured Italy and Switzerland with
Wilkie Collins and Augustus Egg, he had sprinkled a letter to
Georgina with praise of the artist: 'an excellent fellow and full of
good qualities', 'a generous and staunch man at heart', a person

GEORGINA HOGARTH as Lady Grace in
The Lighthouse by Charles Allston Collins
Dickens House, London

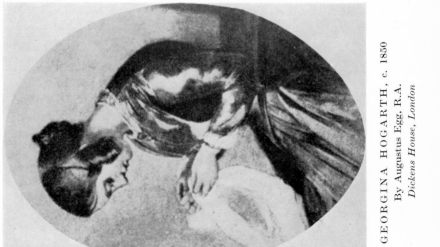

GEORGINA HOGARTH, c. 1850
By Augustus Egg, R.A.
Dickens House, London

with 'a good and honourable nature'.[37] Dickens's motive must have
been quite transparent, for these remarks followed by little more
than a week a pointed observation to Catherine: 'A general sentiment
expressed this morning, that Georgina ought to be married. Perhaps
you'll mention it to her!'[38]

But Georgina had already dismissed any idea of becoming Mrs.
Augustus Egg of Ivy Cottage, perhaps as long ago as 1850, when she
had sat to the painter for the attractive circular portrait which
shows her in profile demurely bending over her sewing. Though she
had refused him, they had remained good friends. Dickens had not
tried to influence her, he declared to Miss Coutts, but had only urged
her to 'be quite sure that she knew her own mind'. He admitted the
desirability of a match with a painter of established reputation—
though, to be sure, Egg was not her intellectual equal. But then,
not one man in five was, for she had one of the 'most remarkable
capacities' he had ever known and was, moreover, 'one of the most
amiable and affectionate of girls'. Having confessed this much,
Dickens unburdened himself further: 'Whether it is, or is not a pity
that she is all she is to me and mine instead of brightening up a good
little man's house where she would still have the artist kind of life
she is used to, about her, is a knotty point I can never settle to my
satisfaction. And I have been trying to untwist it in my mind on the
road here, until it will persist in ravelling itself out on this paper.'[39]

A little later, friends, solicitous for Georgina's happiness, wished
that a match might be made with another painter, William Mulready,
R.A. Gentle, personable, and dependable, he had no enemies. He
was, moreover, on good terms with the family. It is likely, though,
that the faultless Mulready, another 'good little man', seemed too
bland a dish beside Dickens's spice. At any rate, the well-wishers
were to be disappointed: Mulready remained a bachelor, Georgina
a spinster.[40]

Was it attachment for her brother-in-law that made Georgina
reject Augustus Egg and any suitor who may have followed him?
There is no evidence that she thought of Dickens with romantic
ardour. If she knowingly hid any such love in her heart, sublimating
it in sisterly devotion and service, she naturally would not have
confessed it. Modern psychology tends, of course, to find in sex, conscious or not, the only drive powerful enough to motivate such lifelong obsession as this woman's. But of psychoanalysis she lived and
died unaware. For Georgina Hogarth it sufficed that Charles Dickens
was the major planet in her sky, and she, his satellite, had to move
in an orbit fixed by his.

As for her idol, quite aware of his compelling personality, did he

ever suspect his 'best and truest friend' of more than sisterly love?
If so, he may have furnished a hint of it through the parallel with
Agnes Wickfield, who long hid her love under the cheerful guise of
friendship. Near the end of *Copperfield*, but before the culmination
of its unconvincing romance, the obtuse David tells Agnes that there
is about her 'something inexplicably gentle and softened . . .; something that might have been sorrowful in some one else', but that in
calm, cheerful Agnes does not seem so. He then goes on to say that
he believes her able to remain for a lifetime 'faithfully affectionate
against all discouragement'.[41] Dickens could manoeuvre his plot so
that Agnes's love should not remain unrequited but, not being himself disposed to fall in love with her kind, could hardly have done as
much for Georgina Hogarth, had her secret heart matched Agnes
Wickfield's.[42]

> *   *   *

   The decade of the 1850's, for all her pride in the children and
Dickens's expanding fame, for all the thrills of foreign residence, was
an uneasy time for Georgina. The marital discord that had begun
soon after Mamie's birth[43] was growing more and more menacing.
The roster of Catherine's inept and careless acts, each petty in itself,
had so lengthened with the years that her husband's jangled nerves
were now raw. Governing his own life by 'habits of punctuality,
order, and diligence', as he had pointed out in *Copperfield*,[44] Dickens
could not tolerate the lack of these qualities in anyone, much less in
his wife. Nor could he endure her plaintive reproaches or her passi-
vity. Finally, his very intolerance of her burdened him with guilt,
as did fathering such numerous progeny on a woman with whom
he declared himself completely incompatible.[45]
   In the uncomfortable position of a buffer between the two,
Georgina tried alternately to reduce friction and to conceal it. Often
Catherine tearfully inisted that she wished to leave the house and
live apart, but Georgina 'remonstrated, reasoned, . . . again and
again to prevent a separation'.[46] This she had good cause to do, for
not only would such an event mean public disgrace and all the usual
miseries of a broken home; for her it would mean a painful choice,
either alternative fraught with woeful consequences.
   Even under the delights and diversions of Paris raced the under-
current of vexation. In this perturbed time not even Georgina was
exempt from her brother-in-law's carping displeasure. During one of
his London visits he expected word from her about accommodations
in Paris for Wilkie Collins. Her letter was not forthcoming. Since
it was his birthday Dickens must have felt doubly neglected. His

failure to get the expected information, he complained to Catherine, had made him 'look rather foolish' in not being able to tell Collins 'what had been done for him in the way of quarters'. The foreign post had just arrived, he went on, and still no letter from Georgina. 'I cannot conceive what she has been about', he growled.[47] But Georgina *had* written, as he discovered after dinner when two letters from her arrived together. *'Take the Pavilion,'* he advised her tersely in regard to Collins's accommodation. A day later he wrote quite casually about his activities, completely ignoring his pique of the previous afternoon.[48]

Georgina, acutely sensitive to his moods, would have understood his agitation during this period: his feverish exertions in the amateur theatricals and the benefit readings, and his fanatical need for the long, exhausting walks were clearly a desperate attempt to ignore the domestic situation. Some years later he was to write her a letter admitting that this had indeed been the case: 'I feel that if I had not been reading . . .,' he confessed, 'I never could have borne the marriage, and should have excused myself somehow'.[49]

In his hypersensitive state he held his mother-in-law in perennial disfavour. When, during the summer of 1854, she decided on sudden impulse to take out life insurance, he fumed in a letter to Georgina at the 'desperation' of Mrs. Hogarth's 'imbecility' and her impracticality in taking such a step, ridiculously expensive for a sixty-one-year-old woman in poor health.[50] The frankness of his remarks hints that he guessed what side Georgina would take in the event of an open rift. Apparently the crack in the Hogarth family solidarity had already begun.

Especially keen was his irritation on visiting the Hogarths at Tavistock House while they were making a home there for Charley. Unwell and probably never a fastidious housekeeper, Mrs. Hogarth had allowed dust to accumulate till it 'lay an inch thick' on the floor. Only when Dickens remonstrated with her did conditions improve somewhat. And there were also her unpaid bills at the apothecary's for medicines and attendance. Without mentioning the matter to any of the family, he settled the account.[51] As the time drew near for the Hogarths to leave, Dickens could not 'bear the contemplation of their imbecility any more'. For some months he had been 'dead sick of the Scottish tongue in all its moods and tenses'. The sight of his father-in-law at the breakfast table, he complained to Wills, had 'undermined' his 'constitution'.[52]

Once the house was his own again, Dickens and the butler 'wallowed in dust for four hours', getting it in order for the return of the family from France. In the meantime Georgina had discovered that they would all need new passports and had set about getting them. The Tavistock purification rites completed, Dickens reported to his wife that he had 'made a very different place of that establishment. . . .'[53]

It was only natural, indeed inevitable, that the Hogarths' ways should have intensified his dissatisfaction with Catherine, to whom he transferred some of his resentment. Unreasonably depressed, often sleepless, frustrated in his attempts to get on with his work, he found no solace in his wife, in whom he seemed to see the placid, irresponsible nature of her parents. But repose, even such as theirs, he sadly lacked. Yet 'for some men', he wrote to Forster in 1856, 'there's no such thing in this life', adding with startling frankness, 'I find that the skeleton in my domestic closet is becoming a pretty big one. . . .'[54]

To De la Rue the following year Dickens made a similar confession: 'We put the Skeleton away in the cupboard, and very few people, comparatively, know of its existence'.[55] Few did, it was true, for the general public still shared the point of view of Mary Howitt toward the novelist's home life. Shortly after attending the Twelfth Night party at Tavistock House in 1857, she wrote to thank her hostess: 'I want to tell *you*, how inexpressibly beautiful & affecting the whole thing was. . . . It carried me to such a rich revelation altogether of God's best & greatest gifts to humanity—the wonderful power and talent displayed, & the beauty and grace of all those lovely young people, your children.' The climax of this well-meant tribute was an ironic note that must have made Catherine wince: 'I cannot imagine human felicity greater than yours, my heart thanked God for you, & still does, & I think of you and yours as being supremely crowned with the blessings of God's love. Of course I include Miss Hogarth in the lovely family group, where she seems like another daughter.'[56]

Under the necessity of keeping the cupboard door shut on the skeleton, Dickens found a safe outlet for misery in the memorandum book where he had begun in 1855 to keep germinal ideas for his stories. 'A misplaced and mis-married man', reads one of the earlier entries; 'always, as it were, playing hide and seek with the world and never finding what Fortune seems to have hidden when he was born'. Even more desperate was his cry some pages later: 'WE, fettered together'.[57]

*   *   *

Chafing under the fetters in February, two days after his forty-third birthday, Dickens was arrested by a hauntingly familiar handwriting as he thumbed through some mail just delivered. It was the

hand of Maria Beadnell, now Mrs. Henry L. Winter. Through his
mind surged tender memories of his early love affair. 'Twenty years
vanished like a dream,' he wrote to her. In a sentimental glow he
made plans for an early meeting. He would have Mrs. Dickens call
and invite the Winters to dinner. But before the proposed reunion
took place, there were more letters. He was ecstatic, eloquent, nos-
talgic. No one could ever know the heartache that youthful separation from Maria had caused him. What had become of the bundle of
letters returned at her request? He remembered tying it with a blue
ribbon to match her gloves. 'I have never been so good a man
since,' he assured her, 'as I was when you made me wretchedly
unhappy. I shall never be half so good a fellow any more.' Had she
recognized glimpses of herself while following the story of Dora in
Copperfield? Perhaps she had even laid the book down to reflect,
'How dearly that boy must have loved me, and how vividly this
man remembers it!'[58]

But all too quickly came the jarring realization that the image
treasured these many years in memory did not match the reality.
Loath to make their first meeting a conventional visit between the
two families, Dickens and Mrs. Winter arranged, at the latter's suggestion, a prior rendezvous alone. So after a long interval David
again beheld his Dora. Gone was the apparition he had cherished so
faithfully—the lovely creature in a raspberry-coloured dress trimmed
in black velvet. In her place—a shapeless, simpering middle-aged
woman, ridiculous in her affected artlessness, unbearable with her
interminable prattle. All the rapture evoked by Mrs. Winter's first
note gave way to bitter disillusion. Thereafter he evaded her persistent overtures. If she suggested further meetings, he doubted that
he could be at home. If she accused him of avoiding her, he pleaded
his work, insisting that a writer must surrender himself wholly to
his art. When he answered her importunate correspondence, it was
with matter-of-fact notes. These, he told her, would of necessity be
'miraculously few' and 'laudably short'.[59] And therewith he turned
the main responsibility for the correspondence over to his sister-in-
law. It was not the first time that irksome duties had been palmed
off on Georgina.

To her, therefore, fell the courtesy of thanking Mrs. Winter for
her *'most valuable'* suggestions just before Walter had sailed for
India on 20 July 1857. (Now aged sixteen, he had completed his
training at Wimbledon and had been nominated, through Miss
Coutts's influence, to a cadetship in the East India Company.) Mrs.
Winter, to keep affection warm, had written Dickens to urge that the
young traveller be supplied with flannels and medications. Georgina

assured her that this counsel had been of 'essential service', for curiously enough, the need for quinine and the like had not occurred to 'his father, who generally thinks of everything!' She included an account of the sad trial of parting, when Walter had broken down on taking leave of his mother, his sisters, and her. But Dickens and Charley, who had accompanied him to Southampton, had reported him not 'so much cut up again'. Rather, he had been 'set up' by the comfortable accommodations of his ship, the captain's personality, and the presence of an old school fellow on board. 'This is all very cheering, is it not? and reconciles us very much to the separation,' Georgina assured Mrs. Winter. 'Please God he may keep his health and do well!'[60]

A month later the shattered dream image of Maria Beadnell was replaced by the tangible charms of a slight, graceful girl who began rehearsing for the Manchester performance of *The Frozen Deep*. Feeling that Georgina and his other feminine amateurs lacked the vocal power needed to fill the huge Manchester Free Trade Hall, Dickens had found professionals for their parts, engaging at the suggestion of Alfred Wigan, manager of the Olympic Theatre, a Mrs. Ternan and her daughters, Maria and Ellen.[61] It was the blonde Ellen Lawless Ternan, assigned to Georgina's role of Lucy, who attracted Dickens and brought the skeleton out of the cupboard. Only eighteen, Katey's age, she soon entered upon terms of lifelong cordiality with Georgina Hogarth.

Chapter Five
'NO OTHER WAY OUT'

THE Manchester engagement and Dickens's subsequent tour of the Lake District with Wilkie Collins gave Georgina an interval of relief from the bickering of the fettered pair, an interval in which to think. *Gads Hill* Summering at Gad's Hill, the country place which Dickens had bought the previous year, she meanwhile received regular and lengthy accounts of the travellers' adventures. But for Catherine no letters came—not even perfunctory greetings. Her name was not included in the closing formula: 'Love to Mamie, Katey, Charley, Harry, and the darling Plorn'. The letters were otherwise quite Dickensian—in their humour and descriptive detail, even in their note of annoyance with Collins: 'I am perpetually tidying the rooms after him. . . .' Dickens's own fastidious quarters Georgina was asked to imagine as 'airy and clean . . . , perfect arrangement, and exquisite neatness'.[1]

With Charles back again after his two-week tour, she felt the shadow of his dark moods fall once more. Though she had done her best to reconcile him to Catherine, she was now beginning to agree with him that harmony was impossible. Earlier that month he had unburdened himself to Forster, confessing that with each year the marriage became harder to bear for both Catherine and him. He assumed his share of the blame: 'There is plenty of fault on my side . . . in the way of a thousand uncertainties, caprices, and difficulties of disposition. . . .' Again at the end of the month: 'Poor Catherine and I are not made for each other, and there is no help for it'. What a tragedy that he had ever met her and kept her from marrying 'another kind of man'! He knew she would be sympathetic if he were ill, but with his recovery the old barriers would rise between them. '. . . Nothing on earth could make her understand me, or suit us to each other.'[2]

As if to underscore the hopelessness of their life together, he made the wall between them tangible in October. From the country retreat he wrote Anne Brown (now Mrs. Cornelius), for many years their trusted servant, instructing her to have his dressing-room converted into a separate bedroom. The opening between it and

Catherine's room was to be closed off with a plain white door, with specially built bookshelves in the recess. A small iron bedstead, already ordered for his use, would be delivered before he returned to London. He asked Anne to give these alterations no publicity, as he preferred not to have them discussed by 'comparative strangers'.[3] These instructions were carried out while the Hogarths were once more living at Tavistock, thus presumably with their knowledge.[4]

But the new sleeping arrangements did not free Dickens from the conviction that he and his wife would know only misery as long as they lived under one roof. From Catherine came dark suspicions, bitter tears, recriminations as she heard her husband's name linked with Ellen Ternan's. She could not accept his explanation that this was only an older man's innocent attraction to girlish charms. Recalling her fury and ugly accusations in Italy thirteen years before, Dickens poured out his fresh woes to De la Rue: 'Between ourselves, . . . I don't get on better in these later times with a certain poor lady you know of, than I did in the earlier Peschiere days. Much worse. Much worse!' Nor could she get on with the children, he added, no, not even with herself. He mocked at her suspicions: 'She has been excruciatingly jealous of, and has obtained positive proof of my being on the most intimate terms with, at least fifteen thousand women of various conditions in life, since we left Genoa. Please to respect me for this vast experience.' Were it not for Georgina, he insisted, he and the two girls could not have managed. 'She is the active spirit of the house, and the children dote upon her.'[5]

So Georgina continued to preserve the household routine. At least there would be order, whatever the subsurface tensions. But an oppressive atmosphere hung over Tavistock House. Christmas 1857 passed without the usual festivities: there were no parties, no dinners, no ensuing Twelfth Night theatricals to plan for. The shadow 'of change impending' lengthened into spring. In a welter of wretchedness Dickens confessed to Wilkie Collins that he could neither work nor rest, that he had 'never known a moment's peace or content, since the last night of The Frozen Deep'.[6]

In another such escape to his admiring public, then, lay his only hope of relief. On the 29th of April, at St. Martin's Hall, he accordingly embarked on a new venture, a series of readings, not for charity, but for his own profit. The response was tremendously gratifying. But even as he glowed from this public triumph, the private torment became intolerable. The rupture had to come at last.

It was probably precipitated by Catherine's jealousy of Ellen Ternan. When a bracelet purchased for Ellen was delivered by mistake at Tavistock House—Dickens was known to reward his actors with shirt studs and the like, and his actresses with similar personal mementoes—Catherine exploded. So did her mother. Unmindful that her son-in-law had made possible her extended stays in luxurious Tavistock, had helped her husband to a position with the *Daily News*, had paid her medical bills, Mrs. Hogarth denounced him and demanded that Catherine be given her freedom and a settlement. After a half-hearted effort to avoid a public break, Dickens agreed. Forster, as his representative, and Mark Lemon, as Catherine's, were to work out the details. Legal technicalities were to be handled by Dickens's friend and solicitor, Frederic Ouvry, and by Catherine's solicitor, George F. Smith.[7]

In May Georgina, firm in her determination to remain in the relationship to which she had already 'sacrificed the best part of her youth and life',[8] was constantly stung by the reproaches of her parents and her younger sister Helen, who regarded her decision to stay with Dickens as an outrage against the bonds of kinship. Worn by the long conflict in loyalties, she could hardly have borne these weeks had it not been for the heartening devotion of her nieces and nephews—and of their father, when she saw him at all. (During the negotiations he had taken refuge in his living quarters at the *Household Words* office.)[9] The situation eased only a little when Mrs. Hogarth took Catherine down to Brighton, where the final document of separation was presented for her signature early in June.[10]

While the details were being worked out, Dickens felt that he owed an explanation—or defence—to a few close friends. To Miss Coutts he wrote that he and his wife had 'been virtually separated a long time'. Catherine was the only person, he maintained, with whom he could never establish enough common interests for 'communicating'. Moreover, the children felt no affection for their mother, for she had 'never played with them in their infancy, never attracted their confidence as they have grown older. . . .' Even Mamie and Katey, for all their tender natures, had 'their hearts shut up in her presence as if they were closed by some horrid spring'. What had happened, he firmly believed, could be clear only to 'Georgina, who has seen it grow from year to year, and who is the best, the most unselfish, the most devoted of human Creatures'. But Mary Hogarth, who had seen it all begin, had 'understood it . . . well in the first months of our marriage'.[11]

Most of the explanations showered on Dickens's friends were less revealing than this and referred to the trouble only as general incompatibility. Certainly a major source of dissatisfaction had been his wife's scant interest in supervising her home. (More than supervisory

E

duties were not required of her—nor, for that matter, of Georgina.)
Catherine's record of ten confinements and several miscarriages had
not exempted her from censure on this score, for her lethargy had
distressed her husband long before she had borne the last of her
children. It may be that Dickens's natural love for tidy efficiency
had grown to fanatic proportions in order to counterbalance his
wife's slipshod ways. Possibly his repeated insistence on domestic
competence in his heroines (Little Nell, Agnes Wickfield, Esther
Summerson) was an indirect, though not unconscious, way of
prodding Catherine to recognize her own lacks.

A similar covert effort to awaken her to a realization of her shortcomings may be suspected in a letter from Genoa five years before
the separation. His friend Gibbs's wife, Dickens told her, 'never
reads, never works, never talks, never gives an order or directs
anything, has only a taste for the Theatre . . . and buying clothes'.[12]

Dickens may have resorted to still another indirect method
of moulding his wife's character, the kinder and more subtle way of
flattery, such as one might use with a child. Just after the havoc of
the Tavistock House remodelling, when his impatience with Catherine's clumsy helplessness on the premises had been ill concealed
by levity, he had written her, 'I am continually thinking of the house
in the midst of all the bustle, but I trust it with such confidence to
you that I am quite at my ease about it'.[13] But he was dealing with
refractory clay, and no method, direct or indirect, served to remould
it nearer to the heart's desire.

Besides—and it was another irritation to the trim and agile
husband—there was literally too much of that clay! Accustomed to
the accepted practice of eating for two during her pregnancies,
Catherine did not drop the habit (a comforting one, no doubt)
during the brief interims. She had consequently grown fat and
florid before she was forty, and must have presented a somewhat
comical figure riding in her carriage, the 'little pill-box on wheels
which staggers about town with Mrs. Dickens', her husband quipped
to Leigh Hunt.[14]

Another source of dissatisfaction was Catherine's mediocre intellect. Not that Dickens required, or even admired, a bookish or
highly intellectual woman. Nor would the Inimitable have relished
matching wits at his own fireside with, for example, a keen and
caustic Jane Carlyle. He needed, rather, a gentle worshipper, but
one whose mind would respond with real appreciation to his. Catherine did not fit comfortably into his literary and intellectual circle.
Of her he could never have felt—as he did of Georgina—that her
happiness required her having 'the artist kind of life she is used to'

ELLEN TERNAN
*Enthoven Theatre Collection, Victoria and
Albert Museum*

CATHERINE DICKENS   CHARLES DICKENS
Henry E. Huntington Library and Art Gallery

about her. She had no qualities to advance him in that group; hers was a 'weak hand that could never help or serve [his] name'. Those of his circle who regarded her affectionately were prone to mix a pitying indulgence with their kindness for 'poor Mrs. Dickens'.[15] But no one, certainly not her husband and sister, ever saw her faults as other than negative and congenital.

Meanwhile, as the lawyers worked out the deed of separation which would banish Catherine and make her sister mistress of the home, Georgina marshalled her reasons for remaining. Though not unaware of the cost, she would hardly have debated her decision. Once plastic enough to be moulded by Dickens, she was now too firmly set to be shaken from the mould by parents, sisters, friends. Moreover, she liked it too well. As 'the active spirit of the house', she was exercising natural aptitudes developed during a sixteen-year training period. Far more than Catherine she was suited to administer the home of a distinguished author. Furthermore, she was sincerely attached to the children and they to her. They needed her, and no hired governess or nurse, however devoted and capable, could give them the counsel, companionship, and security of permanent affection they derived from her.

And she had to remember the financial aspect. Charles had provided for her generously, amply repaying her services to him and his family. But if she were to withdraw from his house now, he could hardly be expected to make a settlement on her as well as on Catherine. As for her father, a year's bill for her bonnets and crinolines alone would have staggered him. Only four months earlier Catherine had confessed to Miss Coutts that he had been unable to assist her unemployed brother Edward.[16] Besides, if Georgina were to return to the home of her parents, who had relinquished her at age fifteen, it would be to enter an atmosphere hostile to Dickens. Unthinkable!

Of course, she might seek to earn her own independent living. But how was a spinster of thirty-one, a gentlewoman, to support herself? She might, perhaps, become a governess; for such a position her experience in teaching the Dickens children to read and write would have trained her. Her general background and her proficiency in French and simple Italian would also have fitted her for this useful, almost menial, place in some household—one perhaps inferior to that in which she had, except nominally, long been mistress. Another unthinkable solution.

Marriage might provide a blameless exit from the dilemma, but at her age a Victorian woman, particularly a penniless one, found opportunities limited. To be sure, Egg had once proposed to her and might yet think fondly of her as still in youthful bloom, but it is doubtful whether he or any suitor could win her affection now. Dickens was her bright particular star. Dazzled by his radiance, she had from the beginning chosen her orbit and was henceforth not to be moved from it.

So all the arguments, selfish and unselfish, favoured her remaining. Loyalty to the tearful, ineffectual sister facing exile did not deter her. Since there are those who judge Georgina Hogarth to have been an unnatural traitor to the ties of blood, one may raise the question of who would have benefited had she chosen to go with Catherine. Not Dickens, or his children, or Georgina herself—probably not even Catherine, in any lasting or significant way. (Though she would undoubtedly have taken comfort at the time in being vindicated by all her immediate kin.) It would appear that the sisters, though never on unamiable terms, were not really companionable. And Catherine's mild psychotic disturbances, which she herself recognized as connected with the conditions of her marriage,[17] made her pitiably difficult at times. If Dickens's statement can be credited, her mother, her sister Helen, and the younger brother could not have lived contentedly with her, nor she with them. It was 'her misery to live in some fatal atmosphere which slays every one to whom she should be dearest'.[18] Restricted to the sphere of Catherine's mental and physical lethargy and self-pity, Georgina's active spirit could only have wasted into useless discontent, with her sister none the happier for the sacrifice.

In May the strange terms of the legal agreement were completed. Catherine was to have £600 a year and a place of her own. Charley would live with her, the others with their father, but she was to see them whenever she chose. Through her representative, Lemon, then through Forster, then Ouvry, the word reached her husband that 'Mrs. Dickens thankfully accepts the proposal'.[19]

Many another woman, being as blameless a wife and mother— blameless in any legally admissible sense, that is—would have demanded the custody of her children. That Catherine did not attempt to do so may be further testimony to the emotional torpor of which her husband accused her. As she had unprotestingly yielded her body for over twenty years, so she now yielded her children. As the *in*active spirit of the house, perhaps she had neither the desire nor the energy to wrest the care of her offspring from the capable hands of her sister. But if her love for the children was listless, it may also have been generous enough to wish them in better hands than her own.

So it was no objection from Catherine which delayed the signing

of the deed of separation. Just as negotiations reached the final
stage, Dickens was furious to learn that Mrs. Hogarth and her
daughter Helen had circulated 'smashing slanders' about him. The
stream of gossip flowing from their original remarks soon divided
into two main channels: an affair with an actress, an affair with his
own wife's sister! Thus the Hogarths had unwittingly aimed their
shafts at a member of their own family. To be sure, they disapproved
of Georgina's unconventional position in Dickens's home after the
rift, but their accusations had never gone beyond mere folly and a
'mistaken sense of duty'. Certainly they had not intended to compromise her character in a public scandal. But the Georgina rumour
spread. Thackeray heard and denied it at the Garrick Club. To his
mother he ruefully explained how his impulsive denial of the one
intrigue had only confirmed the other: 'No says I, no such thing—
it's with an actress. . . .' A day or so later he called on Catherine
Dickens—'poor matron after 22 years of marriage going away out
of her house!' The visit persuaded him that there was indeed some
'row' or other involving the sister, but 'nothing against Miss H——
except that she is the cleverer & better woman of the two, has got
the affections of the children & the father'.[20]

To Dickens it was unthinkable that the rumours should go unchal-
lenged. He demanded that Mrs. Hogarth and Helen sign a statement
retracting their charges. But he did not 'in the least suspect' his
pathetic wife of any connection with the scandal, he told Ouvry,
adding, 'It would be a pleasure to her (I think) to know that I had
begun to trust her so far; and I believe that it would do her lasting
good if you could carry that assurance to her'.[21] To the Hogarths he
made a threat: no signed retraction, no generous settlement for
Catherine. With the negotiations thus in jeopardy, George Hogarth
tried his hand at mediation. In a statement prepared by Catherine's
lawyer and forwarded to Ouvry, he denied that his family had ever
had any part in the gossip about Georgina: 'I can have no difficulty
or hesitation in assuring you that the report that I or my wife or
Daughter have at any time stated or insinuated that any impropriety of conduct had taken place between my Daughter Georgiana
[*sic*] and her Brother in Law Mr. Charles Dickens is totally and
entirely unfounded.

'It is of course a matter of grief to us that after the unfortunate
differences which have arisen between my daughter Mrs. Charles
Dickens and her husband, my daughter Georgiana [*sic*] should
remain with his family but while we regret what we regard as a
mistaken sense of duty we have never for one instant imputed to her
any improper motive for so doing.'[22]

But this statement did not satisfy Ouvry. In the first place, no one suspected mild George Hogarth of circulating rumours of any sort; his signature, therefore, was not required. A proper retraction would have carried the signatures of Mrs. Hogarth and Helen, who had initiated this scandal. Furthermore, it was Ellen Ternan against whom their gossip had really been directed, but the retraction ignored that aspect of the case. Last of all, Ouvry pronounced the charge against Dickens and Georgina to be of such a 'disgusting and horrible nature' that it should not 'be distinctly written down' in any statement intended for circulation.[23] (Mid-nineteenth-century England looked with pecular horror on intimacy with a wife's sister, such a relationship still being regarded legally as incest.)

The only acceptable statement, then, would be a blanket retraction couched in such general terms as would clear Dickens as well as Georgina, Ellen, or any other woman who might be accused. Drafted by Ouvry and altered by Dickens, such a statement was forwarded to Mrs. Hogarth and Helen for their signatures: 'It having been stated to us that in reference to the differences which have resulted in the separation of Mr. and Mrs. Charles Dickens, certain statements have been circulated that such differences are occasioned by circumstances deeply affecting the moral character of Mr. Dickens and compromising the reputation and good name of others, we solemnly declare that we now disbelieve such statements. We know that they are not believed by Mrs. Dickens, and we pledge ourselves on all occasions to contradict them, as entirely destitute of foundation.'[24]

Then Dickens, taking a very high-handed attitude toward the signers and Catherine's solicitor as well, refused to assent to the latter's proposal of a simultaneous exchange of the Hogarth statement for the deed of separation. Instead, as 'a simple act of justice', he demanded the retraction first: 'I must have that paper at once. I must have it in the course of Monday or not at all'.[25] George Smith complied, reasonably pointing out that he had not intended to bargain, but had merely considered it proper to retain the paper till the completion of the separation details.[26]

The deed of separation at last delivered to Catherine on 4th June, Georgina had to weather Dickens's continued campaign to undo the damage to his reputation—and hers. His action took the bold course of appealing directly to his public with an analysis of the domestic crisis and a strong denial of all unsavoury gossip. The statement drafted, he sent it to Catherine for her permission to publish, adding, 'I earnestly hope that all unkindness is over between you and me'.[27] Catherine obligingly gave her consent.

On 7th June, accordingly, *The Times*, under the heading PER-
SONAL, carried Dickens's account of the separation as an amicable
settlement of a 'sacredly private' trouble, perfectly understood by
his own children. He denounced the 'whispered rumours' as 'most
grossly false, most monstrous, and most cruel', and concluded with
this warning: ' . . . Whosoever repeats one of them after this denial,
will lie as wilfully and as foully as it is possible for any false witness
to lie, before Heaven and earth.'[28] The same statement came out
five days later in his own *Household Words*. On that same day,
oddly enough, it was carried in the paid advertisements section of
the Halifax *Guardian*,[29] the weekly paper edited long ago by George
Hogarth. Had Dickens himself inserted it, possibly with the intention of undermining any sympathy which the community might
have felt for one of its former prominent families? He had even
tried to publish his proclamation in *Punch*, an odd place for such a
communication, as Editor Mark Lemon and its proprietors, Bradbury and Evans, pointed out. Resenting their refusal to print it,
Dickens broke off the long intimacy with Lemon and all relations
with Bradbury and Evans, his own publishers. The latter rupture
was especially awkward because Evans's daughter Bessie and
Charley Dickens, who had grown up together, were planning to be
married.

The result of the proclamation, printed on both sides of the
Atlantic, was to arouse wild speculation in circles that had hitherto
known nothing of Dickens's domestic crisis. Readers were mysti-
fied: What was the 'sacredly private nature' of the trouble? What
'monstrous lies' had been circulated? Who were the 'innocent persons' compromised? Many doubted the propriety of such a public
appeal. The idol of the English hearth had violated its standards of
decorum.[30]

Having addressed the wide world, Dickens did not cease to shower
his friends with explanations. Defending himself for having publicized his intimate affairs, he wrote Macready: 'The question was not
myself; but others. Foremost among them—of all people in the
world—Georgina! Mrs. Dickens's weakness, and her mother's and
her youngest sister's wickedness, drifted to that, without seeing what
they would strike against—though I had warned them in the
strongest manner.'[31] To Tagart he expressed the hope that he might
'live to be good and true to my innocent people who have been
traduced along with me'.[32] With his Swiss friend Cerjat he took a
tone of self-pity, of aggrieved tolerance for the 'knaves and fools' who
had maligned him, philosophically declaring, 'And I hope that my
books will speak for themselves and me, when I and my faults and

virtues, my fortunes and misfortunes are all forgotten'. He concluded with a word on his new domestic arrangements: Mamie
would keep house, assisted by Katey 'and her Aunt Georgina, who
is, and always has been, like another sister'.[33]

But far more detailed than any of these accounts was the one he
sent to his reading manager, Arthur Smith, even before the June
proclamation. In it Georgina's past and present position was clearly
defined: 'Nothing has, on many occasions, stood between us and a
separation but Mrs. Dickens's sister, Georgina Hogarth. From the
age of fifteen, she has devoted herself to our home and our children.
She has been their playmate, nurse, instructress, friend, protectress,
adviser and companion. . . . I do not know—I cannot by any stretch
of fancy imagine—what would have become of them but for this
aunt, who has grown up with them, to whom they are devoted, and
who has sacrificed the best part of her youth and life to them.[34]

'. . . Mrs. Dickens has often expressed to her her sense of her
affectionate care and devotion in the home—never more strongly
than within the last twelve months.

'For some years past Mrs. Dickens has been in the habit of representing to me that it would be better for her to go away and live
apart. . . . I have uniformly replied that . . . the children were the
first consideration, and that I feared they must bind us together "in
appearance".

'At length . . . it was suggested to me by Forster that even for their
sakes, it would surely be better to reconstruct and rearrange their
unhappy home.'

In the future, Dickens explained, all the children but his eldest
son were to live with him, 'in the continued companionship of their
Aunt Georgina, for whom they all have the tenderest affection that
I have ever seen among young people, and who has a higher claim
(as I have often declared for many years) upon my affection, respect
and gratitude than anybody in this world'.

The statement closed with an avowal of the innocence of Ellen
Ternan (unnamed), a 'virtuous and spotless creature . . . pure, and
as good as my own dear daughters'. Attached was a copy of the
retraction signed by those 'two wicked persons', Mrs. Hogarth and
Helen. Arthur Smith was urged to show the entire communication
'to any one who wishes to do me right, or to any one who may have
been misled into doing me wrong'.[35]

Smith thereupon felt free to let a New York *Tribune* reporter see
the letter. As a result, it was published in the *Tribune* of 16th
August, and was soon reprinted in certain London papers. Dickens
protested at once that he had not sanctioned the publication of this

'private repudiation of monstrous scandals' and directed Ouvry so
to assure Catherine's solicitor. To Georgina, whom he kept posted
on the whole affair, Dickens shortly sent word that her sister's legal
representative had written 'a very good note about that published
letter: saying that he was much obliged by the assurance that I had
not sanctioned its publication, but that it was quite unnecessary to
him, as he had been quite certain of that, from the moment when he
saw it'.[36] Feeling that he had vindicated himself, Dickens thereafter
referred to this unauthorized publication as 'The Violated Letter'.
Curiously, the same issue of the *Tribune* that had printed the letter
carried an editorial chiding him for continuing to issue public
denials of the charges against him: 'One more uncalled-for letter
from Mr. D. will finish him', the piece concluded.[37]

Georgina herself added to the stream of explanations that went
forth, for to her naturally fell the task of breaking the news of the
separation to Maria Beadnell Winter. She did so in a letter strikingly
similar in substance and phrasing to portions of Dickens's unfortunate one to Arthur Smith, a communication which antedated hers
by six days. 'Believe me,' she pleaded, 'when I assure you that I am
perfectly convinced that this plan will be for the happiness of all. I
worked hard to prevent it, as long as I saw any possibility, but
latterly I have come to the conviction that there was no other way
out of the domestic misery of this house.' The chief blame she placed
on Catherine: 'Unhappily . . . by some constitutional misfortune &
incapacity, my sister *always* from their infancy, threw her children
upon other people, consequently as they grew up, there was not the
usual strong tie between them and her—in short for many years,
although we have put a good face upon it, we have been very miserable at home. [These remarks are supported by what Katey, as an
adult, is said to have told a friend: namely, that her mother "was
heavy and unregardful of her children."][38]

'My sister has often expressed a desire to go and live away, but
Charles never agreed to it on the girls' account but latterly he
thought it must be to their advantage as well as to his own and
Catherine's, to consent to this and re-model their unhappy home.'

In giving Mrs. Winter a summary of the reorganization of the
household, Georgina took special care to clarify Charley's position.
He was going to live with Catherine 'at his father's request, and not
taking any part or showing any preference in doing it. . . .' (This
was a sore point with Dickens, who had that very day set John
Leech straight on the matter by sending him Charley's own protest:
'Don't suppose that . . . I was actuated by any feeling of preference
for my mother to you. God knows I love you dearly, and it will be

a hard day for me when I have to part from you and the girls.')[39]

In explaining the new domestic arrangements, Georgina did not assume the honours of Tavistock House for herself. Mamie, as the eldest daughter, she made clear, would naturally take 'her mother's place as mistress of the house'. Though Mamie and Katey and she were to work together, 'all the dignity will be Mary's [Mamie's], and she will do the honours modestly gracefully & prettily'.

Such a drastic change in their household, Georgina admitted, would generate wild speculation. ' . . . Charles is too public a man to take such a step without exciting a more than usual nine days' wonder—and we have heard of the most wonderful rumours and wicked slanders which have been flying about town. . . .' He wished a few of his *'real* friends' to know the truth, she concluded, so that they might prove their loyalty by silencing lies with facts.

In making this oblique appeal to Mrs. Winter to take up the cudgels for Dickens, Georgina must also have been aware that her own unconventional position would call forth public disapproval. Even the American press was to condemn her. A typical rebuke appeared in *Harper's Weekly* for 27th July: 'To make the affair still more notorious, a young lady, Mrs. Dickens' sister, has undertaken to "keep house" for Dickens and his daughters. The whole affair is very repugnant to our idea of matrimonial constancy. . . .' And Gail Hamilton added this tart comment: 'England is beating her obstinate head against marriage with a deceased wife's sister, but here it is the living wife's sister superseding the living wife. . . .'[40]

So the blighted home was still not free from tension in the weeks after Catherine had put on her bonnet to walk for the last time down the stairs and through the long corridor, where stood the marble bust of her youthful bridegroom. Georgina continued to be the butt of scandal. As long as the newspapers only reported current opinion as such, Dickens had no power to silence them. But when Colin Rae Brown, a proprietor of the Glasgow *Daily Bulletin,* was accused by one of his writers of having declared Dickens to be 'the outcry of London', where it was said that his 'sister-in-law had three children by him', then the situation called for prompt legal action. On threat of suit from Dickens's solicitors, however, Brown insisted that he had been misrepresented, claiming to be a warm and devoted admirer of the novelist. He had only 'heard a very malicious report in London', he protested, had 'questioned the truth of it', and had rejoiced to find it unsupported. Convinced, perhaps, that a lawsuit could produce only doubtful results, Dickens appears to have dropped the case. At any rate there is no record of any action.[41]

During the turbulent aftermath of the separation, Catherine

Dickens withdrew quietly to her new quarters at 70 Gloucester Crescent, Regent's Park. Thanking Miss Coutts in May for her kindness, she added in a wavering hand, 'One day though not now I may be able to tell you how hardly I have been used'.[42] It may be that she did confide in Miss Coutts during that first agitated summer. If so, the reversal of her husband's softened attitude toward her during the separation negotiations becomes plausible. For in August he assumed a deeply injured tone when he wrote of Catherine: 'As to Mrs. Dickens's simplicity in speaking of me and my doings, O my dear Miss Coutts do I not know that the weak hand that could never help or serve my name in the least, has struck at it. . . . I want to communicate with her no more. I want to forgive and forget her.'[43]

He carried out his threat. After the year of their separation he wrote Catherine only three times—terse, impersonal notes. When she addressed letters to him, he turned them over to Georgina, declaring, 'It is my fixed purpose . . . to hold as little personal communication with her as I possibly can'. As for her daily practical and personal problems, he was determined that she must work them out alone.[44] He was indeed trying to forget. But to forgive the woman he had injured may have been, in the manner of human nature, more difficult.

In spite of rebuffs, Catherine followed the accounts of his new books, his reading tours, the dramatic adaptations of his novels. A note to her from the manager of the Olympic Theatre shows that she was offered a box for the first performance of *David Copperfield* in 1869. And when the adaptation of *Dombey and Son* was presented in the Old Globe Theatre three years after Dickens's death, she was there, moved to tears. That she continued to read his serial publications is borne out by her request to Chapman and Hall while *Our Mutual Friend* was making its appearance: 'Will you with your usual kindness to me send me my husband's new periodical as it comes out each month'.[45]

She bore her banishment with dignity, leaving no record of resentment, no record of jealousy of her sister. Jealous though she had been at various times of different women, she seems to have shown no resentment toward Georgina, perhaps having the feminine instinct to discern how completely unloverlike was her husband's attachment to this sister. As for losing the affection of her children to Georgina, the first pang—if such there was—of that loss would have passed long since. But she must have felt abandoned. Even her faithful maid, Anne Brown Cornelius, who had cared for her for sixteen years 'like a poor child',[46] had resigned the charge. And when it appeared that Catherine might have the companionship of a son at least, Charley left her—first on a business trip to China in 1860, then to start a home of his own. And so the last twenty-one years of 'a certain poor lady' (as Dickens had called her in 1857) were empty ones, except for invitations from a few sympathetic friends and occasional visits from her children, her sister Helen, and, beginning in 1870, from Georgina.

Chapter Six
'A PLACE TO REPOSE IN'

WITH gossip rife during that painful summer of 1858, Georgina could not avoid apprehension about Dickens's future as a professional entertainer. Would he be jeered at, derided, hooted from the platform? She could find reassurance, though, in the reception his St. Martin's Hall audience had given him a few days after the separation proclamation in *Household Words*. Red geranium in buttonhole, gloves in hand, he had walked somewhat rigidly on to the stage to receive a tumultuous ovation.[1] Under too great a strain, Georgina had not dared to be present when he met this challenge.

She need not have questioned the sequel. Even as scandals multiplied to harass him, his provincial audiences thronged the halls during the August-November reading tour. Drawn partly by curiosity, perhaps, they remained to fall under the spell of a great actor playing many roles, the characters who already lived in their hearts. Georgina, summering at Gad's Hill with the children, could temporarily forget her own woes to glory vicariously in Charles's triumphs. Reading his ecstatic accounts from Dublin, she learned that even the men had wept openly over little Paul Dombey's death. And the women had later stormed the platform to collect the crimson geranium petals that had showered from his lapel.[2] His equally enthusiastic welcome at Manchester three weeks later he chose to interpret as 'affectionate recognition of the late trouble. . . .'[3]

Such a heartening reception everywhere was not the only gratification. Georgina knew the increasing demands on the household budget well enough to understand Charles's elation over his earnings. His August profit alone had been one thousand guineas.[4] The audience in industrial Halifax was so responsive that he could have read for nothing, he told her, adding reassuringly that he 'didn't do exactly that'. The town itself, though, was 'as horrible a place' as he had ever seen. But he had found interesting his encounter there with a music seller who had once played duets with her father. The man had told him much of George Hogarth, Dickens reported, not divulging the nature of the information.[5] There was no hint of rancour towards his father-in-law, that emotion now being confined to the two Hogarth women, whom he was determined never to forgive, 'alive or dead'.[6]

Along with the news of the reading tour Georgina gleaned other details of a sort that would henceforth bulk large in Charles's letters to her: minute bulletins on his health, vivid bits about people, and, always, instructions on the management of affairs at home. She must order him a fresh supply of 'Voice Jujubes' and 'Astringent Lozenges'. She must look up the boys' school bill that had somehow been neglected.[7] And as she received the regular cheques for her household budget, she must see that all obligations were met punctually. Fatigued and hurried though Dickens was while on tour, she could always count on his timing the money for her housekeeping expenses so that she would have it by Monday.[8] Her personal allowance was a separate matter. This was received quarterly.[9]

Interspersed with these practical matters were entertaining passages, such as the story of how Dickens had tactfully set 'Katey quite right' in the matter of an unwanted suitor, Andrew Gordon. His father, Sheriff Gordon of Midlothian, had, it seemed, shown 'smirking satisfaction' at the lad's being 'sweet . . . upon a certain young lady. . . .' But Dickens had dashed these hopes. ' . . . The difference is so obvious between a boy of 18, and a young woman of 19 or 20,' he had told Gordon. 'And I like Andrew so much, and should be so heartily grieved if he were to make himself unhappy.'[10] Auntie doubtless relayed this word to popular Katey, whom she chaperoned to balls at Chatham and wherever such attendance was required.

In the autumn Georgina ended her stay in the country. Accompanied by her nieces and the two little boys, Harry and Plorn, she returned to Tavistock House. (With Charley no longer under that roof, Walter in India, and the three middle boys in school— except during holidays—the family had dwindled to four children.)

Once the crucial year was over, Georgina arranged affairs at Tavistock to accommodate Dickens's new series of London readings and his sittings for a portrait by Frith. She and Mamie went with him to the studio the first time and stayed the full two and a half hours. Both Dickens's friends and the artist would have preferred to see the portrait begun several years earlier, before his moustache had hidden the sensitive lines of his mouth. They had hoped that the 'hideous disfigurement' might be only a passing fancy, but when it was followed by a chin beard, all felt that the sittings must begin at once while there was still some face left to paint.[11] Finished in March, the portrait was exhibited that summer at the Royal Academy. The demonic pace of Dickens's activities, the steeling of his heart against Catherine, the strain of facing what followed the separation—all were mirrored in his painted countenance. The beard could not hide the nervous intensity that burned in the eyes. The expression brought an astute comment from Landseer: 'I wish he looked less eager and busy, and not so much out of himself or beyond himself. I should like to catch him asleep and quiet now and then.'[12] Dickens's own reaction was no less discerning: 'It has received every conceivable pains at Frith's hands, and ought on his account to be good.' At the same time he noted: 'It is a little too much (to my thinking) as if my next door neighbour were my deadly foe, uninsured, and I had just received tidings of his house being afire; otherwise good.'[13] Georgina particularly disliked the portrait.

One month after the completion of the painting, Dickens's new periodical, *All the Year Round*, appeared to replace *Household Words*, which had been discontinued as a result of the rupture with its publishers, Bradbury and Evans. In sympathy with Dickens's animosity towards his former publishers (Evans in particular), Georgina undoubtedly read with satisfaction his gloating account of the clever stratagem by which he had forced the sale of *Household Words*, only to buy out Bradbury and Evans's one-fourth interest himself for a mere £500. Time was never to soften the opinion which she had formed of Evans in 1858. In any matter which concerned Dickens she could be as inflexible as he.

And now, this affair settled and the first anniversary of the separation upon him, Dickens needed to escape from London for the summer to concentrate on *A Tale of Two Cities*, intended for publication in the weekly numbers of his new periodical. His retreat was Gad's Hill, the wholesome, airy haven in rural Kent where Georgina had spent the past two summers. It was to be her home for the next decade, the richest and most active of her life. Because the family had first used it as a summer residence the year before the separation, Catherine had spent a few months in this rural Eden. At that time such a good face was still being put upon the domestic crisis that Hans Christian Andersen, visiting Gad's Hill, had seen only felicity. Catherine's passive lethargy had impressed him as 'womanly repose'.[14]

Dickens had owned the property for three years now. Back in the spring of 1856, when Georgina had received his letter announcing the purchase, she well knew it to be the fulfilment of a lifelong dream. She had often heard the story-book tale: Charles, a little lad walking past the impressive red brick mansion on the Old Dover Road; his father telling him, 'There, my boy, if you work hard and mind your books, you will perhaps one day live in a house like that';

the successful novelist still thinking affectionately of the house with its two ancient cedars of Lebanon across the way. For many years he had coveted the place, but it had never been on the market. Then had come the miracle. One morning about the middle of 1855 Wills, his sub-editor, had rushed up to him, exclaiming, 'It is written that you were to have that house at Gad's Hill'. Only the previous night at a dinner party Wills had learned from a Miss Lynn (the authoress known after her marriage as Elizabeth Lynn-Linton) that her father, the owner of Gad's Hill Place, had recently died. She now wished to dispose of the property.[15]

Though begun at once, negotiations had dragged on for months. Before committing himself, Dickens had cautiously set his architect brother-in-law, Henry Austin, to investigating the soundness of the house. It was not old, dating from 1779, but required careful inspection. It also needed considerable equipment and repair. During the final haggling over the price, Georgina, then in Paris, had been kept informed of negotiations. Knowing Charles's superstition about Friday as his lucky day, she must have smiled at his announcement, dated 14 March 1856: 'This day I have paid the purchase-money for Gad's Hill Place. After drawing the cheque, I turned round to give it to Wills (£1790), and said: "Now isn't it an extraordinary thing—look at the day—Friday!"'[16]

At that time Georgina could not have guessed how much she was to love the place, or even that it was to become the family home. In spite of his sentiment for the house, Dickens had at first regarded it chiefly as an investment.[17] A few months later, however, he had become interested in it as a summer retreat, and in 1857 had begun the extensive improvements which Georgina was to witness at intervals until his death.

Many of these tedious and costly operations had been carried out during the first summer's occupancy. An ample supply of water being required by the large household, a deep well had been drilled. By means of an ingenious pumping engine, operated by a blind-folded pony following a circular track, the reservoir to meet the daily needs could be filled in twenty minutes.[18] Then the roof had been raised to provide more rooms. Dickens had characteristically insisted that all remodelling be done 'without pause or postponement'. The whole business should require only six weeks, he had felt. Meanwhile he had begun to collect furnishings. By sending his servant John 'to buy them as for himself—and permitting him to bring them away ignobly, in vans, carts, barrows, trucks, and coster-monger's trays', he had cleverly saved a substantial sum. Henry Austin had been forewarned that if he should 'meet such a thing as a Mahogany dining table or two marble washing-stands, in a donkey-cart anywhere, or in a cat's meat cart', he might know whose purchase it was.[19]

In that first Gad's Hill summer Frank, Alfred, and Sydney had come home from school to stampede in and out with eight-year-old Harry. Plorn, only five and still in kilts, had been confined more or less to a nursery programme. 'Baby . . . calls "auntie" all over the house,' his father had written to Hans Christian Andersen. Of the older four he had remarked ruefully to Macready that a trip down to Gad's 'for rest . . . means violent cricket with the boys'.[20]

The children had had a chance to watch the fascinating repairs for much longer than the six weeks their father had optimistically allowed. Endless troubles had developed. First the well had gone dry in June and had to be drilled deeper. By August the men had still been drilling, at two-pounds-a-day wages. Then the drains had clogged. The man in charge had pronounced the difficulty to be a big pipe meeting a little pipe 'what can't carry it off', with consequent blocking at the elbows. He had advised introducing two little cesspools, one at the 'elber', the other at the washers, to receive 'any sileage as may appear to flow and leave the water free to pass, which likeways, if anything should be wrong then, why you only takes up a stone or whatever you thinks most proper instead of making this here frightful mess'.[21]

By the ensuing June, when Georgina had gone down after Catherine's final departure from Tavistock, Gad's Hill had been in a more livable condition. In that most difficult summer she had found balm in the country after the estrangement from her family and the exposure to speculative stares from the curious. Dickens had also found refuge there. 'The blessed woods and fields', he had written Cerjat, 'have done me a world of good.' The little estate was, he had told Macready, 'a place to repose in'.[22] For the boys, of course, repose had been the last thing desired. That had been the summer when Plorn, promoted to trousers, had joined the lively ranks of the older four. Auntie had hoped to delay his debut until his father's return from the reading tour, but in September had received permission to advance the date: 'My best love to the noble Plornish. If he is quite reconciled to the postponement of his trousers, I should like to behold his first appearance in them. But, if not, as he is such a good fellow, I think it would be a pity to disappoint and try him.'[23]

Though Georgina had received a few sympathetic family friends that summer whenever Dickens could spare an interval from London before the start of his reading tour, a normal social life did not begin until 1859, the following year. Then visitors came and went

F

continually: Wilkie Collins, the Forsters, Mrs. Watson, Lotty White
(a friend of Mamie and Katey), and others. And though Mamie bore
the title of hostess, it was Georgina who took over the details of
hospitality.

A guest coming by train from London could make the journey,
less than thirty miles, in about an hour. At the little station of
Higham-by-Rochester, he might be met by his host's basket carriage
drawn by the pony Newman Noggs, whose harness bells tinkled
merrily as he trotted the one-and-a-half miles to the house. Sometimes a 'trim, sparkling, slap-up *Irish jaunting-car*', bought in Belfast to 'astonish the Kentish people', would meet the train. (Ill-
natured gossips, sneering at Dickens's vanity, hinted that the
painted device on the back was meant for the trumpet of fame.)[24]

As the vehicle topped the rise of Gad's Hill, to the left lay the
tract of dense shrubbery and magnificent cedars which Dickens called
his 'wilderness'. Straight ahead across the Dover Road stood the
plain red brick dwelling with its white frame belfry and small white-
pillared porch. Entering the semicircular driveway, the guest would
find himself on an ideal little domain of landscaped lawns and
kitchen gardens, recreation grounds, stables, coach house, pumping-
room—everything needful for use and delight. On the porch Georgina
and Mamie would be waiting to welcome him.

In July of 1860, before Gad's Hill was completely furnished as a
permanent home, Georgina took part in the first important celebration there, Katey's marriage to Charles Allston Collins, Wilkie's
brother. Twelve years older than the bride, nervous, conscientious,
of a slight figure topped by masses of carrot-coloured hair, the groom
was a minor Pre-Raphaelite artist and an occasional contributor to
Household Words and *All the Year Round*. He had seen a great deal
of the Dickenses, dining with them daily during their 1856 sojourn in
Paris.[25] Though Dickens did not altogether favour the match—he
sensed that Katey was not really in love—his vivacious daughter
looked upon the marriage as a means to independence. Possibly,
too, she was ill at ease and confused in her loyalties after the separation. 'Lord, how time and Life steal on!' reflected her father as the
marriage day approached. It was but yesterday, it seemed, that
Katey 'always had a scratched knee, and it was but the day before
yesterday when there was no such creature'.[26]

Georgina was in a whirl with the wedding preparations. And what
with the exhibition of the bride's gifts, the decorations and provisions for an elaborate wedding breakfast, the trousseau finery, and
the flowers everywhere, Dickens could scarcely find space in the
house to sit down and write a letter the day before the wedding.

That night the family was in a state of wonder at the shots being fired in the neighbouring village of Higham. It developed that a local blacksmith who had erected a triumphal arch for Miss Katey to drive beneath on the way to the church, had also thought of the gunfire as another suitable way to honour the nuptials. In the morning villagers crowded the little Church of St. Mary the Virgin for the ceremony and strewed flowers in the path of the bridal couple. Mamie, as the elder sister and one of the bridesmaids, may have reflected that she should have been the one to marry first. There is a story that she was in love at the time, but had docilely submitted to her father's objections to the match.[27]

At the house Mamie had made the table one unbroken expanse of bridal white. During the ensuing festivity there, Georgina and Dickens acted as 'Universal bootleholders'. When the time came for farewells, Katey wept in her father's arms and Mamie also gave way to a flood of tears. By this time the groom's face, understandably, was blanched and drawn. Above the chorus of 'God bless you's' that followed, boomed Forster's pompous 'Take care of her, Charley. You have got a most precious treasure.' In a shower of old shoes the couple left for Dover, whence they embarked on a Continental journey.[28]

Absent on this family occasion was Katey's mother. Though never mentioned, she must have been in everyone's mind. Thoughts of her may have added to Dickens's noticeable strain after the wedding breakfast, a state which erupted in an argument with the best man, Holman Hunt, over the merits of a painting hanging on the wall—'The Sphinx' by Roberts.[29] Later that day, after the guests had gone, Mamie found her father in the bride's empty room, his face buried in the folds of the wedding dress. 'But for me,' he sobbed, 'Katey would not have left home.'[30]

Barely recovered from the recent flurry, Georgina prepared for the arrival of the Tavistock furniture. Very likely the London home had oppressed the family with dark memories. At any rate, it had been sold in August and had to be cleared early in September. For several weeks she oscillated between town and country, helping with the moving, salvaging discarded curtains and coverings, choosing what furnishings were to be transferred.[31] Though the work was exhausting, it was an antidote to introspection, and she had the satisfaction, before long, of seeing Gad's Hill transformed into one of the most sumptuous places for miles around.

The visitor to this house in its heydey entered a large square hall. On the right wall hung the huge backdrops painted by Stanfield for the Tavistock productions of *The Lighthouse* and *The Frozen*

Deep. On the left rose a handsome staircase, its solid balustrade enhanced with colourful painted designs applied by talented Katey. Eighteenth-century prints ascended the stair wall, and on the first landing an illuminated plaque called attention to the rich literary association of the site:

> *This House*
> *GAD'S HILL PLACE*
> *Stands on the summit of Shakespeare's*
> *Gad's Hill, ever memorable for its*
> *Association with*
> *Sir John Falstaff, in his noble fancy.*
> *But my lads, my lads, to-morrow morning, by four o'clock,*
> *early at Gad's Hill! There are pilgrims going to Canterbury*
> *with rich offerings, and traders riding to London with fat*
> *purses; I have vizards for you all; you have hopes for*
> *yourselves.*

Conspicuous in the lower hall was a letter-box big enough to receive books and manuscripts. On it the post-collection times were painted in large letters.[32]

The room to the right of the entrance was Dickens's library and study. Beyond it was the billiard room. On the other side of the hall were the recently enlarged drawing-room and the dining-room, the latter opening into a greenhouse. Large plate glass mirrors from Tavistock reflected the luxurious furnishings, a blend of old and new.

The two upper floors provided ample quarters for guests, family, and servants. But though the house was adequately staffed, visitors noticed that servants were not often in evidence—except in the dining-room and, naturally, their own quarters. As part of her responsibility Georgina kept the bedrooms so well equipped that attendants need not be summoned to fetch such requirements as writing materials or a cup of tea. Each bedroom provided a collection of books, a large writing-table with a lavish assortment of stationery of different sizes and kinds, and complete tea-making facilities—cups and saucers, a teapot, a filled tea caddy, and milk and sugar. In the fireplace hung a well-polished copper kettle. There was also a bathroom shower, such as Dickens had installed at Tavistock—a real luxury, except when the pipes froze during the cold Christmas of 1860 and remained 'in a stony state for five or six weeks'.[33]

When a guest came to Gad's Hill for the first time, he was taken almost at once to the stableyard, where the dogs were properly introduced to him. This was a necessary ceremony, as four large mastiffs

GAD'S HILL PLACE
Henry E. Huntington Library and Art Gallery

THE GAD'S HILL DINING-ROOM
Henry E. Huntington Library and Art Gallery

or Newfoundlands—Turk, Linda, Bumble, and Sultan—were kept for protection against the numerous vagrants along the Dover Road. Once formally presented to a guest, however, even the fiercest canine guard would ever after uphold the hospitality of the premises—that is, all except Sultan, a ferocious Irish bloodhound who had to be shot for attacking a little girl. He had also disgraced himself by an unfriendly approach to Mrs. Bouncer, Mamie's little white Pomeranian, but had 'only swallowed Bouncer once, and temporarily'.[34] No less than the human residents, the animal population at Gad's Hill enjoyed every comfort. On warm days the larger dogs retreated into the cool tunnels thoughtfully provided under the brick wall by the coach house. Daily they and Mrs. Bouncer feasted from the five plates of dinner prepared for them by the cook. But once, just before meal-time, Bumble, a Newfoundland pup, stole into the kitchen and finished off all five heaping plates, then fainted dead away. Discovered in that condition, he was promptly revived under the pump.[35]

In the congenial surroundings of his country home, Dickens could temporarily escape occupational strains and private worries. At times he surrendered himself completely to the relaxed atmosphere of the place. Even his short notes relating to household matters were sometimes playful, humorous. One to his clockmaker, for example: 'Since my hall clock was sent to your establishment to be cleaned it has gone (as indeed it always has) perfectly well, but has struck the hours with great reluctance, and after enduring internal agonies of a most distressing nature, it has now ceased striking altogether. Though a happy release for the clock, this is not convenient to the household. If you can send down any confidential person with whom the clock can confer, I think it may have something on its works that it would be glad to make a clean breast of.'[36] So pleased was Dickens with this whimsy that he virtually repeated it six months later in his request to a chimney sweep: 'Since you last swept my study chimney it has developed some peculiar eccentricities. Smoke has indeed proceeded from the cowl that surmounts it, but it has seemingly been undergoing internal agonies of a most distressing nature, and pours forth disastrous volumes of swarthy vapour into the apartment wherein I habitually labour. Although a comforting relief probably to the chimney, this is not altogether convenient to me. If you can send a confidential sub-sweep, with whom the chimney can engage in social intercourse, it might be induced to disclose the cause of the departure from its normal functions.'[37]

Such matters also commanded much of Georgina's attention, as did the supervision of a large staff of indoor and outdoor employees. Altogether, the Gad's Hill property comprised some twenty acres to be tended. From the flight of steps at the rear of the house, one looked over an expense of well-kept lawn to a stone balustrade salvaged from the old bridge at Rochester. A handsome stone wall and terrace divided the lawn from a field beyond, which could be entered through the heavy iron gates and over a ha-ha. To the left were the kitchen gardens, extending to the road in front; to the right was the vinery, with croquet grounds between it and the road. To staff and maintain such a place called for a sizable budget. Furthermore there was the constant round of house guests and parties. In planning all such expenditures, Georgina was an expert. Schooled in a long apprenticeship under Dickens, she knew exactly what bills had been paid, what debts were still outstanding, what repairs were pending. During his frequent absences on reading tours or editorial business, she assumed complete charge. In his letters she found constant business assignments: '. . . a staggering bill of Thomas and Homan's [an auction and estate agency in Rochester], which just doubles my rough idea of it. Before you pay it, I wish you would look to the end of it, and see what they have allowed for the change in the cottage bedstead. . . . Pray have this out with them and have it clear, before you pay.'[38]

Besides relieving Dickens of such irksome responsibilities, Georgina gave sympathic attention to his personal problems: his attacks of illness, his discouragement over unsatisfactory progress on a new book, his disappointments in his family—on all such matters he unburdened himself to her. Small wonder that he wrote to Cerjat in 1860, 'Miss Hogarth, always Miss Hogarth, is the guide, philosopher, and friend of all the party. . . .' And to Mrs. Watson the following year: 'Georgina is, as usual, the general friend and confidante and factotum of the whole party.'[39]

As chief hostess at Gad's Hill, Georgina set in motion a thoughtfully planned daily routine for visitors. The morning usually passed in relaxed fashion. A guest came down for breakfast as he pleased: it was on the table from nine to ten-thirty. If he appeared early enough he might eat with his host and perhaps accompany him afterwards on the usual inspection of the house, gardens, meadows, kennels, and stables. If the tour allowed a glimpse of the library before Dickens began work, the guest would note there the same ingenious device that had graced Tavistock House—a door lined with the familiar dummy book backs to give the appearance of shelves. The actual volumes lining the walls displayed the owner's engraved bookplate, a crest with a lion holding a Maltese cross in its dexter paw. Since the family was not entitled to a coat of arms, the crest may have signified Dickens's pleasure in the appurtenances of gentry. On the desk in the bay window was an array of familiar objects: a pair of bronze frogs posed for a rapier duel; a gilt leaf with a rabbit sitting on its haunches; a large paper knife, often held during the public readings; and a little decorated cup of fresh flowers.[40]

At lunch time plans for the afternoon were suggested. Frequently the guests walked through nearby Cobham Park, the owner (Lord Darnley) having given Dickens the keys to all the gates. The hardier of the male guests took longer jaunts, past neighbouring villages and over great stretches of countryside. With their host setting his usual pace, they could cover ten miles in a few hours. Sometimes a party set out in carriages for a picnic, their appetites whetted by the lavish 'hampers and wine baskets blocking the steps of the house' as the vehicles were being loaded. On such expeditions their host saw to it that no lobster shells or other debris remained to litter the wooded site chosen for their lunch.[41]

If, however, an afternoon at home was scheduled, the guests might play croquet or bowl on the lawn. Whatever the day's entertainment, they came to dinner confident of an expertly planned menu. 'His admirable sister-in-law saw to this for him,' said Dickens's young friend Percy Fitzgerald, 'and many were the tit-bits we enjoyed.'[42] Humour and gaiety flourished at the table and afterwards in the drawing-room. Sometimes Mamie sat at the piano, playing her father's favourites: ballads, national airs, lively dances, Mendelssohn, Chopin, Mozart.[43] Often there were guessing and memory games. Sometimes the guests listened as Dickens read, especially when he wished to have their critical judgement on his programme repertoire. Later the men might have a game in the billiard-room and sample their host's supply of high-quality cigars. (Georgina thought she could recognize certain brands by their aroma.)[44]

In spite of the heavy responsibility, Georgina seemed to thrive on the constant entertaining at Gad's Hill. No visitor doubted the genuineness of her welcome. One, the Irishman Francis Finlay, editor of the *Northern Whig*, pronounced her 'a really delightful person, plain, unassuming, totally unaffected and of singularly pleasant and easy manner'.[45] Another house guest, a Frenchman, made to feel at home by her fluency in his language, commented admiringly on her mastery of idiom.[46]

Of all the conviviality at Gad's Hill, Georgina enjoyed Christmas most. Then the house so overflowed that some of the men had to be quartered at the historic Falstaff Inn across the way or in 'the bachelors' cottage' nearby. Unwilling to miss the excitement of all the preparations, Dickens usually took the whole week off. Christmas morning the guests found the dining-room hung with holly and ivy. Later Georgina hovered admiringly as Mamie decorated the table for the main feast. Christmas dinner—it was unforgettable! Seated round the large mahogany table with the family were the house guests and a few near neighbours. With his ready humour the host sparked the conversation, keeping the servants in a titter whenever they waited on him. The climax of the meal was the entry of the flaming Christmas pudding. Holly-trimmed and resting on its special dish of *repousse* china, it was placed before the host to the accompaniment of spontaneous applause. And of course the dinner could not pass without Dickens's traditional toast: 'Here's to us all! God bless us!' His Christmas benediction Georgina recorded for ever in her heart:

> *Reflect upon your blessings—of which every man has many— not on your past misfortunes, of which all men have some. Fill your glass again, with a merry face and contented heart. Our life on it, but your Christmas shall be merry and your New Year a happy one!*
>
> *So may the New Year be a happy one to you, happy to many more whose happiness depends on you! So may each year be happier than the last, and not the meanest of our brethren or sisterhood debarred their rightful share in what our Creator formed for them to enjoy.*[47]

New Year's Eve brought another memorable observance. A large party always assembled in the drawing-room, passing the time with games and conversation until midnight. A few minutes before the hour struck, the butler played chimes on the dinner gong, threw open the house door, and ushered everyone into the large, square hall. With Dickens keeping an eye on his watch, there was a hushed wait for the village bells. At the first peal he exclaimed, 'A happy New Year to us all! God bless us!' What handshaking then, what congratulating, what kissing of the old year out and the new one in! The ensuing frolic always included a dance, the host sometimes starting off with the cook as his partner. After these exertions there was a great demand for lively draughts from the punch bowl, mixed by Dickens himself.[48]

While these festivities brightened Gad's Hill, Catherine Dickens waited in her London home for the Christmas season to pass, living in retrospect, perhaps, the years when she had presided—nominally, at least—over the holiday preparations. Georgina, though, may have found the rush of activity a welcome reprieve from similar memories of the old time. But in quiet moments her sister's vague defencelessness may well have returned to haunt her, even though she might have told herself that Catherine in exile was no more unhappy, no more pitiable, than Catherine in her marriage—indeed, less so. For in the stagnant shallows of her life at Gloucester Crescent, she was no longer exposed to the tides of her husband's criticism or her own jealousy and sense of inadequacy. Now she could tranquilly indulge her old self-pity. The servants would not point out her faults to her or hold her up to ridicule. And she could take comfort in the dignity her reticence had given her in the public eye.

But for all that, Georgina could hardly have avoided some self-questioning, the more for being 'one of the most amiable and affectionate of girls'. Besides, she would have harboured the suspicion that a few acquaintances might have accused her of cunning manoeuvres to usurp her sister's place—a thought far more disquieting than all the wild and scandalous surmises of strangers. Not that strangers and their covert stares would have failed to vex her: Dickens's face was so well known that he was pointed out wherever he went, and anyone seen with him became a secondary target of curiosity—especially the sister-in-law who had sparked so much gossip. Though the first blaze of scandal had died down, the fires were never to be entirely extinguished in her lifetime. Should she be invited to leave Mamie in charge of the boys and come up to London for Sunday dinner with Dickens, or to join his fiftieth birthday celebration with three other friends in a public restaurant,[49] she could hardly accept with any security against unfavourable notice.

The estrangement from her own family was another grievous aspect of her situation. Whatever stinging reproaches her mother had uttered to her in May of 1858 must have rankled in the years to come, particularly if coupled with venomous judgments of Dickens. To avoid an emotion too uncomfortably like hatred of her own mother, Georgina would have had to sink all such bitter recollections far below the surface of consciousness.

Another emotion to be suppressed was the sense of thwarted womanhood. As long as she had been young enough to fulfil her natural destiny, Georgina could have rejected it and contented herself with the substitute she had freely chosen. But as the birthdays sped by and she sometimes lay sleepless in the summer nights at Gad's Hill, she must have felt her feminine birthright irrevocably slipping away. There were times, she confessed in later years, when she debated the wisdom of her choice and wondered whether her life was '*all* a mistake—and a waste'.[50] Dickens, too, was a prey to ambivalent emotions on the subject. 'I doubt if she will ever marry,' he confided to Cerjat when she was thirty-three. 'I don't know whether to be glad of it or sorry for it.'[51]

But Georgina was far too busy to allow gossip, wounding memories, or frustrations to prevail for long. She became more and more indispensable as Dickens was increasingly absent from home. He called on her to send him parcels of books and papers, and even expected her to look after the requirements of his wardrobe. If he needed his umbrella with the ivory handle, or a replenishment of belts, hosiery, waistcoats, trousers ('also any clean things that you know or suspect I may require'), she must send them. An order for 'two or three white shirts', to be delivered by Frank, called for their being carefully 'packed so that he can't tumble them, or he certainly *will*. . . .' On one occasion she received explicit directions for a bit of ingenious dry-cleaning: 'In the middle drawer of my wardrobe are a dress coat and a pair of dress trousers—*the upper pair* (for there are two)—lying together. As I dare say both have suffered from my beard during the various banquets, will you with the end of a clean towel and eau de cologne from my scent case—cleanse them, *by day light*, where they are splashed.'[52]

Frequently she had to carry out specific orders for household management. An envelope case was needed for the library table in the rear of the dining-room. (But perhaps that had already occurred to her, Dickens added, for she thought of everything.)[53] She was also subjected to anxious queries about the wine cellar, from which she sent Dickens—often on short notice—replenishments for his London office quarters. She was urgently charged to have the stable man add a supplementary padlock to the cellar door. Was she positive no champagne had been 'abstracted'? Before leaving Gad's Hill, Dickens had learned from a neighbour that champagne corks had recently been 'flying in the liveliest manner' at a cottage in Higham. It was suspected that the Gad's Hill cellar might be the source of supply. And indeed, he had been somewhat surprised upon learning from her last inventory how little champagne was left. Apparently, though, even the additional padlock did not check the pilfering, for there was continued concern over dwindling supplies.[54] It was not until some years later that he finally hit upon a foolproof plan for preventing the thefts. 'I have been constantly thinking about that cellar-key, and I will tell you how we will keep it,' he announced to Georgina. 'Order . . . one of the ordinary little iron cash boxes to keep it in. To that cash box have 2 keys, both electrotyped gold. Of those keys you shall always wear one, and I will always wear the other, and the box itself shall be kept, not in your room but in mine, in some drawer that we will settle upon. Then, I think, we MUST be safe.'[55]

As she acted upon the instructions in Dickens's letters, Georgina had always to anticipate his return and have everything in readiness, his odds and ends properly disposed of in his room, and a cheerful fire blazing. Even when his plans were indefinite she must not fail him. 'I am not sure whether I can get home tomorrow, or not,' he once informed her. 'On the whole I rather think yes. The best way will be to proceed as though I were coming, and to be equally prepared for my not coming.'[56]

In complying with all these exacting demands, did Georgina ever feel imposed upon? Sixteen months after Dickens's death she was to look back on the Gad's Hill years and wonder why she had ever allowed petty irritations to fret her, important though they might have seemed at the time.[57] The exact source of the irritations she did not define, but it is reasonable to assume that some, at least, originated with the master of Gad's Hill. On the whole, however, she seems to have accepted cheerfully, even proudly, his heavy reliance on her. Hers was not the position of a paid housekeeper: she was hostess of Gad's Hill—even more, she was the Galatea a famous man had moulded to be his confidante, counsellor, best friend.

The easy freedom of Dickens's letters to her testifies that there was no need for reserve or caution between them. If his humorous reports on acquaintances and friends were indiscreetly frank or intimately detailed, he knew she would be amused. Long ago on an Italian tour with Egg and Wilkie Collins, Dickens had dwelt on Wilkie's tendency to deliver interminable smug discourses on art, interspersed with doubtful tales of self-glorification. The *pièce de résistance* had been the account of his first love adventure, which had 'proceeded', Dickens reported, 'to the utmost extremities'. Making some calculations on this episode (whose details Georgina was spared), Wilkie's travelling companions had discovered him to have been little more than twelve years old 'at this precocious passage in his history'.[58] (Georgina, brought up in the freedom lingering from the Regency, would have seen in this titbit nothing to invite a blush.) Dickens also trusted her discretion enough to tell her, for instance, about meeting one of their acquaintances at Torquay with 'the most disagreeable woman . . . I ever saw in my life. I was afraid it was his wife; but . . . it was his sister'. Similarly forthright was his comment on that 'wretched Being', that 'medical Donkey', Harrison Tuke.[59] Nor did he ever need to hesitate in lauding himself to Georgina—as, for example, when he had overpowered Macready by reading

Copperfield. Such a triumph was a real proof of his dramatic genius, he admitted, as he reminded her that the old actor was not 'too prone to praise what comes at all in his own way'.[60]

As for her own letters to him, their tone and substance can be gauged only by Dickens's replies, for unfortunately it was his habit to destroy, at intervals, all correspondence from anyone whatsoever. Clearly, Georgina's letters, like his, were detailed and, at times, voluminous. (He had jestingly threatened to subtract from her quarterly allowance the heavy postage he had paid on her letters to him in Italy in 1853.)[61] Again and again he expressed his delight in her 'amusing and interesting letter', her 'capital letter', her description of Sydney ('excellently told') or of Plorn ('most delightful').[62] Always he depended on her for word sketches of the children and their doings. For though he had deplored the prospect of each new infant beyond the first three or four, he was extravagantly fond of small children and doted on his own, marking with fond fascination all their antics and sayings.

From the tenor of his replies one may gather that Georgina's letters seldom, if ever, included such wails of despair and frustration as his own inflicted on her. She was obviously of a more even disposition than he, and, like Agnes Wickfield, calmly cheerful, though endowed, one can be sure, with more verve than the Misses Wickfield and Summerson. Certainly she needed all the cheerfulness and moderation she could command not to be unduly agitated by the outbursts of woe and exasperation, the alarmed concern over his health that stood hand in hand with his comic passages. All too faithfully he sent her the verdicts of his friend and physician, Frank Beard. To allay her fears he softened the direst of these monotonous bulletins at times: 'Frank Beard thinks me decidedly better today'; 'Frank Beard is in spirits about me this morning . . .'; 'Frank Beard was again in spirits about me this morning. I have not taken the objectionable medicine since last Friday.'[63] But if he needed nursing, he promised to turn to her 'sooner than to anybody on earth'. More often, though, doubts intruded: 'I hope I am still better. My face aches at times, but very little.'[64]

But in the spring of 1862 Georgina herself was in such precarious health that Dickens in alarm dropped his preoccupation with himself. With Katey married, all the younger boys by now in school, social-minded Mamie constantly on the go, and Dickens frequently absent from home, Georgina had more time to herself, probably, than in any period since she had entered that active ménage at the age of fifteen. But the release, ironically, had not brought well-being. In May and June she suddenly began to alter distressingly,

losing 'all that clarity and "cheer of spirit" that used to distinguish
her. . . .' Even the 'distraction and the disturbance . . . of a few
visitors in the house' proved too much for her.[65] As late as Whitsun-
tide, however, she tried to carry on her duties as hostess, even to
joining guests in an afternoon walk and getting drenched in a pelting
rain. That night she stayed up to make one in a game of whist.[66]
During the ensuing weeks she declined alarmingly. Finally the
eminent Dr. Elliotson was called in, the physician of whom Dickens
had once vowed: 'I *know* that, under God, there does not live a man
in whose hands you would have as much reason to hope for a perfect
restoration to health. . . . If my own life . . . were in peril tomorrow,
I would trust it to him, implicitly.'[67] About the same time, evidently, Dr. Frank Beard was also called in for consultation.[68] The
diagnosis, Dickens told Macready, was 'degeneration of the heart'.
In his distress he admitted to his sister Letitia that he was so 'altogether dazed' by it that he could not 'remember one word' of her
last letter—in fact, was not even certain whether he had ever read
it. Repeatedly his anxious reports stressed the shocking change in
Georgina's spirits, the loss of 'alacrity' and vivacity: '. . . She is
very low about herself almost as soon as one has ceased to speak to
her after brightening her up.' It was perhaps well for Georgina that
she would not have read his July letter to Macready, with its statement that 'I (who know her best, I think) see much in her that fills
me with uneasiness'. His summary of her illness ended in almost the
tone of an obituary: 'You may imagine with what solicitude Mary
Katie and I watch the condition of our best and dearest friend—the
most unselfish, zealous, and devoted that ever lived on earth, I
thoroughly believe. No one can ever know what she has been to us,
and how she has supplied an empty place and an ever widening gap
since the girls were mere dolls.'[69]

Three weeks later Georgina was still 'very, very poorly. Excruci-
ating pain in the left breast is the last symptom. It seized her at
dinner yesterday, and she seems . . . to grow steadily worse.' In
September she continued 'very weak', though much improved. She
had rallied to the point of reading the second volume of Wilkie
Collins's *No Name*, had taken 'the deepest interest' in it, and had
enjoyed seeing how strongly Dickens admired it. And, in London
for a few days, she had gone to a play at the Adelphi with Dickens
and Leech.[70] Still, the least excitement or exertion took its toll:
'Georgina being left alone here the other day, was done no good by
a great consternation among the servants', reported Dickens to
Letitia Austin. 'On going downstairs, she found Marsh (the stableman) seated . . . in an arm-chair, and incessantly crying out: "I am

dead". To which the women servants said, with great pathos (and with some appearance of reason): "No, you ain't, Marsh!" And to which he persisted in replying: "Yes, I am; I am dead!" Some neighbouring vagabond was impressed to drive a cart over to Rochester and fetch the doctor, who said (the patient and his condolers being all very anxious that the heart should be the scene of affliction): "Stomach." '[71] Whatever the damage to Georgina, it obviously did not prevent her from recognizing the comedy of the situation.

As early as July Dickens had conceived the idea of taking her over to Paris with Mamie to try the effect of a change of scene in the autumn. This time she was not to have the supervisory responsibilities that former residence abroad had entailed. 'I am not going to have any establishment there,' he told Wilkie Collins, 'but intend the dinner to be brought in on a man's shoulders (you know the tray) from a Restaurant.' As the date of departure approached in October, Georgina was alone again for a few days, but Dickens, finding she had been left thus, gave up a meeting with Collins in order to return to Gad's Hill to keep her company. Besides, he wished to see Dr. Beard, who was coming down for his final professional visit on the 14th.[72]

On the morning of the 16th Dickens went over to Paris alone to find living quarters. Georgina and Mamie, with the bright-eyed Mrs. Bouncer in tow, followed on Sunday, taking the boat from Folkestone, although storm conditions that day had cancelled at least one other Channel crossing. The passage proved so turbulent that their boat was unable to dock at Boulogne that evening, but ran in to Calais instead. There, undaunted, Georgina and her niece dried themselves out to spend the night, having telegraphed Dickens, who had waited five hours for them on the storm-buffeted pier at Boulogne. The next morning they rose to greet him at Calais as if they had only 'been passing a mild summer there'. Having feared that they might be 'half-dead', he hardly believed his eyes to see them 'elaborately got up to come to Paris by the next train. . . .'[73] (In a letter to Miss Coutts a few days later, he mentioned the gale but said nothing of Georgina's reaction to it, or of her health subsequently, or even of the reason for the Paris sojourn. Nor did he add her regards in the complimentary close as had been his custom before his domestic rupture. Miss Coutts, who pitied Catherine and several times sought to persuade him to a reconciliation, would hardly have been among Georgina's champions.)[74]

Soon Georgina was comfortably settled in 'a most elegant little apartment' which Dickens had found for the three of them. It was

in their old familiar neighbourhood near the Champs Elysées, where
'house-rent is awful to mention'.[75] On their second Sunday Bulwer-
Lytton, devoted to Georgina since her girlhood, came to dine with
them. A few days later Wills arrived from London, having been
promised 'a Restaurant Dinner, and Box at the Play'.[76] They had
also the half-rueful amusement of observing poor little Bouncer,
muzzled in accord with the Parisian police regulations—'a wonderful
spectacle to behold in the streets, restrained like a raging lion.'[77]

Whatever the exact clinical nature of her ailment, the invalid was
decidedly better by the end of December. The trio—and a freed
Bouncer—returned to Gad's Hill just in time for Christmas Day.
Though the holidays were 'pervaded by boys' home from school,
each one 'apparently in fourteen pairs of creaking boots', Dickens
could report to Mary Boyle on the 27th that 'Georgina continued
wonderfully well'.[78]

Early in the new year Georgina was alone once more at Gad's
Hill. Dickens had returned to Paris shortly after Twelfth Night,
and Mamie was enjoying the gaieties of London. During this time
Georgina opened all mail addressed to her brother-in-law, forwarding whatever was necessary and herself answering any she deemed
within her province.[79] Apparently, though, Dickens was still taking
care not to burden her unduly. When he wrote her and Mamie
on the same day (Mamie having returned home by 1st February),
it was to his daughter that he entrusted a simple commission of
the sort that had invariably been in Aunt Georgy's department:
'I enclose a short note for each of the little boys. Give Harry ten
shillings pocket-money, and Plorn six.'[80]

When, after spending his fifty-first birthday on French soil, he
was ready to return to England, he wrote Georgina to send his unfor-
warded mail to his London quarters. If she herself could not be
there to greet him, he expected to find a note from her. As he suspected that Mamie and Mrs. Bouncer might be on the go again, he
chose to announce his arrival (*'between 11 and 12 on Monday night'*,
16th February), 'to you who are sure to be at home'.[81] Georgina
would relay the word to Mamie.

By April she was 'all but quite well' and almost ready to take up
the duties of hospitality again—or so Dickens assumed when he
wrote Carlyle that her health now enabled him to look for 'that long-
delayed visit from you and Mrs. Carlyle this coming summer'. Like
a refrain this optimistic note kept recurring in his letters. A month
later he could announce to Cerjat, 'I hope that Georgina is almost
quite well'.[82] Had Doctors Elliotson and Beard been versed in
psychosomatic illness, they might have suspected that hers was, at

least in part, such a case. Certainly the originating undercurrents
were not lacking. And added to the obvious ones may have been a
hidden one even more devastating. Georgina must have suspected,
perhaps known, that in the Ellen Ternan affair Dickens had only
exchanged one heartache for another. Nelly, though dazzled by the
older man's fame, flattered by his admiration, mindful of the luxury
of his attentions, apparently did not respond with the whole-souled
devotion he craved. Dickens was no libertine. Though drawn to her
by the surface attractions of youth and fragile beauty, he longed for
a warm-hearted woman with the courage to glory in a permanent
relationship with him. Ellen, if she had submitted to his advances
after the separation, seems to have done so coldly and with a worried
sense of guilt.[83] Such a capitulation could only have tormented
Dickens with a still keener sense of his own guilt.

Georgina, exempting her hero from the restrictions placed on
ordinary men, had, very likely, entertained idealistic notions of his
finding happiness at last in high romance—a Tristram-and-Iseult
kind of love worthy of transcendent genius. In nothing less could
she have found justification for accepting Ellen Ternan. Disillusion-
ment would have dealt a shattering blow. But even as she had
gained strength and spirits early in 1863, there had come from
Dickens a disquieting corroboration of such doubts. Attending a
production of Gounod's *Faust* while in Paris, he had been much
moved by the mournful blue light that fell on Marguerite's garden,
fading the blossoms and withering the leaves after the ill-fated
maiden had accepted the jewels from her elderly lover. 'I could
hardly bear the thing,' he confessed; 'it affected me so, and sounded
in my ears so like a mournful echo of things that lie in my own
heart.'[84]

During the early summer, when Georgina was finding her way
back to serenity, she received few guests at Gad's Hill and had no
large house parties to cope with. In the first week of August,
though, she lived through an event which could only have renewed
a five-year-old trouble: her mother died. Catherine immediately
wrote to Dickens for permission to bury Mrs. Hogarth beside Mary
in Kensal Green. Answering in a businesslike note from Gad's Hill
the following day, he gave his consent, but did not include even the
briefest phrase of conventional sympathy. What Georgina's behaviour was at this time is not a matter of record. She could hardly
have expected a warm welcome from the black-garbed Hogarth clan
gathered around the grave. She would have had to journey alone to
Kensal Green, where she might have been exposed to chill stares
from her own kin and possibly curiosity and slurs from any others

present. In all likelihood she did not risk such a reception. It is more credible that she remained at Gad's Hill, busying herself with preparations to receive the De la Rues on their arrival from Genoa the following week.[85]

It was about this time that she sat for her portrait to R. H. Mason, the photographer whom Dickens employed for his own publicity photographs. Having undergone such recent anxiety about her health, her brother-in-law and the girls had probably pressed her to give them such a token. In September Dickens wrote Mason, 'We are all very much pleased with Miss Hogarth's portrait'.[86] By mid-December, after a year and a half of semi-invalidism, she was in the midst of normal holiday activities again, bustling about to receive 'a houseful gradually accumulating for Christmas'.[87] After 1864 there are no further references to the mysterious heart malady. Her later illnesses, till the onset of the final afflictions of age, seem to have been minor. From her recovery until 1870 she continued active at Gad's Hill, so active that the loved home was, for her, seldom 'a place to repose in'.

G

Chapter Seven
'ENORMOUS DRAGS'

THOUGH Georgina was to look back on the Gad's Hill years as the summit of her lifetime, the period was permeated not only by hidden traumas, but also by Dickens's mundane anxieties. Not the least of these was the race to keep ahead of financial demands. The drain on his pocketbook came not only from his children, from Georgina (who in any event earned her keep), and from Catherine (who drew her yearly £600); it came as well from two brothers, the indigent widow of a third, a sister, and his senile mother. Augustus, his youngest brother, had deserted a blind wife and run off to America with another woman.[1] From there he appealed to Dickens for funds. And Fred, who had required material aid in the early years at Doughty Street and Devonshire Terrace, now also applied repeatedly for help.[2]

When Alfred, his oldest brother, died in July of 1860, Dickens assumed responsibility for the widow, Helen, and her five children, bringing them to Gad's Hill immediately after the burial and settling them temporarily in a neighbouring farmhouse. When, pushing aside his own pressing commitments, he began untangling Alfred's financial affairs, he found them in sad condition.[3] Meanwhile Gad's Hill was darkened by six 'black figures, little and big, coming in and wistfully questioning' him what should be done 'in this wise or that'. Aided by Georgina on at least one occasion, Dickens inspected London dwellings with a view to finding a home for the bereaved family. By the end of August a suitable house had been located on Haverstock Hill, some distance north of Regent's Park. (The landlady, on learning that it was Charles Dickens 'who would pay the rent, . . . brightened considerably'.) It was Georgina who brought the widow to London, Dickens having given her full permission to manage matters as she thought best in the event of his being absent from the office on her arrival. The affair was arranged barely in time to avoid a conflict with the dismantling of Tavistock House.[4]

Though at first Dickens had praised the widowed Helen as 'patient, uncomplaining, self denying, and quietly practical', the strain of carrying her responsibilities along with too many others finally told on him. In desperation he turned her over to Georgina. 'Mrs. Alfred was here on Wednesday,' he complained from the office in January 1862, 'and I must consult you when I come back touching the best means of making known to her that I wish her in future to communicate personally with you, or with you and Mary. I really can not bear the irritation she causes me, and the strife she gets up in my uneasy mind about the whole business. I was completely disgusted and worn out by her on this last occasion.'[5]

The year after Alfred's death, Henry Austin, the brother-in-law who had given advice on the Tavistock and Gad's Hill purchases, died, leaving Dickens's sister Letitia to face reduced circumstances. As the trustee of the estate, her brother was burdened with the settlement of her affairs. Finally, after circulating a petition and carrying on a tedious two-and-a-half year correspondence with influential persons, he lightened his own financial responsibility by obtaining a pension of £60 a year for her as the widow of the Secretary to the London Sanitary Commission.[6] While the grant was still pending he offered what consolation he could by letter. Upon the approach of Letitia's first wedding anniversary after her bereavement, Georgina called his attention to the date so that he might send another thoughtful message.[7] (It was mid July of 1862, when the alarm over her heart malady was at its height.) In later years she continued her interest in Letitia, bolstering her morale and reporting on her welfare. 'Georgina's account of you is as cheerful and reassuring as I could hope, on the whole,' Dickens wrote his sister in 1868. 'I am off to-morrow to face my heavy spell of work. Georgy will tell me how you get on.'[8]

Concurrent with other expenses of the decade, Dickens's invalid mother, widowed since 1851, was totally dependent on him. Though her mind wandered in her last years, she could rally enough to recognize the source of her support. Visiting her in 1860, Dickens wrote to Georgina that 'the minute she saw me, she plucked up a spirit and asked me for "a pound"!' She died at the age of seventy-four, in a 'frightful' state, six weeks after Mrs. Hogarth.[9]

With all these calls for assistance, it is no wonder that in 1861, on receiving a 'begging letter from that Robert Barrow—a very bad one by the way—with an awful affectation of Christian piety in it', Dickens complained of being 'chained . . . by the enormous drags' upon him. '. . . I seem to stop sometimes like a steamer in a storm, and deliberate whether I shall go on whirling, or go down,' he groaned.[10]

Georgina marked how often he was touched with melancholy in these

years. Recurring deaths in the family and among friends were nar-
rowing his circle. His valued companion and reading manager,
Arthur Smith, had died only a few days before Henry Austin. It
was, he said, 'as if my right arm were gone'.[11] The following year
Augustus Egg also died, a bachelor, at age forty-seven, having
only recently attained the rank of Royal Academician. Dickens
mourned 'the dear gentle little fellow' and 'his pretty house . . .
to be laid waste and sold',[12] the house which Georgina might have
graced.

For Dickens a depressing aspect of such events was his attendance
at funerals. Georgina knew well his aversion to all the hired trap-
pings of woe inflicted by the undertakers on such occasions. At
Arthur Smith's funeral, though, this outrage to his feelings had been
somewhat lessened when, as 'the body was to be taken up and
carried to the grave, there stepped out, instead of the undertaker's
men with their hideous paraphernalia, the men who had always
been with [Smith in his work]; and they, in their plain, decent, own
mourning clothes, carried the poor fellow away'. But he had been
distressed by a service read without feeling or clear articulation.[13]

No less trying were the clouds of relatives and intimates who
darkened the bereaved homes on such occasions. Georgina, who
had not gone down to Ealing for Austin's funeral, had missed
Letitia's first appearance in her widow's cap, of which Dickens 'only
observed that it had very broad strings to tie it by'. But he sent
her a full report of the dismal assemblage at the home, a gathering
not without its humorous aspects: 'The manner in which everybody
sat against the wall, was wonderful. And there was the usual Ghoule-
like indispensability of cake and wine, and old Mr. Austin had a
conviction deeply rooted in him that everybody wanted coffee (which
was also there), and in particular that *I* wanted coffee, and must
have it administered, whether or no. . . .

'. . . I suspected (God forgive me!) the young cousin of getting up
a demonstration now and then. In pouring out the tea he rattled
the teapot against the cups, and the like, and was more jerky than
seemed natural. Also he fell into reveries that I thought too sudden
and profound.'[14]

*   *   *

With the Dickens children widely scattered now, Aunt Georgy was
active in 'holding them all together and perpetually corresponding
with the distant ones'. It was mainly through her that their father
kept in touch with them all, he acknowledged to Cerjat.[15] Unfortunately, she could find in the communications from her nephews

little relief, either for their father's melancholy or for his pocket-book.

Charley, it was true, had begun rather well and for a time appeared to be established in business. Financed by his father, he had gone to China in 1860 to buy tea. Returning early in 1861, he set himself up as an Eastern merchant. He would do well if only he could find 'continuous energy', Dickens told Cerjat. This was an echo of earlier concern over his eldest son's staying powers. 'All he wants, is a habit of perseverance,' Dickens had written Miss Coutts when Charley was fourteen. Some two years later another letter to her had complained that the boy had inherited from his mother 'an indescribable lassitude of character'.[16] His later career was to give his father cause for still further pessimistic reservations.

Another unsatisfactory aspect of Charley's situation—unsatisfactory only to his father, probably—was the marriage to his childhood sweetheart, Bessie Evans. Estranged from Bessie's father after the separation, Dickens did not attend the wedding. (With Catherine present, he would not have done so in any event.) He had not, however, tried to prevent the marriage, nor did he transfer his antagonism to his daughter-in-law. He and Georgina always welcomed Charley and Bessie at Gad's Hill, especially at Christmas. Soon another generation came with them 'to peep above the table'.[17]

The affairs of Walter, Dickens's second son, cast a heavy shadow over the household. Two years after he had first been sent to India as an ensign at age sixteen, he had been promoted to the rank of lieutenant in the Forty-second Highlanders. But soon he showed signs of following the old familiar pattern set by his paternal uncles and Micawberish grandfather. Constantly in debt, he was placed low on the list for a captaincy. Charley, while travelling in the Orient in 1861, had spent a fortnight with him and had, presumably, paid all his accumulated debts. But before long there were more. Apparently discouraged about his future in India, Walter considered volunteering for home service, but finally heeded paternal advice against thus reducing his income. Urged to live within his means, he wrote Mamie that there would be no further letters until he was out of debt. After a long silence he sent word that he was ill. Months later another note stated that he was being sent home on sick leave.[18] (This was in the autumn of 1863, the season marked by the death of both his grandmothers and the optimism over his Aunt Georgy's rapidly improving condition.) The next communication came from the officers' hospital in Calcutta. 'It is my most painful duty to inform you of the sudden death of your son Lieut. Walter Landor Dickens . . .,' it began. The message was not received until 7th

February, 1864, Dickens's fifty-second birthday,[19] though Walter had died on 31st December—the night Gad's Hill had been seeing the New Year in with charades and music and dancing.

One part of the Calcutta letter, its diagnosis of Walter's fatal illness, was kept from Georgina because, as Dickens explained to both Miss Coutts and Macready, she was suffering from 'the same disorder'.[20] Walter's death, it was learned, had been caused by 'the rupture of an extensive Aneurism of the arch of the Aorta', and had been mercifully quick. 'He was talking with other patients in the Hospital and became rather excited about the arrangements he proposed for his homeward passage, when a violent fit of coughing came on and the Aneurism burst into the left bronchial tube and life became extinct in a few seconds by the rush of blood which poured from his mouth.'[21] He was buried in the Bhowanipore Cemetery, Calcutta.[22] 'I could have wished it had pleased God to let him see his home again,' his father wrote to Miss Coutts, 'but I think he would have died at the door.'[23]

A few months later arrived the all too familiar evidence of reckless spending—Walter's unpaid accounts. Georgina, still somewhat under the strain of illness, saw Dickens harried by conflicting demands, but could do nothing. He had been unable to finish the tenth number of *Our Mutual Friend*, he complained to her, because he had spent his time settling 'the regimental part of poor Walter's wretched affairs—utterly incomprehensible, as they always have been'.[24] As long as possible he had postponed facing this miserable business. From Walter's commanding officer had come a humiliating assortment of bills. 'I feel I could not do my duty if I withheld these from you,' the officer had written, adding for Dickens's consolation: 'Let me take this opportunity of saying that the death of your son caused us all sincere sorrow; for he was a favourite with us all; and not all his difficulties in pecuniary matters, which appear to have begun immediately after he came to India, affected or in any way diminished our regard for him. And this perhaps is another reason why I now trouble you with these affairs.'[25]

Among his possessions Walter had left nothing of value: only a small trunk, changes of linen, some prayer books, and a coloured photograph of a woman believed to be a member of the family.[26] (It may have been his Aunt Georgy's recently taken portrait. There would have been time for it to reach him before his death.) According to his captain, everything else had been turned into cash in preparation for the return to England. What could Walter have done with his money! The officers' mess, the regimental store, the billiard table, the native servants, a merchant or two—all remained to be

paid. The claims against him, not including the servants' wages for
£39, were in excess of £100.

But in all this dreary and depressing affair there was one light
touch—a native creditor's request for fourteen rupees and eight
annas:

> *Humble petition of Gunga Rum Cloth*
> *Most humbly sheweth*
> *I most humbly beg to write these few humble lines to your*
> *greate honour*
> *—Honoured Sir—*
> *Your poor petitioner is want 14 Re 8 ans. from April 1862*
> *and he havnt payed to me yet and Sir*
> *I have heard now Dickens is gone to England some days ago*
> *and Sir now I will get these Re with your kind*
> *Should I be so fortunate as to succeed my request for which*
> *act of generiostey I shall ever pray for your long life and*
> *prosperity.*[27]

Dickens could only hope that Frank, his next son, would fare
better in India. In the past, though, the boy's record had not been
heartening. Interested in becoming a doctor, he had been sent to
Hamburg to learn German. But discouraged by his stammer, he
had soon abandoned all ambitions for a professional career and
aspired instead to be a gentleman farmer in Africa, Canada, or
Australia. Brushing this notion aside, Dickens, with some faint hope
of getting his son into the Foreign Office, set him to studying
Italian and reviewing German. But convinced before long that
Frank showed little promise for this calling, he next considered preparing him for a business partnership with Charley. When that plan
failed to materialize, Frank was taken into the office of *All the Year
Round*, being thought to have a 'natural literary taste and capacity'.
Finally, this last experiment proving unsatisfactory, his father got
him an appointment to the Bengal Mounted Police and sent him to
India in the month after Walter's death, but before the news of it
had reached England.[28] Just before he embarked Frank celebrated
his twentieth birthday.

Seventeen months later Alfred, the next son, set out for Australia.
Though he was considered a 'good, steady fellow' and had originally
been prepared for an army career, he could not meet the competition
for the engineers or the artillery.[29] After a short-lived ambition to
prepare for the medical profession, he took a London position with
a large China house. It was after two years of this work that he
sailed for Melbourne at the age of twenty, with introductions

designed to facilitate contacts with some mercantile firm.[30] Behind him he left a welter of unpaid bills. Wearily going through the itemized statements from the haberdasher and the tailor, his father found evidence of appalling extravagance—the curse that had already run through two generations of the family and now plagued the third. Eleven pairs of kid gloves (most of them the finest quality), eight silk scarves, three pairs of trousers, a treble milled coat and vest, as well as cambric handkerchiefs, cameo and onyx scarf pins, a railway rug, two umbrellas (one of brown silk), a silver mounted cane, a bottle of scent—all charged in a period of eleven months! And how were the eight pairs of ladies' gloves to be accounted for?[31] Had any father ever been burdened with so many irresponsible sons?

For Sydney, the one following Alfred, there had been high hopes. As a child he had always been a great favourite with his father and Aunt Georgy. Later, as he prepared for a naval career, he gave them cause for pride. Known in training at Portsmouth as 'Young Dickens, who can do everything', he passed his cadet examination and came home 'all eyes and gold buttons'.[32] Henceforth he was referred to in his family as 'the Admiral'. He was pint size—only three feet tall when he began his cadetship at age thirteen—and, Dickens told Georgina, could easily have lived in his sea chest. On his training ship, where his enormous popularity impressed his father, he was hoisted into his hammock by his mates the first night, but promptly leaped out again and insisted on getting in by himself.[33] In 1861 he got a coveted appointment on the H.M.S. *Orlando*. The next year his father, writing to Cerjat, called the young midshipman 'a born little sailor' who would 'make his way anywhere'.[34] But soon there were ominous signs that Sydney could not resist the family tendency toward extravagance. Rumour had it that while his ship was harboured at Bermuda he made 'prodigious purchases of luxuries'—guava jelly, rahat-lakoum, bananas, boot-laces—much to the delight, of course, of the coloured bumboat woman, Mrs. Dinah Browne, who invited him to have tea with her on shore, where, in her primitive native cabin, she entertained him with 'charming coon-songs in a rich . . . contralto voice'.[35] Evidently this spending orgy was not Sydney's last, for two years later his father, then winding up Walter's pathetic affairs, wrote him a futile letter of admonition.[36]

In sending his sons away one by one, Dickens was greatly concerned that each become independent and self-respecting. Remembering all too painfully his own father's and brothers' improvidence, he refused to spoil his boys with indulgence. He had demanded much of them as children in the way of punctuality, order, and industry—more, perhaps, than they could sometimes deliver without undue anxiety. Still, they themselves testified, when grown, that their father had been generous, loving, and ever ready to frolic with them. And though he stormed at any infraction of domestic rules, he was the very next moment like 'sun after a shower'.[37] From their boyhood he had been convinced that 'the sons of a father whose capital can never be the inheritance of his children must— perhaps above all other young men—hew out their own paths through the world by sheer hard work'.[38] Georgina, chiefly concerned that her nephews be a comfort to Dickens and a credit to his name, fully concurred in this and in whatever he planned for their welfare.[39] She was, moreover, to continue her warm interest in the boys' future after their father's death.

With five nephews out in the world, Aunt Georgy had only two schoolboys at Gad's Hill. Though Harry had begun school at Boulogne, he had been withdrawn because Plorn, a shy youngster, needed his companionship. The two boys were then sent to the nearby Rochester Grammar School.[40] 'Plorn's admission that he likes the school very much indeed, is the great social triumph of modern times,' was Dickens's jubilant response to Georgina's progress report on her youngest nephew.[41] From Rochester both boys went to Wimbledon. But eleven-year-old Plorn, sensitive and unaggressive, soon pleaded that such a large school was too confusing and begged to be transferred. His father attributed the maladjustment to the lad's having been 'a little too long at home with grown people'. Upon the advice of De la Rue, Plorn was next placed under the Reverend W. C. Sawyer's instruction at Tunbridge Wells.[42] In these two younger boys, for a time, and later in Harry alone, the father and aunt found compensation for all the woes inflicted by the other five.

During their vacations Harry and Plorn entertained themselves by editing a small weekly newspaper, the *Gad's Hill Gazette*. It had been organized one summer while Alfred and Sydney were still at home,[43] and in its early stages had been dignified by an office equipped with a bell and staffed by an editor, sub-editor, and office boy (Harry). Though there was little for this last member to do, he was constantly rung for. The first issues were handwritten and duplicated in carbon. Later Wills presented the young journalists with a manifold writer, and still later, with a printing press. This latter piece of equipment Harry learned to operate at the age of fifteen after a period of special training in London. When, according to the *Gazette*, Plorn, 'wearied by the toil of public life . . . resigned his

post' in August 1864, Harry had the sole responsibility for continuing the little paper: he collected the news, solicited contributions,
composed the page, wrote the leaders, set the type, and posted the
copies. At one time there were a hundred subscribers who paid 2*d.*
for each issue.[44] The periods of publication coincided with school
vacations (from late July to late August and between late December
and early February). This journalistic venture ended about 1867,
when Harry was preparing for Cambridge.

He had been only nine years old when his parents separated;
Plorn, six. Thus Auntie had felt a special tenderness in mothering
these two in the early Gad's Hill years. Later, as she followed the
development of the *Gazette* through all its issues, she found a reward
in the keen intelligence and reliability of Harry. He was a well-
balanced lad, too, and became a good cricketer and general outdoors-
man. Happily, he also had the sense of fun to be expected of his
father's child, as shown by his schemes to enliven his little journal.
One such was the series of tilts between editor and readers. 'We are
sorry to state that we have received complaints from *some* of our
subscribers of the printing of the Gad's Hill Gazette,' he editoria-
lized in the issue of 6 August 1864. 'Now if these gentlemen will
inform us of a mode of printing (applicable to our funds) we shall
be most happy to try it.' Of the copies printed by manifold writer,
only one in four was 'the least illegible', he protested. Anyone who
wished to withdraw his subscription could have his money refunded
on application to the editor. This elicited from John Leech an
impassioned defence of the *Gazette*, with a vehement denunciation
of all grumblers.

Dickens, too, entered into the humour of the thing, submitting a
complaint in one number and a reply in another. For these he
invented characteristic signatures: Jabez Skinner, The Skinnery,
Flintshire, was answered by Blackberry Jones.[45] Perhaps he was
reminded of his own schoolboy attempts at writing and circulating a
little newspaper at Chatham. At any rate, he endorsed the *Gazette*
fully. But when Harry tried his hand at sentimental verse, that was
another matter. On the death of Turk the bloodhound in 1865 the
editor had capped the prose announcement of the event with a
poetic threnody. He next attempted a poem in Tennysonian style
and ambitiously submitted it to *All the Year Round*. It was then
that his father quenched the poetic spark, pointing out that Harry
was 'not destined to become a great poet and had better stick to
things mundane'.[46] Thereafter the young editor eschewed literary
embroidery and satisfied himself with reporting Gad's Hill dinners
'served up in the same magnificent and costly manner as usual',

dances, sports, the arrival and departure of visitors, and neighbour-hood news.

Georgina's older nephews were not the only children to call forth solicitude during the 1860's. Mamie distressed her father because, nearing thirty, she had 'not yet started any conveyance on the road to matrimony. . . .' But he dared to believe that she still might, 'as she is very agreeable and intelligent'.[47] It was hoped that she would be attracted to the young Irishman, Percy Fitzgerald (even though he was a Catholic), but Dickens was finally forced to lament, '. . . I am grievously disappointed that Mary can by no means be induced to think as highly of him as I do'.[48] Her continued spinsterhood was a disappointment that her Aunt Georgina was to deplore frequently in later years.

For all Mamie's agreeable and docile qualities and for all her father's indulgence of her, it seems probable that, had she been a boy, her lack of decision and practical industry might have evoked the same censure Dickens bestowed upon his sons. When she revealed herself at times to be as vaguely passive and unpurposeful as her mother, he was not unknown to cloak his annoyance under the same sort of badinage he had used in referring to Catherine. In the summer of his first anxiety over Georgina's illness, he had addressed such a plaint to Thomas Baylis, to whom Mamie had evidently expressed a wish for some ferns to plant at Gad's Hill, around which no suitable nook then remained unplanted. 'After carefully cross-examining my daughter,' her father wrote, 'I do NOT believe her to be worthy of the fernery. . . . When I ask her where she would have the fernery and what she would do with it, the wit-ness falters, turns pale, becomes confused, and says: "Perhaps it would be better not to have it at all". I am quite confident that the constancy of the young person is not to be trusted, and that she had better attach her fernery to one of the châteaux in Spain, or one of her English castles in the air. None the less do I thank you for your more than kind proposal.' Miss Hogarth's illness, he added patheti-cally, was upsetting to all family plans and 'withers many kinds of fern'.[49]

Though he took a tone of amused masculine tolerance towards Mamie's yearly cry to join fashionable London society for the February-May season, he usually deferred to her wishes somewhat protestingly and only from paternal fondness.[50] Mamie, clearly, was something of a butterfly. It is perhaps significant that when Dickens took her and Georgina to Paris for the latter's health, he did not consider setting up an establishment to be supervised by his daughter.

As for Katey—talented, vital, more like Dickens, perhaps, than were any of the others—he had an uneasy feeling, shared by Georgina, that the marriage to Charles Collins had not been entered into whole-heartedly. As his son-in-law was of excellent character and devoted to Katey, Dickens had nothing against him personally, but there was grave concern over his health. By 1864 Collins was so unwell that he and Katey were forced to try a brief residence on the Continent to improve his condition. 'I have strong apprehensions that he will never recover, and that she will be left a young widow,' predicted Dickens anxiously.[51] But though Collins's invalidism meant that Katey had to live in circumstances far more modest than Mamie's at Gad's Hill, she was too proud to add to the 'enormous drags' on her father by accepting his bounty.

*   *   *

With all its burdens life at Gad's Hill had also its delights, none dearer to Georgina in retrospect than the miniature Swiss chalet. It dated from an afternoon in December 1864, when Dickens, returning from London, found a mysterious shipment of fifty-eight boxes piled up outside the gate. Examining this treasure trove, he learned that the crates contained ninety-four pieces of wood to be fitted together like the 'joints of a puzzle'. Even blinds and hardware were included. This amazing gift was a token of gratitude from Charles Albert Fechter, a Parisian actor whom Dickens had induced to make an English stage debut. During the ensuing Christmas holidays, when heavy snow and exceptionally cold weather prohibited outdoor frolics, the master of Gad's Hill and the guests in the bachelor's cottage entertained themselves by unpacking the pieces.[52]

As the weather moderated, erection of the little two-story struc-ture began on the wooded tract across the way. Safely reached through a tunnel beneath the busy Dover Road (one of Dickens's earlier ingenious improvements), this secluded plot provided an ideal setting for Fechter's gift. Once the brick foundation had been laid, the building rose rapidly—except for the intricate wooden cut-out work resembling Swiss embroidery on the outside stairway, balcony, and eaves. As soon as Dickens saw the surprising height of the upper room, he decided to use it as a summer study.[53] In August, when he moved in, he took with him the familiar trivial objects from his library desk: the bronze frogs, the rabbit on the gilt leaf, the paper knife, and the green cup. Georgina made daily trips through the tunnel into the lush wilderness and up the toy staircase to renew the flowers in the little china cup.[54] Picturing his sylvan retreat, Dickens grew lyrical: 'I have put five mirrors in the

Swiss chalet (where I write) and they reflect and refract in all kinds
of ways the leaves that are quivering at the windows, and the great
fields of waving corn, and the sail-dotted river.' For distant vision
he supplemented the mirrors with a telescope. Here, in this delightful study where 'birds and butterflies fly in and out, and the green
branches shoot in, at the open windows, and the lights and shadows
of the clouds come and go . . . ,' he was henceforth to spend his
summer working hours.[55]

Of such solace as the chalet afforded, Dickens had need. He had
come through a difficult winter in 1865, and Georgina was alarmed
over his symptoms of decline. His old 'weak side', the left, had been
troubling him—perhaps an inflamed kidney again. And his left foot
had given him intense pain, though he would not admit gout, insisting that it was only the lingering result of frostbite combined with
irritation from his leather boot on the long walks through the snow.[56]
Augmenting the physical ills was the unremitting work schedule.
For such nervous exhaustion even soothing Gad's Hill was not
always the remedy. So it was that late May and early June saw him
back in Paris on one of his brief excursions. But even on this holiday
the manuscript of his current novel went with him.

Georgina and Mamie were relieved to hear almost at once that
his general health and vitality were much improved.[57] But on 9th
June their optimism was dimmed, when they heard the first reports
of his horrifying homecoming experience. Having crossed the
Channel, he had left Folkestone by the boat train. As the locomo-
tive had sped down the slight gradient approaching Staplehurst, the
engineer had suddenly seen a red warning flag only 550 yards from
a bridge undergoing repairs. Though he had set the brakes the loco-
tive had plunged on over the bridge, leaping a forty-foot gap where
two rails had been removed. Still coupled to it had been the van
and two coaches. The second of these, in which Dickens had ridden,
had hung suspended in precarious balance, its front end resting on
the viaduct, its rear in the marshes below. All the other coaches had
broken from the train and fallen into the shallow stream.[58]

Waiting anxiously at Gad's Hill to hear the whole story from
Dickens himself, Georgina and Mamie had many hours in which to
exercise their imagination. The day after the accident he was still
at his London office, and not until evening did he come home 'to
quiet their minds'. It was then that they learned how he had been
the hero of the occasion. At the moment of the crash he had first
calmed the two women—one old, one young—in his compartment;
then, crawling through the window, he had got from a panicky
guard the key to unlock his compartment and others. He had helped

the two women to safety and, sustained by what he admitted to be 'a constitutional . . . presence of mind', had passed among the injured and dying in the wreckage below, trying to revive them with brandy from his flask and hatfuls of water from the stream. In the midst of bloody faces, deep skull gashes, and general anguish, he had been amazingly collected, even climbing back into his compartment to rescue the manuscript of the last number of *Our Mutual Friend*.[59] But home once more, he found himself nervously shattered by the ordeal.

What the public did not know, but what would hardly have been kept from Georgina, was that the younger of the two women with him had been Ellen Ternan. In the eight years since pretty 'Nelly' had played in *The Frozen Deep*, Dickens had visited her frequently in London and had favoured her family with special consideration, sending her sister Frances Eleanor to Italy to study music and promoting stage contacts for her sister Maria.[60] Georgina and Mamie had received Ellen at Gad's Hill. Katey, however, maintained reservations, and, on being told that Nelly had once joined in cricket there, had given it as her opinion that cricket was obviously not a game which this pretty actress played.[61] Now, as Dickens sought to regain composure after the Staplehurst accident, he directed his servant, John Thompson, to have delivered to Miss Ellen a variety of little gifts designed to revive a young lady convalescing from shock: '. . . a little basket of fresh fruit, a jar of clotted cream from Tuckers, and a chicken, a pair of pigeons, or some nice little bird'.[62]

For the first few days after the accident Georgina took over much of Dickens's correspondence, writing from his dictation answers to the solicitous inquiries of friends who had read the newspaper accounts of his lucky escape. He was 'too much shaken to write many notes', he told them, or even to add the usual flourish beneath his signature. The references to the catastrophe all followed virtually the same phrasing: 'I am shaken; not by the dragging of the carriage, itself, but by the work afterwards in getting out the dying and dead, which was horrible'.[63] Among the dictated letters was one to Maria Beadnell Winter.[64] But to Catherine's kind inquiry he himself wrote one of the brief stereotypes, apologizing for his unsteady hand.[65]

As Dickens, pleading a shaken nervous system and the need to work quietly at home, declined invitations, even far into the future, Georgina narrowed her own social activities to Gad's Hill. Besides Katey and her husband, only a few intimates, such as Frank Beard, Percy Fitzgerald, Frederick Lehmann, and Bulwer-Lytton, were invited to visit. (To Lehmann, Dickens apologized for Mamie: 'I

was vexed that you were put off from coming here by the inscruta-
bility of Mary's arrangements'; to Lytton he jested that Georgina
might prove a 'drawback' as she 'is so insupportably vain on account
of being a favourite of yours. . . .')[66] But for all the relaxed atmosphere at Gad's Hill that summer, Georgina recognized in the lingering effects of the Staplehurst accident one more drag on Dickens's
spirits and vitality.

Chapter Eight
'SAD WORK, WITHOUT THE HEAD'

WITH 1866 Georgina entered on a four-and-a-half-year period of steadily worsening anxiety. Dickens was alarmingly unwell. Ever since the Staplehurst accident he had lacked his old buoyancy and tone. Rail travel agonized him.[1] In February even his heart was misbehaving. Frank Beard's diagnosis, a 'degeneration of some functions of the heart', was—if Dickens reported it to his sister-in-law accurately—couched in the very terms applied to her own case. 'Of course,' he admitted, 'I am not so foolish as to suppose that all my work can have been achieved without *some* penalty. . . .'[2] The report on his condition caused such a flurry of apprehension at Gad's Hill that he used it as his excuse to suggest to Beard the calling in of Dr. Brinton for consultation. Such a measure, he represented, would relieve Beard from bearing any onus in the eyes of the Dickens household.[3] Actually, he had already been disposed to seek a second opinion when he had given Georgina the diagnosis the previous week. Though she probably understood him well enough to suspect what gratification it gave his ego to have someone always ready to worry over him, her concern was none the less acute, her sympathies were none the less harrowed, by the perpetual recitals of symptoms, fatigue, dejection.

And now she was particularly concerned because he was determined to accelerate the pace of the exhausting reading tours. 'I have just sold myself to the Powers of Evil, for 30 readings,' he announced in March.[4] Georgina knew well enough why he had contracted with Chappells of Bond Street for the series at £50 a night, all expenses paid. None of his ventures was more profitable than the readings, none so sure in quick returns. It was not only the multiple expenses that drove him to maintain his earnings at a high level; there was also his compulsion to accumulate a reserve against his children's probable needs. He should have been awarded a prize, he said grimly, 'for having brought up the largest family ever known with the smallest disposition to do anything for themselves'.[5]

During the new reading programme, which covered England, Scotland, and Ireland, Georgina and Mamie lived in a furnished residence in London as was their annual custom during the late winter and spring social season. There, by means of his letters, Georgina followed Dickens in imagination. 'I slept thoroughly well last night, and feel fresh,' she was pleased to read in April at the outset of the tour, only to be cast down by the next sentence: 'What to-night's work, and every night's work this week, may do contrariwise, remains to be seen.'[6] So it went, with ups and downs. But everything she heard about George Dolby, the new reading manager appointed by Chappells, endeared to her that large, bald man, forthright and competent, but hampered by a stammer—particularly whenever the name Cambridge, that 'rock ahead in his speech', appeared in the itinerary.[7] He was of the best: he shared her utter devotion to Dickens. As the tour progressed, she was spared the provincial newspaper accounts, these being 'generally so poorly written, that you may know beforehand all [their] commonplaces'. But from her native Edinburgh, where the audience was, 'as usual here, remarkably intelligent', she received a copy of *The Scotsman* with an article 'so pretty and . . . so true' that Dickens could not resist sending it to her.[8]

For several years now, Georgina had entertained a lurking fear that the reading tours might some day be extended to America. As early as the spring of 1858 there had come overtures from James T. Fields, the Boston publisher and editor. A year later he had reinforced his proposal by calling in person at both Tavistock House and Gad's Hill. However tempting the promises of a new public and huge profits, there were strong arguments, even then, against the undertaking. Dickens would have had to leave much behind: the children and Georgina, the fascinating alterations at Gad's Hill, his newly launched *All the Year Round*. Besides, he admitted, there was 'a private reason rendering a long voyage and absence particularly painful. . . .'[9] Whether this was a reference to Ellen Ternan is, of course, conjectural. Fields did not abandon hope, however, but brought the matter up yearly thereafter.

But now, during the spring of 1866, Georgina was lulled into temporary security on receiving from Dickens the heavily underscored promise, '*You need have no fear about America*'.[10] Comforted by this assurance, she returned to Gad's Hill in June to enter reluctantly on a season cumbered by hospitality. With Dickens absent all spring, she and Mamie had postponed paying social debts. Now, with his sanction, they set out to catch up with the 'accumulated arrears'. But Georgina kept one eye on the harried master of the house and—with Mamie—'would have broken faith all round' had he permitted it.[11]

H

August brought thoughts of Catherine Dickens out into the open again and gave Georgina a distasteful task. For the first time since the Staplehurst accident Catherine had written to her husband. Her plea that he call on her was immediately sent on to Georgina with instructions: 'I find the enclosed at the office here. If you have no objection on your own part, I wish you would reply to it that I have asked you to answer it, and that you think it well to tell her at once that you are absolutely certain that I will never go to her house, and that it is my fixed purpose (without any abatement of kindness otherwise), to hold as little personal communication with her as I possibly can. . . .

'About the house, I can give no opinion. She must decide the question out of her own daily experience of it and domestic knowledge of it. If she has any question to ask me about her boy, she can either write it to me or to you.

'This last paragraph marked with a bracket, will be all you have to say for me, if you don't like to say the rest.

'It is pretty clear to me that she very well knows what is amiss, and has been put up by somebody to trying to get hold of me.'[12]

In the absence of Catherine's letter one can only fall back on sur-mises as to the meaning of Dickens's last paragraph and the refer-ence to 'her boy'. The latter could be explained if Catherine, using the phrase 'my boy', had wished an appointment to dissuade Dickens from having Plorn trained for life in Australia. (Letters to Plorn's tutor nine and eleven months later show Dickens to have been greatly displeased with the 'want of application' and the 'imprac-tical torpor' of his youngest son in 1866 and 1867).[13] One can only believe that Georgina, in transmitting the message to her sister, suppressed her reluctance in the interests of obeying orders.

It was not long until another delicate situation arose. On 3rd November, while guests were in the house, Georgina got a disillu-sioning shock by post. 'If you open this letter in the presence of either of the Stone girls, do not be betrayed into any expression of surprise,' Dickens began. Hastening on, she learned that Scotland Yard, investigating the mysterious theft of eight sovereigns from the office cash box, had found the thief to be John Thompson, a family servant for twenty-five years, his master's valet on all the reading tours, and the attendant currently trusted with the care of the editorial office and adjoining living quarters. 'What I am to do with, or for, the miserable man, God knows,' moaned Dickens.[14]

It was her task to withhold knowledge of the disgrace from the Gad's Hill servants, devising some story to the effect that 'John is going into some small business—anything of that kind. . . .' In the meantime she was to stay away from the office and tell Mamie to do likewise, so that 'no third person . . . who knew him through his old long service' should witness John's shame.[15] At once she took steps to provide a housekeeper for the office living quarters, writing to ask a former servant, Ellen, to fill the post. She was authorized to offer the woman 'a good sitting room at the bottom of the house, three bright airy rooms adjoining each other at the top, coals and candles, and a guinea a week'. Dickens specified her duties precisely: 'to keep the house perfectly clean, to attend to me when I am here, and to Wills when he wants anything—which seldom extends beyond a cup of tea for lunch, or a chop'.[16]

With the shock of John's exposure, the detailed duties in its wake, and the presence of house guests, Georgina became a bit mixed up in one of her domestic responsibilities. At the peak of the excitement over the theft, she had reported the arrival of some French fabrics. Dickens's answer, concerned otherwise with his office housekeeping requirements, urged that 'the curtains and couch . . . be immediately got to work upon'.[17] His next communication, though, must have sent her into a flutter: 'The remembrance of a passage in your letter, yesterday—which I forgot at the time—makes me so very much afraid of your doing something wrong with that French stuff that I go the length of sending a boy down with this, express.

'You write about the sofa not having arrived to be covered and about "the great chair"—or "the arm chair"—being covered. There is no chair whatever to be covered *in my room*. Curtains are to be made to the large windows and the two small windows, and the new sofa is to be covered. That is all. There is no chair to be covered.'[18]

At this hectic time Georgina already knew that another strenuous season of readings was to begin shortly after Christmas. Since the forty-two appearances (contracted for with Chappells for £2,500) would keep him on the road until May, except for the briefest intervals, Dickens did not rent the usual furnished house in London for the season. Hence Georgina wintered in the country, keeping house for Katey and her invalid husband, who had come to Gad's Hill for his health. Mamie, perhaps disinclined to a dull immurement at home, sought diversion with friends in Hampshire.[19]

The bulletins Georgina received from Dickens during his tour held little more brightness than the late winter sky over Gad's Hill. He could not sleep. At Liverpool he felt so faint that he had taken to a sofa before leaving the hall after a performance. He still suffered from the Staplehurst experience, which 'tells more and more, instead of (as one might have expected) less and less'.[20] Only now and then did the sun shine out over his correspondence, as in the account of

lunch with Mr. and Mrs. Harrington of York, both of whom wore
false hair: it had been 'rather comical to see the two wigs presid-
ing . . . opposite each other'.[21] Having so often protected Dickens
from Maria Winter, Georgina must have found further amusement
in his report from Newcastle-on-Tyne. Mr. Winter, having failed in
business, had gone to Cambridge to study for—of all things—holy
orders, had taken his degree at age forty-eight, and was now vicar
at Alnmouth, near Newcastle. 'No news yet of the Winter family,'
Dickens wrote. 'I live in a tremble.' Two days later, having escaped
to Leeds, he sent a second bulletin: 'Thank heaven, there have been
no signs, either of Mrs. Winter or "dear Mr. W.".'[22]

When he went to Ireland Georgina found a new cause for apprehension. There he was travelling in dangerous territory, for it was
the period of Fenian uprisings. His first letter from Dublin intensified her uneasiness by mentioning a threatened 'disturbance between
to-morrow night and Monday night (both inclusive). . . .' But his
next remark urged her not to fret, for 'I shall not put myself in
harm's way'. Hard upon this reassurance, however, came the grim
admission, 'There is no doubt whatever that alarm prevails, and the
manager of the Hotel, an intelligent German, is very gloomy on the
subject'.[23] Georgina was alternately up and down. No sooner had
the seeds of anxiety been planted in receptive ground than she was
charged not to cultivate them. The second letter she received from
Dublin announced 'no new rumours' and concluded soothingly, 'This
is merely to keep you at ease on riotous fronts'; but she could have
found in a letter to Mamie on the same day apprehensions of a possible St. Patrick's Day uprising: '. . . Croakers predict that it will
come off between to-night and Monday night'.[24]

From Ireland also came a reminder of Mamie's regrettable indifference to Percy Fitzgerald. Dublin being his young friend's home,
Dickens wrote of receiving a 'really charming letter from Mrs. Fitzgerald, asking me to stay there. She must be a perfectly unaffected
and genuine lady.' He sent this letter on to Mamie, asking her to
acknowledge its kind messages to herself and to her aunt. 'Percy's
people are of great consideration here, and universally known,' he
wrote wistfully to Georgina some days later.[25]

As always, Georgina had her instructions. She was to replenish
the liquor stocks at the office on her trips to London, so that Dickens
might refresh himself whenever a break in his reading schedule permitted a brief visit there. He had found her inventory of the champagne to be correct. She must remember to bring in some orange
brandy (of her own concocting), as well as a bottle of the aged
brandy. Another time she was directed to bring in six pints of the

best champagne. There was also confirmation of her objection to the exorbitant cost of a dessert service Dickens had ordered. 'But the commission has gone too far to be handsomely receded from now,' he regretted. 'If I had had the slightest idea of its cost I should as soon have thought of buying Strood Turnpike.'[26]

When the readings ended early in May, Georgina relaxed—but only for a day or two. On the 11th she opened a brief note in the familiar hand: 'Expenses are so enormous that I begin to feel myself drawn towards America, as Darnay in the Tale of Two Cities was attracted to the Loadstone Rock, Paris'.[27] She was too well versed in the adventures of Charles Darnay, Dickens must have known, to take from this analogy anything but the direst forebodings. But at the same time she could have discerned in it his characteristic dramatization of his own situation.

It would, of course, be futile for her to try to dissuade him. Once he had decided on a course of action, nothing could stop him. And who recognized more clearly than she the validity of his argument that expenses were enormous—and would probably continue so? Repeatedly she had listened to his pessimistic predictions that the boys would all prove themselves unable to make their own way. This very winter Plorn, having shown no 'continuity of purpose' in his studies, was being prepared for 'a rough wild life' of sheep-farming in Australia, in the hope that he might 'take better to the Bush than to Books'.[28]

In her hopeless opposition to the American tour Georgina was joined by Forster and Wills. They, too, looked on the venture as a grave threat to Dickens's health. To Wills, Dickens minimized his physical infirmities and repeated the financial argument. Where but in America could he make a profit of £10,000 in five months? 'To get that sum in a heap so soon is an immense consideration to me—my wife's income to pay—a very expensive position to hold—and my boys with a curse of limpness on them. You don't know what it is to look round the table and see reflected from every seat at it . . . some horribly well remembered expression of inadaptability to any thing.'[29]

At the same time he admitted to Wills the existence of a real obstacle, one which Georgina possibly appreciated. Writing on stationery bearing the monogram E T (Ellen Ternan), he acknowledged the 'Patient . . . to be the gigantic difficulty. But you know I don't like to give in before a difficulty, if it can be beaten.'[30] ('The Patient' was his designation for Ellen Ternan after her slight indisposition following the Staplehurst accident. According to his pocket diary she had been ill this very spring and thus again qualified for this title.) Nelly, as he usually called her, was now living in Windsor Lodge, Peckham, a villa he had engaged for her. Less than a mile away he had rooms at the Five Bells Inn, where he often stayed during his London visits.[31] His pocket diary for that year contains cryptic entries using the initials 'P' and 'N'. Assuming that these are abbreviations for Peckham and Nelly, the jottings in this journal show that Dickens saw Ellen at frequent intervals. He called on her at Peckham, received her at the office, and occasionally took her out to the theatre.[32] Presumably his attachment to her was now serious enough to be the chief deterrent to the American tour. But only a few knew what she meant to him. To a woman friend, a former actress, he had written the previous summer, '. . . It would be inexpressibly painful to N to think that you knew her history. . . . She would not believe that you could see her with my eyes, or know her with my mind.'[33] Yet Georgina, too, must have striven to see Nelly with Dickens's eyes, know her with his mind.

Throughout the summer Georgina waited for the final commitment on the readings. Then in September Dolby returned from America, where he had been gathering facts and figures on which to estimate the probable success of the tour. The last weekend of that month must have lagged for her. Dickens had gone to Ross-on-Wye for a final conference with Dolby and Forster before cabling his decision to Boston on Monday morning, and it was not until Tuesday that she received his note beginning, 'The telegram is despatched to Boston: "Yes. Go ahead." ' Hurrying on, she came to the characteristic 'I am so nervous with travelling and anxiety to decide something, that I can hardly write'. But at the close she warmed to this assurance: '. . . I send you these few words as my dearest and best friend'.[34]

Again she became a prey to anxiety, for she knew Dickens was unfit for such an undertaking. Throughout August she had been receiving disquieting bulletins: 'My foot is bad again, and I can't walk'. 'I cannot get a boot on—wear a slipper on my left foot. . . .' '. . . Send basket to Gravesend to meet me . . . , as I couldn't walk a quarter of a mile to-night for five hundred pounds. . . .'[35] The trouble, according to Sir Henry Thompson, the eminent surgeon, was friction of the shoe on a bunion-like enlargement, complicated by erysipelas.[36] Even in early September, before a decision on the tour had been reached, she had seen Dickens irritated by rumours that he was in a critical state, that physicians were sending him to America for 'cessation of literary labour!' Messages of sympathy had begun to pour in, followed promptly by his published denials: he was *not* in a critical state, had *not* consulted eminent surgeons, was *not* going to America to rest. But none knew so well as Georgina how wildly exaggerated was his protestation to the Belfast editor Finlay that he had never been so well in his life, that he had not, in fact, had so much as a headache in twenty years![37]

In later life Georgina was to keep as her most poignant memory of this autumn the farewell banquet the week before Dickens sailed for America. For her no other occasion held such proud glory and, at the same time, such tender apprehensions. The affair was spontaneously got up only two weeks in advance by a committee of ten, including Wilkie Collins and Charles Fechter. One hundred celebrities in literature, the arts, and public life were hastily invited to be honorary sponsors, and enough additional tickets were sold at a guinea each to insure a gathering of over five hundred at Freemasons' Hall, London. The one hundred women guests were seated in the ladies' gallery overlooking the magnificently decorated dining-hall. Georgina, resplendent in her best silks and jewels, and still youthful-looking at forty, sat with a little family party—Mamie, Katey, and Charley's wife, Bessie. Directly in front of her was Dan Godfrey, who conducted the Grenadier Guards Band in airs from Mozart, Meyerbeer, Verdi, Strauss, and Offenbach and who endeared himself to her by his obvious relish for the entire occasion.[38]

It was indeed a brilliant scene below. The twenty arched wall panels had been bordered with laurel leaves set on a deep red background. On each panel gleamed the gold-lettered title of one of Dickens's books, the place of honour over the chair being occupied by *Pickwick*. Here also were the Stars and Stripes and the British Standard, symbolically united. Mamie, known to one or two of the Committee as having considerable skill with floral decorations, had been appealed to for help and had responded with a modicum of advice: 'I am afraid I can't help you much with your pretty floral idea. . . . I never had anything of the kind to do. The best way of making the letters is to get some perforated zinc ones (they are made for the purpose) and then nail leaves in places over them.'[39]

As Georgina looked down on the throng awaiting the appearance of the guest of honour, she recognized many of his eminent contemporaries: Gladstone, Tennyson, Anthony Trollope, Millais, Landseer. Some of them she had entertained at Gad's Hill, including Bulwer-Lytton, now Lord Lytton, the Chairman of the Dinner Committee. But she missed Carlyle and Ruskin. Invited to be a sponsor, Carlyle had been unwilling to offer up his digestion on this public altar. 'I must beg you to have me excused at present,' he had written Charles Kent, Secretary of the Banquet, 'as, by health, spirits, etc., plainly unfit.' And Ruskin, only the day before the banquet, had affirmed his deep respect for Dickens, but had characteristically added that he had 'not the least mind to express it Dinnerwise'.[40]

At the appointed moment the ladies in the gallery leaned forward to watch the entrance of Dickens, escorted by the Committee and hailed on all sides. When the time came for her old friend Lord Lytton to propose the toast to the guest of honour, Georgina, unfortunately, could hear little of what one spectator was to call a 'highfalutin' speech.[41] But when Dickens got up to respond—ah, that was a glorious moment! The diners rose with him, tossing napkins into the air and cheering wildly. In the gallery Georgina was enveloped in a flurry of scent from waving handkerchiefs and fans. She saw her Charles, visibly moved, struggling to compose himself before the ovation died down. Then she heard him speak eloquently and gratefully of his faith in the American people, closing dramatically: 'If I may quote one short sentence from myself, let it imply all that I have left unsaid and yet deeply feel; let it, putting a girdle around the earth, comprehend both sides of the Atlantic at once in this moment. And so, as Tiny Tim observed, "God bless us every one!" '
Georgina heard many other speeches that evening, but none so memorable. The banquet ended at half-past eleven, but it was much later before the ladies of the family could expect Dickens's escort. Even as they left the hall, crowds waiting outside in Great Queen's Street cheered him in a final farewell.[42]

Although caught up in the excitement of these days, Georgina could still discern more than one reason that might keep Charles from viewing the trip with elation. Only a few weeks before announcing his decision, on a night when his pocket diary shows him to have been alone, he had written her, 'Last evening I missed you so much that I was obliged to go to the Olympic'.[43] To whom would he turn in America for sympathy and comfortable companionship? Would he not pine for home? Or—might he have secret plans for Nelly to follow him?

That he had probably worked out such a scheme is evidenced by an office memorandum, together with a November entry in his pocket diary. Along with various instructions filed with Wills— provisions for the conduct of *All the Year Round*, for Georgina and Mamie's checking account, for the pension of the old and indigent playwright John Poole—were directions for communicating with Ellen Ternan, then at her married sister's villa in Florence. (In October 1866, Frances Eleanor Ternan had married Thomas Adolphus Trollope, brother of the novelist.) After giving Nelly's address, the memorandum continued: 'On the day after my arrival out I will send you a short Telegram at the office. Please copy its exact words (as they will have a special meaning for her), and post them to her as above by the very next post after receiving my telegram. And also let Gad's Hill know—and let Forster know —what the telegram is.'⁴⁴

How Nelly would interpret his telegram was explained in his pocket diary. There, among some blank pages at the back, he had entered the code they had agreed upon:

Tel: all well means
        you come
Tel: safe and well, means
        you don't come
To Wills. Who sends the Te. on to
Villa Trollope
fuori la porta S'Niccolo
*Florence.*⁴⁵

From Dickens's choice of phrase Nelly would know whether or not she was to undertake the voyage to America, where she had family connections.⁴⁶

That Georgina was aware of the scheme is not improbable, for Wills's orders, it will be recalled, included letting 'Gad's Hill know ... what the telegram is'. It is true that the alternative phrasings of the prearranged message could be understood for their surface meaning alone; but had Dickens intended merely to announce his safe arrival, he need not have specified (as his language clearly implies) that the exact wording of the telegram be transmitted to Gad's Hill—and to Forster, to whose care, along with that of Wills, Nelly had been entrusted.

With the packing and the final preparations for the journey, the five days following the farewell banquet sped by for Georgina. On 8th November she joined the little party that accompanied Dickens to Liverpool—Mamie and Katey, Charley and Wilkie Collins, and a few others. They travelled in the Royal Saloon Carriage that the London and Northwestern Railway had reserved for them as a special honour. All along the way it attracted much attention at station stops. The next day the party saw Dickens aboard the *Cuba*. With him went Kelly (Dolby's assistant), a valet, and all the reading equipment—platform, stand, screen, and gas apparatus. Dolby had gone ahead on an earlier sailing.⁴⁷

As the *Cuba* made the ten-day passage to Boston, Georgina followed it in her thoughts. Her first news, a letter to Mamie from Queenstown harbour the third day out, was cheerful. But it was a long wait for the letters to be mailed from Halifax on the eighteenth. Would they tell of a rough voyage? of sleepless nights? of more trouble with the poor foot? In due time she had her answers, from which she might derive, as she chose, comfort or anxiety. Charles had not been seasick. But he had suffered from headaches and had 'felt faint once or twice'. Also tipping the scale toward the anxious side was the news that he usually lay awake at night and that the foot—it was as she had feared—continued in a 'shy condition' and somewhat painful. Still this might be, as he hoped, merely the result of much walking on deck.[48]

While Georgina waited for the first news to arrive from Boston, Ellen Ternan was waiting, too, at her sister's villa in Italy. But she was not to be kept in suspense for long. During his first three days in America Dickens may have taken counsel with Fields. Careful study of the situation must have convinced him that his plan for bringing Nelly over was too bold. At any rate, the telegram received in London on 23rd November read, 'Safe and well'. Ellen had her coded order: she would not go to America.

Though Georgina may also have gleaned this information from Wills's transcript of the telegram, she had to wait much longer for the first personal message to cross the ocean. But when the letter came it was heartening, spirited, and hopeful in tone. Dickens found himself in fine fettle after the voyage, 'so well, that I am constantly chafing at not having begun [the readings] to-night instead of this night week'. There had been a great demand for tickets, too, though the speculators were on the job, unfortunately. Especially reassuring was the glimpse of Mrs. Fields as 'a very nice woman, with a rare relish for humour and a most contagious laugh'.[49] Perhaps she would help dispel his loneliness. And indeed, later letters were to show that Annie Fields surpassed even the most extravagant expectations.

With the approach of Christmas Georgina had little heart for planning the usual festivities. One thing, though, had to be attended to early in December: a cheery letter timed to reach Dickens by the 25th. He himself made similar calculations, sending his greetings on the 11th with love to 'all the Christmas circle, not forgetting Chorley, to whom give my special remembrance'.[50] (It is not known whether Mamie needed this reminder of her duty to invite Henry Chorley, music critic and old family friend who traditionally ate his Christmas dinner at Gad's Hill. She must have acted somewhat belatedly, though, for in January Dickens was to write Georgina: 'I took it for granted that Mary would have asked Chorley for Christmas Day, and am very glad she ultimately did so.')[51]

To the Gad's Hill party gathered in the holly-decked dining-room, the flaming plum pudding and the traditional ceremonies only served to render the absence of Dickens more poignant. Nor could Georgina console herself that he would be sharing a merry feast across the ocean, for his letter made it clear that he would spend his Christmas Day travelling from Boston to New York. Before her own holiday ended she found time to sit down and dutifully acknowledge on his behalf Mary Howitt's greetings and appreciative comments on the Christmas number of *All the Year Round*. 'We have our annual family party assembled,' Georgina wrote: 'it is sad work, without the Head! But there is immense comfort in thinking of the great success of his undertaking and when once the New Year is turned the time passes on so quickly that we may begin to look forward to his return—please God!—early in June.' She could not resist confiding how substantial had been the profits from the ticket sales, adding, '. . . It *is* very hard work to read four times a week to enormous crowds in immense Halls—and requires the money to be made to sweeten the labour!'[52]

Still wondering whether her Christmas message had reached America in time, she found it hard to wait patiently for the slow trans-Atlantic mail. Her first word after the holiday merely gave the annoying news that Dickens had been 'in a grim state of mind' on 16th December because heavy snow between Boston and New York had held up the mail he had expected by the incoming *Cunarder*. But the letter thus delayed would have antedated her Christmas greeting. Yet she could take satisfaction in the news that New Yorkers were 'a wonderfully fine audience, even better than Edinburgh. . . .'[53]

The arrival of Dickens's next news still did not dispel her suspense over her Christmas letter, though it brought assurance that her delayed earlier one had gladdened his ten-o'clock dinner at the Parker House after a 'detestable' train trip from New York. Best of all, his health was improved, and Annie Fields had been looking after him. She had added books and other homelike touches to his hotel room, even decking it with 'holly (with real red berries) and festoons of moss dependent from the looking-glasses and picture frames'. And because of his scheduled return to New York on the 25th, she had served Christmas dinner on the 21st, with a 'plum-pudding, brought on blazing, and not to be surpassed in any house in England'. Reading all this, Georgina could only concur that Mrs. Fields was 'one of the dearest little women in the world'.[54]

Not until sometime around Twelfth Night did Gad's Hill learn how dismal Christmas Day had been for the absent 'Head'. But—

happy miracle!—Georgina had, through sheer luck or careful study of steamship schedules, timed her second December letter to arrive in Boston on Christmas morning, just before he had taken the train for New York. 'I wanted it very much,' he assured Mamie, 'for I had a frightful cold (English colds are nothing to those in this country), and was exceedingly depressed and miserable.' At dinner that night he had 'made some hot gin punch to drink a merry Christmas to all at home in'. But he had been 'very dull'. Nor was there any reassurance in what followed: 'I have been in bed all day until two o'clock, and here I am now (at three o'clock) a little better. But I am not fit to read, and I must read to-night.' As for the next day, it was to have its own woes, apparently: '. . . I shall probably be obliged to go across the water to Brooklyn to-morrow to see a church, in which it is proposed that I shall read! ! ! Horrible visions of being put in the pulpit already beset me. And whether the audience will be in pews is another consideration which greatly disturbs my mind.' At the end of the gloomy account, which had been addressed to Mamie, was appended a note written the next day: 'I managed to read last night, but it was as much as I could do. To-day I am so very unwell, that I have sent for a doctor; he has just been, and is in doubt whether I shall not have to stop reading for a while. . . .'[55]

The performances continued, however; and Georgina soon had a letter admitting that reading in the Brooklyn church, Henry Ward Beecher's, had proved a gratifying experience after all. There had been an 'ernormously full' house, including the great Beecher himself. The pulpit having given way to the screen and gas apparatus, it had been 'a most wonderful place to speak in'.[56]

Georgina was to have the afflictions of an American winter constantly impressed upon her. What with the severe weather and the heat from the 'intolerable furnaces', hair and fingernails grew dry and brittle. 'There is not a complete nail in the whole British suite,' she was shocked to read in January, 'and my hair cracks again when I brush it. (I am losing my hair with great rapidity, and what I don't lose is getting very grey.)'[57]

Some of the letters reported on the American friends whom she had heard about after Charles's first trip across the Atlantic. Hawthorne was dead now, but he had a 'striking-looking daughter'. Longfellow was living under 'the shadow of that terrible story' of seven years ago, when his wife had died of severe burns, in the very house where he and his daughters now lived. As for the eldest, his grave Alice, it was hard to decide whether she was 'pretty or plain', but 'seeing her eyes looking through a chink, you would say she was lovely'. Cornelius Felton, the Harvard professor whom Georgina had met during his visit to England in 1853, had left two daughters, the elder 'a very sensible, frank, pleasant girl of eight and twenty perhaps'.[58]

In this period, probably more than ever before, Georgina was needed to hold the family together and transmit messages between Dickens and his sons. 'Tell Plorn, with my love', he wrote, 'that I think he will find himself much interested at that college [the Agricultural College, Cirencester], and that it is very likely he may make some acquaintances there that will hereafter be pleasant and useful to him. . . . I am sorry that Harry lost his prize, but I believe it was not his fault. Let *him* know *that*, with my love. I would have written to him by this mail in answer to his, but for other occupation.' She was also charged to tell a neighbour, Mrs. Hulkes, that her letter had been received and that the violet her boy had enclosed still kept its colour. And there was a commission to aid Anne Brown Cornelius, whose husband had been forced to give up his work because of prolonged illness. Nor was the upkeep of Gad's Hill forgotten. A new floor was to be laid in the hall and curtains must be made. Georgina and Mamie were to decide between tile and parquet flooring—they chose the latter—and see that all was 'thoroughly well done—no half measures'.[59] For the most part, though, Georgina received no domestic assignments during the five months of the tour. But it is safe to assume that practical affairs at Gad's Hill went on smoothly, albeit sadly, 'without the Head'. With his tendency to dramatize everything, Dickens probably visualized her as carrying on the household routine like Lucie Manette, for whom 'everything had its appointed place and its appointed time', even while she knew Charles Darnay, 'drawn to the Loadstone Rock', to be in peril of his life.[60]

All through the winter came a steady procession of letters with their foreign postmarks: Boston, New York, Philadelphia, Washington, Baltimore, Syracuse, Buffalo, Rochester, Albany, Springfield (Massachusetts), Portland (Maine). Such distances to be covered! One exuberant little note even hinted that the tour might be extended westward: 'I am quite well, thank God, and everything is most prosperous. We *could not* BE DOING BETTER. Dolby's love. He is just going off to Chicago to look about him. It is only twelve Hundred miles from here!'[61] Would Charles really jeopardize his health by such an extended undertaking? For several anxious weeks Georgina awaited the decision. In February her suspense was broken: 'One of the drollest things . . . is the intense indignation of the West, because I don't go there. Chicago leads the assault with affecting pictures of "my brother's wife and her helpless children", etc., etc.'[62]

Even on the other side of the Atlantic, Georgina reflected, Charles could not escape his family embarrassments. The present furore had, in fact, been anticipated even a year before the plans for the American tour were complete, when it was learned that Dickens's youngest brother, Augustus, had died impoverished in Chicago, leaving several children by the woman who had eloped with him. Having seen a notice of his death, Wills had sent word to Gad's Hill. Thereupon Dickens had replied with some foreboding: 'The news of Augustus, I think may be taken as true. . . . Poor fellow! a sad business altogether! My mind misgives me that it will bring upon me a host of disagreeables from America.'[63] Later, in the hectic days before sailing, he had given his last-minute attention to the details of transferring certain trust funds to Augustus's legal wife in England.[64]

It was distressing to have the matter continue to plague him. In March Chicago was still 'in a frenzy' at being excluded from the reading itinerary. 'They have not only discovered that my "brother's wife and indigent children" are living neglected there,' Dickens wrote Georgina, 'but have (I mean the Chicago papers) circulated a notice that a certain actor who imitates me is going to give Readings for their benefit'.[65] What the Chicagoans did not know—Dickens was usually reticent in such matters—was that after the death of Augustus in 1866, the oldest son, Bertram, received from his Uncle Charles the yearly sum of £50. This aid continued during the novelist's lifetime.[66]

Throughout the late winter months Georgina found in Charles's letters the usual simultaneous low and high spirits. An early account of the Chicago troubles was headed pathetically 'my Birthday, 1868 (And my cold worse than ever.)' But it also brought the heart-warming tidings that Washington, D.C., had not ignored the date: 'The papers here having written about this being my birthday, the most exquisite flowers came pouring in at breakfast time from all sorts of people. The room is covered with them, made up into beautiful bouquets, and arranged in all manner of green baskets. Probably I shall find plenty more at the hall to-night. This is considered the dullest and most apathetic place in America. *My* audiences have been superb.'[67] Among the birthday offerings, though the letter to Georgina neglected to mention it, must have been one from the devoted Annie Fields, whose diary for 7th February records: 'I have sent to Washington to have flowers on his table this morning. I hope it will be properly done.' For her it was a notable day: 'The birthday of our friend! Dear Charles Dickens!'[68]

To no one in America did Georgina feel warmer gratitude than to
Mrs. Fields, for certainly none showed Charles greater kindness or
admired him more. From his first reading Annie had been entranced:
'How we listened till we seemed turned into one eye-ball! How we
all loved him! How we longed to tell him all kinds of confidences!'[69]
Doubtless the Fieldses did confide in Dickens, as he in them. 'He
appears often troubled by the lack of energy his children show,'
Annie observed during the first days of his visit, 'and has even
allowed James to see how deep his unhappiness is in having so many
children by a wife who was totally uncongenial. He seems to have
the deepest sympathy for men who are unfitly married and has really
taken an especial fancy, I think, to John Bigelow, our latest minister
to Paris who is here, because his wife is such an incubus.'[70] Two
months later she took up the subject again: 'Such charity! Poor
man! He must have learned great need for that. He told J. [James
Fields] yesterday in walking that nine out of ten of the cases of disagreement in marriage came from drink he believed.'[71] (But she
did not blame alcoholism for the Dickens rift. Another diary entry
reports how Katey Collins had once confided to a friend that 'her
mother did not drink but she is heavy and unregardful of her
children and jealous of her husband'.)[72]

At once perceptive and sympathetic, Mrs. Fields soon sensed the
eagerness with which Dickens awaited word from home, noted how
his spirits sank when mail was delayed, how they rose when 'modest
letters came from Miss Hogarth and all was bright again.' He let
it be known that his sister-in-law was the heart of his home.
'Georgina Hogarth he always speaks of in the most affectionate
terms,' Annie Fields noted, 'such as "she has been a mother to my
children", "she keeps the list of the wine cellar, and every few days
examines to see what we are now in want of".'[73]

Though cheered by reports of the many kindnesses shown Dickens
by his American friends, Georgina knew he was still homesick and
frequently low spirited. 'I am often very heavy and rarely sleep
much,' he admitted at the end of January. But Dolby and Osgood
(a member of the Fields publishing firm who assisted with the reading arrangements in America) were planning a 'ridiculous' walking
match to keep him in good spirits.[74] Begun as a joke, it developed
into an elaborate affair with Dolby and his American opponent representing their two nations in a twelve-mile walk on 29th February.
A letter of 2nd March brought Gad's Hill an account of the contest.
Big Dolby had begun well, but had fallen behind on the last lap,
while little Osgood had shot ahead 'at a splitting pace'. Afterwards
Dickens had treated eighteen guests, including the Fieldses, to a

sumptuous dinner at his hotel. In the centre of the table was 'an immense basket, overflowing with enormous bell-mouthed lilies; all round the table a bright green border of wreathed creeper, with clustering roses at intervals; a rose for every button-hole, and a bouquet for every lady'.[75]

When early spring came to Gad's Hill and covered the ground with violets and primroses, Georgina gathered a few to enclose in a letter to Dickens. The bond forming between her and Annie Fields was to be strengthened by this token, for when Dickens received the letter he handed the flowers to his hostess, who pressed them between the pages of her diary for April, noting that Miss Hogarth had declared the loveliness of the English spring to be 'something indescribable'. Mrs. Fields also observed that 'dear C. D.'s spirits go up as the days pass; home begins to look very near, but so does our separation'.[76]

On both sides of the Atlantic the days were counted off on the calendar. As April drew near, Georgina had to remember to post her final letter in accord with Charles's specific instructions. If it was to be received before his departure, it must be timed to catch the *Cunarder* sailing from Liverpool on 4th April. Before the month was far advanced there was further news that seemed to bring the date of reunion nearer: 'You will see by the evidence of this piece of paper that I am using up my stationery. Scott [the valet] has just been making anxious calculations as to our power of holding out in the articles of Enchrisma [ointment or hair oil?], Tooth powder, etc.' The staff was being paid off, and 'signs of our approaching embarcation are all around us. . . . We leave on Good Friday.' Reading this letter, Georgina made a mental note of a family duty she must perform shortly: ' . . . to send a present of £25 to Mrs. Alfred's boy, with a letter saying that you have it in charge from me to make him that gift, and to tell him that I hope he will strive to do credit to his name, and will always remember that it is a trust he holds'. Georgina and Mamie were also to reap favours from Dickens's benevolent homecoming mood: 'At the same time I may mention with my best love to you both, that I want the last cheque you draw, to be: "Pay to ourselves Two Hundred Pounds": being a little present of One Hundred Pounds each, from the undersigned Inimitable.'[77]

But a disturbing admission cast a shadow over the eagerly awaited homeward journey: 'I am far from strong and have no appetite'. Also the American catarrh was 'worse than ever!' And at the end of the instalment of 2nd April was a notation which Georgina, reading between the lines, could interpret as one of his darker moods of

reminiscence: 'I don't forget that this is Forster's birthday, or that
it is another anniversary'.[78] (It was the thirty-second anniversary
of his marriage. Secure in not suspecting the future marvels of infra-
red photography, Georgina was later to ink out the second clause of
this sentence.) Mrs. Fields also sensed Dickens's melancholy on this
occasion. *'Thursday.*—Anniversary of C. D.'s marriage day and
John Forster's birthday,' she noted in her diary. 'C. D. not at all
well, coughing all the time and in low spirits.'[79]

The New York Press, Georgina had been told, was to give Dickens
a farewell dinner on 18th April. And now, as the date drew nearer,
Mamie received disquieting news that her father was unable to 'eat
more than half a pound of solid food in the whole four-and-twenty
hours, if so much'. He had, consequently, established a liquid diet
routine: 'At seven in the morning, in bed, a tumbler of new cream
and two tablespoonsful of rum. At twelve, a sherry cobbler and a
biscuit. At three (dinner time), a pint of champagne. At five
minutes to eight, an egg beaten up with a glass of sherry. Between
the parts [of the reading], the strongest beef tea that can be made,
drunk hot. At a quarter past ten, soup, and anything to drink that
I can fancy.'[80]

In America the Fieldses shared the Gad's Hill concern over Dickens's
health during these last days. When his foot became badly swollen
and painful the night before the press banquet, Annie suffered
acutely, too. 'So long as he was above ground, however, it was a
necessity he should go,' she wrote in her diary, 'and an hour and a
half after the time appointed, with his foot sewed up in black silk,
he made his way to Delmonico's. Poor man!' What disturbed him
most about this attack was that the American newspapers were
cabling word of his condition to England, where it would worry his
family—and perhaps Nelly. 'Ah! What a mystery these ties of love
are—such pain, such ineffable happiness—the only happiness,'
reflected Mrs. Fields.[81]

On the day of farewell, 22nd April, this emotional woman felt the
pang of parting too deeply to join her husband and the five friends
who went to see Dickens off aboard the *Russia,* sailing from New
York. 'Rose at six this morning, sleep being out of the question,' she
confided to her diary while alone in her room at the Westminster
Hotel. 'I must confess to sitting down in my night-dress in a flood
of tears.' Two days later she was still sentimentalizing: 'He goes to
the English spring, to his own dear ones, to the tenderness of the
long tried love'. And she thought much of Georgina. 'My respect
for Miss Hogarth grows as I reflect upon Dickens. It is not an easy
service in this world to live near such a man, to love him, to desire

I

to do for him. He is swift, restless, impatient, with words of fire, but he is also and above all, tender, loving, strong for right, charitable and patient by moral force. Happy those who live, and bear, and do and suffer and above all love him to the end. . . . Miss Hogarth has labored for him with remarkable success and for his children. But even now he might be lonely, such is his nature. When I recall his lonely couch and lonely hours I feel he has had a strange lot. May his mistakes be expiated.'[82]

Whatever mistakes Annie had in mind, she had secret knowledge of at least one charitable deed to offset them. The housekeeper at the Westminster Hotel had told her how Dickens had helped a poor Irish chambermaid by giving her $60 to go to California with her illegitimate child. The girl had asked the housekeeper not to divulge her secret, but the woman could not resist telling Mrs. Fields.[83]

On 2nd May, the day after Dickens had reached Liverpool, Annie rhapsodized: 'I cannot help rehearsing in my mind the intense joy of his beloved. It is too much to face, even in one's imagination—and too sacred. Yet I know today to be the day and these hours, *his hours*. Tomorrow Gad's Hill.'[84] The 'beloved' is clearly not a reference to Georgina or to other members of the family, for, according to an earlier entry in Mrs. Fields's diary, they had been requested not to meet Dickens at Liverpool,[85] but would await him at Gad's Hill. On 3rd May Annie noted: 'Today Charles Dickens is at home. Let us be grateful.'[86] (There is evidence to suggest that the Fieldses knew of Nelly Ternan. In December of the second year after Dickens's death, Annie, reminded of his rich association with Christmas, entrusted some tender meditations to her diary: 'Dear, dear Dickens, as the season returns, come back many thoughts of his standing beside us. . . . I heard quite accidently . . . the other day of N. T. being in Rome. . . . I feel the bond there is between us. She must feel it too. I wonder if we shall ever meet.')[87]

There was great rejoicing at Gad's Hill when it was learned that the *Russia* had docked safely at Liverpool. Even the neighbouring villagers shared in the excitement, planning to swarm Higham Station when Dickens's train came in from London. Georgina and Mamie, getting wind of their scheme to take the horse out of the shafts and draw the returning hero's carriage home themselves, quickly sent Dickens warning. Accordingly he was met at Gravesend, five miles away, by basket phaeton. At Gad's Hill the servants, not to be outdone by neighbours hanging out flags, draped the house 'so that every brick of it was hidden'. Had Mamie permitted, they would have greeted their master with a clanging of the alarm bell. 'Linda (the St. Bernard),' Dickens wrote Mrs. Fields, 'was greatly excited; weeping profusely, and throwing herself on her back that she might caress my foot with her great fore-paws.' Little Mrs. Bouncer, too, 'barked in the greatest agitation on being called down and asked by Mamie, "Who is this?" and tore round and round me. . . .'[88]

More than ever, Georgina realized that Gad's Hill must be an anodyne for the intense life Charles was even now planning to resume. She had seen to it that the place was 'lovely, and in perfect order' for the homecoming.[89] Keeping it so would be a joyful responsibility now, rather than 'sad work, without the Head'.

Chapter Nine

'OVER FOR EVER'

IN preparing for the returning traveller, Georgina and her nieces had 'expected a wreck' and were thus, as Dickens told Macready, 'much mortified' to have him appear buoyant and rested from the voyage. But within a few days there was again justification for their anxiety as he plunged into a six-month accumulation of deferred duties at the office. To make matters worse, Wills was at home, seriously ill and 'forbidden even to write a letter'. His absence, complained Dickens to Fields, 'so overwhelms me with business that I can scarcely get through it'.[1]

The chief worry, however, was of a sort that Georgina knew only too well. Her oldest nephew, Charley, was in financial trouble again. Now thirty-one and with a son and four daughters to support, he faced the failure of his paper mill company, a partnership including one of his Evans in-laws. In June Georgina was shocked to learn that 'the "Company's" affairs are far more hopeless than at first appeared, and even as to Charley personally, he owes a Thousand pounds!'[2] As bankruptcy proceedings were initiated, Dickens refused to become involved; he would not be liable for any claims against the company, 'against which and his precious Associates . . . I wrote him a letter of warning when it first loomed in the Evans atmosphere'. With only a 'vague future' before him, Charley was finally taken into *All the Year Round* on a temporary basis, to report on the contents of the daily mailbag and answer correspondence.[3]

Hardly had Georgina welcomed Dickens home and seen him meet these first onslaughts of business than the round of summer hospitality began at Gad's Hill. Mary Boyle and Mrs. Watson, Frank Beard, the Macreadys, Ouvry, and others were urged to visit at various times.[4] Again Georgina busied herself with planning such gastronomic delights as Dickens promised Ouvry: 'We do a little thing or two here—as cock-a-leekie, curry, Scotch collops, mutton a la Don Pedro, and such trifles as relishes with claret—which I am bent on getting you to come and try. . . .'[5] But for Longfellow, his three daughters, and Tom Appleton (his brother-in-law), who came to spend the first week-end in July, Georgina exerted herself particularly, impressing Alice, the eldest daughter, by the lavish variety of the cold buffet set before them.[6] Their host saw to it that they inspected Georgina's special province: 'kitchens, pantry, wine-cellar, pickles, sauces, servants' sitting-room, general household stores, and even the Cellar Book of this illustrious establishment'.[7] And in spite of the brevity of their stay he crowded in sight-seeing tours to Cobham Park and to the Cathedral, the Castle, and other landmarks in his beloved Rochester. Later other American guests, the Charles Eliot Nortons and Bayard Taylor, were also shown the glories of Gad's Hill.[8]

Along with the brisk schedule of diversions, Aunt Georgy kept her cherished Plorn much in mind this summer. Almost seventeen, he was now being outfitted to join his brother Alfred in Australia. Since at the same time provisions were being made for Harry to enter Cambridge, she heard many a groan from the financially burdened parent. Yet she knew well the tenderness Dickens bore his youngest, a feeling disclosed in the letter he handed the boy on the day of leave-taking in September: 'I need not tell you that I love you dearly, and am very, very sorry in my heart to part with you. But this life is half made up of partings, and these pains must be borne.' Plorn was exhorted to leave behind the lack of 'steady, constant purpose' and henceforth 'persevere in a thorough determination to do whatever you have to do as well as you can do it'. He was also enjoined to guide his life by the teachings of the New Testament, packed among his books, and to follow the practice of saying a private prayer night and morning: 'I have never abandoned it myself, and I know the comfort of it'. The letter concluded, 'I hope you will always be able to say in after life, that you had a kind father'.[9]

On the day of farewell Georgina and Mamie sent Plorn off from Gad's Hill in Harry's company. What happened thereafter was reported to them later. Plorn had broken down briefly in the railway carriage after leaving Higham. He had wept again at Paddington Station on being seen off for Plymouth. But it was Dickens, Harry noted, who had broken down the more painfully, with utter disregard of onlookers. He had met the boys in London and, having had a reminder from Georgina, had supplied Plorn with cigars—a rather odd gift for a sixteen-year-old, unless intended for bestowal on travel acquaintances or possibly on Rusden, the boy's sponsor in Australia.[10] To Dolby, himself a father, Dickens poured out his grief: 'When you come (if you ever do) to send your youngest child thousands of miles away for an indefinite time, and have a rush into your soul of all the many fascinations of the last little child you can ever dearly love, you will have a hard experience of this wrenching life'. The ache of parting lingered into October. 'I find myself constantly thinking of Plorn', he wrote Georgina on the 11th.[11]

From this sad farewell it was a relief to turn to the more cheering prospect of getting Harry ready to enter Trinity Hall, Cambridge. Here was the one nephew Georgina could take pride in—the only one who never disappointed his father, the steady lad with a consistently good academic record. Had he not been promoted to the place of Head Censor at Wimbledon? And a few months before, during his father's absence in America, he had capably organized and directed the affairs of the Higham cricket club, calling its working-class members together and addressing them—quite as if, at nineteen he were himself the squire of Gad's Hill.[12]

But for all his youthful promise, Harry must be warned, his father felt, against the family pattern of extravagance. 'Now, observe attentively,' ran the paternal admonition. 'We must have no shadow of debt. Square up everything whatsoever that it has been necessary to buy. Let not a farthing be outstanding on any account, when we begin with your allowance. Be particular in the minutest detail.' The yearly allowance of £250, to cover all expenses, Dickens considered a handsome one, especially since he would furnish Harry's wines. Already there had been ordered and sent to Cambridge 'three dozen sherry, two dozen port, six bottles of brandy, and three dozen light claret'. The father-son relationship was to be built on open confidence: 'If ever you find yourself on the verge of any perplexity or difficulty, come to me. You will never find me hard with you while you are manly and truthful.' As Dickens had done when Plorn left, he urged upon Harry a study of the New Testament 'as the one unfailing guide in life'.[13]

Within a few weeks of his matriculation at Michaelmas, Harry began to justify the hopes of his father and aunt by winning a £50 scholarship. 'I have a great success in the boy-line to announce to you,' Dickens hastened to tell Forster, even daring to predict that Harry might eventually win a fellowship.[14] But there was not to be any spoiling the young man with too much money. As soon as his scholarship began, his allowance was reduced by £50.[15] That winter, while Dickens was frequently absent from home, it was Georgina who received and communicated matters relating to Harry's finances.[16]

In October of 1868 began again the long familiar waiting for letters that alternately alarmed and soothed. Dickens was once more on tour, giving the series of farewell readings that he had recklessly contracted for with Chappells even before sailing for America.[17] Charged with the major responsibility for the weekly appearance of

All the Year Round, and not yet fully recovered from his American exertions, he had to admit to Georgina at the outset of the tour, '*I cannot get right internally, and have begun to be as sleepless as sick*'.[18]

Once he called an old family disappointment to her attention as he regretted that Mamie would not be attending his next London reading: 'I am sorry that Mary will not meet Lynch at St. James's Hall on Tuesday night. But I shall be glad to see him there. . . .'[19] It was William Wiltshire Lynch, a brigade major at Chatham, whom Mamie would not be seeing at the reading.[20] A personable officer seven years her senior, he was considered a most eligible suitor by the family. But for some reason—her brother Harry wondered in later years whether it was her strong attachment to her father— Mamie seemed disinclined to marriage after the thwarted love of her early twenties. Already she had shown a disconcerting coolness to Percy Fitzgerald; now she was to repeat the pattern with Lynch.

All that autumn Georgina, no less than Dickens, had been unwell, suffering from a form of influenza;[21] but with December she nevertheless turned her attention to seasonal matters. Dickens was reading in Scotland; and, though she expected him home for Christmas, she wished to cheer him with some little holiday remembrance appropriate to his sojourn in her native city. Accordingly she had a haggis and some shortbread delivered to him in Edinburgh.[22] His own thoughts, she soon discovered, had followed the same path. Just as she calculated that he would be receiving her token, she opened his letter reading, 'I have ordered for Gad's Hill, a Scotch bun weighing 14 pounds, 6 sheets of shortbread, and some sweeties'.[23]

Meanwhile she and Mamie were making preparations for the usual houseful of Christmas company. They expected Dickens home by the 22nd, when he would be reading in London at St. James's Hall. Mamie, the floral artist, was to meet him at the office at noon that day with all her equipment in a little basket, and he would take her to the hall to decorate his reading-table with holly according to his own specifications: 'If the two front legs were entwined with it, for instance, and a border of it ran round the top of the fringe in front, with a little sprig by way of bouquet at each corner, it would present a seasonable appearance'.[24]

Remembering how lonesome had been the 1867 observance of Christmas, Georgina was determined that this year's elaborate preparations should omit nothing. Soon the house filled with guests. Only Henry Chorley was absent from his usual place at the dinner-table, having at the last moment sent word that illness would keep him in bed.[25] The day after Christmas, when activity was still by

no means relaxed, Dickens announced to Dolby: ' . . . Miss Hogarth
so clearly wants a change, that I think I will take her to Ireland
along with the caravan, as she is a good sailor. . . .'[26]

Shortly before the party embarked for Ireland, Georgina joined
the audience of approximately a hundred specially invited guests
gathered at St. James's Hall to help Dickens decide whether to add
to his repertoire a sensational new reading—a selection from *Oliver
Twist*, reaching a climax with the murder of Nancy and the death of
Sikes. Ever since the previous autumn she had been uneasily aware
that Charles was preparing this programme. Had he not rehearsed
it with hideous snarls and screams in the meadow beyond the back
garden at Gad's Hill? Once Charley, having come there on a brief
business visit, had heard what he took to be violent quarrelling—
perhaps a passing tramp beating his wife unmercifully. Feeling that
he must interfere, he had stepped to the back door and looked out.
There, at the other end of the meadow, was his father, 'striding up
and down, gesticulating wildly, and in the character of Mr. Sikes,
murdering Nancy, with every circumstance of the most aggravated
brutality'. Asked to give his opinion of the reading, Charley had
replied, 'The finest thing I ever heard, but don't do it'.[27]

Indeed, so terrifying was the reading, so overpowering, that even
Dickens himself hesitated to introduce it to his public. Chappels,
too, thought the trial performance a wise precaution. At St. James's
Hall, however, the gruesome rendering was praised extravagantly—
that is after the pallid and trembling audience had been revived by
a champagne and oyster collation. Exhilarated by the results of his
experiment, Dickens refused to consider what price he might have
to pay for frequent repetitions of a reading which made inordinate
demands on his physical energy. But Edmund Yates and Charley
realized, as did Georgina, that such exhausting performances could
virtually set the stage for his own murder.[28]

In mid-January, Georgina, whose health still called forth solicitude,
thoroughly enjoyed the trip to Ireland as one of the reading party.
It was not long enough to tire her, for by 22nd January, her forty-
second birthday, she was home again to receive Dickens's greeting:
'This is to wish you many happy returns of tomorrow, and to send
you my deepest love and attachment'. Her friend Dolby, it seemed,
had grown 'quite "spooney" ' on hearing of the birthday. But her
condition still gave concern. In spite of Frank Beard's assurance
that she was recovered now, Dickens took an attitude of caution:
'I hope the fact stands as he states it. . . . Certainly, if you do not
get *quite rid* of that disagreeable discomfort, we will have another
opinion.'[29]

Whatever other benefits the change of scene had accomplished, certainly the Irish jaunt had not stilled her fears for Dickens. She had witnessed his painful nervous reaction to the perils of railway travel when, between Belfast and Kingston, the giant driving wheel of their engine had flown to pieces, sending a huge fragment crashing down on to the roof of their carriage.[30] And he was taxing his physical reserve by reading the murder scene regularly now, exulting in its electrifying power over his audiences. The birthday letter had boasted 'a tremendous house at Clifton last night, and decidedly the best murder yet done'.

At the beginning of February Georgina prepared for Dickens's birthday, just two weeks after her own. It was to be a weekend visit, his first to Gad's Hill since Christmas. 'I shall be able, please God, to get down to Gad's by the 2.10 (or whatever it is) train on Saturday,' his letter assured her on Thursday. There must be a basket carriage and a luggage cart to meet him and his valet at Higham Station.[31] The Forsters and Wilkie Collins also arrived to join the celebration and drink the health of James and Annie Fields. The eagerly awaited May and June visit of these American friends was already a favourite topic at Gad's Hill, with Georgina and Mamie making hospitable plans for picnics, walks in Cobham Park, and a carriage expedition to Canterbury—the last to be accompanied by red-jacketed postillions in the manner of the old coaching days along the Dover Road.[32]

The brief weekend respite over, late February brought news that Dickens's left foot was aching again. When Dr. Syme of Edinburgh was consulted, he pooh-poohed the idea of gout and confirmed the patient's own judgment that too much walking in the snow had caused a return of the old distress.[33] In April Georgina winced to hear how Charles, groping his way over a dimly lighted stage in Liverpool one morning, had tripped over a heavy galvanized wire brace. He had cut his shin 'rather smartly'—it was his unlucky left leg, of course—and had been required to 'bind it up surgically'. The injury was 'a little unfortunate', he pointed out, 'for it is a bad place to heal'.[34]

But any concern Georgina felt over this mishap faded in the light of vastly more alarming symptoms recounted two weeks later in a letter from Blackpool: 'My weakness and deadness are all *on the left side*, and if I don't look at anything I try to touch with my left hand, I don't know where it is. I am in (secret) consultation with Frank Beard; he recognizes, in the exact description I have given him, indisputable evidences of overwork, which he would wish to treat immediately.'[35] Actually, Dr. Beard had seen in Dickens's condition

far more than mere strain from over-exertion. Going at once to
Preston, where his patient was about to give the seventy-fourth
reading out of the hundred contracted for, he ordered the performances stopped. Gad's Hill had the first disturbing word of this
development in a letter dated 22nd April, beginning ironically,
'Don't be in the least alarmed'.[36]

The arrangements with Chappells were cancelled at once and
Dickens returned to London, where he continued the supervision of
All the Year Round, assisted by Charley, who, in the continued
absence of Wills, was now the acting sub-editor. On 1st May, a few
days before Georgina came in from the country to meet the Fieldses on
their arrival in London, Dickens sent her one of his typically exact
commissions: '. . . I enclose you a key. The key of the top left-hand
drawer in my large writing-table I think, if you will open that
drawer FULL OUT you will see lying at the back of it, a banker's pass
book labelled "Charles Dickens Esqre" fastened with an elastic band
and clasps—and having a line on the label in my writing to the effect
"Important Memorandum within". I want that book when you
come. . . .'[37]

That Georgina was permitted access to and knowledge of Dickens's
private papers suggests that she was enough in his confidence to
know whether he intended any provision for her in the event of his
death. Indeed, leaving her in the dark on this matter, with nothing
to contemplate but pauperism when the long term of her devoted
service should end, would have been little short of cruelty. She must
have had some indication of his concern for her future. And if the
'Important Memorandum' she delivered to the office had anything
to do with this matter, she may well have suspected it. At any rate,
Dickens, impelled by his breakdown, drew up his last will on 12th
May.

The spring of 1869 was a dark tissue of dismal events, shot through
with only a few golden threads, such as the Fieldses' visit. There was
bad news from two of the boys: Sydney persisted in his reckless
spending and Plorn could not adjust to life in Australia. And two
deaths—Macready's daughter and Sir Joseph Olliffe—left a gap in
the circle of intimates. So, for that matter, did the end of 'poor
little Noggs', the pony. Georgina, on reporting his decline, had been
advised 'to have him humanely and promptly killed'. But practical
concerns perhaps cleared the atmosphere of morbidity. Nothing
must be allowed to interfere with the thrifty management of Gad's
Hill. The meadow, for instance, was not to be turned over to the
Higham cricket club as early as in past years. First a hay crop
should be harvested. The cricketers had not previously made such

use of the ground, Dickens reminded Georgina, as would reconcile
him 'to losing another hay-crop'.[38]

If only all economic affairs could have been handled as satisfac-
torily! But so far all attempts to curb Sydney's extravagance and
clear up his mounting debts had failed. His latest plea for help was
painfully familiar. 'I must apply to you I am sorry to say and if
you won't assist me—I'm ruined', began his desperate letter to his
father. To pay his bills preparatory to leaving Vancouver Island,
Sydney had drawn heavily on his agents. If their demands were not
met now, his professional future would be damaged irreparably.
'You can't understand how ashamed I am to appeal to you again,'
he admitted. Still, his father must know how Americans spent
dollars like shillings and how they drank. '. . . *That* has put me
into debt,' he confessed. But he was determined to change his ways.
'If any promises for future amends can be relied on you have mine
most cordially,' he wrote, 'but for God's sake assist me now, it is a
lesson I'm not likely to forget if you do and if you do not I *can*
never forget. The result of your refusal is terrible to *think* of.'[39]

But Sydney's good intentions went no further than empty
promises. No sooner had his father straightened out one set of
arrears than there were others. Time and again there arrived embarrassing reminders from the boy's agents: 'We beg to inform you that
a bill drawn by your son. . . .'[40] Finally Dickens set himself sternly
against the spendthrift. Georgina, her heart heavy, felt more poignantly than ever his disappointment in the boys. This last experience she saw as his hardest—to lose faith in the son who had so
fascinated him as a baby, the 'Ocean Spectre' who had looked so
fixedly out over the sea in childhood, the 'Little Admiral' who had
come home from training, all eyes and buttons. And now Sydney
had to be told that he would not be received at Gad's Hill on his
return to England. It was the last letter his father ever sent him.[41]

Even while Sydney's bills were pouring in, Dickens was writing
to Australia about Plorn's poor judgment in leaving the situation
provided for him. Admitting himself 'quite prepared' for the failure
of this youngest son to settle down 'without a lurch or two', he tried
to defend the boy as having 'more, *au fond*, than his brothers'.
Plorn deserved a 'reasonable trial', for he had 'the makings of a
character restlessly within him'.[42]

Despite such drags on his spirit Dickens was rallying from the
April breakdown with his usual resilience. Though Dr. Beard and
Sir Thomas Watson in consultation had seen him 'on the brink of
an attack of paralysis of his left side, and possibly of apoplexy',
Dickens himself soon insisted that freedom from railway travel had

returned him to normal and that he must, after an interval, give twelve additional readings to ensure Chappells against financial loss. At length it was decided that he be allowed this undertaking, but only after eight months of rest. The performances must be limited to London, as railway journeys were henceforth forbidden. Meanwhile Dickens took care not to tire himself by attending dinners and burdensome social affairs, having—as he excused himself to one hostess—'made Doctorial promises not to do so through the summer'.[43]

Gad's Hill hospitality did not cease, however; for the Philadelphia editor George W. Childs and his wife were entertained before they set sail for home in April.[44] And it was understood, of course, that the ban on social activity would not prevent receiving the Fieldses royally. By mid-May they were in England, accompanied by Mabel Lowell, the poet's daughter. As they were to be shown the London sights first, Georgina, Mamie, and Dickens took rooms at St. James's Hotel, Piccadilly, until 1st June. From there they shepherded their American visitors on rambles through ancient streets, to St. Paul's and historic spots. They also managed a Saturday excursion to Richmond and Windsor Castle. One night, while the ladies entertained themselves more genteelly, Dickens took Fields and a few male companions on a slumming expedition with police protection. 'No dress coat,' he warned one of the guests, 'as it would be a phenomenon in the regions we shall visit after dinner.'[45]

Annie Fields and Georgina took to each other at once and began a lifelong friendship based on their joint adoration of Dickens. Besides, Georgina could not have resisted the comely dark-haired American's humorous sparkle and tender sentiment, a truly Dickensian union of traits which inspired De Wolfe Howe's comment that, except in such rare personalities as hers, 'mirth and mercy do not always, like righteousness and peace, kiss each other'.[46] Georgina's nieces also enjoyed the visitor, as she did them. Mamie struck Mrs. Fields as 'very lady-like and pretty . . . mild quiet and attentive', but less distinctive than her sister, Katey Collins—'more like other people'. Visiting Katey in her London home, the American was entranced: 'She is like a piece of old china with a picture by Sir Joshua Reynolds painted upon it and with manners as piquant peculiar and taking as such a painting come to life ought to have. She wore at our first dinner with her a kind of paradise coloured dress, hanging straight as in one of Stothard's engravings, with an antique lace and muslin cape just drawn over her beautiful shoulders and coming down in straight lines in front leaving her throat and neck uncovered. She has red hair which she wears very high on the top of her head worn with pearls in a loose coil. Altogether the effect is like some rare strange thing, which does not quite wear away in spite of her piquancy; for she is clever enough to be a match for the best of us I am sure.'[47]

Also pictured in detail was the tasteful small house in which this Pre-Raphaelite stunner lived: 'A rug on the wooden floor of her little drawing-room, a couch under the window with a crimson shawl upon it, a quaint round table by one side of the fire behind which she often sits, an antique desk and a tiny piano, with a first-rate landscape by Mr. Collins (the father . . .) and a drawing of herself by a Mr. Prinsep make the chief features of the little place—except the vase of magnolias . . . on her book table and a number of geraniums in pots on a table . . . in a corner between couch and fire. Then in the dining-room which adjoins is the same wooden floor and another bright rug and a bright cloth over the round table and a broad window which is left open to let the trees wave across and to hear the voices of the birds. And more pictures by Collins and sketches everywhere by this distinguished friend or that interesting person. . . .' Such an artistic home, Mrs. Fields pointed out, showed how people of good taste managed in England. For Katey had little money, but preferred the 'deprivations poverty brings to receiving from her father or allowing her husband who is very ill to overwork himself'. She seemed much like her father, 'especially in her indomitable reserve of temper equal to any emergency'.[48]

Throughout this period of social activity in London, Georgina looked forward to showing Annie over her beloved Gad's Hill domain. On 2nd June, the date by which the nightingales were due to reappear, she and Mamie were back home to welcome the Fieldses, Mabel Lowell, and Sol Etynge (illustrator for the American edition of Dickens's works published by Ticknor & Fields). The basket carriage having been sent to bring the guests from Higham Station, the two hostesses hovered in the doorway. Dickens meanwhile walked across the road to the wilderness plot to meet the party. There they alighted and were conducted past the chalet and through the tunnel to the front lawn, where Georgina and Mamie, with Katey and Charles Collins, received them. 'We did not go inside the house for an hour,' Mrs. Fields recalled, 'but walked about lost in admiration over the loveliness of the lawns & ivy and flowers.' After their tea out of doors they played 'Meet Aunt Sally' until dinner time. Writing to her mother, Mrs. Fields rhapsodized on 'the perfection to which the art of dining is carried' at Gad's Hill, 'the old glass and china, the wax candles and quaint devices of spoons and forks. . . . The swiftness of the talk, too, is of a new kind, and the shafts of dinner table wit are very keen.' With its caned chairs and its many pictures, the dining-room had an air of 'thought and refinement'.[49]

Annie was no less taken with the upstairs appointments: 'In each room there are delightful books, and everything the mind of man can conceive to make one comfortable topped off by a little bouquet on each bureau.' Yet she and James did not sleep well. Assigned to Dickens's bedroom, they feared that 'his spirit of wakefulness' had been left behind. For to him, they knew, 'sleepless nights come too often, oftener than they would to a free heart'. Still, it was 'wonderful, the flow of spirits C. D. has for a sad man'.[50]

Mrs. Fields had, of course, been curious about Georgina ever since Dickens had hymned her perfections in America. One morning, the men having gone to London, the guest studied her hostess closely while listening to accounts of life at Gad's Hill and anecdotes of the family. 'I have the deepest respect for her,' was Annie's diary comment on Georgina that night. 'She has been able to do everything for C. D. in his home.' And a letter to her mother spoke of Georgina as 'a strong, simple, noble, devoted creature, equal to her position which is saying everything'.[51]

For the rest of her life Georgina was to hold in her heart this visit from the Fieldses. From this final summer of gaiety at Gad's Hill she stored up memories of Dickens in his most exhilarated mood as he entertained his guests. What would her brother have said to the scarlet-coated outriders who escorted their carriage to Canterbury, he who had laughed at Charles's dress coat with its lining of red silk and had censured his ostentatious adjustment to a higher social caste![52] All along the Dover Road people had run out to stare. And then there was the visit to the marshes of Cooling, immortalized in *Great Expectations,* and the outdoor lunch in, of all places, the cemetery where the fictional Pip's little brothers were buried! Here on a large flat gravestone Dickens spread the picnic fare. Then, struck by the incongruity of feasting in these surroundings, he went on to make the situation still more ludicrous. Ducking briefly behind the stone wall, he disguised himself with towel and napkin as a head waiter, and reappeared to range the plates along the top of the wall. From behind this improvised buffet he summoned his guests to approach and be served.[53]

When the Fieldses left Gad's Hill Georgina and Annie began a correspondence that continued at intervals until 1913. 'I am sure we can never feel as strangers any more to each other!' Georgina wrote the first time, a few days after the June visit had ended. Harry had just come home from Cambridge with a mathematical scholarship. 'I have not seen Charles so happy about anything for a long while,' she reported. 'It is a famous beginning, . . . and I hope augurs well for his future college career. It will be quite a new sensation for Charles to have one of his sons distinguish himself.' She also included a confidential bit about Mamie: 'You should indeed hear a cheerful word from me in the event of any progress being made by our nice military friend [an allusion to Major Lynch, the officer at nearby Chatham], but I am afraid to allow myself to be hopeful about it.' She would not let Mamie know that Mrs. Fields had inquired about Lynch; for, she explained, 'I think harm is done if the interested party gets an idea that her friends are *talking her over*, don't you?'[54]

As her friendship with Annie deepened through the years, Georgina's closely written pages became increasingly intimate and revealing. And Mrs. Fields often meditated on her friend, on Dickens's daughters, and on life at Gad's Hill. But dimming the joy of her first memories was the persistent conviction of an ominous shadow over that household. On the second anniversary of her 1869 visit, reflecting on a recent entertainment in her own home, she confided to her diary that there had been 'more jollity than ever I saw except at Dickens's, and alas! I must say it, with more real lightness of heart than I ever saw at Gad's Hill. The shadow of somewhere already fallen there and there were no *young* people—young in the sense of being innocent of all experience as these are here.'[55]

Annie Fields was as religious in preserving her letters from Georgina as, unfortunately, Dickens was ruthless in destroying all but business documents. In 1860, just as Tavistock was being permanently abandoned, he had sought to wipe out the past by 'burning the accumulated letters and papers of twenty years'. Family correspondence and communications from such notables as Washington Irving, Carlyle, Thackeray, Tennyson—all had been cast into the flames. Katey, Harry, and little Plorn had carried out basket after basket of the precious fuel to the meadow bonfire. Later the boys had 'roasted onions on the ashes of the great!'[56] The letter burning became a periodic ceremony. In March of 1865 Dickens wrote Macready of having made another such 'great fire in my field at Gad's Hill. . . .'[57] And he did so again a year before his death, according to Georgina, who 'helped him in the work of destruction. He had a great horror of the improper uses often made of letters of celebrated people—and there had been some flagrant instance of this just before he made up his mind to do this.'[58]

Following the Fieldses' departure, the activities at Gad's Hill were adjusted to a programme of writing and editing. Dickens was working on a new novel, *The Mystery of Edwin Drood*, for which Charles Collins, though ailing, hoped to do the illustrations. With autumn the pace of living had so accelerated that Georgina was catering to Dickens's overstrained nerves again: 'I intend to drop both tea and coffee in the morning. Please get some of that Homoepathic Cocoa,' she was instructed, 'and let me have a jug or pot of it containing 2 large cups—alys boiled with milk, and no water—on the table at breakfast alys'. She had also to keep an eye on further improvements to the house: 'Ask him [Aldridge], whatever he does to the Billiard room ceiling, to do something DURABLE,' she was directed.[59] The major remodelling, though, was the conversion of the greenhouse into a large conservatory, 'a great ornament and addition to the house', Georgina wrote to Annie Fields in November, 'which is now getting on pretty fast—and will, we hope, be finished before Christmas'. As she and Mamie would be with Charles in London that winter, for the farewell readings, it would not be stocked until their return in the spring.[60]

In the same letter Georgina revealed her pride in Katey, who had been working so industriously at her painting that her teacher, the noted Pre-Raphaelite Millais, had praised her efforts, giving her 'the strongest encouragement to persevere—which delighted her very much—and pleased her Father too'. But Georgina must have been somewhat embarrassed at having to perform a courtesy which her nieces, she feared, had neglected: 'I heard . . . that they were charmed with the pretty presents you had sent them before you left. I don't know whether they have, yet, written to thank you for them—I know they mean to do so immediately.'[61] It was not the last time Aunt Georgy had to apologize for such negligence.

At the beginning of the busy Christmas week she joined Dickens in seeing Fechter off for America.[62] To Annie she wrote merely of the actor's being on his way to New York, 'with good prospects, I hope'.[63] She refrained from adding that Charles's recent efforts in Fechter's behalf had cost too much valuable time and energy. It was only through Dickens that this irritating friend had finally concluded the attractive offer to play in America. Even then it had been necessary to coax him to drop his petulance over the engagements as arranged by his American sponsors. In a hysterical macaronic letter he had fumed, 'C'est plus que "unfair". C'est "ridicule!" et je refuse "emphatically".'[64] Writing to Georgina in November, Dickens had outlined his strategy: 'Tomorrow I give Palmer [the American agent] a little dinner (with only Dolby) in Regent Street. *He will engage Fechter at £90 a night*, if Fechter be not stark staring mad. I have telegraphed to him and written to him, and will settle the engagement at dinner tomorrow, in the improbable event of his turning out sane.'[65] So there had finally

been a meeting of minds, and now Fechter, accompanied by Carlotta
Leclercq, his leading actress, was on his way across the Atlantic.
In the future his affairs would furnish considerable gossip for
Georgina and Annie.

It was the traditional Christmas at Gad's Hill in 1869, and
bitterly cold. The usual houseful of guests had assembled: Charley
and his family, Katey and her husband, Henry Chorley as always,
and a few other friends. But it was not the usual holiday for Georgina. Dickens was not well and, for the first Christmas that she
could remember, did not leave the house. All day she sat with him
in the library, poulticing his left foot. With it bandaged and hoisted
on a chair, he managed to appear at dinner. In spite of discomfort
he kept up the customary cheer of the day.[66] Noting the ravages of
pain and overwork, Georgina may have asked herself how soon his
familiar Christmas blessing would become only an echo in her heart.
After the meal he joined the party in the favourite memory game.
When his turn came to add to the growing list of names, he pronounced 'Warren's Blacking, 30 Strand' in an odd tone of voice.
Harry noticed the queer gleam in his father's eye, but it was not
until two years later that the family, reading the first volume of
Forster's *Life of Charles Dickens*, learned of the bitter childhood
experience in the blacking warehouse.[67]

A few days after the year-end festivities Georgina regretfully
packed up to leave Gad's Hill, Dickens having leased a London house
opposite the Marble Arch in order to please Mamie—though, he
admitted ruefully, '. . . she will probably go somewhere else, the
moment we take possession!'[68] Except for being near him during
the arduous period of the farewell readings in town, Georgina would
have much preferred a quiet winter in the country. Already she was
looking ahead to the return in June, when the handsome new conservatory, finished now except for paint and floor tile, would be
abloom.[69]

January was to be the most tiring month of the readings, she
wrote Annie, as four evening and two morning performances were
scheduled; then in February and March, six evenings altogether—
'the LAST of ALL, thank goodness! on the 15th March!' She heartily
wished they were all over, and deplored Charles's having to wear
himself out by going to the Birmingham and Midland Institute to
present the certificates and prizes, just before his first readings.[70]

Katey's husband, Georgina lamented, was now in such failing
health that he had been forced to give up the illustrations for *Edwin
Drood*—just when his samples promised so well, too. But he had
completed the cover, which was considered so good that it would be

K

used.[71] This piece of news may have caused Annie to reflect on what she must have suspected on her visit to Gad's Hill—Dickens's despair over his vital, talented Katey, in yoke with a semi-invalid whose ailment precluded any return to health, yet allowed him to linger in misery. Later Annie was to receive more light on the situation by gossiping with Fechter in America. Dickens, the actor explained, 'could not understand the prolonged endurance of such an existence and in his passionate nature which must snap when it yielded at all, it produced disgust'. He would look across the dining-table at his son-in-law as if to say, 'Astonishing you should be here today, but tomorrow you will be in your chamber never to come out again'. This attitude toward his brother aroused Wilkie Collins to such resentment that, according to Fechter, he and Dickens became estranged.[72]

In February, replying to Annie's best wishes for Dickens's fifty-eighth birthday, Georgina wrote on black-bordered stationery. 'I hope you will not be startled by my mourning paper,' she began, 'but I think you must have seen that my poor old Father died on the 12th of this month—therefore you will be prepared for it.'[73] George Hogarth, aged eighty-six but still active in journalism, had fallen downstairs at the *Illustrated London News* office. Several weeks later he died at the Gloucester Crescent home of his daughter Helen, now Mrs. Roney, not far from Catherine's residence.[74] In his last years he had continued to impress his associates as pleasant, genteel, and unassuming. William Michael Rossetti, who had often encountered him through journalistic connections, called him 'an affable, simple-mannered elderly gentleman, free from anything stiff or self-assertive'.[75] The death notice which appeared in the 'Obituary of Eminent Persons' column of the *Illustrated London News* for 19 February 1870 confirmed Rossetti's appraisal. Written by one 'who has succeeded him in his office on this Journal, and who was for many years his colleague elsewhere', it eulogized its subject for his 'guileless simplicity of character and never-failing geniality of temper'. As Hogarth had apparently never acted upon, or even shared, the acrimony of his wife and his daughter Helen toward Dickens, Georgina could remember him with tenderness, observing the mourning amenities without hypocrisy. Ironically, though, he could not leave the world clad in the dignity of his own repute only: the newspaper notices, as she pointed out, inevitably mentioned his connection with Charles Dickens.[76]

The winter in London, Georgina's letter to Annie continued, had been 'long, dark and *bitter*', and a curious epidemic of measles had broken out among adults. Poor Mamie had been a victim, but, with only a light case, had suffered chiefly because 'so many of her friends were afraid of her and she was shut out from everything for a little while. . . .' Now that she was well again, she and Katey were going to a fancy ball: 'Mamie is going as Marguerite (Faust)—she has got a lovely dress—and I think it will suit her very well'.[77] (Had the Marguerite costume perhaps recalled to Georgina the anguished confession she still kept among her letters from Dickens?)

Seasonal ailments had attacked poor little Mrs. Bouncer, too, for she coughed terribly with bronchitis. 'I fear she is getting old,' Georgina explained, 'and finds the winter very hard to get through!' At Gad's Hill, though, the dogs were hardy, and had almost killed Georgina with their friendly demonstrations when she went down into the country for a few hours to inspect the improvements on the house. The conservatory, finished at last, was a delight: 'The Florist has orders to fill it—and is to begin soon—and it is to be full of beauty the 1st of June, when we go home. . . .'[78]

Again there was encouraging news about Harry. 'He made his first speech "on National Education" at the "Union"—which is the Debating Club at Cambridge . . .' Georgina announced. 'A day or two afterward a report in the Pall Mall said that at the Union on such a night THE speech of the evening was made by Mr. H. Dickens.' But happiest—and saddest—of all her news, Charles's strenuous reading career was almost at an end. 'Fancy there being only three more Readings now!' She was 'thankful that *the last* of this work is approaching'; still—'there is always something sad about "the last" of anything—and I think he will feel it melancholy to take leave of the public in *that* relation with them. But he will feel the relief after the work is over. Although, on the other hand, he also declares that he will feel the absence of he *money* made by the Readings. . . !'[79]

On the very day that Georgina was writing her February letter to Annie Fields, that voluminous diarist was reflecting on her English friends, recording a conversation which had taken place in her home between Fechter and Longfellow. 'Yes, yes,' Fechter had said of Dickens, 'all his fame goes for nothing since he has not the one thing. He is very unhappy in his children.' What Annie thought on that subject was also confided to her journal: 'Nobody can say how much too much of this the children have to hear. . . . Poor Miss Hogarth spends her life hoping to comfort and care for him. I never felt more keenly her anomalous and unnatural position in the household. Not one mentioned her name. They could not dare, I suppose (lest they might do her wrong).'[80]

Being in mourning for her father, Georgina had not gone out in February, not even to the readings, but the final three she could not miss.[81] On 1st March she heard *Copperfield* for the last time; on the 8th, *Oliver Twist* (the murder scene); then, on the 15th, the final programme, *A Christmas Carol* and 'The Trial' from *Pickwick*. Long before the doors of St. James's Hall were opened, the street outside was jammed. To a capacity throng of two thousand it was a stirring performance, this farewell of an artist to his public. For many, the most memorable moment came at the close, when Dickens returned after a tumult of applause to address his audience briefly and personally. For fifteen years, he told them, he had been cheered by their response and stimulated by their support. But now he thought it best to confine himself to the literary art which had first brought him before the public. Alluding to *Edwin Drood*, he promised to enter their homes again in but two short weeks. He concluded dramatically: '. . . From these garish lights I vanish now for evermore, with a heartfelt, grateful, respectful, and affectionate farewell'.[82]

Georgina, who had watched him fighting to keep his composure during this moving address, noted that even Major Lynch, generally a 'reserved and undemonstrative man', was 'visibly affected'. What a pity that Mamie could not share her father's warmth for such a perceptive young officer![83] Another spectator who reacted to the entire performance with wide-eyed fascination was Charley's eldest child, little Mary Angela, who for the first time saw her grandfather on the stage and was puzzled and frightened by all his strange voices.[84]

Georgina was greatly relieved, as were all the family and intimate friends, to see the readings end. Under tension Dickens had developed a pulse rate so alarming that Dr. Beard had thought it best to attend every performance, asking Charley to be present also, ready to dash up the platform steps at the first sign of need: '. . . If you see your father falter in the least, you must run and catch him and bring him off to me, or, by Heaven, he'll die before them all'.[85] But mingled with the general relief at the safe conclusion of the series was a touch of sadness. '. . . There is always a little melancholy in the thought of a thing *over for ever,*' Georgina admitted to Annie Fields in May, after the readings had already been 'wafted into one of the many Dreams of the past'.[86]

The first week in May found Georgina longing for the country home. The gardener and the workmen, she wrote Annie, were still engaged in getting everything 'all "polished up" and ready for our return on the 1st June'. Mamie, however, did not share her

feeling, being 'very gay—out every night—and not at all tired of it!
She will not be so glad when we give up this home—and will stay
on with Katey a good deal until the end of the season.' It was a
particularly glorious spring for Mamie. She had been invited to
attend the Queen's drawing-room and a Court ball after her father
had made his first appearance at Buckingham Palace, having been
summoned to receive Her Majesty's thanks for some American
photographs he had sent her at her request. He had found Victoria
'strangely shy—and like a girl in manner . . . ,' reported Georgina,
'but with a girlish sort of timidity which was very engaging'. He
had got along well with her, though, and at parting had been presented with a copy of her published journal, *Our Life in the High-
lands*, the Queen saying modestly that 'she was really ashamed to
offer such a book to such a writer'. As it bore the royal autograph,
Georgina speculated that it should be something of 'a curiosity years
hence!' But she was convinced that any honour conferred was upon
the Queen—'which republican sentiment', she felt, Mrs. Fields would
no doubt share.[87] She herself was not invited to Court when Mamie
went—or ever. Having once been the subject of scandalous public
rumours, she could hardly have expected to be received at that
decorous Palace.

Even more agreeable to Charles than the attention of Queen Victoria, she told Annie, was a tribute from an unknown admirer: a self-
taught, once humble man whose gratitude touched Dickens as had
little else in his public career. Shortly after the move to London for
the reading season, there arrived a letter from this stranger. He
had begun his rise to wealth, he said, in some minor job with a well-
to-do Liverpool timber merchant and, being highly industrious and
conscientious, had ultimately become a partner in the firm. Recently
he had acquired the whole fortune at the timber merchant's death.
His phenomenal success he attributed to the 'encouragement and
cheering influence' of Dickens's books, which he had read regularly
since childhood. Now his thoughts turned to his 'Benefactor and
Teacher', whom he begged to accept £500 as a token of 'gratitude
and veneration'. Struck by the genuine tone of this letter, Dickens
replied cordially that he was in no need of money, but would gratefully accept for himself and his children some table ornament bearing a commemorative inscription. In April there arrived two silver
pieces, a flower basket and an elaborate epergne. The basket was
inscribed: 'To Charles Dickens from one who has been cheered and
stimulated by his writing and held the author amongst his first
Remembrances when he became prosperous'. According to the
representative from Hunt & Roskell, where the gift had been

purchased, the base of the epergne had originally been ornamented with figures representing the four seasons. But the donor, 'averse to associating the idea of *winter* in any way with Mr. Dickens', had ordered the design altered to 'leave only the three *cheerful* seasons'. Throughout the negotiations the name of the Liverpool admirer was revealed to no one but Dickens. Even Hunt & Roskell did not learn his identity, payment being made in cash instead of by cheque. 'Is it not an odd and pretty story!' exclaimed Georgina.[88]

But Court recognition and the affection of strangers, as both Georgina and Annie knew, went 'for nothing since he has not the one thing'. In May reports from Australia caused Dickens to fear that Plorn had 'been born without a groove'. To Rusden, the boy's sponsor, he wrote, 'It cannot be helped. If he cannot, or will not find one, I must try again, and die trying.'[89] To Alfred he wrote on the same day: 'I am doubtful whether Plorn is taking to Australia. Can you find out his real mind? I notice that he always writes as if his present life were the be-all and the end-all of his emigration, and as if I had no idea of you two becoming proprietors, and aspiring to the first positions in the colony. . . .'[90]

But the picture was not entirely cheerless, Dickens having had good reports on Alfred: ' . . . They did not surprise me, for I had unbounded faith in you. For which take my love and blessing. . . . This is . . . an assurance that I never think of you without hope and comfort.'[91] Harry, too, was a comfort, as always. On 4th May his Aunt Georgy announced to Annie Fields that he had, on the day of the final readings, brought home the happy news of winning 'the prize for the Essay, *at his college*—much to his Father's gratification'.[92]

The proud new conservatory was another bright note, though by the middle of May Georgina heard murmurs of its costing more than had been anticipated. Returning from one of her spring trips to Gad's Hill, she brought word that the gardener would need more geraniums and lavender plants. Thereupon Dickens wrote an authorization for their purchase, adding: 'Be careful not to get more than are absolutely necessary, as the garden expenses are becoming excessively heavy'.[93]

A flare-up of the old foot trouble that spring brought renewed awareness of omnipresent tensions. The affliction would 'yield to nothing but days of fomentations and horizontal rest', Dickens told a correspondent on 11th May.[94] Georgina worried about some 'little risings' on the ailing foot, but was assured that they were merely blisters from the constant application of hot poultices. (A testimony, perhaps, to her own over-zealous nursing.) Writing her from his office quarters, Dickens reported himself refreshed by a good night's sleep, but only because he had taken laudanum. It was this letter which Georgina was later to label in his own familiar bright blue ink, 'THE LAST May 1870'.

With the end of the month came the return to the loved country home. Never had it looked more inviting. In the front garden blazed two large beds of scarlet geraniums, Dickens's favourites. More brightened the well-stocked conservatory. When Katey came down to see this latest addition on the first Sunday in June, her father promised, 'POSITIVELY the last improvement'. She recognized his little joke; for years every alteration at Gad's Hill had been 'positively the last'.[95]

Though Georgina had confidently relied on the country to restore Dickens's vigour, she was disturbed when her niece called his 'curious grey colour' to her attention. Perhaps it was his noticeable decline that now drew Katey closer to the father whom she had always adored, even as she defied him. For on that Sunday night, after Georgina and Mamie had retired, 'Lucifer Box'—the one who had dared to come down late to breakfast in childhood, had married to declare her independence, had not hesitated to champion her mother—stayed downstairs for an intimate talk with him. She needed money: should she accept a recent offer to go on the stage? Her father advised her not to, promising to make it up to her. Then he spoke of his own affairs. He hoped for the success of *Edwin Drood*—'if, please God, I live to finish it'. Seeing Katey's startled look, he explained, 'I say *if*, because you know, my dear child, I have not been strong lately'. In a low voice he spoke of his past life, baring his soul to the child most like him, herself an Inimitable. When their talk ended at dawn, Katey understood her father, the man who had combated and exposed cruelty all his life, who had taught his children to pray that they might never be cruel even to 'a poor little fly', yet had harboured the tormenting recognition of his own inhumanity to an exasperating, defenceless wife, admitting 'every day more and more, how much I stand in the need of charity and mercy'.[96]

When Katey came down to breakfast in the morning, her father was already at work in the chalet. Knowing how much he disliked partings, she was about to leave for London without bidding him farewell. But as she waited on the porch for her carriage, she felt an irresistible urge to see him once more. She found him bent over his writing. Instead of turning his cheek for the usual light kiss, or dismissing her with casual pleasantries, he held out his arms and embraced her. Returning to the house, she kept repeating to herself,

'I am so glad I went—I am so glad'. Georgina saw her off, accompanied by Mamie, and promised to keep both girls informed of their father's health.[97]

Alone with Charles at Gad's Hill, Georgina asked about *Edwin Drood*. The novel was giving him some difficulty; he felt that he had revealed too much of the plot in the early part. Yielding to her curiosity, she inquired boldly, 'I hope you haven't really killed poor Edwin Drood?' He replied gravely, 'I call my book the Mystery, not the History, of Edwin Drood'. From this answer she could not determine whether he meant the story to remain a mystery for ever, or only until the proper time for revealing its secret.[98]

On Tuesday afternoon, 7th June, she rode with him to Cobham Park, staying with the carriage when he left it to walk home. After dinner that evening she remained in the dining-room with him to enjoy the Chinese lanterns which had been hung in the cool, fragrant conservatory only that day. He talked about his love for Gad's Hill: it was his wish to have his name associated with the place and to be buried near it.[99]

The next day Georgina sensed that he was feeling dull. Though he went to the chalet as usual, he complained that work was burdensome. At six, as she joined him for dinner, she noticed that his eyes were full of tears. Anxiously she watched him. Finally, alarmed by his colour and a change in his expression, she asked whether he felt ill. 'Yes, very ill for the last hour,' he replied. She suggested calling the doctor. 'No,' he insisted with blurred articulation. Then, complaining of a toothache, he clasped his jaw and asked to have the window shut. 'Come and lie down,' Georgina begged after she had closed it. Struggling to his feet, he answered, 'Yes—on the ground'. His last consciousness of this world was Georgina's voice and supporting arm as she tried to help him. After a step or two he fell heavily on his left side. Hastily ordering a sofa brought into the dining-room, she had the servants place him upon it. Then she sent at once for the local doctor and telegraphed Frank Beard. On their arrival both men saw that Dickens was beyond help.[100]

When Georgina left his side hours later to receive Mamie and Katey, come in response to her summons, her face told them that hope had been abandoned. All night she and the girls watched beside the stricken man, placing hot bricks at his cold feet. He never stirred. The next morning Charley arrived, followed by Dr. Russell Reynolds, who found unmistakable symptoms of brain haemorrhage.[101]

Throughout the day the hushed watch continued. From the conservatory came the spicy aroma of the bright geraniums Dickens

loved. Through the open windows floated the heavier scent of
syringa, which for Charley became so inseparably associated with
this hour that he could never again bear to be near these blossoms.[102]
In the early afternoon Mary Boyle arrived. She found the front
door open, but dared not enter or ring for fear of disturbing the
silence, broken only by the chorus of birds. Finally Charley, coming
out for a breath of air, discovered her and led her into the library.
Here Georgina clasped her in a comforting embrace. But the visitor,
feeling that this was not her place, soon left for ever the home where
she had spent so many happy hours.[103]

Ellen Ternan came also. Who had summoned her to Gad's Hill?
Katey had hurried in to London that day to break the news to her
mother,[104] but even in the light of her recent glimpse into her
father's soul, she would hardly have softened to that extent. It is
more likely that Georgina took upon herself the responsibility of
letting Nelly know.

About six that evening Dickens began to breathe heavily. A
little past the hour there was a shudder, a deep sigh—then silence.
Thursday, 9th June—it was five years to the day since the Staplehurst accident. Because air and light and vivid colour had always
been a passion with him, the blinds were not drawn according to
Victorian custom. His body was left in the dining-room with the
June sun flooding over the flowers that had been carried in from the
conservatory—blue lobelias, musk, his favourite scarlet geraniums.[105] 'There was something beautiful and appropriate *to him* in
his lying dead in that bright room,' Georgina wrote Mrs. Fields, 'surrounded by the Pictures and looking into the Conservatory which
had delighted him so much in the last two weeks of his life.'[106]

'Almost stupefied with grief,' Harry arrived from Cambridge two
hours after his father's death. A porter at the railway station had
broken the news. The next morning came two artists: Millais to
make a sketch and Thomas Woolner to take a cast of Dickens's face.
Some months earlier the sculptor, hoping to do a bust of the novelist,
had been put off until *Edwin Drood* should be finished: 'It will be
done by Christmas, and after that I am your humble servant'. Now
the bust would have to be modelled from a death mask. Millais's
pencil drawing was later given to Katey, who declared that no one
else 'could have so perfectly understood the beauty and pathos' of
her father's face.[107]

Catherine Dickens was not among those who looked for the last
time upon the silent figure in the dining-room. Even in this hour
she respected her husband's insistence on an irrevocable separation.

Dickens had often expressed a wish to be buried near Gad's Hill, either in the village of Shorne, or in St. Nicholas Churchyard, Rochester, at the foot of the old Castle Keep. Arrangements were made, therefore, at Shorne. Meanwhile the Dean and Chapter of Rochester Cathedral urged burial there in St. Mary's Chapel, the St. Nicholas graveyard across the way having been closed several years earlier by order of the Privy Council. Accordingly the Shorne arrangements were abandoned and a grave was dug in the Cathedral.[108] But even as these preparations were in progress at Rochester, other plans were forming in London. Learning of Dickens's death, Dean Stanley immediately wrote to Locker-Lampson, his brother-in-law, through whom he had recently made the acquaintance of the novelist. He was prepared, he stated, to receive a communication from the Dickens family respecting burial in Westminster Abbey. Unless such formal application was made, he could take no steps. Locker-Lampson promptly forwarded this note to Charley Dickens. Three days passed without reply. Then there appeared in the London *Times* for Monday, 13th June, a leading editorial urging burial in the Abbey as appropriate for a person of Dickens's distinction. At eleven o'clock that morning Forster and Charley called on Dean Stanley. At first so overcome with grief that he could hardly speak, Forster finally regained his composure to explain that he and Charley had come in response to the article in *The Times*. (The note sent on by Locker-Lampson had somehow gone astray.) The family would defer to public demand for burial in the Abbey, but only on condition that the instructions in Dickens's will for a simple, private funeral be strictly observed. The Dean agreed, enjoining the utmost secrecy to insure such privacy.

At six o'clock that evening, by only a dim light, the grave was dug in Poets' Corner. At midnight came a thundering knock at the Dean's door. A reporter from the *Daily Telegraph*, having heard that Dickens's body was being brought to London, wished to know the hour of the funeral. 'Dean Stanley has gone to bed,' replied the servant, 'and cannot possibly be disturbed.' The reporter left.[109]

The next morning, 14th June, the Gad's Hill household was astir in the pearly dawn. Long before the neighbours had breakfasted, a special train took the family from Higham to London, where they were met at Charing Cross Station by a hearse and three coaches. ('At the utmost, not more than three plain mourning coaches,' the will had specified.) There was none of the undertakers' paraphernalia which Dickens had always hated: the sable plumes, the tasselled black velvet palls, the hired mutes. And the mourners wore only the simple black garb, the will having explicitly forbidden any-one to appear in 'scarf, cloak, black bow, long hat band, or other such revolting absurdity'. In the first coach rode Mamie, Katey, Charley, and Harry, of eight living children the only ones at hand to attend the funeral. In the second coach were Georgina, Letitia Austin, and Charley's wife; in the last, Dr. Frank Beard, Charles and Wilkie Collins, and Edmund Dickens, a nephew. At nine-thirty, with St. Stephen's clock chiming the half hour, the procession approached the Abbey. To the tolling of the great bell the coaches turned into the Dean's Yard. From there the body was carried through the cloisters and into the nave, where the Dean, the two canons in residence, and the minor canons met the mourners. Their arrival had attracted no attention whatever. The doors were closed immediately and the coaches dismissed.

The little band that gathered about the open grave was strangely dwarfed by the vast grey stone building. There was no choir, only subdued music from the great organ. And there was no graveside eulogy. (Only a few months before, Dickens had excused himself from speaking at the unveiling of Leigh Hunt's bust at Kensal Green Cemetery: '. . . The idea of ever being the subject of such a ceremony myself is so repugnant to my soul, that I must decline to officiate.')[110] Attended by none but the Abbey clergy, Dean Stanley began the ancient lines of the burial service: 'I am the Resurrection and the Life. . . .' The words that echo like a refrain through the final chapters of *A Tale of Two Cities* fell on Georgina's heart with the numbing sense of 'a thing *over for ever*'.

As the small group filed out, Dean Stanley asked the last of the mourners whether the grave might be left open for the public. 'Yes,' replied Forster, 'now my work is over, and you may do what you like.' From the cool shadows of the vaulted Abbey Georgina passed into the brilliant sunshine outside. It was one of the first warm days of summer, and beds of red geraniums burned against the green of newly planted gardens in Parliament Square. How right that Charles's special flowers should grow so near his resting-place, she told herself. Returning to the country, her senses drugged by the beauties of June, she took 'some solemn comfort' in the thought that the 'scents and sounds and sights of nature' were a 'faint foreshadowing' of his 'Eternal Peace'. Gad's Hill had never looked lovelier—'so *Cruelly* and unkindly cheerful it seemed!' Yet it was fitting, she felt, that dear Charles 'should be taken away from the world when it was as nearly like heaven as we can ever suppose it to be!' But 'how empty the house felt . . .! We seemed for the first time to realize fully the blank that was made in life.'[111]

PART TWO
1870-1917

Chapter Ten

'A DREADFUL WRENCH'

THE following Sunday Georgina was compelled to renew the emotional strain of the burial by appearing once more at Westminster Abbey, this time for Dean Stanley's public funeral sermon at the evensong hour. Long before the announced time a throng had gathered outside, many from the working classes; and shortly after the doors were opened every available seat was taken. The organ strains of 'Blessed Are the Dead Who Die in the Lord' throbbed softly through the nave as the congregation sat in hushed solemnity, though not indisposed to steal glances at the literary notables present. Carlyle and Tennyson, in particular, drew attention. Then, as the service began, came the faint voice of Dean Stanley, hoarse from laryngitis and barely audible in that lofty space. It was a tense and painful hour: the Dean earnestly trying to project his carefully prepared message, the vast congregation straining to hear. Only the handful nearest the pulpit could have known that the text was from St. Luke, the parable of Lazarus and the rich man. Just as the Great Teacher had demonstrated the instructive power of narrative, so Dickens had dedicated his sacred gift to the betterment of mankind, said the Dean. And as Christ had used the story of Lazarus to impress 'the pungent, pathetic lessons of social life', so the novelist had portrayed the wrongs and sufferings of his own time. 'By him that veil was rent asunder which parts the various classes of society. Through his genius the rich man, faring sumptuously every day, was made to see and feel the presence of the Lazarus at his gate.'[1]

South of the gallery in which Georgina sat, was the flower-laden pavement in Poets' Corner, where the names of Dr. Johnson, Garrick, Sheridan, Handel, and Macaulay formed a guard of honour around the newly made grave. Before it had been closed on Thursday night a continual procession had filed by to drop flowers, verses, and tokens of every kind upon the panelled oak coffin with its simple bold inscription—CHARLES DICKENS. Now many had returned to pay their public homage.

An occasional sob broke from the congregation. Valiantly the

Dean struggled on: 'Many, many are the feet which have trodden and will tread the consecrated ground around that narrow grave; many, many are the hearts which both in the Old and in the New World are drawn towards it, as towards the resting-place of a dear personal friend. . . .' In conclusion Dean Stanley made public for the first time an extract from Dickens's will: 'I commit my soul to the mercy of God through our Lord and Saviour Jesus Christ, and I exhort my dear children humbly to try to guide themselves by the teaching of the New Testament in its broad spirit, and to put no faith in any man's narrow construction of its letter here and there'. It was the 'simple but sufficient faith' in which Dickens had lived and died.

The sermon concluded, the congregation dispersed to the 'Dead March' from *Saul*. But the Abbey emptied slowly. Though all three doors were open, nearly everyone passed through Poets' Corner.

Returning to the emptiness of Gad's Hill that evening, Georgina began to feel the full impact of her bereavement. At first the shock had been '*so* sudden, so awful' that she had been 'stunned and bewildered by it'. She had found it 'impossible to realize— . . . impossible to *think*—at all'. But even now, in the first agony of grief, she took comfort in the knowledge that Charles had died without physical or mental suffering. Again and again she was to give expression to that thought. 'He was in the full vigour of his working powers—in the full height of his reputation,' she wrote Mary Howitt that autumn. 'If he had survived that attack, the doctors assured us it could only have been to live a paralysed man. And who that loved him *could* be selfish enough to wish for such prolongation of life for that great active spirit?' She derived added comfort from 'the universal grief and real mourning for his memory—such grief and mourning as I think were hardly ever given to *one man* in any age or country . . . before. And he deserved it!! for a more Simple Generous Kind *Great* heart never beat, and I should think there has seldom been a case in which Death deprived *so many people* of their best, truest and wisest friend'[2] (*Active spirit, best and truest friend*: the very words Dickens had applied to Georgina herself.)

Because of this universal admiration for dear Charles, she went on, there had, of course, been no alternative but to yield to the national wish for burial in the Abbey, especially when that could be accomplished 'according to his solemn injunctions, with the most perfect privacy and simplicity. And it is *fine* that he should lie there.' Personally, though, she would have preferred Rochester. It would have been a 'sort of shrine for him—he loved the place so much—it was the home of his boyhood—and close to the dear home of his last years.' (As a matter of fact, she did not allow his connection with the ancient city to go unnoticed, for she and Forster, as his executors, ordered a commemorative tablet placed on the south transept wall in the Cathedral there.) And numerous scenes in Dickens's first and last books presented further testimony to his love for the place. Indeed, almost the last lines of *Edwin Drood* were a description of Rochester Cathedral: 'Changes of glorious light from moving boughs, songs of birds, scents from gardens, woods, and fields—or, rather, from the one great garden of the whole cultivated island in its yielding time—penetrate into the Cathedral, subdue its earthy odour, and preach the Resurrection and the Life. The cold stone tombs of centuries ago grow warm; and flecks of brightness dart into the sternest marble corners of the building, fluttering there like wings.' Recalling that Dickens had been at work on this last chapter within an hour of his stroke, Georgina wondered whether he might not have had 'some mysterious feeling of what was impending that day. God knows! but the words are comforting, and beautiful anyway.'[3]

In the first days after the funeral Georgina, Mamie, and Katey responded to a request from Catherine that they call on her.[4] To Mary Howitt, always a sympathetic friend, Georgina wrote in September, 'My sister has been, of course, much afflicted and shocked by her husband's death'. An awareness of speculation as to her relations with Catherine having, no doubt, long weighed on her, she took obvious satisfaction in reassuring Mrs. Howitt: 'You will be glad, I think, to hear that we all went to her immediately and have seen her several times since'.[5] Though the details of this first strange meeting can never be known, Catherine might well have displayed proudly one of her messages of condolence; for it was to her, the widow, that Queen Victoria had telegraphed from Balmoral, 'Deepest regret at the sad news of Charles Dickens's death'.[6]

During the first days of numbing shock, Georgina could spare little time, fortunately, for memories and meditation. The immediate demands of etiquette could not be neglected, lest her nieces and nephews be thought remiss. In her own handwriting, therefore, a weary number of formal notes like the following went out to acknowledge condolences:

> *Mr. Charles Dickens, Miss Dickens, Mrs. Charles*
> *Collins, Miss Hogarth and Mr. Henry F. Dickens*
> *return their sincere thanks for*
> *Mr. Samuel Lover's*
> *kind sympathy*

Gad's Hill.[7]

L

Practical matters also clamoured for attention. In addition to winding up Dickens's affairs and comforting his children, Georgina faced the stern adjustment to a totally different way of life. 'I have a great deal to do but it is a terrible feeling—and a new feeling to me to have to be busy, with no heart or care about being busy any more,' she wrote Mrs. Fields. 'However, the work must be done and there are many things to be thought of and attended to. I find myself constantly waiting still—in my own mind—for his advice and opinion. He was so universally referred to in his home in these matters.' Bleak as Gad's Hill was now without the Head, 'yet we all feel that the pang of leaving this place, for ever, will be a reopening of the wound—and, in fact, a beginning of the reality, which we can scarcely take in yet'. With the property to be sold in August, Georgina had to find a home for herself, Harry, and Mamie. 'She clings to me just now,' wrote Georgina of her niece. '. . . She thinks of nothing but staying quietly with me. So I must consider myself bound to her.'[8] Katey, too, had been at Gad's Hill constantly since her father's death. But poor Charles Collins did not figure in his wife's present plans; he was in London, staying with Leslie Stephen, who had taken pity on him. He looked 'quite broken down and miserable—not that he is ever cheerful', his host wrote Fields.[9] Fechter, having returned to America after a brief visit in England, also explained Collins's pathetic situation to the Fieldses, whereupon Annie reflected in her diary: 'I earnestly hope all will be right with [Katey] soon in this particular for Charles is a tender devoted husband and will be more to [her] now than ever before if she can only bring herself to go back to him'. It was doubtless the intensity of grief, observed Annie, 'which causes her to feel as if she could not give him a thought'.[10]

During these last days at Gad's Hill every corner of the house, every foot of its grounds, 'looking green and pleasant—sadly and cruelly so', revived some beloved memory. There was one hallowed spot, however, that had not been used since Dickens's death—the dining-room. Georgina and the girls lived in the drawing-room now. Almost as sacred as the place where Charles had died was the little study in the chalet, where he had written the last lines of *Edwin Drood*. There, on his desk with the little objects dear to his fancy, stood the register, still open to 8th June.[11]

Much as Georgina dreaded leaving the home where she had spent her happiest years, she anticipated no material want. Charles had seen to that. 'We are *wonderfully* provided for—I think—considering that the provision was all made out of one poor hard-worked brain,' she wrote a girlhood friend.[12] And indeed, Dickens's will had done handsomely by her, leaving her £8,000, duty free. She was also to have most of his personal jewellery, the familiar objects from his writing-table and room, and all his private papers. To Mamie was bequeathed £1,000, with a yearly annuity of £300 so long as she remained unmarried; to Ellen Ternan, another £1,000; to Catherine, the life interest on £8,000. Also amply provided for were Katey and the boys. A special codicil added only a week before Dickens's death left his share in *All the Year Round* to Charley, who had just been officially appointed sub-editor. Even the servants had been remembered with legacies of £19.19s.0d. each. With John Forster Georgina was named joint executor. As a final tribute Dickens's will left her his 'grateful blessing as the best and truest friend man ever had'. It solemnly enjoined his children 'always to remember how much they owe to the said Georgina Hogarth, and never to be wanting in a grateful and affectionate attachment to her, for they know well that she has been, through all the stages of their growth and progress, their ever useful self-denying and devoted friend'.[13]

However sincere this encomium, there were those who felt that it would be misinterpreted. 'Fechter was shocked at the publication of the will,' wrote Mrs. Fields in her diary, 'filled as it is with expressions fitted to give colour to the senseless and cruel accusations against Miss Hogarth. He thought the money might have been conveyed some other way.'[14] Even Wilkie Collins, if he was reported correctly, lent some support to the detractors. Commented John Bigelow, the American diplomat, in his diary for 24 July 1870: 'Collins intimates too that Dickens's sister-in-law, to whom he leaves all his private papers and whom he pronounces the best friend man ever had, was very fond of him. The impression seems to be that they were too intimate.'[15] (Collins, cooling toward his friend in the late sixties, may have transferred some of his resentment to Georgina. Besides, such conjectures about her and Dickens would have been normal to one of his loose morals.)

After the reading of the will, some two or three days before the burial, Georgina had written at once to Frederic Ouvry, the family friend and solicitor: 'I am most deeply touched and greatly astonished by the mark of his affection and trust in me which he has left in making me one of the executors of his will. I wish he had not given me so great a trust and responsibility. If I had ever had the least idea of such an intention on his part, I would have begged him to reconsider it. But as it is, I can only do my best to show that I deserved it from him.

'Some day, I shall ask you to be so good as to give me an hour of your time to explain the will to me—and the nature of my duties. I have no knowledge whatever of large money transactions or legal form, and I would rather have an explanation from you than from Mr. Forster—good and kind as he is.'[16]

But she need have felt no qualms, for it soon became evident that Dickens could not have left his affairs in better hands. She knew exactly where to find all valuable papers, what Gad's Hill fields had been leased and what rents collected, which bills had been paid and which were still outstanding. With her usual promptness and thoroughness, she sent Ouvry all documents relating to trusts, agreements, and investments, as well as miscellaneous memoranda found in various locked drawers. To these, and a desk of papers at the office, she had the keys. Meticulous was her handling of all accounts; Dickens had trained her well. As soon as statements reached Gad's Hill, she checked their accuracy before forwarding them to Ouvry for payment. 'I enclose some bills which came today. They are right,' she wrote in many a letter as she sought to drown her grief in practical concerns of the moment. But even business details occasionally awakened poignant memories: for instance, the bill for twenty guineas from the London specialist who, with Frank Beard, had attended Dickens in his last illness. 'I enclose Dr. Reynolds' demand for his fruitless visit', was her terse but emotionally charged comment.[17] There was also the matter of reimbursing the authorities of Rochester Cathedral for digging a grave and tolling the bell before it had been decided to bury Dickens in the Abbey. To be sure, no payment had been asked, but Georgina felt the obligation as a point of honour.[18] Among other funeral expenses to come out of the estate was a Rochester draper's bill for the mourning worn by Letitia Austin and the Gad's Hill servants.[19] Finally there was the fee of £100. 10s. to the Dean of Westminster.[20]

Few details escaped Georgina. Remembering that Sir Joseph Olliffe had, just before his death in 1869, supplied Gad's Hill with three dozen bottles of French hock and that Dickens had several times intended to ask Lady Olliffe for the bill but had never got around to it, Georgina took it upon herself to settle the business. She wrote the widow, at length received a statement, and immediately forwarded a memorandum to Ouvry: '3 Dozen Hock at 5 francs a bottle making in English money, as I calculate, £7. 3s. 4d.'.[21]

What was to be done, she asked another time, about the dues to the Higham cricket club? She explained that on the day Dickens was stricken, 'that dreadful 8th June—the subscription list for this summer's season was taken to him. He put down his name and his family's . . . for £5. 0s. 0d.—*but did not give the money*.' Should it be paid? 'I think so,' she advised, 'in consideration of his undoubted intentions when he put his name on that list—and also of his love for the neighbourhood. . . .'[22]

Ouvry had to rely solely on Georgina's information in at least one matter—the large loan Dickens had made to Fechter, who, though a brilliant actor, was a poor financier and often lived in the shadow of legal proceedings. During his lease of the Lyceum Theatre he had not only incurred great losses but had quarrelled violently with his acting manager and treasurer, H. Barnett, from whom he had borrowed heavily. Repeatedly put off whenever he tried to collect on the loans, and grossly insulted, Barnett had finally threatened to cash the securities Fechter had given him. At this juncture Dickens had rescued his friend by lending him £1,700, interest free. Ouvry, who had handled this transaction, knew that Fechter, though repaying a large part of the sum before leaving for America, had asked for an extension of six months on the balance.[23] Had this obligation been met? 'My own strong conviction is that Fechter *had paid everything he owed him*,' Georgina told Ouvry. She recalled that shortly before the end of their last winter in London, Dickens had been delighted with a letter from the actor, telling of his American success and also enclosing some money. 'I always told you Fechter would pay,' Dickens had told Georgina, who previously had expressed some doubts on that score. 'Has he paid *all* he owed?' she had asked. 'EVERYTHING,' had come the answer.[24]

Even the self-complacent John Forster had to turn to his co-executor for help on one occasion. Coming to claim the manuscripts of Dickens's novels, left him by the will, he discovered that *Our Mutual Friend* was missing. Georgina immediately wrote to the Fieldses, inquiring whether Charles had ever made them a gift of the missing manuscript. 'If so it is all right,' she hastened to explain. She merely wanted to clear up the mystery.[25] But the manuscript was not with the Fieldses. A month later Forster, seeing it advertised at £500, was infuriated, for he assumed it had been stolen. It was Charles Collins who luckily remembered what Georgina had temporarily forgotten: that Dickens had presented it to the journalist Eneas Sweetland Dallas. '. . . I remember at the time thinking what a pity—and what a waste it was,' she recalled. 'But Mr. Dallas had done some business—I forget what—which obliged Charles. He had also written a notice in the *Times* . . . which pleased him—and therefore he made him this wonderful present.' She admitted that Dallas, whose affairs were now 'in a most entangled condition', had a right to do what he chose with the manuscript. The sale, she had learned, was being handled by Camden Hotten,

'not a very reputable Publisher as I dare say you know', she
remarked to Mrs. Fields.[26]

Georgina's distrust of Hotten probably stemmed from her brother-
in-law's own experience and its current sequel. As a letter of
Dickens to Ouvry shows, the publisher had once asked to use a few
'copyright trifles' in a work on the novelist as a speaker. Receiving
neither the permission nor any acknowledgement of his request, he
had still gone ahead with publication plans.[27] And now, in the
summer of Dickens's death, he brought out a memoir incorporating
much of this material, augmented by hastily assembled information.
Hotten having quoted freely from the letters of Dickens and his
friends, Georgina was undoubtedly indignant at what she must have
regarded as an unauthorized production throughout. It was a
foretaste of the sort of thing she would have to encounter, and
combat, in the years ahead.

Ever mindful of economy during her years of handling the household budget, Georgina could not countenance wastefulness now. To
Dr. Frank Beard she sent a note, asking him to help her dispose of
some elastic stockings—how often she had forwarded replacements
while Dickens was on reading tours! 'I have got a pair of Elastic
Stockings of dearest Charles'—*quite new*. They had been sent to me
from Sparks but a month before his death—and I doubt whether he
ever had them on. His old ones, of which there were eleven pairs—
I have given away to the poor people about here who wear them—
but these seem too good for that.'[28]

On another occasion she was much annoyed when unable to
return some unworn summer clothing. Shortly after the move from
London back to Gad's Hill on 1st June, Dickens's tailor had sent a
light-weight suit and two pairs of lisle trousers to Hyde Park Place,
their winter residence. In that 'careless household' these articles
had lain unheeded for several months. 'If they had been forwarded
immediately,' complained Georgina to Ouvry, 'I suppose Skinner
[the tailor] would have taken them back.' Now she would have to
keep them for Harry, who, being in mourning, could not wear light-
coloured clothes for some time.[29]

Many were the disbursements she handled in her last days at
Gad's Hill: the recent remodelling expenses, the servants' wages, the
nurseryman's bill. This last, she explained, was so enormous because
their new gardener had followed a very incompetent one. Finding
everything in a dreadful state, he had done much replanting. 'I
remember Charles saying that he hoped the garden would produce
something this summer,' she told Ouvry, 'as he should have enough
to pay for what had been put into the ground.'[30] Since there had

been little cash on hand at the time of Dickens's death—£1. 15s. 9d. in the house purse and £6. 6s. 3d. in the pocket of his coat[31]—she made frequent applications to her solicitor for money out of the estate. All this she itemized in her account book.

As exacting and time-consuming as any of her other responsibilities, and more demanding of patience, was her position as family co-ordinator. With Sydney in the navy, Frank in India, and Alfred and Plorn in Australia, she was constantly writing letters—first to comfort her bereaved nephews, later to explain matters pertaining to the estate. When official documents needed signatures, she was expected to forward them. When any of the children needed money, it was she who approached Ouvry. Harry had worked hard at Cambridge and would benefit from a little trip to Belgium and Holland. Might he have £25 for travelling expenses? Mamie would like to know what income she could expect before the end of the year. When would Frederic Chapman pay the children what he owed on copyrights? Dickens having regarded this publisher's way of doing business as 'scrambling', Georgina echoed his doubts, advising Ouvry that Chapman was 'one of those people to whom I should be disposed to show no quarter'.[32]

With her own affairs, too, she was occupied at intervals. Heretofore the money for her personal and household expenses had always been on hand, Dickens's cheques arriving periodically. Now, however, she would have to depend entirely on the judicious use of her legacy. 'As soon as you think it advisable,' she wrote Ouvry, 'I shall be glad to reinvest my money and get as much as I can for it. So that I may know . . . exactly what my income is going to be.' Some weeks later she asked whether she ought not to have a dividend that month. 'I seem to be inveterately stupid about my money affairs,' she admitted on learning that her principal had not yet yielded any interest for her to draw on. She had not realized that much of her legacy was still to be transferred to her account. Gradually she began to penetrate the mystery of finance. 'After I wrote to you the last time, a ray of intelligence on my money matters came to my brain,' she announced. 'I think I can understand, now, that I cannot draw on Messrs. Coutts for the income on my investments, until sufficient time has elapsed for the investments to return money to theirs—and therefore I can only count on the ready money they have of mine up to the end of this year.'[33]

What would Ouvry think of investing her money in American stocks? A friend of Mamie's had recommended Mississippi Bonds at six and a half per cent. That, by Georgina's calculations, must bring her income to £400 a year (after part of her legacy had been spent on a house). But there must be no transaction, of course, of which Ouvry did not have 'a perfectly good and safe opinion'. His advice was strongly against these bonds. 'For personal kindness and trouble privately, I owe you what I can never repay,' Georgina assured the friend to whom she took all her financial problems.[34]

Another imperative concern: who would inherit her legacy, should it not be spent in her lifetime? 'I am constantly haunted by the recollection and impression of sudden death which has been so awfully brought home to us lately—that I want to be provided against my own.' There must be a will. But no sooner had she filed a document, than an afterthought demanded alterations. 'I made it in a hurry . . . when my head was very much confused,' she apologized. The £2,000 left to her infant goddaughter, Beatrice, should have been equally divided with 'her sister, Mary Angela, Charley Dickens' eldest child who is the one I like best—and the most interesting of his children.' (For was not Mary Angela, nick-named 'Mekitty', the one who cherished vivid memories of her Inimitable grandfather?) Could a codicil take care of the matter? And if Charley were named one of the executors of the will, would he thereby become his aunt's legal heir and succeed her as adminis-trator to Dickens's estate? If so, Georgina would much prefer to name Ouvry as better qualified to be a '*well judging* Trustee' in the interests of her nieces and nephews. 'Besides it seems to me that if his Father had considered it desirable to make his son one of the Executors,' she reflected, 'he would have done it. . . .'[35]

Two months later she had misgivings because only her nieces and grandnieces, and not her nephews, had been named her legatees. 'I did not feel comfortable or just about the boys—who are all of them very dear to me both for their Father's sake and their own—and who are all, I think, fond of me and affectionate to me,' she told Ouvry. Now she wished to will each of them £200. Even the banished 'Little Admiral' was to be remembered with the other boys, for 'there can be no harm in letting that unfortunate Sydney share equally in so small a remembrance as this would be.' That would still leave the larger portion to the girls, for whom the money would do more good. A letter of final instructions to Mamie had been lodged in a casket 'which she *must* open, if I were to die (and of which she knows I always wear the key). . . . I have given her directions, first of all to burn her Father's letters to me! (which I have tried to do since his death myself—but find I cannot).' The casket letter also specified how her personal effects were to be distributed. 'I have no doubt I am as little likely to die, at present—as most people—and very probably shall live far longer than I have any desire to do,'

she added, 'but I always feel that I may die—at any moment.
Therefore I want all my small worldly affairs to be in perfect order.'
She feared that she was becoming a nuisance to her solicitor. 'This
will, I hope be the last time I shall have to trouble you with any
alteration of this document!' she promised.[36]

But not for long did her will remain unchanged. Before the end
of the year Forster, as the heir to Dickens's manuscripts, made
Georgina a present of *The Cricket on the Hearth*, requesting only that
it revert to him in the event of her prior death. Though she drew up
her own codicil to record this arrangement, the final details had to
be referred to Ouvry.[37] The frequency with which he was consulted
about the will thereafter became embarrassing. Many were the
changes, many the codicils, in the next few years.

Much in her thoughts, too, Georgina held a sense of duty to
Dickens's closest friends. Only a few days after the funeral, on
reading his will herself, she arrived at a new interpretation of the
clause which bequeathed her 'my personal jewellery' and 'all the
little familiar objects from my writing-table and my room'. Dickens
had said, 'She will know what to do with these things'—and that she
did. 'The meaning I attach to it is that he trusts me to distribute
memorials of his *amongst his friends*,' she informed Ouvry. She had,
accordingly, already assigned the jewellery to members of the
family, keeping a diamond ring for herself. The large collection of
little objects she planned to itemize, listing beside each one the name
of a friend—'when I get time and can clear my stunned head
sufficiently to do it'. Ouvry was invited to make his own selection.[38]

So began another demanding job. Georgina selected relics suitable
to particular friends, made up many a parcel, and accompanied each
with a note. To Frank Beard, whom she sent a cigar case and a
medicine chest, she wrote, 'First of all we think of *you*—in the
memory of what you did for him at Preston—and still more—in the
remembrance of what we all went through together in those last
hours'.[39] To Ellen Ternan went the pen that had been used to write
Edwin Drood.[40] For Carlyle there was a walking stick which,
Georgina pointed out, Dickens had used constantly. 'You did not
meet very often of late years,' she observed, 'but there was *no one*
for whom he had a higher reverence and admiration besides a sincere
personal affection than for yourself.'[41] To the Fieldses she explained,
'I . . . send you what I think you will like all the more from its being
an utterly valueless and shabby little thing. It is a paper knife
that he had given to him years ago in Scotland.'[42] Charles Reade
received a pen tray belonging to the sitting-room at the office, where
it had been 'constantly under [Dickens's] eye, and associated with

his familiar every-day life. You did not meet very often; but I
have never heard him speak of you except with the heartiest and
most cordial expressions of admiration, respect, and personal
affection.'[43] To Bulwer-Lytton, whom she sent a package of photographs, she used almost the same phrasing. Including pictures of the
writing-table in the chalet and in the library, both associated with
Dickens's last afternoon's occupation, such a parcel of mementoes
was dispatched also to the Fieldses and other friends. In this manner
Georgina's distribution continued for many years as she thought of
other deserving associates or decided to part with some of her own
prized keepsakes.

In the early weeks after the funeral much of her time was given
over to preparing for the two important sales: one of the pictures
and art objects, the other of the Gad's Hill property and furnishings.
The first of these took place on 9th July, in Christie's auction rooms,
London. Here had been assembled a variety of oil paintings, water
colours, and household curios, some of them of no great intrinsic
value. Yet so eagerly were they sought after, so frantic was the bidding for even the merest trifle, that the auctioneer could readily have
sold the seventy items ten times over. Crowded into the room with
the usual types of auction frequenters—the collector, the connois-
seur, the speculator—were many persons from the lower middle class,
a sort seldom seen here. The event was charged with all the drama,
suspense, and comedy of a scene from Dickens himself. 'No living
Englishman for certain, and perhaps no Englishman of the Future,
will ever see such a sale again,' predicted one reporter. Things went
for unbelievable prices: 1,000 guineas for Frith's *Dolly Varden*; 990
guineas for Stanfield's *Eddystone Lighthouse* (a souvenir of the Tavistock House theatricals); 510 guineas for Webster's *Dotheboys Hall*. As
bidding proceeded on the lesser articles, the auctioneer's porter
grinned in amazement at the sums offered: 5 guineas for a little
match box worth scarcely 5 shillings; £120 for the mounted figure
of Grip the Raven; 31 guineas for an ordinary little gong. 'He was
always very fond of gongs,' observed one of the spectators confiden-
tially to a stranger, as if addressing his closest friend. 'Don't you
remember the weak-eyed man and the gong at Dr. Blinker's?'[44]
(Three days earlier Georgina had given Ouvry a chance to acquire a
gong for himself prior to the public action. 'Charley reminded me
to-day,' she wrote, 'that there is *another* gong at the office—and in
fact, the original and more interesting gong of the two. It was at
Tavistock House, and was used in the Plays. Mr. Homan [the auc-
tioneer] was greatly excited by finding it at the office, and that it was
to come under *his* Hammer. Why should you not go in for that

gong? and I should think you might arrange with Homan, without
any difficulty to buy it in, at some fair price arranged between you.')[45]
The auction over, well might Georgina exclaim, 'What astonishing
prices the things fetched at the sale yesterday! We are all very
thankful.'[46] John Forster was equally exuberant. 'The sale has
been a success far beyond the most exaggerated expectation,' he
wrote Carlyle. 'I should have thought £5,000 a fair, even a great
result: and we have obtained £9,460. The pictures all went at prices
far beyond their value; but the other smaller things brought prices
even more disproportionate; bits of china obtainable for 10s. or 20s.
going for 20 and 30 guineas!'[47]

For the sale that followed at Gad's Hill Georgina naturally
assumed a major responsibility. Painstaking was her inventory of
all chattels, both at the house and at the office. Dickens's favourite
cane chairs, sofas, beds, tables—all were assembled at Gad's Hill,
repaired, touched up and polished. In view of the prices brought by
the bric-à-brac at Christie's, she even salvaged from one of the office
mantelpieces a little bronze *tazza* with a broken handle, and had it
mended and added to the list. Many items besides furniture and
ornaments figured in the sale inventory. 'What about the cellar full
of wine?' she asked Ouvry. But the orange brandy, of which there
was a quantity on hand, she would not sell. 'As you remember,' she
explained, 'I always made it every year. Charles was very fond of
it.' This she would distribute among those who would 'care to have
it as a remembrance of the dear old place—and the dear old happy
days'. But the flowers in the conservatory—should they not be sold?
Within only the past three months they had been added at great
expense. Surely they should not go as plants in the garden. Had
the carriage and stable properties been valued, she asked an apprai-
ser, when a 'probate' was made of the house?[48] In her zeal to overlook
nothing of possible value, she acted solely in the interest of her nieces
and nephews, for none of the proceeds from the sale would go to her.
Her only part in the estate was the £8,000 legacy.

'It *was* agony!'—that period when 'shoals of people came three
times a week to see the place—very often 12 at a time,' Georgina
wrote Annie Fields. 'Of course we shut ourselves in one room, and
did not see them in the house, but we could hear them tramping up
and down on the stairs and in the rooms, and see them walking about
the garden—often with children and little dogs, making quite a
pleasure trip of it.' Meanwhile there was the 'gradual dismantling
of everything, the auctioneers here arranging the furniture to show
it off, and going about making their catalogue.'[49] Part of Georgina's
share in this enterprise was to help prepare a bill of sale, replete

with lavish description, a diagram of the main floor plan, and photographs of the house, chalet, and grounds. Under her critical eye passed many a proof submitted by the photographer. The completed prospectus was an enticing one, setting forth such features as the locality—in 'a fine healthy part of the county of Kent'—and the 'Doubly Historic' site, 'First as the scene of one of Shakespeare's most celebrated pieces of humour, and Secondly, as the abode of the greatest English Humourist who has lived since Shakespeare's time.' Nor were the tangible assets of the property forgotten: the 'capital stables for four horses with patent fittings and hot and cold water laid on', 'the paved yard with glass roof', and the 'well of pure water of great depth'.[50]

With all in readiness for the sale of the house, scheduled for 5th August—furnishings and wines to be auctioned off on the three days following—Georgina faced the inevitable parting from the only place ever to give full scope to her active spirit. Bracing herself against the 'dreadful wrench'—she and Mamie were to leave Gad's Hill on 1st August—she handled business details to the final moment. She would delay filling in the amount on the last cheque until all housekeeping bills were in, wages paid, and receipts taken, she told Ouvry. Two servants should stay on at Gad's Hill after the sale, she suggested: the gardener to look after the house and the groom to take care of the horse that was to be sold. At last, on the eve of departure she gave way to her feelings. 'This is a hard, hard day for us!' she admitted. 'How very, very much better, it will be when we have left this dear home.'[51]

The next morning was an even greater trial, with the farewells to neighbours and staff 'and all the poor people crying'. But such sympathy—'*that* was comfort'. So, too, was the letter from Annie Fields in the last post. But even on that final morning, business intruded. In her nervous flurry Georgina wrote twice to Ouvry. Dispatching a parcel of accounts to him by messenger, she had to enclose a brief note explaining the absence of a receipt inadvertently packed in her desk, which had already left the premises. She concluded pathetically, 'We go away quietly—by ourselves this afternoon. I am sure you think of us, and feel for us today.'[52]

Moments thereafter she suddenly woke to a belated consciousness of a lapse of duty. George Woolley, the young under-gardener, had not been included with the other legatees! Except for Anne Cornelius and her daughter Catherine, not of the Gad's Hill staff, no servants had been named in the will, which provided merely that the legacy of £19. 19s. 0d. be given to anyone who was in Dickens's employ at the time of his death and had served at least a year. It was Georgina's task to compile the list of those who qualified and to set up trust funds for all minors, two of whom, Catherine Cornelius and Isaac Armitage, she had included in her calculations. Young Woolley had been about the place since childhood, first as 'ostel boy', and for the past two years as the gardener's assistant. Though he did not sleep or board in the home, might he not qualify as a domestic servant anyhow? 'He is a very good steady respectable boy. His mother is a widow, a hard working honest woman, who has been our charwoman here, whenever we have wanted one, these twelve years,' Georgina wrote in her second letter that morning, the twenty-ninth to Ouvry since Dickens's death. 'So it is a dreadful blow to the poor mother and the boy, losing us all, of course. And £19. 19s. 0d. would be a small fortune to them. *Of course I have not said a word to them*, but I thought I would put the question to you.'[53]

Finally, all duties finished, Georgina, Mamie, and Katey had the house to themselves. Having sent the servants away early that morning, the three women spent their last hour 'going into every room, and saying goodbye to every dear corner'. So, as Georgina wrote Annie, they 'walked about the place *alone*, and came quietly away alone in the afternoon'. And Mamie added her recollection of the leave-taking: '. . . We three, who have been best friends & companions all our lives, went out of the dear old Home, together'.[54]

Toward the end of the hectic dismantling, Georgina and Mamie had hastily taken a Weybridge dwelling, Monument House, to be their home until they could find suitable quarters in London. Georgina had baulked at the rent, four and a half guineas a week, but 'could see *nothing* cheaper that was fit to live in'.[55] The Weybridge place was attractive, though, 'very airy and clean, and prettily situated' about a half mile from the Thames. The locality was identified for Annie as 'only about ten miles from Windsor so you know the sort of country. . . . It is close by all the water-meadow country, which you know well, by description, in Our Mutual Friend.' Frequently she and Mamie rowed on the river with Harry, who was to live with them whenever he was not at Cambridge. For the first few days Katey stayed with them before going to Scotland with her husband for a rest.[56] Mrs. Bouncer, aging and asthmatic now, was naturally a permanent member of the household.

In Weybridge Georgina found some measure of peace. The environment was what she desired, 'a quiet country place which was new to us and which had no association with past happiness'.[57] Yet the home was not altogether strange, for she and Mamie were using furniture, plate, and linens which they had purchased from the estate, along with what was left of the summer store of candles and provisions laid in just before Dickens's death.[58] And three of the Gad's Hill servants had come with them: Emma, the maid; Catherine, the cook; and Isaac Armitage, the houseboy. 'It is less desolate for us to have all those faithful and kind faces about us in our new home', Georgina wrote to Mrs. Armitage, reporting that 'Isaac is quite well, and cheerful and happy. He is a most good boy, and a great comfort to us'.[59] As a matter of fact, Isaac was in ecstasy at the prospect of donning livery in his new situation.[60]

Georgina soon had the satisfaction of being allowed to put the £19. 19s. 0d. legacy in trust for the other servant boy, Woolley. Sending his receipt on 12th August, she told Ouvry, 'I had a most grateful letter from his mother and himself'. Since the lad was exactly as old as Plorn—born on the same day—she felt certain that she would not be likely to forget his coming of age.[61]

Accompanying the heavy duties of London house hunting and business and social correspondence were the ever present memories of Gad's Hill. 'I think of the place and Charles inseparably, and I think of both, day and night,' Georgina confessed to Annie Fields. 'But I am thankful to do so, both of him living and dead. It is the most peaceful, happy remembrance . . . , and I am glad to think that he owed the happiest and most quietly happy part of the latter years of his life, to the love and interest he felt for that pretty home.'[62]

Mamie also reminisced as she wrote Mrs. Fields of the 'dreadful wrench' she and her 'dear faithful little Auntie' had undergone in leaving the place her father had so loved. And she eulogized him as one who 'never had anything to do with a living soul without attaching them to him. If strangers could so love him you can tell what he must have been to his own flesh and blood. It is a glorious inheritance to have such blood flowing in one's veins.' Then she added, 'I am so glad I have never changed my name'[63]—a curious remark in view of her father's dismay at her remaining Miss Dickens.

As for Georgina, her reminiscent mood gave way momentarily to a less tender one when Gad's Hill Place was sold during her first week in Weybridge. She and Forster had hoped it might go for at least nine or ten thousand pounds. In fact, they had arranged with the auctioneer beforehand to buy it for the estate if the bidding did not exceed eight thousand pounds. But their careful scheme came to naught, wrote Forster to Carlyle, because of Charley: 'Not communicating with me in any way beforehand, not knowing there was a reserved price, most unwisely and most unbecomingly Charles Dickens (representing his father alas! in no one particular but his name) showed himself prominently in the crowded sale-room—very

GEORGINA HOGARTH
Diclens House, London

MONUMENT HOUSE
Now Lavender Cottage
By courtesy of Felix Aylmer

probably deterred many from bidding—and, from the slow and comparatively small offers at first made, believing (this is his own
account apologetically made to us after) that the property was about
to be sacrificed, was induced to take up bidding himself—bid on,
quite unconscious that he was bidding only against the auctioneer
representing *us*,—and had the whole knocked down to him at the
next bidding above our reserved price. . . !'[64]

Georgina blamed Ouvry somewhat for allowing Charley to take
this action. The very presence of the oldest son at the sale, she told
Mrs. Fields, had stopped competition, discouraging prospective
buyers, who thought he was bidding for the family. How could he
afford to live at Gad's Hill? Where would he find money to pay the
estate? If, by October, he could not raise the £8,647 he had offered
for the property, it would revert to the heirs, but, of course, depre-
ciated in value. If he resold it at a loss, he would have to make up
to the estate the difference between his bid and the purchase price.
Should he sell it at a gain—here Georgina began to suspect his
motives. 'Unless he intends that his Brothers and Sisters should
share in the profit, I shall always consider it a dishonest transaction,'
she maintained to Ouvry. What right, she asked, had Charley to
step in, no matter how low the bids were going? 'Nothing will
shake my belief that Charley has taken an unfair advantage of his
Brothers and Sisters in interfering with the sale of Gad's Hill *at all*,'
she fumed a few days later. 'It would have been far better for us to
leave the property *unsold* for the present—and have bought it in,
for the Estate.' When Ouvry reminded her that Dickens himself,
according to Wills, had once considered £7,000 a fair price, she argued
that after its noted owner's death it should bring 'far and above its
market value'. And she remarked tartly, 'We can hardly say it was
sold very well—as we have not got the money for it yet'. It must also
be borne in mind, she pointed out, that the recent improvements—
£1,000 for the conservatory and £500 for alterations to the house
and stables—had greatly enhanced the value of the property. She
was glad, she admitted in September, that Charley had 'not yet
secured the house'. She hoped that he would let it go back to the
heirs, 'for his own sake—as much as anything else', for he had made
a grievous mistake.[65]

Unlike Gad's Hill Place, the furniture and wines sold far in excess
of estimates. 'I fancied and foretold we would get £2,000 for it, and
we got £2,200 odd,' Forster reported to Carlyle. Actually, the final
figure was roughly £2,270.[66] Besides the satisfaction of seeing her
tedious preparations well rewarded, Georgina had one touching
testimony of public regard and sympathy. Several days after the

sale she recounted to Ouvry the story of a little relic, possibly the very *tazza* she had taken pains to have mended: there had arrived 'a pleasant little note from a *Mr. Simpson* an entire stranger to us, who said he had become the purchaser of a little bronze Tazza which the auctioneer had mentioned he had been desired to retain for Miss Dickens, if possible. Mamie and I had told him we would give £3. 3s. for it. It was a pretty little thing that used to be at the office. We saw in the Telegram that it had sold for £7. 15s. Well, this gentleman said he had only one motive in buying it, when he heard that Mamie wished to have it. Which was to restore it to her and he wrote to ask me if she would accept it—and when he should send it. Was it not kind of him?'[67]

By the end of August Georgina and Mamie had found a sizeable London residence at 81 Gloucester Terrace, Hyde Park. 'We have seen so many *nasty* houses at very little lower rents,' Georgina told her solicitor, 'that I certainly do think that the rent of Gloucester Terrace (which is a nice house decidedly) is very reasonable.' There was, however, one decided drawback; they would have to pay an additional premium for the fixtures, many of no conceivable use to them. 'Cornices are things we have a particular objection to,' she complained. 'We never had one in our house.' And the blinds were frightfully dirty and ugly. But she would have Homan, of the Rochester auction agency, represent her in arriving at a fair appraisal of all such items. Some weeks later she announced the shocking result of this negotiation. 'Mamie and I have had a great blow,' she exclaimed on learning that the fixtures had been valued at £71. 16s. 'We were horrified—as we should have thought half that sum large enough.' Even the assurance that Homan had obtained a reduction from the £85 originally demanded, did not placate her. 'It is a breach!' she insisted. But it would be pointless, she agreed grudgingly, to incur the expense of another valuation. 'Therefore we must leave it alone.'[68]

In entering upon her own first major transaction, Georgina exercised her usual caution. Would Ouvry be sure that the lease was made out to her and Mamie jointly? For her part she found it difficult to feel exhilarated about housekeeping under her altered circumstances. 'I hope the house will work out all right—and I wish with all my heart I could get myself to feel any interest as to whether it does or not!' she confided. 'I suppose it will come. Mamie is pleased, I hope—which is a good thing.'[69]

While the workmen were making the necessary repairs and alterations at 81 Gloucester Terrace, there was a quiet interval of waiting. With too much time to think, there came a rush of memories. Some found their way into letters to Annie Fields. One gave the history of the little New Testament which Dickens had written for his children. Georgina thought its sixteen short chapters, 'chiefly adapted from St. Luke's Gospel—most beautiful—most touching—*most* simple, as such a narrative should be'. She was sorry that it must never be published. Only last year she had asked Dickens's permission to make a copy for Charley's children. At the same time she had urged to have it printed—at least for private circulation. Charles had considered the matter for a week or two. 'At the end of the time he gave it back to me,' Georgina recalled, 'and said he had decided *never to publish it—or even to have it privately printed*. He said I might make a copy for Bessy, or any one of the children, *but for no one else*, and . . . he also begged that we would never lend the MS., or a copy of it, to any one to take out of the house. So there is no doubt about his *strong feeling* on the subject, and we *must* obey it.' She had given the manuscript to Mamie, considering it proper for the oldest daughter to own this precious work.[70] (Being one of the private papers left Georgina by the will, it was hers to give.)

As she tried to adjust to her altered circumstances, she was often discouraged. '. . . It's every day I feel more and more what a blank is left in life!' she lamented. 'It is not the first agony of such a grief that is hardest to bear. It is the beginning the old routine of life again—and going on from day to day—and being *obliged* to live and try to take an interest in life for the sake of the people about one—that is the hard, hard trial—and *that* seems to get worse instead of better as time goes on!' How painful had been the awakening, 'when we all returned to our old routine of life, and had to make our plans, and to live our lives, and eat and drink, and see the world go on—and *know* that he is gone!'[71]

Though Georgina had earlier told Annie that she meant to recall only the cheerful past—'only the remembrance of the happiness for all' at Gad's Hill[72]—it was inevitable that she should look back self-reproachfully on the times when she had doubted her happiness there. 'My life has been a curious one—and not the ideal of a happy woman's existence,' she admitted. 'And I have often felt it hard—and wondered whether it was *all* a mistake—and a *waste*! *Now* I feel that with all its difficulties and drawbacks, I would not change it—I would not have it altered for the brightest and most prosperous existence any woman could have had.' This conviction was to be her solace in the years ahead—almost half a century. '*My* comfort is now,' she assured Mrs. Fields, 'in the feeling that I would not give up *a day of the past*—in which, IN MYSELF, I live now!'[73]

M

Chapter Eleven
'MAKING THE BEST OF IT'

'WE are going in to our home tomorrow,' Georgina announced to Ouvry at the end of October, 'as the only way of forcing the work people *out*—but it is not nearly ready to receive us—and we shall be very uncomfortable for some time to come.'[1] Like Dickens during numerous renovations, she had begun to chafe as the painters and carpenters had fallen behind schedule. And now, the move already delayed by a month, she forestalled further dallying by camping temporarily in one little room on the kitchen floor. In this way she and Mamie would be on hand to supervise and hasten the final stages of alteration. At last, by the third week of November, they were quite settled.

Filled with their Gad's Hill furniture, the place looked like home, 'pretty and graceful', Georgina wrote her American friend, whom she now addressed familiarly for the first time as Annie. She hoped that Mamie, who found real pleasure in the new arrangements, might soon work at her music—they had bought a new piano—and get a 'resource and distraction out of that'. And, though her niece was already a spinster at thirty-three, perhaps she would still 'make a new interest in life for herself. I feel that she wants it very much,' her aunt remarked, perhaps uncovering a submerged regret for her own celibate existence, 'and that she will, by and bye, miss the change in her *position*, which does not make itself felt, yet, while the great grief swallows up all minor losses and troubles'. Referring to Major Lynch, who had written her a 'kind, feeling' letter of condolence from his new station in the West Indies, Georgina still deeply regretted that nothing had come of his attentions to Mamie: '*That*, as you know, was a disappointment to me, and I have never been able clearly, to understand how it was that it fell to the ground. I had a strong suspicion that some mischief was made, which I could not make you understand, without entering into a long history.'[2]

Georgina could not whip up much interest in the pleasant new surroundings at 81 Gloucester Terrace. 'Some day I hope I may get *some* feeling of home here—but as yet, I feel more desolate *than* I

have done yet,' she wrote Annie. 'The London streets are so mournful and haunted to me, and as I walk about them the memories of
the *long* past are almost more than I can bear, and I feel too, such
a yearning for the dear old country home, the country roads and
walks, as I cannot describe. But it must be borne, *and kept to myself.'*
Since Mamie also lived in a void without the 'centre and sunshine
of the *old* home life', Georgina felt that she herself must 'set the
example of cheerfulness—and of making the best of it. But it is so
difficult!' Already she dreaded the year-end holidays. 'We shall
have nothing to do with the festivities of course,' she insisted, 'but
it will be impossible to avoid seeing the evidence of them all around
us, and Christmas had always been such a celebration with us, and
is altogether so inseparably associated with his memory that this
first one, without him, will be almost too agonizing.'[3]

But she reproached herself for being 'selfish' and 'wicked' in
dwelling thus upon her private woes 'when half the world is in
sorrow and so many poor families must be desolate this Christmas.
God knows I think of them all, and sympathize with my whole heart,
but one *must* feel the weight of one's own burden.' With the arrival
of the new year, she hoped, there would come some relief, not only
for herself, but for the whole world. On the subject of the Franco-
Prussian War she vented her horror: 'Is it not *awful*! Fresh rumours
of wars, and troubles which will involve every nation, apparently,
before this bloody struggle is ended!' How could two Christian
countries wage this conflict in the season of 'peace and goodwill
towards men'? England, too, she observed, had felt the impact of the
war. 'Our *own* charities are suffering this winter because people have
given so much to the sufferers by the war, and they cannot afford
their usual charities at home. Also a great many people are thrown
out of employment because the Refugees are being employed. This
especially applies to Servants, Dress Makers, and even governesses,
because people like French nurses and teachers for their children,
and of course Dress Makers like French *hands*, and they are to be
had now for half the money they would take at other times. I think
this is very bad and wrong.'[4]

But from the international scene her thoughts must return, per-
force, to Charles. She agreed with Annie that *Edwin Drood* was
'worthy to be the last work, and to stand out as a sort of monument'.
She had not found the courage, however, to read it again. 'Nor can
I venture yet, to read any of the dear Books,' she admitted. 'I hope
time will be good enough so far to harden, and heal the wound, as
to permit that solace. Just now it is agony to read the familiar
words. It seems to bring him *to life*, too terribly, and to make the

stern reality less endurable.' It was painful enough, she complained, to be constantly reminded of 'poor Gad's Hill', now standing 'empty and desolate'. Charley had been unable to sell or rent it.[5]

Seldom, however, did she allow thoughts of the past to crowd out practical considerations. Finances she had always to wrestle with. In fact, she had borrowed fifty pounds from Ouvry during the summer and had worried about the debt in the brief interval before she had funds to repay it. Now she expressed to him her concern over keeping a required balance in the bank. 'If I were living *alone*, I should not have *any* doubt on the subject,' she declared. 'You see we are starting expensively, certainly—more so than I would have done for myself, and much more than I care for at all. But I have not liked to thwart Mamie in this—as to worldly matters. The change to her, poor girl, is more trying than to any one, and she has expensive tastes, especially as to house and furniture, which I have not had the heart to refuse to join her in indulging.' Georgina hoped that, once all bills were paid, their joint housekeeping would not exceed four or five hundred pounds a year. 'Mamie has plenty of sense,' she pointed out, 'and understands . . . the necessity of keeping our household expenses small. Her extravagant tastes are not of that kind, and she is quite prepared to acknowledge the necessity of our having no company and living altogether within a limit, as far as regards what we pay *jointly*.' About her personal spending Mamie could, of course, do as she chose. There was also the question of what Harry should contribute to the household budget. So long as he was in college he had his own heavy expenses, naturally. But when he stayed with them during vacations, what might he reasonably be charged for room and board? 'He wouldn't come on any other terms,' Georgina explained.[6] In a later letter she thanked Ouvry for suggesting a figure, though what it was is not clear from her reply.

Compared with her active days at Gad's Hill, life at Gloucester Terrace was strangely quiet, she found, once her routine was established. 'I am up and have no *work*, that you would call work!' she wrote Annie in outlining a typical day. But she was not idle. 'In the morning I work, and read and write, and do odd "house" matters —and in the afternoon I generally have business of *some* kind out of doors, and friends to go and see, several *Invalid* friends, whom I have to go to see regularly, at least twice a week, and as people all live in such opposite directions in London, it is generally only possible to make one visit in a day. So life slips away, with very little variety. . . .'[7]

A few days before the first lonely Christmas Annie Fields wrote that a spiritualistic medium had communicated a message from

Dickens to Longfellow's brother-in-law, Tom Appleton. Georgina was indignant. '. . . I have not the slightest belief in spirit rapping *mediums*,' she replied. Not that she discounted the possibility of communicating with the departed. 'God knows I think nothing *impossible* in connection with the great mystery,' she declared. 'I never know whether I *wish*, or not, that the spirits of our beloved Dead should have any knowledge of us, our poor troubles and weaknesses, after they are taken to their eternal rest. For their own sakes, I think I hope *not*, as it seems inconsistent with the notion of the peace and repose to which we all look forward. . . . But for ourselves it is well I think that we should live with the idea that our lives may be seen by those we loved and honoured beyond all the world, and there is something that makes life more bearable, and worth living *on*, when one can feel that. When I sit in the Grand Old Abbey, where I go nearly every Sunday afternoon, to the Service, I like to feel that his spirit *may* be somewhere near me, and I can think of him, and of God together, more peacefully and happily with that thought. . . .' But she found utterly 'degrading' any communication through paid mediums 'performing antics' with their chairs and tables. Had Charles wished to reach a friend, she maintained, 'it would be possible for him to impress himself directly *on that friend*, not on a woman on the other side of the Atlantic, who is to give the message to a slight acquaintance like Mr. Appleton, to be handed on to Mr. Forster!' Compounded of details and names appearing in published sources, the medium's story was too transparent to dupe even the most credulous person.[8] Georgina's position on spiritualism was precisely that of Dickens. 'It is not at all in accordance with my reverence for the Great Mystery of Death and the existence beyond the grave,' he had written in 1864, 'to put them [questions to the dead] myself through the interposition of any human creature.'[9]

Whether or not the 'beloved Dead' might be aware of the living, for Charles's sake Georgina would never neglect her responsibilities to his sons. Shortly after settling at Gloucester Terrace, she became increasingly occupied with their affairs. For Sydney, still hopelessly entangled in a skein of debts, she felt compassion. His bills were finally paid out of the estate, but she feared that he had already seriously damaged his professional prospects. To Ouvry, who handled his business, he wrote contritely, 'I feel exceedingly obliged to you for your advice, but no one than myself can better understand the misery of being involved in debt and difficulties'.[10] And to his Aunt Georgy he presented himself 'very miserably and remorsefully'. 'We can only hope and trust that he may take a lesson from the awful calamity which has fallen upon him,' she decided. 'It is

impossible to judge, until we see him, what reason there is for hope—
or the reverse—about him.' In December he arrived in England.
'Sydney was here yesterday evening,' she reported to her solicitor,
'in a *most* wretched state, poor boy! and full of good intentions—
which I hope and pray he may keep! He brings a good character as
a first-rate officer—from his last ship (this we have heard, *not* from
himself) which is, so far, hopeful.'[11] He was expected to remain in
England for a month or two.

From the two nephews in Australia came a request that Georgina
commission a portrait of their father as a gift for G. W. Rusden, their
Melbourne sponsor. He had been 'more than kind' in helping the
boys adjust to life in a strange country, she explained to Ouvry in
justifying the expense of the portrait, 'and their own dear Father
was deeply grateful to him, and had the highest regard and respect
for him. Therefore I think this slightest mark of gratitude from
Alfred and Plorn to him is perfectly right.'[12] This evidence of her
nephews' thoughtfulness delighted her.

But there was no concealing that Plorn gave her some anxiety.
She remembered too well how Charles, only a few weeks before his
death, had been gravely concerned over this youngest son's indifference to making a future for himself in the new country. Understandably, therefore, she searched all letters from Australia for hope that
Plorn might adjust to the life in this land of opportunity. Since he
was still a minor, his affairs required her close supervision. 'Perhaps
it would be dangerous to put him in possession of his income, before
his age,' she observed cautiously. Ouvry must realize how little the
boys were 'to be trusted with money—almost all of them'. Plorn
should, of course, have a yearly allowance; she suggested £100.
Learning later that he was in debt, for he had worked without salary
on a sheep ranch, she felt it stupid of him not to have asked for help
sooner. All the nephews were 'generally so very ready to mention
when they want money, that I thought his not applying for it was a
sure sign he did not want it!' A year later he complained that his
allowance was too small, utterly inadequate to allow him a holiday.
'I wrote him that it was his own money we were economizing for
him,' Georgina reported to Ouvry, 'and that the amount of his
allowance had been carefully considered as being surely sufficient for
his expenses in the Bush.' If he really needed more, however, he
must send her a business statement of his specific requirements, for
she could not present a vague request to Forster, her co-executor.[13]

Frank, the oldest of the four absent nephews, returned from India
in March of 1871. He had lost his stammer by now and was a handsome young officer with a golden moustache. Having been with the

Bengal Mounted Police for seven years, he looked forward to his six months' leave. But Aunt Georgy found his eagerly awaited visit somewhat disappointing. 'We don't see much of him,' she complained to Annie Fields. 'He seems affectionate and pleased to see us when we do, but I don't think he cares much about any one.' Yet there was some gratification to be derived from his enthusiasm for India. He liked his service and would be quite willing to go back, she felt.[14] A hint of unsteadiness, however, portended ill: without explanation he had failed to appear for an appointment to go over his affairs with Ouvry. 'I hope . . . that he had merely forgotten . . . ,' she wrote apologetically.[15] Before long she was to be sadly disillusioned in Frank.

But the bitterest disappointment of all was Charley. Unable to dispose of Gad's Hill, he sold the Swiss chalet for exhibition all over England and possibly in America. On reading in a newspaper that the hallowed little building had already been moved to the Crystal Palace for this purpose, Georgina became frantic. 'The notice of the chalet is too dreadful,' she exclaimed to Ouvry. And to Annie she poured out her vexation: 'I cannot imagine *how* Charley could do such an indecent action. Also, I maintain that he had no right, to do it—without consulting the family. *Legally*, of course it was his own as he bought the property—but *morally*, he had no business to compromise *us all* . . . because when this dear sacred little place where his Father spent his last living day comes to be puffed and hawked about, ALL his family will be held responsible—and will be disgraced by it.' As soon as she and her nieces could learn the name of the purchaser, they hoped to buy the chalet back, should it be within their means. If not, they would take 'steps to disavow . . . all knowledge of, and participation in, this shameful transaction'. Should Annie hear any mention of this disgraceful affair, would she rise to their defence? '*Please* speak as plainly and emphatically as you can, on the subject—for *our* sakes. Say that you *know* that to Charley Dickens *alone* belongs the discredit.' He had, Georgina added, decided to live at Gad's Hill himself. 'Of course, that is his own business and no one else's,' she admitted, adding doubtfully, 'I surely hope the experiment may be successful.'[16]

Persistently she urged Ouvry to negotiate with Charley over the fate of the chalet. She herself was so disgusted that she refused to see her nephew. She directed, further, that her will be rewritten to remove his name as one of her executors. 'I do not like the idea of having left him any right to interfere in my own small private affairs after my death,' she explained. And she reduced her legacies to his daughters from £1,000 each to £500. Herself amused by now at the frequent changes in her testament, she remarked, 'I think it appears as I was going to spend all my substance on *will making*!' As for the chalet, nothing would induce her to 'let the *matter* drop, or to be contented with anything short of a solemn assurance that the Exhibition of the place is *altogether abandoned*'. It would be most satisfactory, of course, for Charley to cancel the sale and so withdraw himself from the 'disgraceful transaction'. There could be no objection, certainly, if the chalet were sold to someone who did not intend to exhibit it. If, however, it had to be shown, Forster had suggested that it might best be sent to America. 'But *this* we would much rather not do,' Georgina insisted, 'and if we were obliged to do it, it would only be a consent accompanied with the *strongest private protest*. But to any exhibition in the United Kingdom *we will never consent at all*.'[17]

At one time the situation looked hopeless. A note from Charley's lawyer maintained that 'the contract entered into with the Crystal Palace Company must be carried out unless some satisfactory arrangement be forthwith completed'. This Georgina interpreted as a demand that the chalet be bought back for a prohibitive sum. 'It would be nonsense for Mamie and Katey and me to offer "compensation" to the amount of £1,000 ! ! ! as we could not afford it,' she exclaimed. 'I foresee no end of family misery arising from that wretched business, all for the fault of one, and the most favoured and considered one, in the will at all events, of the children! It seems very hard and cruel, and gives me such an opinion of Charley as I am sorry to be obliged to entertain of any of his Father's children.' Mamie had tried to see him at his office. Finding him out, she had left a note asking him to call on her. 'He never appeared,' Georgina told Ouvry. 'I never thought he would!' But what would have been gained by speaking to him?[18]

As for having the heirs publicly repudiate the sale of the chalet, she now realized that it would be better to let the matter rest. 'I confess I shrink from the idea of any newspaper affair,' she wrote her solicitor. 'I think that kind of scandal would be almost as irreverent as the transaction.' But she wanted it understood that 'I have no feeling about *Charley* in the matter, nor any desire to save him from the stigma which I am sure he richly deserves. *My* own feeling . . . is for the name and beloved memory which I think we should be helping to drag through the mud—if we allowed ourselves to be led into any newspaper controversy amongst ourselves before he has been dead twelve months!' But nothing should prevent their protesting privately against Charley at every opportunity.[19]

At the point of greatest frustration, negotiations took a sudden turn. 'The miserable business of the Chalet is completed—thank God!' Georgina reported to Annie Fields. 'We have carried our point, and have saved the dear little place from the profanation to which it had been destined by its owner.' The whole affair had been 'MOST painful', she declared, 'really too shameful!' Plans for exhibiting the chalet had been abandoned only because the representative of the Crystal Palace Company had pointed out that, unless it were furnished with relics, no one would pay an extra shilling to go inside when the exterior could be viewed from the grounds. 'I think *Charley* felt that it would be a little "too strong" if he undertook to put any sacred memorials inside . . . ,' Georgina concluded, 'and he agreed to accept the sum we offered.' This was £250, £200 for the chalet itself and £50 for the expense Charley had incurred in moving it to London. 'You will be glad to know that, directly our dear Harry heard of the business, he offered *at once* to pay his share,' she informed Annie. As for Frank and Sydney, they 'have no more *feeling* in the matter than Charley has'. It was hard to believe this of Frank, just home after his long absence. What a grief and shock it was, after she had eagerly looked forward to his visit! 'We thought it right, *for their own sakes*, to ask all the boys,' she explained, 'but we begged them to understand that we wanted no one to join who did not see the matter in the same light as we do. . . . It is a sad disappointment to find so *many* unworthy sons of their great Father, isn't it!'[20]

After its repurchase, the chalet was given to Lord Darnley, who accepted it with 'pride and pleasure' for his private garden at Cobham, where it would 'be held sacred, and not exposed to being scribbled over, according to the custom of the British Public, as it would be, if it were placed in an open part of the Park'. Georgina felt that, next to Gad's Hill, there could be no spot more appropriate than Cobham, which Charles had 'loved and haunted so much, and where he took his last walk, the day before he was stricken with death'.[21]

In due time she had an answer from the Australian boys to her letter about the chalet. 'They both say *just what they ought to say* about it—and are most willing to join us in the expense of the redemption of the poor little place', she wrote Annie. 'You may imagine that this is worth much more than the money to us, although the money help is acceptable, too. It is a comfort that *three* of the six boys share our feeling, and have a proper respect and veneration for their Father's memory.'[22] In gratitude to these three nephews Georgina changed her will again. She instructed Ouvry to add a statement that 'in consequence of the sale and re-purchase of the Swiss Chalet in April 1871' she revoked her bequest of £200 to each of the six sons of Dickens and left £400 instead to Alfred, Harry, and Plorn. She also willed the manuscript of *The Cricket on the Hearth* to Harry, 'as Mr. Forster has . . . begged me to revoke the sentence in my will which turns it back to him or his Executors'. Realizing that technicalities would necessarily delay the Australians' contribution to the chalet fund, Georgina made herself responsible for their sum. '*I have the money ready for you* and shall be most glad to pay it, and have it done with,' she notified Ouvry. 'As I have calculated, our respective share will be £41. 13*s*. 6*d*.'[23]

Unfeeling though Charley appeared in this chalet affair, his financial position makes his conduct understandable. To raise the purchase price of Gad's Hill, he had mortgaged the place for £5,000 and added another £3,000 from his share of the estate.[24] Burdened with the support of a large family, forced to maintain a costly house, and faced with diminishing income from a journal that had once flourished because of his father's prestige, he stood on perilous ground. In addition, he had found it necessary to buy out Wills's one-eighth share in *All the Year Round*. There had been an altercation, Charley insisting on a dual salary as editor and sub-editor, since he was now in sole charge. He stipulated, furthermore, that no dividend would be paid unless this salary (£924) had first been met. Wills objected strenuously. 'This,' he fumed, 'after my having presented him, through his father, with £600 a year when he was a bankrupt and out of employment!' Regretfully, because he found it 'not convenient . . . under the circumstances', Charley paid the £500 asked for Wills's one-eighth interest and became, in January of 1871, the sole proprietor of the journal as the 'best way to settle the question without further trouble'.[25] It was under this pressure that the chalet was sold two months later.

Concurrently with the chalet transaction Georgina was occupied with another family affair. This stemmed from her affection for Charles's sister Letitia Austin. A widow with only the small pension Dickens had obtained for her, she was forced to live frugally. Georgina, in one of her numerous will changes, had bequeathed Letitia £250, at the same time remarking to Ouvry: 'Mrs. Austin is *very much* my senior, and is not in the best of health. Therefore in all human probability I shall survive her. . . . But who can tell! I might die any day, although I am strong and she is weak.' A few days later she persuaded her nieces and nephews to a scheme for helping their Aunt Letitia. A contribution of £125 from each one was agreed upon. 'It is very much on my mind that the children should carry out their intention of giving their Aunt the sum of money as soon as they can,' she wrote to Ouvry in urging action.

'For I feel so keenly that the omission of his only sister's name in his
will is the *one action* of his life which I *think unjust*—and unthought-
ful on the part of my dearest Charles—especially as I know he had a
great respect and regard for her—and that she was the one member
of his family who had never asked for anything of him, nor had any
substantial help from him during his life. I can only account for the
omission of any provision for her by his never taking into account
that she should survive him.'[26]

The scheme was complicated by Plorn's being a minor. But surely,
Georgina argued, she and Forster could legally pay his share from
the estate or make some provision so that Mrs. Austin need not wait
two years for his contribution. If necessary, she would make herself
responsible for his share. Apparently, though, she was not required
to do so. Triumphantly she wrote Ouvry: 'After all, it seems I was
not so *very* wrong in my suggestion that the money could be taken
by some arrangement being made by me and Mr. Forster! But you
snubbed me in such a severe manner for making that suggestion that
I thought there could be no way out of the difficulty except my
lending the money for two years.'[27]

Before the matter was finally settled, however, she was again disappointed in one of her nephews. Through his lawyers Sydney indicated that he was 'not disposed at present to place this sum in the
hands of Mrs. Austin' and requested that the cheque for £125 be
forwarded to him. 'It *is* too disgusting,' Auntie exploded. 'I have
no words to express what I think. . . .' But she had the satisfaction
of seeing six of the children make their contributions. 'What a bore
business is!' exclaimed Katey in empowering Ouvry to handle her
contribution. 'Of course I sanction everything that you have done
with regard to Aunt Letitia.' To which her husband appended a
note: 'I sanction too and *don't* consider business a bore!'[28]

As for Sydney, he would not disappoint his Aunt Georgy again.
Within the year the family received word that he had died on
2 May 1872 aboard the *Malta* on his way home for sick leave. Only
twenty-five, he had succumbed to bronchitis, to which he was subject. He was buried at sea, according to the doctor in attendance,
'with all the honours due to him, not only as an officer in the Service
—but also as being the Son of one of the most distinguished men
in England'. Georgina was grateful that Dickens had been spared
this shock. In her letter to Annie she recalled that 'poor Sydney's
life was his Father's most bitter trial and grief for several years
before his death—and I fear we *must* feel that his being taken away
early is the most merciful thing that could have happened to him,
but it is very, very sad to have to feel this'. She would always

believe that this nephew's deterioration was somehow connected
with a hard fall on board ship during his first cruise. A brain con-
cussion, followed by African fever, must have affected him both
mentally and physically. 'Well, he is gone, taken away, in his youth
from further folly and *certain misery*,' she observed philosophically,
'and is more mercifully and tolerantly judged now, than he could
ever have been by his fellow creatures, and I am thankful he is at
rest. Peace be with him.'[29]

She could think tenderly of him now. Because of his diminutive
size, the young officer had often aroused an amused protectiveness.
She recalled how Leech, who usually took the boy to dine at the
Garrick Club after each cruise, had once professed himself horrified
at the sight of little Sydney eating his dinner with the huge silver
knife provided. Leech had remonstrated with the waiter, demanding
smaller knives, 'after which, he and the officer messed with great
satisfaction, and agreed that things in general were running too large
in England'.[30] And her memories went back to the child at Broadstairs
who had always cast a far-away look at the ocean. Was it not sad
and curious, she pondered, that he should now be buried at sea?[31]

His death had come as a great shock to his mother, who, without
any preparation, had learned of it from the captain's letter. Sydney
was a favourite of hers and had often been with her during his
leaves in recent years. Immediately after getting the news, Georgina
and the girls had gone to comfort her. On learning this, Annie
Fields could not refrain from comment. Her curiosity brought a
prompt and forthright response. 'As to my sister, it is a subject I
don't want ever to say much upon,' Georgina stated, 'but I hate all
false pretences so I must just, *once and for all*, make a remark upon
that allusion . . . in your letter.' It was not the first time, she
assured Annie, that they had seen Catherine. They had been visiting
her occasionally ever since Dickens's death. 'She comes to dine with
us, and we go to her, from time to time. I cannot say we get much
pleasure out of it, but it is better it should be so,' Georgina admitted,
adding that she and the girls always stood by to help in any emergency or sickness. As to the present sorrow, Catherine had felt it 'as
much as she can feel anything, but she is a very curious person—
unlike anyone else in the world'. Annie probably would not understand: 'Naturally, as you don't know her. Therefore I should feel
myself to be hypocritical if I did not say these few words. We dined
with her on Saturday. She was very well, and seemed to be in very
good spirits again.'[32]

What a contrast between Sydney's sad history and Harry's record
of achievements! Time and again Georgina applauded the triumphs

of her favourite nephew. 'He is so bright and pleasant and sensible, and feeling besides,' she told Annie, 'that he cheers us up and comforts us greatly.' During his last year at Cambridge he worked harder than ever. It was hoped that he might fulfil his father's expectations and win a fellowship when he took a degree early in 1872. Harry himself, though, begged Aunt Georgy and Mamie not to be 'too sanguine' over his prospects, for it was a good year at Trinity Hall, with many industrious and clever men in the competition. 'But at any rate,' Auntie decided, 'I think from what we hear of him, we may feel pretty confident now that he will take a good and honourable degree, and finish his college career with credit to himself—and to his name. He is doing his *very best*, I am certain, and the best can do no more.'[33]

When the London *Times* announced the results of the examination, Georgina promptly sent the information on to Annie: 'Harry is the 29th *Wrangler*—a most excellent and honourable degree'. Though he had not won the fellowship—he had to be among the first twenty for that—she was entirely satisfied and felt certain that 'his dear Father could have been quite contented and pleased with him'. Harry himself was somewhat disappointed, but she maintained that those who knew the circumstances expressed only 'pride and pleasure' in his record. What with the unusual competition, he had come out with the 'greatest credit and honour'. After a three-month tour of Italy and Germany he would make his home with her and Mamie while pursuing his law studies at the Inner Temple. 'I am sure you would like him,' Georgina told Annie. 'And I think he would remind you of his dear Father—*in manner*, especially. I see that more and more as he gets older. I don't think he is like in the face, but he has a carriage of his *head*—and a quick turn of it—which sometimes strikes me as being *very* like. He has a most intense veneration for his Father, and love for his memory, I am thankful to say, which I hope will be a blessed influence to him through his life, and a stimulus to working on steadily to do credit to his name.'[34]

Georgina was also much interested in Katey and her painting. Now working with models, her niece had improved so much that Millais had encouraged her to enter the Winter Exhibition of the Water Colour Dudley Gallery in Piccadilly. Her picture, 'Song without Words', had been accepted. A study of a single figure seated at the piano, the painting displayed skilful drawing and 'a good deal of sentiment'.[35] But the happiness in this achievement was dimmed by the failing health of Charles Collins. Since Dickens's death he had grown steadily worse and was often in great pain. 'His is a sad

existence!' Georgina lamented to Annie in 1871. The following year
he seemed to be 'better and worse alternately'. His behaviour, too,
became rather trying. Katey, her finances improved through her
legacy, had finally persuaded him to rent a larger house in a pleasant
neighbourhood. But, after the workmen had gone in and she had
furnished a top room as her studio, he had suddenly insisted that he
could not bear the thought of moving, and had halted all preparations. 'And so he goes on,' complained Georgina. 'He won't make
up his mind either to live in it, or to give it up! . . . In the meantime they are paying *two* rents, and taxes, the most unsatisfactory
of all ways of spending money, I think.' Through all this Katey
had 'behaved quite *admirably*', though their small abode was highly
undesirable for 'two such delicate people', since they had to live in
London the year round now and had 'no country home always open
to them as she had in her dear Father's life time. She won't let us
go and *shake* C.C.! which we would like to do—morally at all events
—and I should like some one to do it bodily, too!' Allowances must
be made for his poor health, Georgina admitted, but in this instance
he had certainly exceeded the bounds of forbearance. The unsatisfactory state of affairs continued. 'They still have the *two* houses on
their hands!' she exclaimed four months later. How exasperating
Collins could be! He had even turned down two or three offers for
the second place.[36]

But on 9 April 1873 the sore trial ended. 'Poor Charley Collins
is dead,' Georgina wrote Annie. During his last days his condition
had suddenly entered a new stage, enabling the doctors to diagnose
as malignant ulcers of the stomach an illness that had long puzzled
them. Suffering intense pain for many hours, he had at last fallen
into a short sleep and died peacefully. He was only forty-nine. For-
given, now, were his shortcomings. 'Poor Charley Collins! it is very,
very sad to think what a suffering life he must have had even more
than we supposed, for many, many years,' reflected Georgina. 'And
certainly the gentleness and patience with which he bore his bodily
suffering were most admirable.' Condoning his recent 'gloom and
indecision about everything', she held the opinion that his mind as
well as his body must have been affected. 'Poor fellow! No one who
knows him can feel anything but that he is mercifully released from
a sad suffering life.'[37]

For Katey the last ten years had been a 'weary existence'. At the
end she had gone through 'the great trial, very bravely', refusing
help and staying at her husband's bedside four days and nights.
Quite exhausted from sleeplessness and 'brought down to a shadow',
she was in the country now, the doctor having ordered complete

rest. She felt the loss of her husband '*very* sincerely', according to her aunt, 'and fully appreciates the great love he had for her— although it was shown in a very trying manner, of late years, poor fellow!' But Katey was still young and would doubtless 'begin life again and make fresh interests and ties for herself'. More than ever, she was determined to work hard at her painting, 'a great resource to her'.[38]

Interspersed with the accounts of Charles Collins's last months was more pleasant news: Alfred, the older of the Australian boys, had been married early in 1873. For this nephew Georgina felt a particular regard because he had thoughtfully inquired of Ouvry whether she and Mamie might not welcome some financial aid from his share of the estate. Though she had declined the proffered help, replying that she had 'no need, thank God!' she was, nevertheless, deeply touched by his consideration. 'I can't help remarking,' she had told Ouvry, 'that he is the only one (except Harry) to whom it seems to have occurred that Mamie and I have had some little difficulty to go through in making our great change.'[39] And now he had married the belle of Melbourne, Jessie Devlin, a captain's daughter. 'We know all about the young lady—as she is a connection of some kind neighbours of ours at Gad's Hill,' Georgina informed Annie. 'So it is all right in *that* way. Alfred of course says she is "beautiful and accomplished" and we hear, from other sources, that she is a very nice pretty girl who is likely to make him a good wife. . . . And it is a great comfort to us to think that as he is obliged to pass so much of his life in that distant colony he should be going to make a *home* there, to take away the feeling of exile which one cannot [help] having for young men who have to work so far from home.' Barely twenty-eight, Alfred was doing 'extremely well in the money way' with the London and Australian Agency Corporation Limited, so that there was certainly nothing 'improvident in his taking this important step in life'. Mamie's 'nice letter from her new sister-in-law' strengthened the conviction that his marriage was 'the greatest blessing to *both*' and that the bride, whose photograph showed her to be 'very good and pretty', must be a 'perfectly nice, unaffected girl'. For Plorn, too, the new domestic arrangement would be a good thing, in giving him a home to visit. Auntie was grateful that he had finally decided to make a career for himself in Australia.[40]

*   *   *

Every summer Georgina pined for the country. For her part she would have preferred to live there all year round, though for Mamie's sake she supposed 'it would not have been wise . . . to have made a home anywhere but in London'. But when the August heat came during their first summer in town, her niece drooped. 'She never knew what it was *in her whole life before*, to stay in this large hot city after the pleasant cheery time is over. . . .' Unable to get away from what Dickens had always called 'the great oven', Georgina dreamed of walking in Kentish lanes with the cool breath from fresh green fields upon her. She sadly missed her accustomed exercise. 'I have quite lost my walking powers,' she was to complain a few years later. But with the expense of the new home and the repurchase of the chalet, even a simple rural cottage was beyond their means that first summer.[41] In 1872, though, they got away for a time through the kindness of Ouvry, who offered them his cottage at Maidenhead.[42] The next year they spent most of the summer with Katey, who had a great deal of business to see to after her husband's death. Once she had disposed of her two houses and put her furniture in storage, only a brief holiday was possible, for which they chose Ramsgate, near Broadstairs. What memories the old seaside home recalled when Georgina visited it again! 'The last time we were there, I was a young girl, and Mamie a child,' she wrote to Annie. 'It seemed so strange and sad to see everything exactly the same—and to feel myself so utterly different. . . . The first time it made me so wretched I could hardly bear it. Every house, every stone in the place, seemed to be so vividly associated with Charles, and with all my youthful days of carelessness and happiness, that a succession of ghosts seemed to rise up in the paths as we walked about the place.'[43]

*   *   *

As Georgina had foretold at the time of Charles Collins's death, Katey was young enough to begin life again. Through her art circle she met Carlo Perugini, a rising young painter of her own age, and within the year was betrothed to him. Italian by birth, he was a naturalized citizen and, according to Georgina, spoke English 'as well as we do'. Though the family had known for some time of her engagement, Katey permitted no announcement until after the anniversary of Collins's death. In breaking the news to Annie, Georgina characterized Perugini as 'a most sensible, good, honourable and upright man, and *devotedly* attached to Katey. Every one likes him —he is so *perfectly* unaffected, simple and straightforward.' He would be 'a good and tender guardian' of his bride's 'future life and happiness'. Though he had only what he made by his art, his pictures sold well. 'I hope she is going to begin to get some happiness out of her new life,' continued her aunt fervently. 'Poor girl! she had many dreary years in her youth, in her first married life!'[44]

Katey and Carlo were quietly married at St. Paul's Church, in Wilton Place, London, on 4 June 1874.[45] 'We would not have it in the *second* week, of course,' declared Georgina, for whom nothing must conflict with the sacred anniversary of Dickens's death. Besides Mamie and Aunt Georgy, only Frank, Harry, and Millais attended the ceremony. Radiant in 'the very palest grey silk with some beautiful lace on it, and a pretty little bouquet to match it with a long white spotted veil', Katey looked so 'young and bright and happy' that it was impossible to think of her as having been married before—nearly fourteen years earlier. Since Charley Dickens was out of town and had received too late the invitation which pursued him, Frank gave the bride away. Afterwards the small group, augmented by Forster and Ouvry, gathered at Gloucester Terrace, where Mamie had 'charmingly' decorated the rooms 'with quantities of white flowers everywhere'. After the festive breakfast, which featured 'a pretty wedding cake on the Table', the bride packed and wrote a few notes while the groom transacted business with Ouvry, who had brought some settlements to sign. Carlo behaved handsomely, Georgina thought, in insisting that Katey's money be set aside for her own use and for their children. Later in the afternoon the bridal couple visited the grave in the Abbey, dined with Carlo's parents, and left for their honeymoon in Paris.[46]

For the second time Catherine Dickens was not present at her daughter's marriage nor at the subsequent breakfast. In her letter to Plorn she gave the odd excuse that Katey had wished the ceremony to be quite private and that her own presence would have made it necessary to add the groom's parents to the guest list. Katey had sent her a note, however, and with this Catherine professed herself satisfied.[47]

During this happy turn in her niece's life Georgina thought constantly of Dickens. 'This marriage of Katey's would have been a great comfort to him,' she told Annie. 'For many years he had been much concerned and troubled about the dreary unfortunate fate of his bright handsome younger daughter and he had been especially occupied in mind about her—and had been speaking of her a good deal the two or three last days of his life. This blessed change in her existence would have greatly eased and brightened *him*, I know— and he would have much liked her Husband who would I know have appreciated and loved *him*.' What a pity that he had never met Carlo, who had an 'intense veneration and love for his memory, although he never even *saw* him'! She felt certain that Katey would

N

often talk about her father and was perhaps even now, 'in the midst of all this new happiness', thinking of 'that awful day and night when we three watched him dying'.[48]

While the Peruginis were still abroad, the Fieldses' wedding gift arrived, a signed photograph of a painting by their friend William Morris Hunt, the American artist. 'What a charming picture!' exclaimed Georgina in her note to Annie. 'I cannot tell you how much I like it. I have been obliged to *sit and look* at the sweet graceful girl figure—and it is so beautifully framed, too.' It would make a 'delightful remembrance' to hang in the couple's 'new *artist* home'. Katey was sure to be pleased and, on her return, would tell Annie so. But as the weeks passed without any expression of thanks, Georgina explained apologetically, 'She has so many letters she *must* write—that she is putting off writing *any*, I think. But she is none the less grateful to her friends.' Auntie's own enthusiasm over the picture seemed somewhat more restrained than in her earlier letter: 'It is a very nice one; of course the idea is not quite original, but it is very sweet.' Finally, after four months, the situation had become embarrassing: 'Katey is a very naughty girl not to have written to you, and I have not a word to say on her behalf! The only thing to be said is that I think she has behaved equally ill to every one she knows, almost.'[49] (It is interesting to speculate on the reaction of two artists to a framed picture not of their choosing. Writing an enthusiastic note of thanks may have posed some difficulty.)

As Georgina rejoiced over the happiness of the newlyweds, a happiness reflected both in Katey's remarkable improvement as an artist and in her appearance—she looked 'ten years younger'—there was, again, the old wish that Mamie, too, might still enjoy a full, rich life. Earlier, on receiving Annie's announcement of Mabel Lowell's marriage, Georgina had replied feelingly, 'I wish, oh *how* I wish! that I were likely to have similar news to send you of *my* girl, but alas! I begin to give up hope of that'. Now, seeing Katey blossoming, she declared once more, 'I wish Mamie would make such happiness for herself! although I would miss her sadly, still it would make her happier if she *filled up her life* as she ought to have done. She would be such a good wife and mother! But I fear she is not likely now, to marry.'[50]

In the ensuing months Georgina was again distressed about her older niece—not only because of Mamie's rather delicate health, but also because of her extravagant grief over the death of her aged pet. After ailing for several years, Mrs. Bouncer had died within three months of her fifteenth birthday. How dreadfully Mamie missed

her loyal companion! And Georgina herself mourned for Bouncer.
'It was not only the death of the little creature,' she explained to
Annie. 'It was quite extraordinary how it stirred up and re-
awakened *the* grief and sense of loss which is always present.' She
recalled how 'very, very kind and sweet to her' Charles had been.
On the day of Mrs. Bouncer's death she and her niece had both
remarked how sad he would have been to see the 'little favourite
lying, as she did, so meekly dying on Mamie's bed, all those hours!
and the little dog was so connected with all the eventful years of
our later lives—all the joys and sorrows—and with the deepest
sorrow of all—and so associated *especially* with dear Gad's Hill
where she used to trot about like a little white shadow after Mamie,
and walked in the lanes with her dear Master and the big dogs! You
cannot imagine how it all came back as we sat and watched by the
little patient grateful creature!' Mamie had padded a box with the
old cloak and shawl kept for Bouncer's bedding, and had placed
the tiny body inside with some flowers. A kind Gad's Hill neighbour
had given her a grave in the prettiest part of his shrubbery. The
spot was soon marked by a stone with Mamie's inscription:

> *This is the Grave of*
> *Mrs. Bouncer*
> *The Best, the most loving, the most faithful*
> *of little Dogs.*
> *Her happy life was passed with the*
> *exception of the last 4 years of it*
> *at her home*
> *Gad's Hill Place*
> *Higham*
> *By Rochester.*
> *She was born 5th November 1859*
> *and died 9th August 1874.*[51]

It was painful to see Mamie fretting 'about her little companion—
she had made such an occupation of her for years'. But Georgina
tried to take no notice, explaining to Annie: 'I did *fully* sympathize
at first, and perfectly understood how much more than the usual
loss of a *dog* the death of little Bouncer was to Mamie, but I cannot
go beyond a *certain amount* of sympathy for grief over the death of
an animal, and I *have* expressed all I have to express on the subject'.
She was glad that her niece did not intend to have another dog.[52]

Percy Fitzgerald, married now and long removed from the ranks
of possible suitors, composed twelve stanzas, more light than elegiac
in tone, celebrating the charms of 'Miss Dickens' Pomeranian',

whose 'ears seemed lined with crinoline'. Only the final triplet referred to Mrs. Bouncer's demise:

> *Alas, so furry, warm, and white,*
> *From this cold world she took her flight,*
> *No more on rug, by fireside bright,*
> *Dear Bouncer sits.*[53]

Along with her concern over Mamie's health and spirits, Georgina had yet another worry—the utter ruin, financial and professional, to which Frank was recklessly drifting. Having overstayed his leave in 1871 from the Bengal Constabulary Force, where he had an excellent seven-year record, he had finally given up his appointment. A disastrous speculation in indigo lost him a large part of his patrimony; the rest he squandered. His aunt reported the situation to Ouvry: 'I know very little of Frank—and all that I know is most sad and hopeless. . . . What he intends to do, I have not the faintest idea. It seems of no use making any effort to help him. Both his sisters have tried and so have I to put him in the way of getting employment—but it is in vain. He has appointments made for him with men who seem likely and willing to be of use to him—and he does not keep them. So it all ends in his giving offence—and bringing discredit on those who endeavour to do him good. I think he is mad—I really do.' Penniless, he disappeared.[54]

After a search of some months Georgina and Mamie located him, 'very miserable and very penitent and anxious to do *any* work to begin *life* again'. Mamie appealed to a few of her father's friends for help. To George W. Childs, the Philadelphia publisher who had visited Gad's Hill in 1868, she wrote that her brother had never asked Dickens for a penny or given him any anxiety after leaving for India. Even now, though he had squandered his own money foolishly, he had taken nothing that did not belong to him. 'He is now thirty—clever, well educated, a gentleman,' she pointed out. 'He is fully alive to his folly . . . & is sincerely grieved & ashamed to have come to us for help.' Mamie felt certain that Childs would do whatever he could to find her brother a situation.[55]

A similar appeal to Lord Dufferin, the Governor-General of Canada, secured Frank an appointment in the Northwest Mounted Police, a post congenial to him, as he liked outdoor work. Georgina sent Annie a report on the generosity of Mamie, Katey, Harry, and the two Australian boys in advancing the capital to start Frank *'fully* and as a gentleman' on his new life. Katey's new husband, too, had been exceedingly kind and helpful: 'He represented what the elder brother *should* have been in the matter, for Charley stood aloof, and declined to help in *any* way, either with money, or advice or trouble of any sort'. Georgina firmly believed that Frank would repay his brothers and sisters every penny. 'I daresay it will be *long before he* can send even the first instalment,' she admitted, 'but that does not matter, so long as he does it *when he can.*' In October 1874 he sailed for Quebec. 'Poor fellow! the parting was a sad one,' his aunt told Annie. 'We all went to see him off at the station. Harry went with him to Liverpool, and said he was very much "cut up" at last—but he was *most* anxious and thankful to go.' Georgina herself was hardly less thankful. 'I cannot tell you what a relief it is to have got this place for him.'[56]

Absorbed in the complex affairs of her nieces and nephews, she no longer dwelt on the bitterness of her sorrow. (One of the outward symbols, the black-bordered writing paper, she had dropped in the autumn of 1872.)[57] But the sense of loss she kept alive. 'Nothing will ever fill up that empty place,' she insisted. 'Nor will life ever again have any *real* interest for me.' The past held the only meaningful happiness, and this the years could not take from her. Each anniversary of Dickens's birth and death, each Christmas season, each family event brought its flood of memories—too poignant at first, but mellow and tender in later years. At such times she admitted Mrs. Fields to the privacy of her deepest emotions. For more than any other friend, Annie had also come under Charles's magnetic spell and would understand. That she did so was shown by the sympathetic timing of her letters by the three anniversaries: Dickens's birthday, the day of his death, and Christmas.

'How strange it is that in such a grief as ours, any *one day* should seem more melancholy than another!' observed Georgina in answer to her friend's first birthday letter. 'And yet it certainly is the case with a Birthday. . . . It shows how our lives are made up of association and imagination.' Did Charles know that he was 'held in such tender remembrance' by those he had left behind? Here Georgina had mixed feelings, 'because if he knows things that would please him, there must be knowledge of *pain,* too, and it is inconsistent with the hope of *perfect peace,* which is *my* great hope of hereafter, that there should be any knowledge of trouble. However! the comfort is, the conviction that it is *all right,* however it may be, and that if he does see and knows everything of what he has left behind him, it is with such a different knowledge! and such a purified sense of the insignificance of all mortal things, that his peace cannot be troubled by any of them.'[58]

In answering the first of the punctual letters timed to arrive by 9th June, she could not help recalling the Fieldses' visit as among the 'last *happy* days' of her life. But Annie must not think her 'gloomy or morbid'. 'Indeed I am not—I am quite cheerful now—and can be *contented* and am willing to take a sort of passive pleasure out of life—but *happiness* is over for ever.' She was thankful, though, for her creed of the 'eternity and immutability of love'. Were it not for 'that belief, and the *certainty* that our Beloved Dead are safe and blessed, life would be a poor business indeed!'[59]

And it was good to know that among the living, Charles would never be forgotten. Was not his stone in the Abbey annually covered with tributes from those who 'kept green' his beloved memory? Besides the two wreaths that Mamie placed on his grave each 9th June—one bright and cheerful, the other made up entirely of white flowers sent by some kind neighbours at Gad's Hill—there were always many bouquets, chiefly roses, all brought by different hands. Georgina liked to think that the little bunch of 'common looking flowers', laid on a corner of the tomb, came from some poor person. 'I hope I may never live to see that stone *without* flowers!' she declared fervently. On this 'saddest of days' she liked to sit in the grand old Abbey, 'so cool and *calm*', and thank God that Charles had found 'everlasting peace and rest!' He had been spared 'decay of mind and body—for that I thank God every day and hour'. To growing old, that 'hardest part of life', he could never have resigned himself.[60]

Of the three special days Georgina found Christmas the most painful—at least in the early years of her bereavement. So completely had Charles dominated the holiday preparations and festivities in his household, so inseparably had he always been a part of any year-end celebration that December gaiety now without him would be mockery. She was always glad to see the '*sad* merry season' end. 'It can never be anything but a sad anniversary now,' she maintained, 'but I hope I shall never allow myself to let it be a gloomy one—in my own spirit, I mean.' On Christmas Day she liked to be alone. One year she meditated for an hour or two in the vast silence of the Abbey, where the grave in Poets' Corner was appropriately decked. In the evening she had a favourite book by her fireside. 'This is really the way I believe I would always prefer now, to spend the day, whose gay associations are all *buried*. But like all the other memories which hang over that grave, they are all tender, beautiful, and full of hope, and I would not *forget* anything if I could.' For Mamie and Harry, though, the season should be cheerful. She encouraged them to leave town for the holidays and to enjoy a festive Christmas dinner with their friends.[61]

Even more vividly than the anniversaries did Forster's *Life of*

Charles Dickens recall the past. As one by one the three volumes
made their appearance from 1872 to 1874, Georgina felt the 'skin of
the old wound . . . perpetually torn off'. Yet she admitted that such
a work on a major novelist had to be written; and Forster, because of
his material, knowledge, and power, was the only person qualified
to do it. She was pleased to have him read some of the chapters to her
and Mamie as he wrote. After the first volume was out, she characterized it as 'delicately, skilfully, and lovingly done'. But the publicity it received was 'agonizing'. Because Dickens had died while
still comparatively young, his biography had to appear while 'so
many people are living to whom all these private details of his life,
which must be told, are so sacred, and so painful to have made
public property'. She would be grateful when the book was completed, 'the painful record made, and become History, and all the
the newspaper criticism and hard *unloving* comments . . . over'. Not
that she ever read the reviews. Against that she had determined
from the first. All the same, she knew that the comment was there.
'Well, it is a tribute, in a way, and we must bear it,' she agreed,
'remembering . . . that he belonged to the whole world, as well as to
us, and that every one is entitled to speak of him as they please.
The comfort is that though there will always be *some* to detract and
to find unloving faults, I am sure the *many* will always love and bless
his memory.' The second volume, with its vivid account of the
happy times in Italy and Switzerland, brought her girlhood into
such sharp focus that 'I seemed to awake from a dream to the
reality of present things, and to a great *blank* when I closed the
book'.[62]

The most difficult volume, Georgina realized, had still to be
written. But Forster had 'such a love for the subject, and a desire
to present him in the most noble light to the Public, and yet with
such a consideration for the feelings of living people too' that it
would be 'ungenerous' not to trust in his treatment of the separation. There would, of course, be disappointed readers because the
book would give '*no gratification to scandalous curiosity*'. Having
discussed the matter with Forster, she knew that he would be 'wise
and judicious' in handling the domestic rift. 'What I feel to be *hard*
is that proper justice cannot be done to Charles,' she complained,
'while it is imperative (as, of course it is in her life time) to give no
picture of his wife, and to make no comment on the peculiarities of
her character, which, if they could be fairly set against *his* would I
think require no comment, and would be an explanation for a great
deal. But alas! every body—except Him—is living, and therefore
this is impossible—and as little must be said as possible, and that

is all. I am always anxious and unhappy about the whole thing, and shall be *wonderfully* relieved and thankful when the volume is out, and the "Nine days" talk, over. Everything passes quickly, in these rapid days!'[63]

When the third volume of the *Life* finally appeared, Georgina was convinced that Forster had taken 'the wisest course . . . , and indeed the only course possible to him while my sister lives'. He had told 'just as much *and as little* as must be said'. Still, there were those who would like to probe 'private points' and 'would be only too glad to be able to pick a hole in that glorious mantle'. What a relief that there were no more volumes to come! Each one had been 'an annual tearing open of a wound, and a trial . . . which it is impossible to assess'. Though 'no book could do Charles justice—or could give a living picture of what he was,' this one had been 'admirably done'. Presented with 'love, *truth* and fidelity', it would be 'better appreciated and understood years hence, when we are all dead. . . .' She was thankful that Forster, ailing for some time, had lived to finish it.[64]

Georgina's admiration for the *Life* was underscored by Mrs. Fields, who, after seeing the first volume, recorded her enthusiasm in her diary: 'We hardly breathed until we had read every word. I think if people will ponder this life of Dickens they will discover a greatness in the man which they were before ignorant of. Such unending power of work, such universal care for others, such intensity of absorption in whatever was before him, has never been portrayed before. Were there a life of Wm Shakespeare we should then doubtless see a parallel experience. Both lived many years in one, and the lives of both closed before the usual number of days had passed allotted to the lives of mortal men. The fun and pathos of this book brings his dear presence back to us again with intense vividness.'[65]

But on the critical front all was not so serene. Though Georgina read none of the reviews, Forster occasionally reported the adverse comments he had seen or heard. 'I do not think he cares, at all, for the ill natured things that are said about his book,' she told Annie, adding that he had 'plenty of appreciation' from those whose judgment 'he *does* value'. It is a foregone conclusion that he would not have valued the opinion of Wilkie Collins, who had encroached in later years upon his monopoly of Dickens. That Wilkie, for his part, bestowed no praise on the work is borne out by John Bigelow's diary. During an American reading tour in 1873, when Collins visited the diplomat and 'enjoyed his dinner, but his brandy after it yet more', he spoke freely to his host about the biography. 'Forster he thinks more hipped than sick,' Bigelow noted. 'His Life of Dickens worries him because of the criticism it has provoked. He has presented the selfish aspects of Dickens' character. This seems to be in consequence of Forster's plan to give only his own letters. Collins has a great many which Forster proposed to use, if he could use them in the same way, but that did not suit Collins and he retained them. Collins says he has a letter from Dickens assigning his reasons for separating from his wife. He thinks Forster very injudicious in publishing what Dickens says about his mother, who after all, behaved quite sensibly in insisting that this boy should contribute toward the family support by sticking labels on blacking bottles so long as that was the best remunerated work he could do. Collins said he would not have published these letters.'[66]

*   *   *

Reliving the past, as she did constantly now, Georgina was chagrined at having once let trivial matters alloy her happiness at times. She should have been 'too thankful' to worry about anything. 'I suppose it is always so in life,' she wrote Annie, 'that we never appreciate *to the full* our greatest blessings and sources of happiness until they are taken away from us. However, thank God! I do not murmur now. *I am peaceful*—and cheerful—and thankful, above all, for his everlasting peace and rest.'[67]

With this philosophic calm had come some serious reflections on faith. Her belief in the hereafter strengthened through sorrow, she held firmly to her creed. 'Like you,' she observed to Mrs. Fields, 'I have been brought up—at least since I was old enough to *understand* things—in a very liberal atmosphere, with more of church influence than you, very likely, but always out of the pale of strict creeds and dogmas. I scarcely know *what* I believe! but I know I do faithfully and earnestly believe in the Almighty and in our Saviour and have a perfect faith and trust in a *Hereafter*—and in the future state being blessed and *peaceful!*' On science and religion, the subject of many a heated controversy in her time, she also spoke with conviction: 'Why Science—which simply illustrates and discovers more and more every day the beautiful sides and arrangements of all things from the *beginning*—which must be from God! should be supposed to be incompatible with belief and trust in God—is one of the things that I never can understand. But it is so—and always will be so with what are called "Church people" I imagine.'[68]

*   *   *

The Christmas season of 1875 brought a new interest to vary the pattern of holiday quiet and solitude which Georgina had established for herself. Katey was expecting a child. On 28th December Auntie took up her post at her niece's home for 'a day of miserable anxiety and *waiting*'. Katey, in her thirty-seventh year now, 'suffered very long and very much' before being delivered of 'a *splendid* Boy', Leonard Ralph Dickens Perugini, soon to be called Dickie. Mamie, for the fourth time spending the holidays with her favourite friends in Hampshire, was happily spared the strain of that day and received the news in a telegram. To Annie Fields, of course, went proud bulletins from time to time. Katey's motherhood had followed shortly the success of her two paintings at the Suffolk Street gallery: both had sold and the larger 'could have sold . . . four or five times over!' Georgina was exultant: 'I am always thinking HOW proud and pleased her Father would have been—and how delighted with Katey's little Boy!' After several months she fancied a resemblance to Charles. 'The child even now has a remarkable look of him about the eyes. I do *so* hope it will grow with him! . . . He begins to "take a great deal of notice" . . . and has always such a bright smile for Mamie and me. . . .' It was a joy to observe Katey in her devotion to him; she made a 'most excellent and practical little mother'.[69]

But all too brief was her delight. At the age of seven months Dickie died of a bowel inflammation. 'I cannot express to you what grief it is to Katey,' Georgina told Annie. 'Her love for the child was a revelation to *herself*, of a power of loving which she did not know she had in her.' The baby had been everyone's pet—a 'fine, *noble* engaging creature—with the sweetest nature—so patient in his suffering! I think he was one of those children who are not *meant* to live. He looks so pretty in Death.' Since he was to be buried at Sevenoaks in Kent, the funeral would be delayed a few days. 'Which I am sorry for,' added Georgina. 'It is such a *gloomy* time for our poor girl.'[70]

In the ensuing year Katey found her painting a blessing 'in helping her out of the desolate state of grief into which she fell after the death of her little Darling'. Her work continued popular and sold well at the exhibitions. But Aunt Georgy declared herself anxious to have the first anniversary of Dickie's death pass. At least Katey would be in the country at Sevenoaks on this occasion—'near the pretty little grave, and not in the home where the child died'.[71]

As heartening as Katey's artistic success was the start Harry had made in his profession. Called to the bar in November of 1873, he took up his work with enthusiasm. At the end of the month his Aunt Georgy reported, 'We have not seen him in his wig and gown, as he has not brought them home, but we mean to go one day to

Westminster and see him in all his glory!' Exactly twelve months later she announced proudly that he was 'really getting on *capitally*', having 'done a great deal more in his first year of practice at the Bar than is usually the case with young Barristers'. The next autumn she again wrote fondly of him as a 'bright good fellow' who always brought 'life and spirits' into her 'quiet home'. Once more she dwelt on his resemblance to his father in 'manner and carriage, and a sudden turn of his head. . . .'[72]

But in September of 1876 the happy living arrangement with her favourite nephew came to an end with his marriage to Marie Thérèse Louise Roche, granddaughter of Ignaz Moscheles, an artist and composer. 'We missed our dear bright *good* old fellow dreadfully at first,' Georgina testified some months later. 'However such partings are in the natural order of things—very different from *bereavements*, thank God! and we are reconciled to the loss of Harry by the hope that he is going to be very happy in his marriage.' Though she liked Marie and for the most part approved of the match, she recognized one drawback: the bride was a Catholic and any children would have to be brought up in their mother's faith. Recalling Dickens's repeated strictures on Roman Catholicism, Georgina declared that Harry's father would have found this a 'terrible blow'. (She seemed to ignore that Dickens had once hoped to see Mamie wedded to Percy Fitzgerald, also a Catholic.) 'But there is no help for it,' she concluded, 'so we must make the best of it.' Otherwise the marriage should work out well, she felt. Harry's professional success, together with Marie's prudent and modest start in housekeeping—there would be only one servant—promised financial stability.[73]

With Harry no longer sharing their household expenses, Georgina and Mamie were forced to leave Gloucester Terrace for a smaller home. After six years it was a great trial to break up the place to which they had become attached. While the search for new quarters went on, they lived temporarily in lodgings. 'We want to get part of a house, unfurnished, in a nice section,' Georgina explained to Annie. But everything they had looked at was either too expensive 'or very nasty!' She refused to despair, though. Something would turn up soon: 'The longer I live, the more I feel that Micawber's is the true philosophy!'[74] And in this frame of mind she continued until she found the house exactly suited to their needs.

Chapter Twelve

'THE MANY FRIENDS WHO LOVED HIM'

ON leaving Gloucester Terrace at the age of fifty, Georgina became a property owner. A search of several months having yielded no suitable home at a moderate rent, she had almost discarded her Micawber philosophy. Then 'one day a kind of inspiration came to me that I might use some of my money to buy a nice little house', she wrote Annie Fields, 'Mamie paying me half the interest of the money every year and I living rent free to represent the other half'. Ouvry heartily endorsing her plan, she finally decided on 11 Strathmore Gardens, Kensington, just below Forster's home. She considered this an ideal site and felt she had made a good investment. Another alteration in her will would leave the property to Mamie, 'if she outlives me, as I trust most fervently she will!' Should her niece marry—Auntie had not abandoned hope—the house could either be let or sold at a profit, for it was in an 'improving' neighbourhood. 'So I don't feel that I have taken at all a rash step!' she maintained.[1]

But she proceeded cautiously in concluding the transaction, for she had little confidence in the agent with whom she was dealing. 'He seems to be such a slippery individual,' she complained to Ouvry. 'However, I suppose he is not much more than the generality of his class.' In any event, she was pleased to learn that the purchase money would not be required until the first week in July, after most of her large investments had paid their dividends.[2]

While awaiting the completion of alterations before moving into the new home, Georgina quietly observed another 9th June. 'This year's anniversary . . . was wonderfully like the time seven years ago,' she told Annie. 'The weather was *so* lovely! on *the* day; and on *this* last day, it was perfect summer—so bright and hot, and yet so fresh and beautiful. Even in London everything looked so sweet and peaceful. . . . I like it best so, although the contrast was hard and sad in a way, too.' More flowers than ever had decked the grave this time. 'Thank God for it! I get every year more and more jealous of the tender *personal* remembrance of him,' she declared, '. . . as the years roll on and put him, *himself*, further and further away!'[3]

The seven years had not dimmed her interest in Charles's children. What a satisfaction to see Katey achieving new recognition! One of her pictures was not only accepted by the Royal Academy, but 'passed with Acclamations'. 'Beautifully hung on a place of honour in one of the best rooms,' it received '*universal* praise' and sold on the first day to a 'perfect stranger'. 'Ah! *how* pleased and proud her dear Father would have been!' exclaimed Georgina. 'I don't know anything that could ever have pleased him *more!*' Carlo, too, was as proud as if the success were his own. His pictures were not selling well at this time. It was a bad year for art—'war and rumours of more wars are always destructive to all peaceful pursuits', painting being a luxury which could be 'cut off with less sacrifice than any other'.[4]

There was pleasant news of Harry, too. He and Marie had a baby girl, Enid Marie, born in June. 'Harry is *very* proud and delighted with his *Daughter*—I need hardly say! It seems absurd to us that he should be a Father! He looks so very young, almost a boy still.' But there was a hint of dissatisfaction in his aunt's letter to Annie because the child had not been a son, to carry on the great name: 'It is wonderful the number of *girls* in this family! This is the *10th* grand-*daughter* of Charles's—and as yet, only the one boy, Charley Dickens' "little Charley"; Charley has *seven* daughters! Alfred in Australia has two—and now this one of Harry's!'[5] As the months passed, Georgina reported that little Enid Marie, looking at first like her mother's family, had begun to favour Katey. And Harry was getting on well professionally. 'I always feel so proud of Harry', she added. 'He is such a *worthy* representative of his Father, thank God! and is growing more like him as he gets older. His wife is very nice and good, and quite devoted to her Husband and child.'[6]

By Christmas Georgina was completely settled at 11 Strathmore Gardens. Replying to Annie's seasonal greetings, she observed, 'It is always delightful and comforting to think how many people all over the world! are thinking of what fills *our* hearts at the Christmas season.' What a deep satisfaction to have 'such loving memories' shared by Annie, who had been associated with one of Charles's last Christmases! This year Georgina had dined quietly with Katey and her husband, as had Harry and his wife. Mamie, as usual, had been in the country.[7] Her long and frequent absences were soon to become a trial.

The next memorable anniversary, 7th February, was a 'fresh Spring Day, with beautiful sunshine, and that indescribable Spring feeling—a mixture of hope and sadness—in the air. . . .' It seemed somehow appropriate, Georgina felt, that Charles's birthday should be bright and cheerful: 'He loved so much all that was bright, and fresh and *wholesome* in the world, that I have, still, a kind of superstitious feeling of joy or sorrow, according to the weather on the anniversaries of his Birth and Death'. How reassuring that thousands now thought lovingly of him on the day—many, like Annie, '*still* with real personal love'![8]

*   *   *

To all who had loved and admired Charles Dickens, Georgina was for ever bound, her devotion to them being in the ratio of theirs to him. Even casual acquaintances held her special regard if they had valued him or if he had honoured them by his esteem. Determined to overlook no one, she made it her business to send out a constant stream of greetings, commendations, congratulations, and condolences to all who had so won her favour. For many years she maintained her contacts with this circle. But long before the close of her life—she was to survive Dickens by forty-seven years—most of them had joined 'the beloved memory'.

One of the first to go was old John Poole, the playwright for whom Charles had obtained a government pension in 1850. His death brought no sorrow, for he had long lived in mean lodgings, his health broken, his mind enfeebled. Georgina could not fail to recall how it had been necessary for her to revive her brother-in-law with brandy after his visit with Poole in 1869. The old man had been 'so dirty, smelt so ill, and scratched himself so horribly', Dickens later told Wills, 'that he turned my stomach'.[9] Two years earlier, just before the American tour, Poole had entrusted Dickens with £25 for funeral expenses. This had been duly noted in the memorandum left with Wills. But after Dickens's death the money could not be accounted for. Learning that it had not been turned over to Ouvry as she had supposed, Georgina recommended that the sum be made up from the estate. 'Alas!' she added poignantly, 'to think that that wretched, useless poor old man should be the survivor. . . !'[10]

When Poole died in 1872 Charley Dickens was in charge of the funeral arrangements. Of the £25 provided, there remained a balance of £10 after all expenses were paid. This, Georgina suggested, should be used to place a small headstone on the grave in Highgate Cemetery. But even as the cost of such a marker was being investigated she made an appalling discovery. 'I cannot tell you how shocked I was—as Mr. Forster was, also, to find that Charley had put old Mr. Poole into a *common* grave!' began her letter to Ouvry. 'I feel as if we had neglected our duty in leaving the arrangement of the old

man's burial entirely to Charley, but he had been in communication
with him constantly since his Father's death, and he seemed the
natural person to do it. And who would have supposed he would
have executed, even so small a trust, in such an indecent manner!'
Every effort was made to have the body moved to another lot purchased for the purpose, but the cemetery authorities, hampered by
technicalities, could not grant the necessary permission. Feeling that
it would be still 'more indecent to make such a stir about the
matter', Georgina contented herself with seeing a stone placed on
the recently acquired plot of ground, the inscription giving Poole's
name, date of death, and age. But in an unmarked pauper's grave
rested the remains of a man whose chief concern in old age had been
to provide for his burial.[11]

Another friend whose life ended in loneliness was Henry Chorley,
the music critic. From 1854 on, when he had responded enthusias-
tically to Dickens's appeal for help in promoting a plan to pension
needy writers, he had been in close association with the family. A
frequent guest at Gad's Hill, he seldom missed the Christmas festivities there. 'I believe he loved my father better than any man in the
world,' Mamie wrote of him in later years.[12] His tribute to Dickens,
published in the *Athenaeum,* was one of the most sincere and
eloquent utterances that followed the novelist's death. Though
Georgina acknowledged Chorley's addiction to drink and admitted
that she could never care much about him—'I mean as a personal
friend'—still she did not deny him a certain regard, 'knowing his
great affection for Charles and gratitude to him'.[13]

By the terms of this old friend's will, Mamie was left an annuity
of £200 for life. Another instance of his sentiment for her and Gad's
Hill came to light upon his death: in the coffin with him lay two
dried, brown branches. These she had gathered for him, at his
request, from the two large cedars just before leaving Gad's Hill.
His wish to have the branches buried with him had apparently been
communicated to his servant.[14]

A far more personal loss to Georgina was the death of Bulwer-
Lytton. Her fondness for him had begun more than twenty years
earlier, at the time of the Knebworth dramatic festival. 'Georgina
is deeply impressed by the profundity of your occult knowledge,'
Dickens had written him about this time. 'She thinks that man . . .
who took you for a wizard knew better than we thought he did.'[15]
The Lytton personality, with its resemblances to Dickens's own, had
cast something of a spell over Georgina. She had appreciated also
the constant kindness of this old friend after Charles's death, particularly his inviting her and Mamie to escape to Knebworth during

the oppressive London summers. Her observance of Dickens's birthday in 1873 was additionally saddened, therefore, by Lytton's death early in January. Ear treatments which had considerably improved his hearing of late must have brought on the fatal brain abscess, Georgina believed. 'I sincerely loved Lord Lytton,' she mourned. 'If I had no other reason to do so, for my own sake (which indeed I had, for he shewed a never failing regard for me—from the time I first knew him when I was quite a girl to the time of his death), I should have had a grateful affection for him for the fact of his real, earnest admiration for my dearest Charles. He never had a warmer, more generous, ungrudging appreciator and admirer as an author than he had in Lord Lytton. . . .' Forster, too, she felt, had undergone a grievous shock, having given Lytton a place second only to Dickens in his heart.[16]

No such shock, certainly, was the passing of Macready three months later, for 'he just died out', after having 'been worse than dead for many years'. In the autumn of 1871 Georgina had gone to Cheltenham to spend a week with him and his young second wife, the former Cecile Spencer. At the time of their marriage in 1860 he had been sixty-seven, she thirty-four. On first meeting her, Dickens had thought her not 'half so pretty or buxom as poor Mrs. Macready dead and gone', but he had none the less made clear in his letter to Georgina that the diminutive charmer, very French in manner and appearance, had won him by her gaiety as well as by her tact and competence in dealing with her ailing husband and his rather difficult children. Her lack of stiffness and pedantry he had also thought worthy of remark.[17] (He had doubtless expected someone like her sister Lizzie, a severe dragon who had served as governess to Macready's lively daughter Benevenuta.) Georgina, only a few months older than the bride, had subsequently won her gratitude by serving as her social mentor when she was first introduced in London as the new Mrs. Macready.[18] On her return from the Macreadys in 1871, Georgina, in one of her faithful reports to Annie Fields, extolled the virtues of this 'admirable and devoted second wife. She is young enough to be his daughter, and now that he is so completely "fallen into the sere, the yellow leaf", the difference between their ages seems enormous, and hers is a trying life. But she is so fond of him, and so good to his children, and is of such a bright and cheerful spirit herself, that she makes the best of it all, and is quite an example of the bearing of such a position.'[19]

Georgina had found the aged actor 'a sad spectacle of infirmity and decay'. But an occasional spark, such as the mention of Dickens or the theatre, had fired his old vivacity and intellect at times, and he had enjoyed conversing with her. At the account of Dickens's death, however, he had shed many tears, 'such sad tears to be from so old a man'. At last he had exclaimed, 'Oh! happy, happy dearest Dickens! how much better such a death than such a life as *mine* is now!' So Georgina could feel no regret when his end came—only the melancholy that accompanied 'the breaking of another link with the past' and the thought of *'how* touched and affected dearest Charles would have been by the death of this friend than whom he had none dearer'.[20]

When Macready's reminiscences appeared two years later, she relived in them many of her own 'young—and *happiest* days'. But she questioned the wisdom of publishing the more private meditations from his voluminous diaries. The religious bits as well as the confessions of his struggles to control a furious temper had caused some readers to suspect him of cant in writing with a view to publication. Though she herself was convinced that he had set these matters down in deep sincerity, she deplored the public exhibition of a human soul. Private material 'written in confidence between the man and his own conscience', she firmly believed, 'never should be published *at all*'.[21]

Some five months after Macready had gone, the death of Sir Edwin Landseer snapped another link with the past. Once more old memories were stirred up, though Georgina admitted having regarded him as no more than 'a most agreeable and amusing man—and a charming companion'. Recalling how the artist had grieved over Dickens's death, she gave it as her opinion that 'Edwin was fonder of Charles than Charles of him'.[22]

But with Georgina such personal acquaintance was not necessary for personal interest, if only there was some Dickens connection, however remote. So it was with the novelist Charles Kingsley, in whose father's church Dickens and Catherine had been married. In the seventies Georgina sometimes went to hear the younger Kingsley preach, noting sympathetically how worn and weary he had appeared after his American trip. His death several months later at the age of fifty-six called up the inevitable comparison with her dear Charles: 'It is inscrutable and wonderful that these strong useful lives should be cut off in their maturity—and so many poor old withered branches left hanging on to the very, very last,' she meditated in a letter to Mrs. Fields, who had entertained Kingsley during his American visit. But Georgina did not question Divine Will. '. . . I think every one can find and acknowledge in the case of their own bereavement, that it was wise and well . . . that the loved one was taken,' she concluded. 'There is always much "evil

o

to come" from which one can thank God He—or She—is spared! I know it has been so in our case.'[23]

The following year, 1876, brought the death of one of the inner circle, John Forster. Having worked with him closely as co-executor, having followed with mingled eagerness and pain his preparation of the *Life*, having, in fact, turned to him in the past six years for advice on numerous personal matters, Georgina had come to regard him as a close friend. Much as she had respected his judgment, how-ever, their relationship had not been entirely free from friction. Especially at first she had now and then, like Dickens, found the manner of this 'arbitrary gent' rather irksome. On one of these occasions she had bared her annoyance in a letter to Ouvry: 'I think, between ourselves, that he sometimes forgets that any one ought to have a voice in any of the business [of the estate], except himself'.[24]

But the memory of such irritations had faded with her concern over Forster's failing health—at first because she feared that the *Life* might not be finished, later solely because of her regard for an old friend. In her letters to Annie she detailed his bouts with bronchitis, his desolation after Lytton's death, his exhaustion after Macready's funeral.[25] After he was gone she felt profoundly the dissolving of another bond with the past.

Again some of the precious relics must change hands. To Carlyle went the watch and chain which Dickens had left Forster. And to the Victoria and Albert Museum at South Kensington were sent the manuscripts of Dickens's works as well as Forster's library and art treasures. These Georgina saw displayed at the private view—'a very sad and touching Exhibition!' She was pleased, though, to find everything shown to good advantage; protected under glass, the manuscripts were secure against careless handling by the public. It was best to have them there, to be '*much* appreciated and most affectionately and eagerly looked at'. Her only regret was that Frith's 'horrible' portrait of Charles formed part of the Forster collection. Having captured the Dickens whom she refused to recognize, it was, she fumed, 'odious—vulgar and commonplace—not in the least *like* . . . and giving no idea of the character *at all*'. What a pity there was no good likeness of him in the National Portrait Gallery, which should have bought the one by Maclise rather than the Ary Scheffer portrait. She recalled the objection by the committee making the selection—that the Maclise was not like the man most people knew. That, she felt, was a 'very foolish' argument. Dickens 'had altered so much certainly in his later life', she agreed. 'But what did that signify to future ages! as it was an exact portrait of the *young* man of 25.' Forster would have bought it at one time, had he not been restrained from bidding by the definite understanding that the National Gallery intended to have it. 'It was a *Muddle* altogether,' she lamented to Annie, adding that the Maclise painting had gone to a clergyman in Suffolk.[26] In 1898, however, she was to have the satisfaction of seeing it deposited on loan in the National Portrait Gallery.

For Forster's friend Thomas Carlyle, Georgina had always shared Dickens's admiration. Early in her bereavement he had written her a letter which she valued above any other consolation received in that 'dreary time'.[27] She saw him occasionally after moving to London, once at a Christmas dinner with the Forsters in 1873—a rare exception to her custom of not dining out on that day of memories. Though three weeks past his seventy-eighth birthday, he impressed her then as 'just as clear-headed and fresh in mind altogether as ever —and with very little appearance of the infirmity of age upon him'. A few months after Forster's death she remarked, 'Dear old Mr. Carlyle is *wonderfully* well! looking strong and bright and vigorous but I suppose he cannot be expected to live *many* years more'.[28] Two years later at age eighty-two he called at her home one March day while she was out. 'I am more sorry than I can confess to find that I have missed the honour and pleasure of a visit from you,' she promptly wrote him. When the first edition of *The Letters of Charles Dickens* was issued, she presented him with a copy. 'Offered to Mr. Carlyle, with much respect and regard—and best wishes for the New Year,' read her inscription dated 1 January 1880.[29] Thirteen months later, during the week of Dickens's birthday anniversary, he died at the age of eighty-five.

To none of Dickens's friends did Georgina devote more space in her correspondence with Annie Fields than to Fechter. In spite of his muddled finances, his shabby treatment of his wife, his exasperating unreliability, both women were at first irresistibly drawn by his magnetic personality. Obviously his ardent admiration for Dickens was a further recommendation. When, within two months of his first arrival in America, he had received the cabled news of his friend's death, he had given touching evidence of his devotion by cancelling his engagements for a period of self-imposed mourning.[30] During the dismantling of Gad's Hill he had returned to England briefly and offered sympathy, but had wounded Georgina by departing without a word of farewell. 'I did expect a line from him before he sailed,' she wrote Annie.[31]

From this point his affairs, both professional and private, became chaotic and dishonourable. Though convinced that his troubles were entirely of his own making, Georgina could not at first withdraw all sympathy. 'I can never cease to take an interest in him . . . in remembrance of the strong affection my dearest Charles had for him —but I confess I am very much disappointed in him,' she told Annie in 1871. Eventually Fechter placed himself beyond all pity when he failed to deliver a letter and a parcel of Dickens relics which she had entrusted to him for his wife and children. Disturbed because there had been no acknowledgment of these remembrances, she asked Madame Fechter whether they had reached her. 'Never!!!' came the emphatic reply. Inquiry of a servant revealed that Fechter had opened the letter and parcel and had appropriated part of its contents. As a further outrage, he had left behind in his London house some of the precious objects Georgina had lovingly tendered him: 'the *cloak* . . . which Charles used to wear, and a little table ornament, and even the bit of hair!!! . . . It is a most extraordinary and dishonourable action,' she exploded, 'and I cannot forgive it.' Her message of astonished protest, sent Fechter through his daughter, went unanswered.[32]

Thereafter Georgina was coldly unsympathetic as reports of his decline reached her. And when he neglected to call on her during another visit to England, she wrote Annie, 'I cannot say I am sorry. . . . If he had come here we would have given him a very cool reception, and I would have told him the reason, we did so.' Both she and Annie had concluded by now that Fechter was no gentleman. Looking back, Georgina recollected that the defection had begun even while Dickens was alive. 'I remember the first time we were struck by a *visible* impression of his deterioration—all of us, Charles, Mamie, and I—was on the day that Fechter came to the Hotel to meet you and Mr. Fields. We had not been seeing him for some months previously, and I remember we all exclaimed about him directly he was gone, and found we had all three been shocked in the same way by a revolting change in his appearance and manner. And Charles was very much vexed about it because it was just when Fechter was deciding to go to America and he wished him to make a favourable impression on you and Mr. Fields.'[33]

Her sympathies went out to Madame Fechter: 'She is a good woman—and a good mother. If she was not a good wife, it was from some unsuitability between them—and from *no fault* of hers.' Her thoughts doubtless reverting to another domestic crisis, Georgina dismissed marital difficulties as a subject 'on which *no outsider* has ever a right to have, or to express an opinion'.[34]

Her last recorded comment on Fechter came four years before his end: 'He has made a sad muddle of his life altogether. . . . I always think how sorry Charles would have been.'[35] Alienated from his friends, dejected, miserable, the actor died virtually destitute in 1879 on his little farm in Pennsylvania.

Another of Dickens's younger friends to go on tour in America was Edmund Yates. Capitalizing on his former association with a famous novelist, he embarked on a series of literary lectures in 1872, when the great age of the lyceum was in full swing in the States. As his comments on noted writers were to be supplemented by gossipy recollections, particularly on Dickens and Thackeray, Georgina was not at all certain that his talks would be 'in good *taste*'. As for herself, she was sure she 'would rather not hear them', but she hoped Annie might like them, as Yates was 'pleasant and clever and very amusing'. Though he was admittedly 'a warm hearted good fellow', she considered him 'a *harum scarum* creature . . . , not a man to be relied upon at all', one whom Charles had 'helped . . . out of a good many scrapes into which his own rashness got him'. (Here she may have been thinking of the unhappy Garrick Club affair, which had estranged Dickens and Thackeray.) In her opinion he was 'very weak, uncertain and easily influenced'. Yet she would 'always retain a feeling of affection for any one to whom dear Charles was kind, and in whom he showed an interest'. Besides, Yates had his own good qualities; she judged 'one of his very best points to be his love for dear Charles, and gratitude to him, and appreciation of him'. After Yates's return to England Georgina received with amazement the news that his success had warranted plans for another engagement.[36]

Some years later she and Annie aired their opinion of his weekly journal, the *World*, which Georgina received regularly by courtesy of the editor. Portions of it she considered '*very* objectionable'. She disliked especially 'all that *familiar* and private gossip' (perhaps recalling again how Yates's unflattering article on Thackeray had involved Dickens in the Garrick Club affair). Yet she found many delightful things also, such as 'the *constant* quotations and allusions to his dear *great* friend'. And sometimes there were excellent articles. Mamie, for instance, had contributed one called 'Ladies under Canvas', an account of her two-week camping expedition on the Thames in the summer of 1878.[37]

American audiences saw still another of Dickens's younger friends, Wilkie Collins, who was, incidentally, also an intimate of Fechter. Georgina, herself so often an echo of her brother-in-law, had long regarded Wilkie as a feeble copy of the Inimitable.[38] Now again, hearing that Collins was about to emulate Charles by giving readings from his own books, she was all scorn: 'I cannot imagine that he is fitted for the work in any way,' she maintained, 'nor can I conceive how *his* books could bear being cut up into *portions* for Reading. They seem to me to depend so entirely upon the excitement and interest of the *whole plot*.' Still, as Annie would undoubtedly meet him if he went to America, Georgina recommended him as 'very agreeable and easy to get along with'. At the same time she could not resist a mention of his 'conceit and self-satisfaction', warning that no one 'can think Wilkie a greater man than Wilkie Collins thinks himself!'[39]

James T. Fields had already confided to Longfellow that Collins 'must be a strange fellow and I hope he won't come to America'.[40] But come he did, in September of 1873. The Fieldses met him in November. 'Our first visit with Mr. Wilkie Collins—a small man with an odd figure and forehead and shoulders much too large for the rest of him,' read Annie's diary appraisal. 'His talk was rapid and pleasant but not at all inspiring. . . . A man who has been feted and petted in London society, who has overeaten and overdrunk, has been ill, is gouty, and in short is no very wonderful specimen of a human being.'[41]

With such negative physical qualifications it is not surprising that he suffered from the rigours of the tour. 'His health is always wretched,' Georgina replied to Annie's report of his illness. But the account of his favourable reception brought disbelief: 'I cannot imagine that any reading of his would ever give me the slightest pleasure. He seems to my ideas—and from my knowledge of his *acting*—not to have any single qualification for it!' A subsequent announcement that he was concluding his tour after the sixth month did not surprise her: 'I suppose his readings have not been very successful. I never imagined it was possible they *could* be.'[42] Her judgment was borne out by the relatively small earnings from his American venture: probably no more than £2,500, as compared to Dickens's £20,000 for a similar period.[43] But she regarded Wilkie's presumption tolerantly and was later more than willing to accept his help in editing her brother-in-law's letters.

With many of Dickens's American friends she maintained contacts, especially with any who had shown particular kindness on his last visit to the States. Chief of these, of course, were the Fieldses. But she had also grown fond of Charles Eliot Norton, the editor, author, and educator whom Dickens had met through Fields. When Norton had brought his wife and five children, his mother, and his two unmarried sisters, Jane and Grace, to England in 1868, her affection had embraced the entire group. Early in 1872, during a brief residence in Germany, Mrs. Norton died following the birth of her sixth child. When the bereaved husband and his family returned to England, Georgina found them a pleasant furnished home just behind her own in Gloucester Terrace. Thereafter she and Mamie saw much of them during their year in London. 'The good sweet sisters . . . , devoted to their brother and the poor motherless children,' Georgina pronounced 'a touching sight'. So fond did she become of Grace Norton that she gave her an inkstand which had belonged to Dickens. Her December letter to Annie sympathized with the widower's loneliness: 'I am sure he feels his *first* Christmas and New Year a terrible trial. I know too well what the feeling is after such a grief.' Finding the family depressed again in February, the anniversary of Mrs. Norton's death, Georgina drew on her own experience once more: 'I do not think the freshness of grief is the hardest to bear; it is the continuance of living without *the* thing that made life interesting and *worth* living!'[44]

When the Nortons returned to America in 1873 she entrusted them with a gift for the Fieldses: 'The Photograph [of Dickens] which I have put in a little case to stand on your Table is, I think, a remarkably good one. It is so quiet, and has not the hard stern look which so many of his Photograph portraits have. But better than the Photograph you will like what I have put inside the case; if you raise the velvet at the back you will find a little lock of hair cut off after his death.'[45]

To Norton, Mamie, ten years his junior, sent a farewell letter with a similar token: 'Being a coward in the matter of saying good-bye today to you dear people, & with the remembrance of my last good-bye upon me, I have to write this line, instead of coming to see you, & send you in spirit, the same kiss as I gave you then. I also send you a Photograph of my beloved Father. At the back of the portrait you will find a lock of his hair. I cut it myself off his beautiful, dead head.'[46]

If it ever occurred to Aunt Georgy to consider Mamie as a possible candidate for stepmother to the six little Nortons, she apparently kept the thought to herself. She did not allow her interest in the family to wane, however, after their departure. Frequently she discussed them with Annie. Once she expressed concern for Norton's spiritual state. Was it true that he did not believe in the hereafter? If so, she would pity him deeply, for 'the sorrow of this world would be indeed unbearable—and without alleviation if that hope and faith did not lie beyond!'[47]

In 1877, after the death of Jane Norton, Georgina must have seen in the position of the remaining sister a parallel to her own. For Grace was now, more than ever, indispensable in the home of her brother. 'Dear Grace Norton does *indeed* live a life of utter self-devotion and self-forgetfulness,' Georgina agreed with Annie, 'and I hope and pray that she may have her reward.' Then followed a possible reflection on her own circumstances: 'But (*as a rule*) I confess I have not much faith as to the reward coming from love and devotion to *other people's children*—or indeed, *always*, from one's own. However, there is recompense to a great and sweet nature like hers in the mere fact and action of giving her love and care.'[48]

In Longfellow and Lowell Georgina also continued her interest. She looked forward to reading each new work of Longfellow's and shared his joy in his daughter Edith's marriage. With Lowell's appointment as minister to Spain she was well pleased, feeling that his sympathy for the Spanish people fitted him for that post. Several years later, when he was minister to England, she commented on his great popularity: 'I don't remember any American minister who was more liked—hardly any so much'.[49]

Less agreeable were her reflections on Henry Ward Beecher when the notorious Tilton *v.* Beecher trial aired the alleged adultery of the celebrated preacher. Like Annie, she earnestly wished to believe him innocent. Though only casual acquaintances, he and Dickens had engaged in amiable conversation in the vestry of Plymouth Church during the readings there—enough in itself to tip the scales slightly in Beecher's favour. Besides, remembering the unsavoury rumours circulated about her Charles in 1858, Georgina naturally sympathized with the accused rather than the accuser. Naturally, too, she vented her indignation against the English newspapers, which had 'taken up the matter and given publicity to all those odious details'.[50] She might have reined in her sympathies, however, had she known that the matter of Dickens's Christianity had been raised as a doubtful issue at one of Beecher's Friday evening prayer meetings.[51]

Among her women friends one or two were valued for their association with the Tavistock House days. There was particular warmth for Anne Thackeray, the novelist's daughter, who had been an occasional guest at the children's parties in the early fifties. She had married her cousin Richmond Ritchie, young enough to be her son— a 'novel venture' which Georgina pronounced 'very risky', believing 'even a *few* years disparity on the *wrong* side is dangerous—because a woman is always *older* than a man, even if they are the same age'. Still, she tried to hope that 'poor Anne' had 'made a new life for herself' to compensate for her desolation after the death of her father and her sister.[52]

But Georgina took no such tolerant view of the ill-assorted marriage

between Marian Evans and J. W. Cross in 1880. In an exclama-
tory sputter she gave Annie Fields the sensational details of the
recent match: 'London—or rather I should say *literary* London! has
been much convulsed by the extraordinary marriage of "George
Eliot" aged 62, and supposed to be quite inconsolable for the death
of G. H. Lewes, with a Mr. Cross, a stock broker, aged 35—tall, fair
and good looking, and with a special reputation for his Lawn Tennis
playing! [Rumour had exaggerated; actually, Cross was forty and
George Eliot only sixty.] Wonders *will* never cease! especially in the
matrimonial line! and they were married at St. George's Hanover
Square! all in the regular way! I should have thought, at all events,
she would have made her wedding a very quiet and retired one.
Did you ever see her? She is a singularly ugly woman—as ugly for a
woman as G. H. Lewes was, for a man. I confess I can't reconcile
myself to these violently unnatural *disparities* in marriage—especially when the disparity is on the female side.' (As James T. Fields
was seventeen years older than Annie, Georgina did well to qualify
her remarks by adding that last clause.) Compared with the Evans-
Cross match, Anne Ritchie's paled somewhat, for there the difference in ages had been only eighteen years, with the bride just forty.
'I believe she is the happiest of the happy,' Georgina reported two
and a half years after she had first felt some doubt about Anne's
marriage, 'and she has two beautiful children'.[53]

Again there was an expression of disapproval, though of a milder
sort, when Tennyson accepted a barony in 1883. Though never his
intimate friend, Dickens had always been his admirer, reading his
poems as they were published and even asking him to stand god-
father to Alfred. And Tennyson, Georgina remembered, had presented himself at the Abbey for the funeral sermon for Dickens.
'What do you think of Tennyson's peerage!' she demanded of Annie
Fields. '*I* think he was better without the title—and that, especially at his age, it is a pity he should make the change.' Then she
added indulgently, 'But I suppose his sons like it'.[54] She was probably comparing Tennyson with Dickens, who, repeatedly declaring
himself against such distinctions, had never accepted a title—
though gossip had it that Victoria had offered him one in the spring
of 1870, a rumour categorically denied by Forster.[55]

*   *   *

Georgina found a major satisfaction in continuing Dickens's bene-
factions to Anne Brown Cornelius, who was still in financial straits
because of her husband's illness. This loyal maid and she had both
entered the Dickens household in 1842 and had spent sixteen years

together in growing confidence before the separation.[56] Though Anne had been Catherine's personal maid, she had continued at Tavistock House after 1858 and had served the family intermittently thereafter. 'My dear good Anne' she had been to Dickens, who had valued and rewarded her devotion as he had that of all who adhered to him. As long as he lived he had kept the Cornelius family going. Later Georgina, Mamie, and Katey had shouldered part of the burden. But this encumbrance proving too great to be borne indefinitely, outside help was solicited. 'I am going to address you now for the first time—and I hope the *last*! in the character of a beggar!' Georgina appealed to Annie Fields in October 1871. She explained that she and Mamie hoped to get up a subscription which would assist Anne in the event that her husband did not regain his health. Meanwhile they were educating Catherine, the daughter, to be a schoolmistress. In a few years she should make substantial contributions to her parents' support. 'We do not like to leave any stone unturned on behalf of poor Anne,' Georgina wrote, 'and, after all, our friends can only *refuse*, and we shall quite understand if they do that they have *Annes* of their own whose claims must come *first*.' She and Mamie had spent three days in writing to old friends who had known Mrs. Cornelius and been served by her. Would Annie Fields give what help she could and perhaps approach Longfellow for a contribution? 'I do not like to intrude upon [him] personally,' explained Georgina.[57]

Many of the friends appealed to responded handsomely. 'You talk of your help being *"little"*!' Georgina expostulated with Annie. 'I assure you we should have thought very, very much *less* a most liberal subscription—and most acceptable addition.' She was grateful, too, for Longfellow's donation of £5. For 'her present exigencies' Mrs. Cornelius had been given over £50. But of the nearly £100 'in hand' she must not be told just yet: 'We intend to make a little investment of this sum—and have it to fall back upon when the *very* dark hour comes'.[58]

For the next few years Georgina's plan succeeded admirably. 'It is always pleasant to know that any good work you have helped in has had good results,' read her progress report. Anne had a steady income from letting lodgings; her husband was somewhat improved, though he would never be able to work again; and Catherine had just passed 'a most triumphant examination' before the government inspectors. Already on a small regular salary as pupil-teacher, having begun as a third-year student instead of a first, she would get pay increases until she was nineteen. Then, if she did well on her next government examination at a college, she would qualify at twenty-one for a school of her own. 'She is a good, industrious, clever girl, and we can consider that her career is *safe*—unless she should fall into bad health,' Georgina wrote with assurance.[59]

But in her optimism she had not reckoned with one aspect of normal girlhood. Early in 1874 the neat plans were upset. 'This morning we heard to our great surprise that the young girl, Kate Cornelius . . . is going to be married immediately,' Georgina wrote Ouvry, who had also contributed generously to the fund for Anne. 'We knew she was engaged, but she is not 18 yet and we understood that there was to be no question of marriage for two years, and we strongly advised that there should *not* be. However it seems our advice is not to be taken; and we can do no more than protest. The young man she is going to marry is steady and industrious, so I hope it will turn out well.' Since Georgina had in trust the legacy of £19. 19*s*. 0*d*. which Dickens had left the girl, she asked whether it might not be turned over at once. There would be a long wait until Catherine came of age, and the money would be well timed now for wedding expenses. This, Georgina maintained, was her own idea; she had not mentioned it to the parents or the daughter before consulting Ouvry. He agreed to the suggestion, and the young bride, happily surprised, found herself with enough cash on hand to buy her trousseau and begin housekeeping comfortably.[60]

A further opportunity to serve an old friend came in 1880, when Georgina negotiated the sale of a valuable manuscript for Amelia Fillonneau of Paris. The sister of Dickens's deceased brother-in-law Henry Austin, Mme. Fillonneau was now a widow in reduced circumstances. For thirty-four years she had kept the manuscript of the Christmas book which Dickens had given her in exchange for the manuscript of a play written in his youth. On Amelia's behalf Georgina now approached George F. Harvey, a London bookseller, for advice: 'A lady, a connection of my late Brother-in-law, Mr. Charles Dickens, to whom he gave the MS. of the "Battle of Life", has written me, today, telling me that owing to very grave pecuniary difficulties she is, reluctantly, obliged to make up her mind to try to sell the precious MS.' The owner, she continued, did not wish to part with it under £200, that being the figure for which the manuscript of *A Christmas Carol* had sold. Later Georgina assured Harvey that the treasure would be brought from Paris within the month. She vouched for its authenticity and guaranteed that no erasures had been or would be made.[61]

Meanwhile, with Harvey's approval, she also offered the manuscript to Dickens's Philadelphia friend, George W. Childs. But Childs, having recently acquired the manuscript of *Our Mutual*

Friend, was not interested. He advised her to see Scribner's London agent, who made such purchases for America. Ultimately, however, the manuscript went to Harvey, whose original bid of £100 was not exceeded by that of Scribner's agent. To Childs Georgina declared herself dissatisfied with the outcome, foreseeing that 'someone who wishes to possess the MS. as a curiosity and a relic will some day, give the dealer more for it than he gives Mme. Fillonneau.'[62] Her prediction proved correct. The manuscript was sold for £150 to William Wright of Paris, at whose sale in 1899 it went to Henry Sotheran of London for £400.[63] Today it forms part of the Dickens Collection at the Pierpont Morgan Library.

In turning over this treasure to Harvey, Georgina complied with his request for information about its history. She recalled that Dickens had always written on sheets, or 'slips' as he called them, which had gone from his hand directly to the printer. 'An average day's work with him was 2–2½ of those sides . . . of MS.,' she explained. 'A very, *very* hard day's work was 4 of them. The sheets were returned to him, with the proofs, and it was, usually, his habit to collect them and have them bound, with memoranda relating to his titles and names, etc., etc., after the publication of his books.' Having completed her part of the transaction, she could not restrain a tender recommendation: 'I hope most earnestly that you may dispose of it well—and that it may fall into good and appreciative hands.'[64] Many years later the experience gained through these negotiations was to suggest to her a more important sale which would bring another manuscript to the Pierpont Morgan Library.

*   *   *

With three women who had figured prominently in Dickens's life Georgina maintained occasional contact. Of the three—Maria Beadnell Winter, Mary Boyle, and Ellen Ternan—it was Mrs. Winter, least valued by Dickens in his later years, who was the least regarded by his sister-in-law. But when Maria died in 1886 Georgina dutifully sent condolences to her daughter Ella. 'Accept my truest sympathy, my dear Ella,' she wrote after several months' difficulty in getting the right address; 'although it is late, it is none the less heartfelt.'[65]

With Mary Boyle, Dickens's staunch defender, her relations were more personal. The two women saw each other at intervals and also kept up a correspondence. When Mary was preparing a book of reminiscences Georgina came to her aid by suggesting that Annie Fields send her some materials. Annie responded with a helpful letter and some photographs which, Georgina assured her, 'are a valuable contribution to her Book'.[66] This association continued until Mary's death in 1890.

It was Ellen Ternan whom Georgina evidently held in the warmest affection, perhaps more for what Nelly had meant to Dickens than for what he had meant to her. The friendship continued even after Ellen's marriage—Dickens had then been dead six years—to George W. Robinson, a clergyman who later became headmaster of a school in Margate. Here Georgina and Mamie occasionally visited her.[67] In turn Ellen called at Georgina's home and in the 1880's sometimes brought her daughter with her. The daughter still remembers Georgina as 'the sweet, kind old lady', one of her mother's special friends, who gave them some photographs of herself.[68] Ellen Ternan Robinson died in 1914. Though Georgina frequently rallied to defend 'the beloved memory' from one charge or another whenever by her own knowledge or belief she could honestly correct a misrepresentation, she apparently never made any statement as to what the Dickens-Ternan relationship had—or had not—been.

The attachment she displayed for women of whom Dickens had been fond—romantically or otherwise—suggests that her own devotion, though fervent to the point of obsession, partook of no jealous female possessiveness. Evidently she had always welcomed whatever service or solace any other woman offered her idol, feeling no compulsion to reserve for herself all rights to minister to him. Regardless of sex, age, or condition, 'the many friends who loved him' were for ever assured of her grateful remembrance.[69]

Chapter Thirteen
A NEW BOOK FROM THE 'DEAR DEAD HAND'

In the spring of 1878 Georgina announced a plan which had gradually taken form during the past several months. Frequently suggested by friends, though already occurring to her, it was a proposal to edit, with Mamie's collaboration, a collection of Charles's letters. The scheme may have suggested itself as early as 1871, when Fields had reproduced some of Dickens's correspondence in 'Our Whispering Gallery', then appearing in the *Atlantic Monthly*. 'The letters are —as all his letters were—charming from their reality and simplicity; they are *bits* of *himself*,' Georgina had observed at the time. 'Ah, me! What a sad dream it seems when one reads these letters—so full of life and brightness and brave enduring spirit.' Whatever its inception, the design was now sufficiently advanced to warrant publicity. 'It will be a sort of supplement to Mr. Forster's "Life," ' she explained to Mrs. Fields. '*That* was exhaustive as a *Biography*, leaving nothing to be said ever more, in my opinion. But I believe it was universally felt to be incomplete as a *Portrait*, because the scheme of the Book, as Mr. Forster wrote it, prevented his making use of any letters—or scarcely any, besides those addressed to himself.' A collection of Dickens's correspondence to numerous persons and on a variety of subjects should, then, 'supply a want', Georgina was convinced, and 'make a very charming and interesting book'. Having decided on this labour of love, she had no illusions about its difficulty. 'It will take a long time,' she admitted. 'We are rather terrified at the magnitude of the task we have undertaken but, as I feel sure it is a right and good thing for *us* to do, I hope a way will be shewn to us to do it *well*.'[1]

Undaunted by their lack of editorial experience, Georgina and Mamie began the arduous work of assembling the letters. They advertised in numerous periodicals for the originals, promising to return them with as little delay as possible, just as soon as usable extracts had been copied. Fields was asked to insert a similar announcement in American newspapers and journals.[2] There was also the tiring correspondence with many of Dickens's friends who might be willing to lend their letters. Since all this was done with no secretarial help, it is not surprising that Georgina, addressing

Charles Reade, asked him to excuse her penmanship. 'I have so much writing to do just now,' she complained, 'that my, always, illegible hand I fear must trouble my friends more than usual.'[3]

By June, three months after initiating the project, she felt as if she had been writing to every 'public character' in the world. In England the response had been tremendous, though from America, oddly enough, there had come only 'a fire of applications for Autographs!' This year, because of all the work on the letters—'so fresh and bright and full of life!'—the anniversary of Dickens's death seemed more poignant than ever. 'It is sometimes difficult even now,' Georgina wrote Annie, 'to realize that the hand that wrote them is dust! and the fresh bright heart and brain still for ever.' She found her present occupation 'deeply, intensely interesting', though 'mingled with a great deal of pain', for it meant reliving her whole life. There was also the perplexing problem of deciding what to incorporate in the edition. 'It will be heart breaking,' she remarked more than once, 'to reject any of the letters of *public* interest . . . for all are beautiful and interesting. We feel it will be terribly *our* fault, if the Book is not a very welcome and a very successful one.'[4] From their own treasured letters, available without the effort of collecting, the editors were to choose fifty-seven to Mamie and seventy-seven to Georgina, altogether comprising roughly one-sixth of the total to be published in the three volumes.

For months they copied stacks of holographs—about nine hundred by the time the third volume went to press. Even during the summer holiday the work went on, Georgina receiving and transcribing manuscripts in Devonshire during August and later at the seaside. Mamie took her share of copying along on an outing by the Thames, an expedition which brought clucking protests from Aunt Georgy: camping out and sleeping in a tent would be likely to endanger her niece's delicate health. Visiting the camping party for two days, Georgina occupied a bed 'in a charming little Inn—like a Christian!' She had to admit, however, that Mamie was thriving—and 'burned brown, like a gipsy'. By October both women planned to be back in London, when they hoped that all the material for their edition would be in. Then the real work would get under way. Publication was tentatively set for spring.[5]

In spite of much exacting labour, the days were enriched by the associations that had spelled all of life for Georgina. 'Certainly there never was so charming a letter writer,' she told Annie. 'There is hardly a little note from him in answer to an invitation or something of the slightest possible consequence, that has not some little graceful turn or pretty compliment—or little joke that makes it unlike all other people's notes—and marks it with his own original stamp. Then the *letters* to various people are so different in style—bright, earnest, serious, playful—really wonderful! Unless we spoil it *woefully*! I do feel we ought to produce a wonderful Book—like a new one from the dear dead Hand! The life in letters is so wonderful and so sadly touching now!'[6]

But from her absorption in the past, harsh realities recalled Georgina to the present: serious obstacles all but blocked progress on the edition. First, the constant reading and copying of closely written letters, many in bright blue ink on the light blue note paper Dickens had used for his personal correspondence, had imposed such a severe strain on her eyes that periods of rest had become necessary. An even more disturbing delay resulted from the prolonged illness of Catherine Dickens, dying of cancer, according to the verdict of two doctors. 'We have been *quite* stricken by this sudden announcement,' Georgina wrote Annie, not naming the malady. 'We are afraid to shew, *to her*, too much solicitude—for, as yet, . . . she does not believe there is anything to be alarmed at, in her condition, and she is *quite* cheerful (which is almost the saddest part of the matter!)'[7]

The case was pathetic indeed. Writing at this time to her brother Robert, Catherine gave her own account of her illness: of being confined to her sofa except for an occasional drive; of going down to Gad's Hill—when well she had frequently visited Charley and his family there—in the expectation of a beneficial change, only to grow worse; of consulting, at her children's request, a second physician. 'He quite agreed with my own doctor's treatment,' she added optimistically, 'and so he gave me fresh hopes of recovering although my disorder is a most tedious one.'[8]

Two months later Georgina reported to Annie, 'My poor sister suffers *very* much. She is as gentle and patient as it is possible to be and bears her great pain wonderfully. But sometimes it is very, *very* hard to bear.' The only relief came from opiates, which insured her the 'unspeakable blessing' of a restful night. 'It is heart-breaking to go to see her,' lamented Georgina, 'and to feel that there is *no hope* of cure!'[9] On one of her earlier visits, according to a friend in Katey's confidence, the two sisters had undergone an emotional reconciliation in which any lingering bitterness over the past had been dispelled.[10]

In letter after letter Georgina described Catherine's fluctuating condition: intense suffering alternating with periods of apparent improvement. Mamie and Katey began to take turns in watching at her bedside, for the doctor had warned that the end would be sudden. Though Georgina considered it right for them 'to fulfil this duty themselves,' she thought the exertion 'a great trial of their strength'. The 'Poor Book', she grieved, had to be put 'sadly to one side' now. Under the circumstances work on it was almost impossible, though a friend was helping with some of the copying. Hopes for an April publication were dashed.[11]

Only a comparatively small number of Dickens's letters to Catherine had been chosen for the edition. Katey found a packet of others, as well as a picture of her father and a lock of his hair, when, during one of her sickroom vigils, she was called to her mother's bedside and instructed to open a drawer. 'Give these to the British Museum,' said Catherine of the letters, 'that the world may know that he loved me once.' Twenty years later Katey was to carry out this commission, with the proviso that they were not to be made public during the lifetime of any of Dickens's children.[12]

During her mother's last years Katey, conscience-stricken, tried to make up for her earlier neglect. She remembered with shame how she and Mamie, as thoughtless young girls in the Tavistock days, had taken music lessons across the street from the home of their mother in Gloucester Crescent, but had never gone to see her. And as a mature woman Katey had made her occasional calls only at the insistence of her first husband.[13] It may have been duty more than congeniality which brought her to Gloucester Crescent in later years, for she seems never to have been irresistibly drawn to her mother as to her father, though at times she had taken Catherine's part from a sense of justice. Very likely the meek and colourless mother, with her lifelong tendency to regard herself as a pitiable object, had aroused in the vivid daughter something of the half-guilty impatience of Dickens himself. However that may be, mother and daughter agreed never to mention him, the subject being too poignant. Except for the transfer of the letters, the pact was broken only once—and that in Dickens's lifetime. 'Do you think he is sorry for me?' Catherine had asked pathetically—and characteristically.[14]

Now, as she lingered, a younger brother, Edward Hogarth, and his wife were both dying of 'galloping' consumption. 'To see these two poor *patient* gentle Invalids together—both dying! and then to go from their home to my Sister's, is the most tragic experience I have ever gone through in my life—and it is all my life just now!' Georgina observed to Annie. With the years her Hogarth family ties had been resumed—even with the younger sister Helen, who had so aroused Dickens's wrath. In 1874 Helen's little girl, May, had come to spend Christmas week with Aunt Georgy, and had been commended as a good and considerate child.[15]

The three Hogarth invalids were not the only ones to prey on

P

Georgina's mind during her occupation with the letters. Of Charley, too, there had been disturbing news. The pressure of maintaining Gad's Hill and supporting a large family on a precarious income, together with the physical strain of travelling to work in London, had finally impaired his health. ' . . . His mind is more ill than his body,' Georgina contended, 'and I do not think there is a chance of one being better, until the other is easier.' Much as his past conduct had infuriated her, she was all tenderness to him now in his misfortune. Her heart went out to his 'poor little wife (who is *most* good, helpful and devoted) and his *eight* children! seven of them girls!' It was her fervent prayer that his illness might be 'taken in time—and that he will pull through'.[16]

Her hope was realized: once Charley had followed his doctor's advice and given up Gad's Hill, his health improved. But there were harsh adjustments as he and his wife and two of the daughters lived temporarily at the office, the other children having been scattered among relatives. The oldest, Mekitty (Mary Angela), stayed with Georgina and Mamie.[17] It was 'sad and desolate' to think of the country house standing empty now while Charley tried for months to dispose of it. Finally it was to be sold at auction. Georgina hoped that it would fall 'into tender and reverent hands'. A year later, however, when another June anniversary reminded her of the happy days at Gad's Hill, she exclaimed, 'To think it should have fallen into common vulgar hands! but it won't bear thinking of'.[18]

Unceasing seemed the family anxieties and sorrows that hampered work on the edition of letters. In February of 1879 the Australian mail brought word of an 'entirely unlooked for, and most terrible misfortune'—the death of Alfred's wife. Thrown from her carriage when one of her ponies bolted, she had fractured her skull on the curb and died within a few hours. Georgina wondered what poor Alfred, once 'so happy and fortunate in his marriage', would do with his two motherless little daughters, Kathleen and Violet. He had written, three days after his wife's death, 'a perfectly heart broken and heart *breaking* letter—all the more touching from its manly resignation and *truly* religious tone.' This tragedy was a terrible blow to Plorn also, for he had always made his home with Alfred and Jessie 'whenever he chose in that far away country'.[19]

Not many months after, there was fresh cause for anxiety—the serious illness of Charley's Mekitty. Just seventeen, she had, according to one doctor, a fatal spine disease. Georgina could only hope that the diagnosis was wrong, for hitherto this physician had been 'very stupid' in his treatment and judgments. There was to be a consultation with some London specialists, but she could not feel too sanguine. She recalled that Mekitty had stayed at Gad's Hill a great deal as a child and that Dickens had been very fond of her. The only grandchild who remembered him, she cherished some *'wonderfully* and delightfully *reverential'* reminiscences.[20]

During this troubled period another June anniversary arrived. 'We . . . always keep the day in the same way,' Georgina informed Annie, 'taking flowers to the Abbey in the morning, and going again in the afternoon, so that we spend nearly the whole day there.' Once more the stone was bright with flowers. 'It always gives me a peaceful, almost happy feeling, this setting the day *apart* from all the other days in the year! and this year, especially, we are in the midst of so much gloom and sadness, that the sort of *calm* on the 9th was a relief.' And there was consolation, too, in the assurance that Charles had been removed from all the worries visited upon his family.[21]

Happily, it developed that Mekitty was not suffering from a fatal malady; she gradually recovered her health and spirits. It was comforting, furthermore, to see Charley feeling much better, his family all living together again in Regent's Park near his mother. His *Dictionary of London*, a cleverly designed guide book, had enjoyed great success, Georgina told Annie with pride. (It was to be followed later by similar works on Paris, Oxford, Cambridge, and the Thames.) The other cheerful news came from Harry, who was happy in his family life and had made real strides professionally. He now had a 'son and Heir!' born 7 October 1878. 'I am glad it is a boy *this* time . . . ,' exclaimed Auntie.[22] Christened Henry Charles Dickens, the baby (called Hal) was to be followed by three other sons whose names would also terminate in the magical 'Charles Dickens'.

*   *   *

In spite of constant interruptions, the editing of the letters had somehow gone forward. 'The work *must* be done, and *shall* be done, please God!' Georgina had insisted in the early stages of Catherine's illness, 'and we must keep ourselves ever strong and as brave as we can, to continue [?] all that we may have to do!'[23] Persistently she and Mamie selected, copied, and arranged chronologically such correspondence as they could use; added brief explanatory notes only when necessary; and, as connecting links between the years, inserted prefatory narratives. The one for 1858 and all that followed completely ignored the separation. As for Georgina's connection with recorded events, it was introduced when essential, but was frequently omitted when it might well have been considered apropos. For example, the account of Dickens's illness on his last Christmas Day did not mention her poulticing his foot. Nor was it brought out that she had accompanied him on his final excursion to Cobham Park.

By the end of June 1879 the first volume was ready for the printer. '. . . Ah! dear, how thankful we shall be, when it is *out*,' Georgina wrote Annie. 'The book will be *"our very own"* and I need not tell you how intensely anxious we are that the "setting" of our notes shall do no injustice to the gems which most of the letters certainly are.' At least it was a relief to have the 'unqualified approval' of their work from Wilkie Collins, who alone had been consulted for editorial advice. His few 'trifling alterations' had been 'very good ones—and easily made'.[24] Apparently any former coolness between Wilkie and Georgina was not to affect their present relations, for he responded generously whenever she required his helpful suggestions. He also offered a few of his Dickens letters for the collection. (Many more of them would be printed in 1892 after his death, the selection to be made by Georgina, whose permission as the only remaining executor was necessary for publication.)

Pushing the volumes to completion entailed much more than the actual editing. There were in addition the tedious, often exasperating, negotiations with the publisher, F. Chapman, whose preliminary estimate promised Georgina and Mamie a profit of £1,400 on a sale of two thousand copies at £2 each. He also made overtures of reducing his own commission from the usual twelve and a half per cent to ten. When, however, he returned to the higher figure in his calculations several months later, Georgina poured out her indignation to Ouvry, on whose advice she relied heavily throughout the negotiations. 'No!' she sputtered, 'I should say F. C.'s terms will *not* suit us at all!' And she threatened to approach Macmillan if she and Chapman could not not reach an agreement.[25]

There was also a question about the publisher's solvency. Wilkie Collins had suggested a 'private enquiry' to ascertain the facts. The results of this investigation were not reassuring. 'I don't feel quite easy in my mind, I must confess, . . . and doubt whether it will be well for Mamie and me to cast in our lot with a firm whose "pecuniary position does not amount to a certainty",' Georgina wrote Ouvry. 'We *must* stick to immediate cash or not go in with [him] *at all*,' she insisted. 'But I suppose if he agrees to the ready money bargain we cannot draw back, for we cannot appear to doubt his credit.' It was a 'worrying and anxious business', she complained. 'Of course I know quite well that *even* you cannot insure our coming out right if F. C. has no money to pay with!'[26]

Also perplexing was the decision regarding the retail price of the volumes. As opposed to Chapman's suggested £2, Collins and Georgina inclined to £1. 10s. This lower figure had the support of another publisher, George Bentley, whose opinion had been solicited without Chapman's knowledge. After interminable correspondence and wearisome consultations Georgina and Chapman finally came to terms. While the formal agreement was being drawn up, Collins gave Georgina the benefit of his own considerable publication experience and suggested some shrewd changes in several of the clauses.[27]

The bargaining had been complicated because Georgina and Mamie were paying their own production costs. In this their motive was a charitable one, prompted solely by a wish to help Charley Dickens. To reduce his business expenses, he had decided to print *All the Year Round* himself, establishing for this purpose the Crystal Palace Press with F. M. Evans, his brother-in-law. With this firm Georgina and Mamie contracted for the printing of the letters. Here again the business details were handled by Ouvry, who generously advanced the money for full payment of the bill (£730) on delivery of the first two thousand copies, so that the editors could realize a discount of five per cent on half of the total printing charges. At Charley's suggestion further savings were effected with stereotypes for subsequent printings.[28]

Not without misgivings, however, did Georgina award the printing contract. She could not forget that Charley's partner was the son of the Evans who had grievously offended Dickens at the time of the separation. It must be made unmistakably clear, she demanded, that, though her business was with the Crystal Palace Press, she would deal personally only with her nephew. 'Charley quite understands this,' she assured Ouvry. 'Indeed if he would not understand it we would not have given him the Book to print. It will not be necessary ever I hope, that Mr. Evans should be present at our signing of the agreement? I don't mean that we should not speak to him, as Charley's wife's brother—if we did this in an ordinary way—but on *this* business I will not meet with him. It is quite painful enough to have his name joined to "Dickens" on the page of our Book, and it required *all* my feeling of a desire to be helpful to Charley to make up my mind to that connexion!'[29]

As the publication date neared, there were further negotiations with Chapman, who now proposed to pay the editors in three instalments, the last a few weeks after the delivery of the volumes. 'I suppose we *must* agree to that?' Georgina asked Ouvry, 'especially as I suppose he won't be paid by "the trade" for the first ten weeks?'

She and Mamie did not want to be 'female Shylocks'. 'If you will write to him . . . saying you agree under protest, to our desire of making the concession to him,' she advised, 'I think it will do?' But she cautioned Ouvry against arranging to receive payment on 30th November, that being a Sunday; it must be the 29th. In the same letter she expressed her approval of his suggestion that a copy of the *Letters* be specially bound and sent to the Queen.[30]

A sobering thought, as Georgina waited for the volumes to come off the press, was her sister's pathetic condition. Though the end had seemed near in January, Catherine had rallied surprisingly and was still alive in November. 'My poor sister is very, *very* ill,' Georgina told Ouvry. 'I do not think—and indeed I cannot hope— that she will live long. I am glad to say that she has taken the greatest interest and the greatest pleasure in the Book. I really think it has been of much joy and comfort to her. Under the sad circumstances this has been a real pleasure to Mamie and me.' It seemed unfeeling, Georgina admitted, to be writing about business at this time. But 'the business *must* be attended to—and she is in so bad a state, now, that I feel it all the more necessary and import- ant to get all this done while I can'. Of course, Catherine might rally again, but not for long. 'God knows it is not to be desired for her sake, poor soul!'[31]

For six days more the passive spirit considerately delayed its flight. On 21 November 1879 the first two volumes of *The Letters of Charles Dickens* were issued. At eight-thirty the following morning Catherine Dickens died. To Georgina she had willed her blue enamel snake ring, a present from Count D'Orsay.[32] Though some have found the bequest appropriate, Catherine was hardly the sort to have made it through any ulterior design.

In 1881 a third volume of the *Letters* was ready for the press, Dickens's correspondence to Bulwer-Lytton and Austen H. Layard having been made available since the earlier printing. Also included were two of the less personal letters to Maria Beadnell Winter. 'Do you not think those *two* letters to Mrs. Winter quite wonderful?' Georgina asked Annie Fields—'the one about *himself* and the other one after the death of the baby.' Absent, for obvious reasons, were the reminiscent letters addressed to Maria in February of 1855, in which Dickens had revealed himself unabashedly. Even if they had been offered for inclusion in this volume, Georgina would hardly have published such intimate documents. Her restrained comment on Mrs. Winter identified her merely as 'a very dear friend and companion of Charles Dickens in his youth'.

In 1882 the three volumes were brought out as two in a cheap

edition, with the letters of the third introduced in their chrono-
logical order. 'We have cut and condensed *remorselessly*,' Georgina
reported, 'but I hope and think, *wisely* and *well*. We have left
everything that it most interesting. . . .' This edition, she was convinced, would take its 'stand with the other precious books' of
Dickens. It was, in effect, 'his *last* Book. We are proud and thankful
to have produced it,' she exulted to Annie.[33]

Whether the venture was a financial success is difficult to determine, since there are no longer any records for this particular publication at Chapman and Hall. From Georgina's letters it appears
that the first printing of two thousand copies sold out before the
actual date of issue. Whether the second printing of three thousand
did as well is doubtful. And the popular edition of 1882 added
further production costs. 'I hope I shall get a *good deal* of money
from the Letters,' Georgina wrote to Annie in December 1882, 'to
help me to make up that Bill—as to which Charley has proved such
a *very* hard and tradesmanlike creditor! . . . I much prefer to pay
it and to let Mamie owe her half of it *to me*, rather than to renew the
Bill—and carry on such very unpleasant relations with Charley and
his Partner.'[34] It would appear that her generous impulse toward
her nephew had received a jolt.

*   *   *

Without previous experience or any actual knowledge of publishing procedures, with only an ardent wish to honour 'the beloved
memory', Georgina and Mamie had brought out the first important
collection of Dickens's letters. It included general correspondence
addressed to approximately two hundred persons from 1833 to 8 June
1870, most of which the Forster biography had not used. The
selection was aimed, so Georgina told a Birmingham friend, at giving
'a new *and right* idea of his great heart and mind' to supplement
Forster's work, which, however 'faithful' and 'very acceptable' as a
life, 'fails entirely in giving a picture of my dear Brother-in-law; at
any rate, it gives only one view of him'.[35] There was an unfortunate
gap in the family letters, for all of Katey's from her father had been
destroyed in 1873 by the great fire at the Pantechnicon, where most
of her chattels had been stored following Charles Collins's death.
From a window at Gloucester Terrace Katey had watched the flames
with her aunt and sister, not dreaming what building was being
consumed.[36] So her share in the book had to be limited to an appearance in the dedication: *To Kate Perugini, this memorial of her father
is lovingly inscribed by her aunt and sister*. From Harry came a most
useful contribution, a meticulous index for the letters.

What editorial practices characterized this work? As Georgina and Mamie had from the first chosen to exclude all matter which they did not consider to be of a general nature and of justifiable public interest, the scope of the edition was necessarily limited. Such a policy resulted in alterations of text, deletions of particular passages, and omission of entire letters. Since many of the manuscripts to which the editors had access are still extant, it is often possible to check the printed versions against the originals. Such a comparison sometimes reveals startling differences.

A few changes were dictated by Victorian decorum, as in the letter to Georgina which refers, in veiled terms, to Dickens's haemorrhoids. The original passage reads: 'Yesterday morning I was so unwell with an internal malady that occasionally at long intervals troubles me a little—and it was attended with the sudden loss of so much blood —that I wrote to Frank Beard. . . .' In the Georgina-Mamie edition this becomes simply: 'Yesterday morning I was so unwell that I wrote to Frank Beard. . . .'[37] Here, as elsewhere frequently, the omission is not indicated by ellipsis periods. Similarly, there is nothing to show that Dickens's account of Wilkie Collins's youthful love adventure has been expunged from a letter written during the Italian jaunt in 1853.[38] The omission of this passage stems, of course, as much from the avoidance of private details about living persons as from any ban on indelicacy. Certainly the editors did not insist on any extreme prudery of expression. At the close of a letter to Macready, for instance, they allowed this message to stand: 'Kate sends her tender love; so does Georgy, so does Charley, so does Mamey, so does Katey, so does Walter, so does the other one who is to be born next week'.[39] And the description of an insane Mrs. Crowe was left unaltered, except for the omission of her name: 'Mrs. —— has gone stark mad—and stark naked—on the spirit-rapping imposition. She was found t'other day in the street, clothed only in her chastity, a pocket-handkerchief and a visiting card. She had been informed, it appeared, by the spirits, that if she went out in that trim she would be invisible.'[40]

As for profanity, the editors had to deal with only the mildest of examples, none naming the Deity. Though they once allowed *damnable* to remain,[41] they usually emasculated such expressions by means of dashes which seldom concealed the wording of the original, 'the damndest inn' becoming 'the d——dest inn'. The harmless *deuce*, however, they did not permit to retain so much as its initial consonant in 'will play the —— with all public gaieties'.[42]

In such deletions and alterations Georgina and Mamie were only following current practice. And they were observing accepted custom

in any time by eliminating disparaging comments on their contemporaries. The reference to Harriet Martineau as a 'wrong-
headed woman' and 'such a humbug', the imitations of Dolby's
stammering, the portrayal of Forster as ridiculously arbitrary and
egotistic—such details had to yield to the canons of good taste.
Surely the editors would have been unnecessarily tactless to print
in full Dickens's opinion of one of his amateur actresses: '. . . Miss
Daly knew best what she was about, yesterday—to my unbounded
amazement. But she is too old for Grace [in a dramatization of *The
Battle of Life*], and not pretty enough'.[43] Similarly, in giving
Dickens's characterization of Cecile Macready as 'exceedingly winning' and 'sensible, gay, pleasant, sweet-tempered; not in the
faintest degree stiff or pedantic; accessible instantly', the editors,
averse to deflating a friend, understandably deleted the unfavourable comparison of her pulchritude with that of the first Mrs.
Macready: 'not half so pretty or so buxom'.[44] The same tact
accounts for their withholding the name of a woman referred to in
a letter dated from the diminutive Paris apartment occupied by the
Dickenses in 1856: '. . . I live in terror of asking —— to dinner, lest
she should not be able to get in at the dining-room door. I *think* (am
not sure) the dining-room would hold her, if she could be once passed
in, but I don't see my way to that.'[45]

Reputations also had to be protected, of course. Thus Dickens's
comments to Georgina on John Blackwood called for excision:
'. . . I think I told you that I saw him three times in Edinburgh and
always extremely drunk. Your estimate of him I take to be quite
correct'.[46] Likewise omitted from a letter to Wilkie Collins was a
reference to Caroline Graves (Wilkie's mistress), her daughter, and
the Collins-Graves ménage on New Cavendish Street, even though
couched in such veiled terms that only the initiate could have understood: 'I am charmed with the Butler. O why was she stopped!
Ask her flinty mother from me, why, why, didn't she let her convert
somebody! And here the question arises—Did she secretly convert
the Landlord?'[47]

Just as Blackwood and Collins required protection, so Wills and
Forster needed to be exonerated. An 1867 letter to Wills was
inserted, therefore, possibly out of deference to the suggestion which
he had pencilled across the top: 'This letter so illustrative of one of
the strong sides of C D's character—powerful will—I think ought
decidedly to be published, in justice to Forster and myself, who dis-
suaded him from America—which killed him eventually'.[48] Accordingly Georgina reproduced those paragraphs in which Dickens had
answered the opposition of his sub-editor to an American reading

tour. Omitted, naturally, were the personal references, like the one
to Ellen Ternan as 'the Patient'.

In their insertion or rejection of material, the editors expended
their zeal chiefly to enhance Dickens's own reputation. Carefully
pruned were passages which might in any way tarnish the idol that
they—and, for the most part, the world—had enshrined. Hence
references to feasting and drinking were frequently struck out.
Because Dickens had displayed in his books an obvious relish for
good eating and the making of gin punch, a minority had repeatedly
accused him of gluttony and drunkenness. Even after his death
these aspersions continued. In Boston, for instance, Annie Fields
was shocked, shortly after his funeral, to hear announced from the
Tremont Temple pulpit that 'indulgence in drink killed him. Abstin-
ence and rest might have given him two decades more of life. He
tried these a year ago, and at the same time staved off the threatened attack, but his old habit of life and work returned. His fuel was
required to keep up the flame.'[49] Such derogatory statements may
have impelled Fields to assert in 'Our Whispering Gallery' (*Atlantic
Monthly*, August 1871) that Dickens had really been extraordinarily
temperate in his eating and drinking habits. Commenting on this
'true, delicate, and discriminating' vindication of her idol's character, Georgina confessed to Annie that Charles had often made her
angry by his indifference to public opinion and that she had 'sometimes laughingly begged him not to speak about his dinners—in a
joking way he had . . . before certain stupid people who did *not*
understand him, and thought it rather wonderful that he should
attach such importance to his meals'.[50]

Aware of Dickens's reputation for self-indulgence, Georgina ruth-
lessly suppressed all instructions in his letters to her for stocking the
wine cellar. Why should the public know the extent of his orders of
sherry, Moselle, champagne, brandy, and gin? Not every mention
of alcoholic beverages was obliterated, however. When it was a
matter of showing his conviviality or generous social impulses, the
references were usually allowed to stand. For example, Dickens had
once written Wills about witnessing a play by a humble strolling
company in a schoolroom at Dartford. Having to leave early to
catch a train, he and Mark Lemon had sent their hotel landlord back
with the makings of a celebration for the troupe. The items as listed
in the letter were printed in full:

1 bottle superior old port,
1   do.   do.   golden sherry,
1   do.   do.   best French brandy,
1   do.   do.   1st quality old Tom gin,

1 bottle superior prime Jamaica rum,
1   do.   do.   small still Isla whiskey,
1 kettle boiling water, two pounds finest white lump sugar,
Our cards,
1 lemon,
                    and
Our compliments.[51]

Also allowed to remain was the following remark in a letter to
Wilkie Collins: 'What a pity I am not with you to make a third at
the Trois Frères, and drink no end of bottles of Bordeaux, without
ever getting a touch of redness in my (poet's phrase again) "innocent
nose".'[52] Any number of similar examples might be supplied.

Though not in the damaging category of references to liquor,
financial details were also ruled out. They did not come under the
heading of what the editors considered legitimate public interest,
nor did they enhance the dignity of a major literary figure. In fact,
some of them played into the hands of those detractors who considered Dickens mercenary. His exuberant reports of enormous
profits from the reading tours, his explicit comments on the household
budget and family expenses, his complaints about exorbitant bills—
all such mundane references had to be deleted. That money had
bulked large in his daily concerns could not be gathered from the
Georgina-Mamie edition of his letters.

Nor would readers know how much Dickens had depended upon
his sister-in-law. Why should the world be told that he had frequently written to her for shirts, elastic stockings, clean dinner
jackets, and other changes of apparel? Why give publicity to her
examining and forwarding his personal correspondence and valuable
papers? Whose concern was it that he had communicated with her
regularly about the management of Gad's Hill—the hiring and
reprimanding of servants, the arranging and repairing of furniture,
the harvesting of hay crops?

It was not the intention of the editors, however, to suppress the
picture of Dickens as a private citizen: their Preface made clear that
the more intimate letters were published 'with the view of showing
him in his homely, domestic life—of showing how in the midst of his
own constant and arduous work, no household matter was considered too trivial to claim his care and attention. He would take as
much pains about the hanging of a picture, the choosing of furniture,
the superintending any little improvement in the house, as he would
about the more serious business of his life; thus carrying out to the
very letter his favourite motto of "What is worth doing at all is
worth doing well".' One of the letters included from the humble

Doughty Street days, therefore, shows his detailed concern for the practical aspects of a country cottage which he had rented for his parents—its 'coal-holes, fowl-houses, and meat-safes out of number'; the reasonable rent (£20 a year); and the delightful luck of finding an upholsterer with two second-hand carpets for sale.[53] Though full of the financial transactions involved in securing and furnishing the cottage, the letter stands uncut as an endearing portrait of a great man observing necessary frugalities in his youthful beginnings. Equally endearing, his editors must have felt, was his plea for bright colours in the children's bonnets.[54]

But warily pruned were references to the more private family matters: the lack of enterprise in his sons, his burdensome relatives, his marriage troubles. Though the natural anxieties of an affectionate father are evident in letters to Alfred and Plorn and to G. W. Rusden, understandably deleted was the passage in which Dickens, three weeks before his death, had reluctantly admitted that his youngest son had been 'born without a groove'. Too poignant for the public eye was the paternal resignation: 'If he cannot, or will not find one, I must try again, and die trying'.[55] Yet, as if to uphold Dickens against those who found fault with him for sending a mere adolescent so far away, the editors carefully included his own defence: that the boy had 'qualified himself for no public examinations in the old country, and could not possibly hold his own against any competition for anything to which I could get him nominated'.[56] But excluded throughout the edition were the more bitter passages of disappointment. Missing in a letter to Wills, for example, is the mention of 'my boys with a curse of limpness upon them' and their 'inadaptability to anything'.[57] Allowed to stand, however, were playful deprecations of parenthood, such as that addressed to Mrs. Cowden Clarke in 1884: 'I loathe domestic hearths. I yearn to be a vagabond. Why can't I marry Mary [a character in *Used Up*]? Why have I seven children—not engaged at sixpence a-night apiece, and dismissable for ever, if they tumble down, not taken on for an indefinite time at a vast expense, and never,—no, never, never,— wearing lighted candles round their heads [as did the fairies in the amateur production of *The Merry Wives of Windsor*].'[58]

As far as Georgina was concerned, Forster's *Life* was the final published word on the separation. Dickens's letters to his wife during this crisis, his references to Ellen Ternan, his furious statements about the Hogarths could only gratify prying curiosity. Besides their deletion from the printed text, comments on Ellen were so heavily inked out in the originals as to be illegible to the unaided eye. Occasionally portions were cut from the letters with scissors. Some, perhaps many, manuscripts were completely destroyed. Georgina told Ouvry in 1879 that she had felt no hesitation in burning seven or eight of Dickens's early letters referring to the affairs of his father or his brother Frederick. (This was part of the correspondence addressed to Mitton, a lawyer friend.) A letter dated 21 September 1842, with 'some remarks about his Father in it, but otherwise . . . a pleasant little note', she informed Ouvry, she had 'patched up', cutting part away and making two sheets into one. Unwilling to subject this manuscript to further snipping, she had resorted, according to her own admission, to inking out a passage.[59]

An examination of the ink and the pen strokes in this early cancellation, hers without question, makes it possible to recognize the same hand in subsequent obliterations. From a comparison of this key letter with others, it would appear that Georgina herself scratched out all the damaging lines in her own correspondence from Dickens, but that two assistants dealt with the remaining holographs. In ink, in geometric patterns, even in the characteristic sputter of the pen, several of the blottings closely resemble those in Wilkie Collins's *Armadale* manuscript. And since Wilkie was credited with suggesting a few 'trifling alterations' in the edition, it may reasonably be assumed that he helped with some of the cancellations.[60] Very likely the third hand recognizable in the obliterations was Mamie's.

Not all of Georgina's inkings were made for the sake of the family's good name. Of those that have yielded up their secrets to infra-red photography, one shows her care to preserve the honour of a personal friend and fellow Dickens worshipper. 'I have also an incoherent letter from Mary Boyle—or I should say rather gincoherent,' Dickens had written his sister-in-law in 1869.[61] (It was not his only joking reference to Mary's letters.) Later Georgina heavily crossed out the last clause, even though the letter itself was omitted altogether from the published collection.

That the editors used comparatively little of Dickens's correspondence to his wife has been cited as an instance of Georgina's unfeeling attitude toward her sister. It has been stated, furthermore, that tender and affectionate passages to and about Catherine were not reproduced. Can these charges be substantiated? Though it is true that only twenty-three of the letters to Mrs. Dickens were published, this is a fairly representative number, considering that Dickens had addressed only a few notes to her in the last twelve years of his life. Besides, it is the sad truth that in writing to his spouse he had seldom appeared as an Inimitable. Georgina was concerned, moreover, to use only letters of general interest, a test met by the twenty-three to

Catherine included in the edition. As for endearments, except for the usual affectionate formulas in the salutation and the closing, there were few—chiefly the playful 'dearest Pig', 'dearest Titmouse', and 'darling Tatie' of the courting days. From this period, in which the correspondence is particularly flat and monotonous, and seldom indicative of a young man in love, only two samples are given. One deletes a dull final paragraph explaining why Dickens might not be able to come to Brompton on Friday and assuring his fiancée that he would, in any event, be out early on Saturday. This sort of material, utterly devoid of interest, the editors omitted from many a letter to anyone whomsoever.

The other sample is printed without the opening and the closing portions—roughly two-thirds of the whole. The unpublished final passage, a long one of scant interest, contains, it is true, an affectionate postscript: 'I wish you were a fixture here—I should like to have you by me—*so* much'. But it is the deletion of the opening third which is more significant in showing the attitude of the editors. Throughout the premarital correspondence one note is sounded over and over: Dickens's discontent with his 'Tatie's' pettish jealousy of his work and her bursts of ill-tempered suspicion whenever his commitments kept her lover away. This is the subject of the omitted portion. Whether its inclusion would have won any champions for Catherine need hardly be asked: 'My dearest Life You must not be "coss" with what I cannot help. I like the *matter* of what I have done to-day, very much, but the *quantity* is not sufficient to justify my coming out to-night. If the representations I have so often made to you, about my working as a duty, and not as a pleasure, be not sufficient to keep you in good humour, which you, of all people in the World should preserve—why then, my dear, you must be out of temper, and there is no help for it.'[62]

In all the known correspondence to Catherine during the wedded years, only a few expressions of strong affection and approval stand out. The most unmistakable of these are kept by the Georgina-Mamie edition. A notable instance is the close of a letter written after two and a half years of marriage: 'God bless you, my darling. I long to be back with you again and to see the sweet Babs. Your faithful and most affectionate Husband.'[63] Even the unessential though tender bits used as closing formulas—for instance, 'Take care of yourself, and God bless you'—are not sacrificed in the interests of compactness.[64]

Nor did Georgina and Mamie delete a rare commendation of Catherine for being in a 'methodical, businesslike, and energetic state'. But they kept out of print the contrary picture—the inept, careless wife who could not even address an envelope properly.[65] In making this omission, the editors did a favour, it must be admitted, not only to Catherine but to Dickens, who otherwise might have been judged as a carping and hypercritical husband.

As for the accusation that affectionate remarks about Catherine are missing in letters to other correspondents, it can only be pointed out that, except for the routine courtesy of enclosing her love or her compliments, Dickens seldom mentioned his wife. Included, however, is his praise (to Mitton) of her hardihood and courage on the Vesuvius expedition.[66] But an occasional trifle which might present her in an unflattering light is ignored: for instance, the remark that she is described in a book by Harriet Beecher Stowe, who 'is of opinion that she is "large" . . . !'[67]

As the editors tinkered with their materials, they developed still another technique, one naïvely aimed at improving the originals. Sometimes this involved tightening up the loose and rambling accounts Dickens had sent Georgina during his reading tours. Thus five paragraphs could be reduced to one.[68] Occasionally two or more letters of different dates were telescoped as a single entry. Such patchwork methods enabled the editors to combine scattered short notes or to throw together the more interesting portions of longer letters. Needless to say, the reader was kept in ignorance of these liberties.

One highly successful product of this method is a New Year's greeting to Wills, dated 2 January 1862, and made up entirely of expressions of affectionate good will. It begins: 'My dear Wills, Being stationed here for an hour, on my way from Leamington to Cheltenham, I write to you.

'Firstly, to reciprocate all your cordial and affectionate wishes for the New Year, and to express my earnest hope that we may go on through many years to come, as we have gone on through many years that are gone. And I think we can say that we doubt whether any two men can have gone on more happily, and smoothly, or with greater trust and confidence in one another.' At the side of this sentiment in the original Wills had pencilled a note to the editors: 'It would gratify me to see this passage in print. HWW'.

They allowed him this gratification—and more. Into limbo they cast the remaining three paragraphs of the original, made up of odds and ends of office business, and attached instead three others concerning a gift which, had Dickens thought of it in time, would have made an appropriate New Year's token to his sub-editor. But it was not until four months later that he had actually written to announce: 'A little packet will come to you from Hunt and Roskell's, almost at the same time, I think, as this note.

'The packet will contain a claret-jug. I hope it is a pretty thing in itself for your table, and I know that you and Mrs. Wills will like it none the worse because it comes from me.

'It is not made of a perishable material, and is so far expressive of our friendship. I have had your name and mine set upon it, in token of our many years of mutual reliance and trustfulness. It will never be so full of wine as it is today of affectionate regard.'[69]

Other examples of the editors' mosaic work may be found here and there, the letters to Wills and Collins furnishing the principal opportunity for their skill.[70] Such liberties sometimes necessitated the rewording or the addition of a phrase or sentence. Since Georgina and Mamie were following a fairly common nineteenth-century practice, however, they felt no compunctions over methods which must have driven many a later student of the same material to the verge of madness.

It is true that the editors now and then inserted a row of asterisks to indicate a lengthy deletion, or the customary three ellipsis periods for a briefer one, but their practice was sporadic and inconsistent. If it grew out of any recognizable policy, it would seem to have been one of throwing dust into the reader's eye. That is, a row of giant asterisks or a period triplet might conscientiously indicate the omission of such dull and trivial matter as 'I walked over to Maryport today, to see what letters were there, and to ask the Postmaster to send any more he might have over here. I found none from you, but hardly supposed I should so soon.'[71] Anyone whose curiosity, thus aroused, urged him to look up and examine the original would soon find the game not worth the candle. But interred without a trace was many a reference to titillate the reader —and, more important, to reveal what manner of man the writer was. Among the more significant of such deletions was Dickens's confession of finding in *Faust* 'a mournful echo of things that lie in my own heart'.

How was the edition received? If contemporary reviews are any indication, the reactions ranged from unqualified praise to mild disapproval. The *Westminster Review* commended the work for increasing the readers' 'affectionate regard for Dickens' memory' and thanked the editors for having produced 'another book from Charles Dickens' hands'.[72] The *Athenaeum*, sedate organ of critical opinion, considered the letters necessary to clear up Forster's *Life*, and observed that no pains had been spared to make the collection

complete.[73] By the *Saturday Review* it was likewise hailed for its
information about those portions of Dickens's life of which his
biographer had had little knowledge. 'A sort of irregular biography,'
the reviewer called it.[74] William Minto, writing for the *Fortnightly
Review*, insisted that 'no formal portrait could be half so vivid'
because the book brings us 'nearer to the man as he was than any
biographer could have brought us'.[75] For an appraisal in the London
Times Georgina waited impatiently. 'Of course we want a notice in
The Times, and it is odd they don't give us one,' she fretted two
weeks after the release of the first printing. 'I should think *The Times*
should hardly be likely to be the only paper that does not notice a
book with that name!'[76] When the tardy review finally appeared
within the month, it delighted her by lauding the edition as 'virtually
a new biography' to supplement the 'strangely incomplete' *Life* by
Forster.[77]

Of the negative notices, that in the *Atlantic Monthly* was perhaps
the most outspoken. (By this time Fields was no longer connected
with this journal.) Chiefly it criticized the letters as 'not very dis-
creetly edited' because they brought out Dickens's patronizing attitude toward America and in the main emphasized his 'astonishment
and exultation at the success of his readings' there.[78]

More moderate in tone was the valid judgment of Matthew Browne
as pronounced in the *Contemporary Review*. After pointing out that
'published collections of private letters are usually disappointing
things, and these two large volumes . . . constitute no exception', he
criticized the edition for not giving the reader the key to Dickens's
'interior life', for presenting only those features already well known,
such as his love for the young, facts about his health, and the
routine of his activities. 'If about half of the collection, as it stands,
were omitted,' Browne concluded, 'and such of the more private
letters as could properly be made public, were printed, we should
receive a much more nearly perfect impression of the man.'[79] This
cogent criticism gets at the underlying weakness of the work, a
weakness that stemmed from Georgina's worship of her idol. Intent
on suppressing many intimate details of Dickens's private life, she
kept the whole man from emerging in his letters. Her policy
amounted, virtually, to canonization. It was this protective concern
that prompted the late Count de Suzannet to characterize the
edition as 'somewhat disingenuously bowdlerized'.[80]

*　　　*　　　*

During her long occupation with the letters, Georgina still felt
Dickens to be the mainspring of her life. 'Ten years ago!' she

Q

exclaimed in June of 1880. 'It seems in one way, impossible, it can be so long—and in another view, it appears but yesterday! . . . Every year only seems to make his *presence* more actual. I suppose, in a degree, it may be accounted for by his passing away as he did in the *very fullness of his life*, with no previous decay of mental or bodily powers—but I can never think of him but as a Being full of life, and brightness, and influence over everything and everybody about him. I am thankful that it becomes *intensified*, instead of modifying as the years roll on.'[81]

Only that bright memory remained constant, for each year wrought changes in the family. The Australian mail in June of 1880 brought the news of Plorn's coming marriage to Constance Desailly, the daughter of a prominent settler. Now that Plorn was in possession of his inheritance from his mother, he saw no reason to postpone the event to the year after her death. 'Why should you, after all?' Aunt Georgy reassured him. It was right, she told Annie Fields, that he should have a wife and home in the distant country where he had his occupation. The announcement set her to reminiscing on the boy who had been 'his Father's pet'. 'God bless him dear old Fellow! I hope and pray he may be very happy in his marriage.' She wrote to Plorn to ask what wedding gift he preferred—'something that will last for ever'. To the bride she sent an affectionate welcome into the family.[82]

A year later Georgina's letters to Annie began to pour forth consolation drawn from her own experience, for in April James Fields died. Faithful Annie nevertheless remembered the solemn 9th June that her friend would be observing. 'I *knew* you would not forget!' Georgina answered. 'On the contrary, I felt sure that as you say, you "never remembered so much or so keenly", but I did not expect that you would write.' She appreciated fully Annie's 'utter inability to go on'. For it was not at first, she knew, 'that the full bitterness and realization' of such grief were felt. 'But you *will* be better, my dear Annie! believe me,' she wrote reassuringly. 'I *know* you will. You have a strong, wholesome nature—and "Time will be good to you" as it always is to those who do not *insist* on morbid self indulgence or sorrow.' And from her own heart she added, 'Of course the happiness of your life is over! it would be vain to speak of the possibility of a return to *that*—but you will gain peace. . . .' She marvelled at Annie's courage in undertaking and completing within the year her biographical work on Fields. It must have been a 'blessed occupation . . . , although mingled with *bitter* tears!'[83] But for James Fields, no immortal, the two Dickens idolaters refrained from establishing the annual rituals of mourning in perpetuity.

In 1882 Annie, accompanied by Sarah Orne Jewett, visited England. 'Indeed we shall *not* forget to be glad to see each other!' Georgina promised on receiving the news of the proposed trip. And after Annie's first call on her at 11 Strathmore Gardens, she sent word, 'It was sweet and pleasant to have you—although there were sad memories revived by seeing your face, with its gentle sorrowful expression, in *our* changed lives!' Annie once more urged Georgina to visit her in Boston, an invitation issued many times since Dickens's death. But however appealing the prospect of seeing her friend's Boston home, Georgina declined again. Of an ocean voyage, she admitted, she had no fears, for she was never seasick. But financial considerations argued against such a long trip.[84]

While Mrs. Fields was still in England, Georgina wrote her of a 'heavy trouble and anxiety' that had befallen. Returning from a trip to Boulogne with Harry and his wife—more and more she was to accompany them on their travels—she learned that Mamie was in an Edinburgh hospital, recovering from an operation for glaucoma. Though the patient preferred to have none of her family with her, Georgina lived in constant readiness to heed the first call. Happily, the surgery proved successful, without leaving any serious disfigurement of the eye as had at first been feared.[85]

By the end of 1882, the year in which the final volume of the *Letters* was published, Georgina was able to find something of the old delight in Christmas again. After church she spent the day with Harry and his family. 'We had lunch, and the sweet chicks had their Christmas dinner with us,' she wrote Annie, 'and afterwards, they had a Christmas Tree with a few more children and some grown up "family" added to the party—and the little ones were *so* happy that it was impossible to help feeling *reflected* Christmas happiness in being with them and in living.' But there was also a hint of perplexity, for Mamie's restlessness had put Georgina in a 'wretched state' as to her own future living plans. She wished something would force her to a decision. 'In short,' she admitted, 'I suppose it is rather the Micawber frame of mind—hoping and trusting that something will "turn up" to show me a *clearer* path ahead!' Her comfort in this perplexity she declared to be the sense of 'the Beloved Dead' remaining in some mystic way 'a sympathy and a help with our poor everyday troubles'.[86] It was like the touch of the 'dear dead Hand'.

Chapter Fourteen
GUARDIAN OF THE 'BELOVED MEMORY'

RULED by the one obsession, Georgina found that 'life slips away, with very little variety, but the years seem to pass with *wonderful* quickness!' She was gradually growing a little less active physically, a little plumper, a little more inclined to cluck maternally over her nieces and nephews—and all the grandnieces and grandnephews with their teething troubles, whooping cough, and other childhood ills.[1] And she was growing increasingly crotchety whenever non-worshippers dared approach her idol's shrine. After Dickens's death, anticipating the volleys of irreverent journalists, critics, and scandal-mongers, she had built a wall around his name; and she zealously devoted the remaining forty-seven years of her life to repairing the breaches in this defence. In time her position won public recognition. Declared a caption under her portrait in *Nash's Magazine*: 'No one living has so wide or intimate a knowledge of Charles Dickens, or exercises a more loving guardianship of his memory'.[2]

Suspecting that even a trivial detraction from his dignity might upset Georgina, Annie Fields had approached her apologetically in 1871 on the subject of the *Atlantic Monthly* 'Whispering Gallery', which had been devoting considerable space to Dickens, including an account of his part in the ludicrous walking match between Osgood and Dolby in 1868. 'You need have no fear of "a barrier being raised" between us by the "Whispering Gallery",' Georgina had reassured her friend. 'There *are* some things Mamie and I would rather not have had published, as you may imagine. The Walking Match, for one thing—it was so entirely a *joke*, that it seems to me as if the Public had no business with it. However, it matters little, after all, and I am *sure* the whole thing is done, as you say, in the spirit of tenderest love.'[3]

Some two years later, though, while Forster was still living, the same periodical offended again, this time gravely; and as a result Georgina became involved in a rather embarrassing correspondence with the Fieldses. She had been commissioned, she wrote after the second volume of the *Life* had appeared, to inquire about a review in February 1873, 'an *article most contemptuous and disparaging* of

Charles—not only of Mr. Forster or of his book, pray understand, but of *Charles himself*'. Though she had not seen it—she never read anything of the kind, she protested—what Forster had told her of its 'tone' filled her with indignation. How could a journal edited by Osgood 'be allowed to contain any depreciating and disrespectful mention' of Dickens? Had he not always spoken of Osgood 'with such hearty good will and kindness'? It was unthinkable that the publisher who had made many of the arrangements for the American reading tour and had travelled everywhere with Charles in 1868, could sanction such detraction. Did Fields still have any connection with the *Atlantic Monthly*, or any power over it? Georgina assumed not, but Foster would like definite assurance. He wished it understood, furthermore, that he did not object because of any criticism disrespectful to himself. It was solely because of what had been written about Dickens that he wanted to know where to place the responsibility. 'I hope you will be so good as to send me a note in answer to this—*exclusively*,' Georgina suggested, 'that when we return to our usual correspondence together this painful subject need not be alluded to, at all.'[4]

How offensive was the article that had stirred up this trouble? Objecting to the attitude Dickens had expressed towards Americans (in letters quoted in the *Life*), the reviewer had dared to call him 'a high-pressure egotist . . . eager for gain, and dismayed by smaller profits than he expected. . . .' He had condemned Dickens's 'fatiguing' exaggeration and deplored his consummate self-absorption. 'A man of unquestionable genius,' chided the review, 'his material, at its finest, was never of the finest. The melodramatic was his notion of the dramatic, the eloquent was his idea of the poetic; his humour was burlesque; his pathos never too deep for tears.' There was harsh criticism, too, of Forster, the 'jealous and greedy intimate', for quoting principally from the letters to himself, as though he 'did not like to connect any other name with Dickens's'.[5]

What Annie wrote in response to Georgina's query has not been preserved. Since Fields had given up his connections with the *Atlantic Monthly* before the review appeared, he would, of course, have been absolved from blame. But there were ruffled feelings. 'I told Mr. Forster just what you said in your letter,' Georgina answered Annie. 'He is sorry that you should have taken his message as "*an attack*" on Mr. Fields, and assures you that he had no intention of making an attack.'[6] This had been, assuredly, a delicate situation, not to be mentioned in subsequent letters.

Even as she corresponded with Annie Fields about this matter, Georgina was in high dudgeon over another issue. For on 19

November 1873, while scanning the theatrical notices in the London *Times*, she had been startled by the following item:

> CHARING CROSS.—*Charles Dickens—the only farce that was ever written by this great humourist, and which is entitled* The Strange Gentleman *will be revived tonight, and until further notice.*

Who could have authorized this performance? Certainly the executors had never been approached on the matter. *The Strange Gentleman* was an early attempt at dramatic authorship which Dickens had been especially concerned to suppress. Written as a practical joke for a friend, the comedian John P. Harley, it had not been revived since its only appearance at St. James's Theatre in 1836. Seven years later, considering it a blot on his career, Dickens had averred that he would not have it repeated for a thousand pounds.[7] And now it was on the boards at Charing Cross! Distressed, Georgina clipped the notice from her paper and sent it to Ouvry, with a note urging immediate action.

The solicitor set to work at once. First he obtained the name of the producer, W. H. C. Nation. At the same time he learned that the advertisement in *The Times*, though only just noticed by Georgina, had been appearing regularly since 27th October. Then, determined not to overlook any technicalities, he inquired of Chapman and Hall, the publishers of the farce, whether Dickens had disposed of the copyright.

While Ouvry waited for his answer, Forster, also alerted by Georgina, lost no time in launching his own investigation. On 19th November he wrote to the producer, challenging his legal rights to the burletta. The next day brought an answer from Nation. *The Strange Gentleman*, he wrote, had been placed in his hands by one of the late managers of Sadler's Wells Theatre, with the understanding that it had ceased to be Dickens's property. Should this assumption be wrong, the piece would be withdrawn from the bills as soon as another could be rehearsed. 'I may add,' he remarked solicitously in a postscript, 'that were you to visit the Theatre I think you would be pleased with the manner in which the farce is acted, though of course this does not affect the question as to whether it ought to be acted at all.'[8] Forster forwarded this reasonable letter to Ouvry, adding some comments of his own. 'Here is a cool Epistle, just come, from the Gentleman question G. H. [Georgina Hogarth] will . . . have sent you,' he pontificated. Though damages could probably not be collected, 'the fellow must be made to stop the thing'. But the estate was not to be committed to 'certain Expenses'.[9]

Georgina also kept prodding Ouvry to bring Nation to terms. 'He is in a wrong position altogether and could, I should imagine, be easily frightened into withdrawing the piece, without more ado— supposing no penalties were insisted upon,' she contended shrewdly. With 'a little *mild and judicious* (not peremptory!!) legal intimidation' he could be brought to halt the production, she believed.[10]

Forster lent further encouragement to this suggestion of intimidating Nation. There was, of course, still the unanswered question as to whether the acting rights of the farce belonged to the family. But Nation must be made to think that they did. 'Just put a bold face upon it as if you had every proof you have not,' Forster urged Ouvry, 'and you will see that he will make *immediate suppression*.'[11]

Forster was right. Threatened with legal action, Nation yielded. 'In my letter to Mr. John Forster I asked him if he would feel satisfied with my withdrawing the farce "The Strange Gentleman" as soon as I could get another old farce rehearsed,' he wrote Ouvry, 'but he has not had the courtesy to send a reply.' So, rather than risk litigation over a production which had 'proved anything but remunerative', Nation had decided at 'much inconvenience' to remove 'it *at once* from the boards'.[12]

It was a real victory for Georgina and Forster. So effectual had been their strategy that all performances were cancelled abruptly only four days after the notice in *The Times* had come to their attention. There had not even been a sufficient interval for a reply from Chapman and Hall to Ouvry's query about the copyright. The answer would have made little difference, however, for the publishers' records failed to show whether Dickens had held on to the acting rights. It was on questionable legal grounds, therefore, that the unauthorized revival of the farce had been quelled. But Georgina had no qualms about the validity of her tactics. All that mattered was that Charles's wishes had been respected in the theatrical demise of *The Strange Gentleman*.[13]

Much less agreeable was the aftermath of an episode occurring three years later. At the home of a friend one day Georgina picked up the April 1876 issue of *Temple Bar*. Flipping through its pages, she came to an article on Forster, who had then been dead two months. She read just enough, she later wrote Annie Fields, 'to be *more* than angry—deeply hurt, and wounded—not so much by what he says of Forster as by the use of Charles's name—and even of mine. . . .'[14] The author of this inflammatory piece was R. H. Horne, a former contributor to *Household Words* and at one time a friend of Dickens. From 1852 to 1869 he had been an inspector of lands in Australia, leaving his wife behind in England. Once on intimate terms with a number of the Dickens circle, he had thrown together his recollections for this offending biographical sketch.

It mocked at Forster's 'pompous airs and dictatorial voice' and at the 'imposing hauteurs' which had amused even the 'most intimate associates'. Dickens, for one, had secretly enjoyed his friend's ridiculous posturing and had smiled indulgently at his 'pomp and dignity of behaviour'. A case in point was his reaction to the hidden bath Forster had devised for the space under his window seat—a specially constructed tub, neatly lined with zinc. 'A fine thing that —I flatter myself . . . for a refresher before breakfast,' had been the owner's proud boast. But Dickens, amused, had declared privately to Horne that Forster could never get into his tub: 'If he did, he would squeeze every *drop* of water out of it!' Another time Forster had convulsed the Dickens household by demonstrating the steps learned a few months earlier in private dancing lessons. Appearing in glazed leather shoes whose toes extended at least two inches beyond his own, he had waltzed with a younger member of the family to impress the seated onlookers. Bent over his small partner, his feet 'thrust out in a peculiarly marked style, at every turn', he had looked so ludicrous that Dickens, to conceal his astonishment and suppress incipient guffaws, had retreated to another room. And Georgina, in response to Horne's remarks on Forster's antics, had exclaimed, 'I really can't tell you, but his absurdities are a constant source of amusement to us. I don't know what we should do without him.'

Incensed by the use of Charles's name and her own in this unflattering sketch of a friend, Georgina denounced Horne as 'one of the most contemptible and disagreeable of mankind'. Because of his disgraceful treatment of his wife, whom he had never sent a penny during his seventeen years in Australia, Forster and Dickens had both refused to see him or correspond with him after his return to England. This article, then, must have been intended as his revenge.[15]

That 'such a little old, conceited, selfish miserable specimen of a man' should have used the name of Dickens in this deplorable fashion did not surprise Georgina. 'I often used to tell Charles that he was too open with many people—and too much in the habit of judging other men by himself,' she recalled, ignoring her own verbal indiscretions, 'also that he did not remember how small things and sayings of his were noted down by those about him—to be used some day—and little jokes which he may have made without the smallest unkindness or idea of disloyalty to his friends, in moments

of confidence, look and sound so different when they are seriously
and maliciously written down after the death of both men!'[16]

Some years later Georgina was again infuriated, this time by an
article published in an American newspaper. It was called to her
attention when Annie Fields, who collected all manner of items for
her Dickens scrapbook, inadvertently slipped one of her clippings
into an envelope with her letter. Challenged, Annie promptly
explained that she had not read the cutting before it got away. This
newspaper story evoked a heated response. '. . . It annoyed me
very much—and was *all* a lie!' Georgina insisted as she summarized
its contents for her friend. 'It was written by some one who *professed*
to have had from Charles's own lips! some most extraordinary revelations and confidences as to his (C's) experiences of *mesmerism*—and
also his (C's) avowal of himself as *spiritualist*!' What could be more
absurd than charging Dickens with a belief in spiritualism? 'You
know what his opinion was of all *that* imposture!' As for his mesmeric
demonstrations, they had been fully treated in the letters to Forster
in the *Life*. Any departure from the facts as there presented was a
deliberate distortion of the truth. How preposterous the claim by
the author of this article that Charles had given him magnetized
shirt fronts and collars, or had caused a Sheffield woman, under a
hypnotic spell, to experience 'amazing visions and contortions'!
Dismissing these fabrications as of 'no real consequence', though
they had angered her at the time, Georgina appealed to Annie to
contradict such stories at every opportunity.[17]

A ruder jolt was the unauthorized publication in 1883 of some
early Dickens letters to Thomas Mitton. Since they dealt in part
with such strictly private matters as the financial embarrassments of
Charles's father and brother Fred, there were sordid details whose
circulation distressed her. Why should the general public be given
more information about this unfortunate chapter in the family
history than had already been divulged by Forster in the *Life*?
Little had Georgina suspected, while examining these letters four
years earlier, that they were soon to see print. At that time they
had just been purchased by Ouvry, a great collector of autographs,
and she had been asked to go through them. Though hard pressed
to get on with her edition of the Dickens letters, she had spent many
hours on this assignment, determining dates wherever possible for
the undated manuscripts, repairing the torn and mouse-eaten places,
and arranging the whole chronologically. Seven or eight of the
strictly private letters she had burned without scruple. Some
others dealing with the same family affairs she had hesitated to
destroy, however, because they were especially interesting specimens

of Dickens's early correspondence. 'But I trust, if you see there is any impropriety in any of these letters being kept, you will destroy them,' she had advised Ouvry.[18]

But he had not destroyed any of them. Instead, he had assembled them with a number of other letters by and to Dickens, as well as some engraved portraits of the family, and had ordered the collection mounted and bound in dark morocco to form two large quarto volumes. Two years later, in June of 1881, he died suddenly. When his executors sold his valuable library the following year, the recently bound letters were purchased by Sotheran and Company, who in turn offered them for sale at two hundred guineas. They went to an American, J. W. Bouton. In 1883 selections from this collection were printed in the New York *Tribune*.[19] At this point Georgina re-entered the picture.

'A "Dickens Correspondence" of great interest has just passed into the hands of Mr. J. W. Bouton, the well-known publisher of Broadway, New York,' she read in the London *Times* for 27th October. The news item announced that these letters would 'throw much light upon the early struggles and first literary achievements of Dickens' as selections appeared in the *Tribune*. There was also a reference to Georgina's part in arranging and dating the manuscripts. 'We shall give the gist of the most interesting of these documents, or quote the letters themselves,' *The Times* promised. Thus did Georgina learn that some of the strictly personal correspondence which she had handled for Ouvry was now being made public. Would it appear, then, that she as Dickens's executrix had sanctioned such publication? Stung by this suggestion, she rushed into action.

'I beg emphatically to state that I have nothing whatever to do with the publication of these letters, or am in any way connected with it,' she declared in an announcement which *The Times* inserted for her on 29th October. 'In my capacity as executrix, I denounce the making public in England of this correspondence as an infringement on my rights; and on behalf of every member of Mr. Charles Dickens's family, I wish it also to be well known how utterly repugnant to our feelings is the publication of some of these letters.' But out of loyalty to her old friend she absolved Ouvry of any blame for the unauthorized appearance of the letters. 'He was a man of the finest tact and delicacy of feeling,' she maintained, 'and I can only imagine that his ill health during the years that preceded his sudden death must have prevented him from leaving due instructions as to the disposal of his correspondence.'

And apparently it was true that he had never thought of making his collection public. According to Thomas W. Newton, who had assisted him with his library and had prepared the Dickens manuscripts for binding, the two quarto volumes had been valued solely as personal reminiscences of a great author and friend and had never been intended for the press. Any letters Ouvry considered fit for publication had already appeared in the Georgina-Mamie edition.

To her belief in him as a friend who had meant well Georgina gave further support in a letter to Annie: 'Yes—it was indeed, a worry and a shock, about Mr. Ouvry's letters! I assure you it made me ill. Indeed, I think I have been . . . as much vexed for dear Mr. Ouvry's memory as for our own share of the annoyance. He was the *very last* man who would ever have dreamed of allowing the publication of private letters. He was one of the most delicate, most discreet and judicious of men. The only blame I allow to *him* is that he *ought*, certainly, to have made some special disposition in his will as to these letters—both his own, and some letters that he bought after the death of a Mr. Mitton. . . .' This oversight, she assumed, was probably the result of his bad heath and failing memory in later years. Having made his will in 1876, he had not touched it again before his death. 'So I shall always believe that he *did* intend to have made some specific disposal of them and, like many men, put it off—until his sudden death stopped all his earthly plans!'[20]

But for his executors, one of them his brother, she had only reproof. Without looking over the letters, they had simply sold them in a lump to a dealer. 'There was nothing in any of these which reflected anything but credit *to Charles himself*,' she admitted, 'but the private affairs of his Father and family, which were never very creditable, were freely written of . . . and we would *never* have sanctioned their publication.' Had Ouvry's executors applied to her, as they should have done before selling the documents, she would have interdicted the sale of the more private ones. Of the rest they could have made any disposition they pleased. 'It was a shameful carelessness,' she charged.[21]

Ten years later the same old family skeleton was on exhibit again. This time it was Percy Fitzgerald who perpetrated the offence. 'I was very *much* surprised and I had better confess at once, VERY much annoyed when I saw in yesterday's "Globe" a letter of old Mr. Dickens to Chapman & Hall—published by you,' Georgina wrote him. Had Fred Chapman given him this letter? If so, there should have been a stipulation not to make it public. 'Quite enough statement has already been made on the subject of Micawber being taken from C. D.'s Father,' she complained, 'and if this publication should bring forth any more Disagreeable statements, I shall be most sorry

—and angry.'[22] The letter in question was one which John Dickens had written to Chapman and Hall in 1837, asking for an advance of £15. 5s. on a bill due his son two months hence. What concern, demanded Georgina, could the public possibly have in the matter? How incensed Charles had always been when the lives of great men and their families had been raked up in this fashion!

It was not Fitzgerald's last outrage against the Dickens family. In April of 1902 *Harper's New Monthly Magazine* carried his article entitled 'Dickens in His Books'. Part of it was devoted to an analysis of the novelist's affection for Mary Hogarth. It raised the question why Mary's 'charms—she was more attractive *and had always secretly loved him*—did not appeal' to Dickens before his marriage to Catherine (mistakenly referred to in the discussion as the younger sister). Could the answer be found in *The Battle of Life*? Had Mary, knowing Catherine's feeling for Charles, hidden her own affections? This speculation, Fitzgerald maintained, was the '*only one*' that would '*rationally account*' for Dickens not marrying the girl he loved'.

On this occasion Henry Fielding Dickens rose to the defence of his father, doubtless with the concurrence and advice of Aunt Georgy. In a devastating letter to Harper's, published by the editors with due apology for giving offence to the family, Harry took Fitzgerald to task for his errors in fact and his absurd speculation. Mary was not the older sister; she was only fifteen at the time of Dickens's marriage and still in school. At the age of seventeen she died. This information Fitzgerald could have found for himself, had he 'taken the most ordinary precautions to verify facts', either by consulting Forster's *Life* or, 'better still, by communicating with some member of the family, before speculating in public upon matters connected entirely' with Dickens's private life. His article was 'obviously calculated to give an entirely false impression' of the novelist's affection for his young sister-in-law.

It was something of a trial to Georgina, this deserved reprimand to Percy Fitzgerald. He was actually a sincere Dickens admirer, with whom she had carried on a warm correspondence through the years as occasion dictated. She had condoled with him on the death of his father, had congratulated him on an article in the *Illustrated London News*, had appealed to him when she wished to make a gift to 'an old lady, a very dear friend of ours, Mrs. White . . . living in Devonshire', who had 'taken quietly to amusing herself with acrostics'. Where, Georgina asked, might she find a book of acrostics like Percy's own? In time the well-meaning Fitzgerald, having twice been slapped on the wrist, was restored to favour. At the age of eighty-four Georgina was still corresponding with him, inviting him to 'see my small flat' and thanking him for reviving her 'departed' energy by bringing up Dickensian topics afresh.[23]

In the late 1880's Georgina stood guard like a dragon over the treasure of Dickens's honour while F. G. Kitton was collecting materials for his *Dickens by Pen and Pencil*. She carefully watched the preparation of the bulky folio, exercising her right as executrix to hold back any pictures or letters which she deemed unsuitable for general circulation. As the work went to press she diligently read the proof sheets. She also directed Kitton to valuable sources of information and pointed out inaccuracies in his work. 'But for her aid,' he stated in his warm acknowledgement, 'many errors might have disfigured these pages.'[24]

Chiefly, she corrected faulty assumptions that had somehow gained varied degrees of acceptance, like the identification of Bleak House with Fort House at Broadstairs. She blasted the claim that Dickens had used this seaside cottage as his original, pointing out that he had not written a line of *Bleak House* there, that the story very plainly indicated a locale near St. Albans, Hertfordshire, and that the description did 'not in the least resemble' Fort House.[25] Such 'silly little false statements', she wrote Annie Fields, '*do* annoy me!'[26] She also corrected the impression that Dickens had acted in Planché's *A Romantic Idea* at Drury Lane on 11 May 1855, under the name of George Warwick. That he had not appeared in the play, she affirmed, was borne out by Edmund Yates, a member of the cast.[27] And she bristled at a statement by a former pupil of Wellington House Academy that Dickens, as a boy, had shown no musical ability, his teacher 'declaring it was vain to teach him the piano'. She insisted that 'he was very fond of it [music] in after life, and had a most excellent ear and a good voice, but I daresay it would have been useless to have taught him music at school'.[28]

Her protective zeal further asserted itself in withholding a facsimile page from the manuscript of a juvenile dramatic piece, a travesty of *Othello*, which Dickens had written in 1833 for his family and friends. She considered the work unworthy of his later stature. (Curiously enough, though Kitton was prevented from using the manuscript, Robert Langton had already published a facsimile page some years earlier.)[29]

Though Georgina made every effort to keep objectionable material out of Kitton's book, she was not consulted, apparently, during the preparation of a supplement, to which a number of Dickens's friends contributed reminiscences. Not subjected to her censorship, some of these entries included items which would certainly not have seen print had her consent been asked. There was, for example, an account by Arthur Locker of how Dickens had resuscitated the nearly drowned John Leech by 'making mesmeric passes', sparks shooting from the ends of his fingers.[30]

Piqued by the publicity given such absurd details, Georgina dashed off a note to the publisher. 'I can only repeat that you and Mr. Kitton and I see the subject from totally different points of view!' she expostulated, 'and that personalities which you consider interesting and which are, I suppose, found interesting to the Public are painful to Mr. Dickens' family, because—on the whole—they give an entirely false impression of him!' Though she recognized the author's desire to 'show all reverence' and 'do justice', she felt that Kitton had been 'too ready to accept contributions from *everybody*! Whether they really knew anything of Mr. Dickens—or whether they did *not*!' And she reminded the publisher that the work had so far enjoyed the sanction of the family, that she had read the proof and 'kept a great deal of matter out of the work that was *absolutely untrue*', that she and Katey had contributed various portraits of Dickens, and that Mamie had written one of the entries.[31] The tone throughout her letter was one of aggrieved astonishment over the utter disregard of family feeling.

It is interesting to speculate on her further shock when she discovered the footnote supplied for a description of a photograph of Dickens at Gad's Hill, 'leaning against a column . . . holding in his right hand a glass of wine'. The wine glass, Kitton's note pointed out, had been 'omitted in the wood-cut reproduction in Forster's *Life*, and replaced by a book in an enlarged American copy'.[32]

It was to be expected that Georgina would hold inviolable any details about Dickens's early romance with Maria Beadnell and his later attachment for Ellen Ternan. What consternation, therefore, when in 1908 his letters to Maria appeared in an unauthorized publication by the Boston Bibliophile Society! In 1905, almost twenty years after Maria's death, her daughter Ella had sold the precious packet of correspondence tied up with a faded blue ribbon. Shocked by the printing of these intimate and tender missives, Georgina, with the concurrence of Harry, banned the Boston publication in England. But one copy passed the customs and came into the hands of B. W. Matz, then editor of the *Dickensian*, who could not understand why Georgina had always opposed his use of any letter to Maria in his journal. Even her name had been taboo. After he had shown Georgina his copy of the Boston book, she privately recorded her recollections of Maria and her husband. This note ultimately found its way into print when at long last the Beadnell letters were brought out in an English edition in 1934, seventeen years after Georgina's death.

The possibility that Dickens's relations with Ellen Ternan might be subjected to prying scrutiny was even more repugnant than the publication of his letters to Maria. On learning, therefore, that Thomas Wright was collecting materials for a biography of Dickens, Georgina appealed to him by letter to preserve certain privacies. Though Wright did not publicize the exact contents of this correspondence, she apparently had asked him not to divulge a story Canon Benham had told him of Ellen's confessing to intimacies with Dickens. 'But there was no need for perturbation,' Wright remarked later, maintaining that it would have been cruel to make such revelations at that early date, when his 'conscience would have been a greater barrier than Miss Hogarth's letters'.[33]

Of all the stories Georgina felt called upon to contradict, that linking Dickens's name with the notorious Druce trial was the most fantastic. Though the case did not actually reach the courts until 1907, it had its beginnings in 1896, with a petition for the opening of a coffin in one of the vaults of Highgate Cemetery, which, according to the records, held the remains of Thomas Charles Druce, a London tradesman with whom Dickens had dealt. The burial there in 1864, the petition alleged, had been falsified; the coffin would be found empty. Druce, it was charged, had in reality been the name assumed by William John Cavendish Bentinck-Scott, fifth Duke of Portland, after the mysterious death of his older brother, with whom he had quarrelled. Fearing for his own safety, so ran the testimony, he had transferred to himself vast properties from his estate at Welbeck Abbey and had begun life as a merchant at the Baker Street Bazaar in Tottenham Court Road, London. Finally wearying of a tradesman's life, he had staged his death as Druce and assumed madness as the Duke of Portland, so that he could fall back on the plea of insanity if he should ever be accused of murdering his brother. Many persons believed this preposterous story and invested in bonds (to be repaid in the event of a favourable court decision) to underwrite a suit by Druce's son to have his claims as the sixth Duke of Portland legalized and the present incumbent ejected.[34]

One of the key witnesses was a Mrs. Mary Robinson, who testified falsely that she had met the elder Druce in 1862. During a period of residence in America, according to her statement, she had visited Dickens when he read in Boston in 1868. At his suggestion, she asserted, she had returned to England and applied to Druce at Welbeck Abbey for an appointment as 'outside correspondent'. Eventually Druce had hired her to post his letters· From further contacts with Dickens in April of 1870 she had learned that her employer was actually the Duke of Portland, that he was 'one man in two bodies', that his workmen called him 'Resurrection'. To give weight to her testimony, she spoke with assurance whenever questioned about her claim to friendship with Dickens and burst into tears at the mention of his death. She had been in Westminster Abbey, she said, to hear Dean Stanley preach the funeral sermon.

Shocked by the references to Dickens in the hearings, Georgina asked the newspapers to publish a statement denying that he had ever known the Duke of Portland. Nor did the Druce furore subside before it had subjected her to an unpleasant encounter. Returning by rail to London after a visit at Foxwold, the home of a friend who lived near Westerham, Kent, she was approached at Dunton Green Junction by a bustling magnate, one of her acquaintances, who asked her officiously, 'Well, Miss Hogarth, what about the Druce case, eh? Think your friend Charles Dickens knew anything of it?' Bridling, Georgina replied emphatically, 'He was my brother-in-law, and these people's stories are all lies'.[35] As, in fact, they were. The case broke down when it was learned that Mrs. Robinson had come from New Zealand in response to an offer of £4,000 to tell her fabricated story from the witness stand.

We *were very* much annoyed by the Druce Case! and the *lies* by that odious woman!' Georgina wrote an old friend. 'I wonder she dared! I suppose she thought there were no survivors left of Charles Dickens' family!' Now, unfortunately, it would probably be necessary to open the Druce grave. (When it was opened all was in order; the coffin held a shrouded figure.) As to Druce, Georgina remembered him well—'*as a tradesman*'. Dickens had bought considerable furniture from him for Gad's Hill; it was excellent merchandise. 'As proof of which, I have a great deal of it which came from Gad's Hill in my Dining room here in this house,' she added. Charles had always found Druce 'a very superior *Tradesman*', but had known him 'in no other way!' Nor had her brother-in-law ever seen the Duke of Portland or gone to Welbeck Abbey '*in his life*'.[36] So ended an affair unique among the carking episodes which beset the guardian of 'the beloved memory'.

Chapter Fifteen
'HOW THE YEARS MELT INTO EACH OTHER!'

In her fifties Georgina underwent a period of indecision and depression. Once the letters had been given to the world, she had time to nurse a growing dissatisfaction with her domestic life. When in February of 1883 she went alone into the Abbey to keep the annual birthday tryst in Poets' Corner, the gravestone in the dismal late winter light 'looked sad and dreary—as I felt!' she confessed. But she cheered herself by leaving some bright flowers before returning to the tensions developing at Strathmore Gardens. Mamie had been growing more and more unstable emotionally as she sought in changes of scene—in alcohol, even—some anodyne for the dissatisfaction which plagued her. After her father's death she had found no abiding or dominant interest and purpose in life, though a lurking religious element in her nature had begun to turn her in the direction of Christian social work.

'It is merciful for me that I have Mamie to love . . . ,' Georgina had vowed to Annie Fields in 1874; yet in view of her niece's present behaviour—erratic, puzzling, pathetic—it was easier to indulge that love at a distance. Though Mamie was at home now, it would be for one of her short stays only. Before Easter she would be back in Edinburgh for another visit to her friends, the Whites. Her prolonged intervals of absence kept her aunt in a fret over maintaining a large and expensive home unnecessarily. Georgina calculated that her own half of the upkeep came to much more than she would spend in a small place suited to herself alone—especially as she fancied a quiet life in simpler surroundings than would content Mamie.[1]

Now that aunt and niece were briefly together once more, the interminable discussions resumed, with nothing settled. 'I have *again* put it to her . . . that she is spending too much money for her share of a house she uses so little . . . ,' Georgina confided to Annie, 'and I, again, suggested that she should set up her own *home* as the place where she likes best to be, and only come to me as a *visitor*—when she is inclined—in some much smaller place that I would take for myself *alone*.'[2] But Mamie remained unwilling, perhaps regarding the less elaborate establishment that she could afford to maintain by herself as somehow unworthy of her social position.

Annie, it seems, had sympathetically advanced the idea that Dickens would have wanted his sister-in-law to follow her own desires. Georgina agreed: 'I feel all you say about our Beloved, who are gone, wishing us to do the best for our own welfare and happiness. But you see, in *my* case, my life is so bound up with this other —*his* Daughter—whose welfare must also (if it is possible that such things can be known and can affect those who are gone from us!) be his desire! that I have this peculiar feeling which binds me more to Mamie than my feeling for *herself*, does. Because I must own that, though I *love* her as much as ever, I feel that she has shown, and *does* show, so little consideration for me, that . . . I sometimes get so angry that I think I will make up my mind to think only of myself! and insist on breaking off, and going my own way. Then this other thought and love comes in, and, until she wishes it, too! I cannot make the separation.'[3]

But by the end of the year the decision was made. With Mamie still spending more time in Scotland than in England, it was absurd to go on maintaining the costly home. 'I have a board up! which looks melancholy! and many people come to see the house,' Georgina announced. Her plan was to move into a small flat and keep only one maid. Mamie, during her brief London intervals, would also live there. In this way the two could cut expenses drastically. A few months later, however, Georgina was forced to change her plans: '. . . I have been decided—and undecided! and decided *again*! about my house!' She had received an offer for the property, but it had been too low to warrant a move, except into a place so very small that there would have been no room at all for Mamie. When for the '100th time' she approached her niece on the desirability of dissolving their partnership altogether, there were strong protests again. 'And I *cannot* bring myself to say that I should much prefer to live really by myself—as I do virtually!' Georgina admitted. On the advice, therefore, of Ouvry's successor, who agreed that she could only lose money by selling out now, she decided to continue the old arrangement as a matter of business prudence. And she would have the satisfaction of keeping both her maids. For how could she have parted with Emma, who had been with her for seventeen years? Having come to Gad's Hill just before that lonely Christmas when Dickens was in America, she was 'a link with the old days'.[4]

The memory of those days became especially vivid in February, as always, though, after all, 'one thinks of the dear beloved Dead EVERY day!' But for the first time in the fourteen years, the birthday anniversary found her unable to go to the Abbey. A chill fog, the worst of the season, had settled over London, and she dared not venture out because of an obstinate cold that had hung on since Christmas. She tried to regard the matter sensibly, realizing that it was 'foolish to risk one's health for a sentiment which is only a satisfaction to [one's] own self!' But it was sad to think of the stone bare of the usual early blossoms, such as brightened Gad's Hill every February.[5]

Two more years passed before the domestic question resolved itself and aunt and niece went their separate ways. It was depressing to note the change in Mamie. Gone now was the daintiness that had once marked her, the fragile charm of the Miss Dickens whom Henry James had met through the Nortons in 1869 and described as 'lady-like (in black silk and black lace) and the image of her father'.[6] Yet the loss of her exterior attractions may have had inner compensations. Possibly in the hope of redeeming a hitherto empty life, she had, even before permanently quitting her aunt's roof, set up an abode with a clergyman and his wife, in whose company she was now to carry on philanthropic enterprises among the poor in Manchester. More than likely she was urged on by a sense of continuing her father's efforts for social betterment. But Georgina, who had previously remonstrated with her on other grounds (as had Katey), felt that there was renewed reason to deplore the way Mamie was managing her life. The clergyman and his wife, it was suspected, were manoeuvring to get her niece's money from her.[7]

An unexpected development soon focused Georgina's thoughts on another of Dickens's children, Frank, who had undergone a dozen years of frontier hardship with the Mounted Police in Canada. It was the period of tense alarm over the Indian uprisings. In 1883, following an outbreak of new danger on the Saskatchewan River, he had set out, with twenty-five men under his leadership, to establish a post at Fort Pitt. The assignment had ended disastrously when, outnumbered in a fresh Indian revolt (the Red Rebellion), he and his men had been forced to escape by the river. Left behind were all the cherished letters from his father, the photographs, and the other relics. His spirit broken by this experience and his efficiency reduced by growing deafness, he resigned his commission in 1886 and planned a year's travel in the United States.[8]

By June he was in Moline, Illinois, where he had been asked to speak before a dinner gathering of the Friday Club on his experiences in the Red Rebellion. On the appointed day the mercury stood high, and Frank, overheated by the horse-and-buggy ride to the meeting place, took a long drink of ice water on reaching the table. Immediately he suffered acute distress. 'It was the water,' he gasped. 'When I drank it I felt as if I had been stabbed.' Fifteen minutes later he died. The seizure was later diagnosed as heart paralysis. He was buried at Moline, and his effects were disposed of according to instructions from Charley, who, as head of the family, handled the necessary correspondence.

Dead before their time were three of Dickens's sons. For Georgina this last loss released another flood of memories—tender memories of how Walter, Sydney, and Frank had once come to her with their childish problems, their early lessons, their evening prayers. But she could not let her thoughts dwell on the past, for the immediate concerns of daily living intruded, now that she and Mamie had at last dissolved partnership. Taking her valued maid and companion Emma with her, she moved into a flat at 70 Wynnstay Gardens, Kensington. But she could not feel settled there. Before her lease expired, she sublet the place furnished and went to live temporarily at Harry's home, 15 Tedworth Square, where Emma came to be with her during the day. 'I *am* very happy here—with my dear Harry and his kind, sweet wife, and my darling pets,' she told Annie Fields. But in this household a new 'pet' appeared every year or so (the two and a half years between the fourth and the fifth she called 'a longer interregnum than usual'), and soon Auntie had to give up her quarters. 'In October Marie expects *another* Baby! I am sorry to say—so I shall have to leave this home, as my room will be required,' she wrote in the summer of 1887. She would get rid of her flat on the expiration of her lease a year hence and find something more to her liking. Happy though her life had been at Harry's, she felt that she would be 'for many reasons . . . glad to have a little place *of my own again*'.[9]

This she managed according to plan, taking a small house at 55 Oakley Street. From now on her life revolved around Harry and his family. Whenever they moved, she did too, selecting a place near theirs; when they holidayed at the seaside or travelled on the Continent, she went with them; when they observed Christmas and other special occasions, she always joined the group. To Harry's children—there were seven in 1889—Auntie was a stout kind lady in a lace cap. The three little girls admired her frilled caps with their pretty ribbon bows, sombre-coloured in the daytime, gayer at night. Often a bracelet made from one of Dickens's watch chains encircled her plump wrist. She loved jewellery, and her fingers twinkled with masses of rings as she sat knitting long black silk stockings for her grandnieces and grandnephews. Like Dickens, she enjoyed inventing nonsensical names for children: Harry's Olive was Olivey-Polivey; Elaine, Bobilow-Bobs; young Hal, Halikins-Balikins; and Philip, like his namesake in *Great Expectations*, Pip. The youngsters found her always affectionate and sweet-tempered, unruffled by their antics and mishaps. One day five-year-old Olive, carrying a dish to the table, spilled custard all over Auntie's pretty clean dress. 'There, there,' the frightened child was comforted, 'it's nothing, nothing at all!' Of no one was Aunt Georgy fonder than of their mother, often patting her hand and exclaiming, 'Dear Marie!'[10] She characterized Harry's wife as 'a most devoted mother' who 'not only brings children into the world, but works for them in every way—incessantly after they come'.[11]

But Georgina's keen interest in the third generation never crowded out the past. The children heard her speak constantly of their grandfather, who had died before they were born. And for many years, until infirmity and old age made such trips inadvisable, the family counted on her to be in Poets' Corner for the three special anniversaries. The sacred June observance, they were aware, was not confined to the 9th alone; Auntie proclaimed the whole week 'from the 8th, the day he was stricken down, to the 14th, the day he was buried', to be the anniversary.[12]

In June of 1887, however, the Abbey was closed to the public during the special preparations for the Queen's Golden Jubilee. For the first time in seventeen years the two wreaths would not adorn the grave on the 9th. The Dean of Westminster would have escorted Georgina to Poets' Corner himself, had he not felt that she would have been distressed by the *'desecration* of the place'. All the stones were boarded over. Worst of all was 'the thought of the *noise*, confusion and disorder going on in that quiet corner' where it was usually 'so calm, cool and tranquillizing'. The anniversary that year, she noted, came on the very day of the week and brought the same 'bright and lovely' weather as in 1870. 'How vividly it all comes back! every year more and more so,' she wrote Annie, adding that she was *'thankful* to feel it so!'[13]

In the ensuing autumn and winter she followed with mixed feelings Charley's American reading tour. Hard pressed to support his seven daughters and one son, Charley had already hit upon the expedient of reading from his father's books in England. A successful provincial tour encouraging him to continue the venture in the States, he sailed in October, accompanied by his wife and their third daughter, Sydney Margaret. He began his engagements at Chickering Hall in New York City, before an audience that filled the auditorium and part of the stage as well. Reading 'Doctor Marigold' and scenes from *Pickwick*, he created for many of his older listeners the illusion of the novelist himself come back. Even so, his performance was no 'servile imitation of his father', one review pointed out. He had perfected his own technique.[14]

'I don't profess to like the idea of Charley's reading his Father's books—and I *cannot* believe it is anything remarkable in the way of reading,' declared Georgina on receiving Annie Fields's favourable reports. The whole performance, she felt, could be little more than an imitation. 'Still he has a right to do it, if he chooses—and if people are content to go and hear him and put money in his pocket! I can only be *very* glad,' she admitted. 'For with all those *girls*, he certainly wants as much money as he can get.' And she agreed that it was well for him to make friends in America, 'where his Father's name is a support of *love!*' But she acknowledged that he would also be liked for himself, for he was a 'good fellow'.[15]

Apparently he did enjoy popularity in his own right, for he was deluged with invitations. Perhaps his most memorable visit was to the home of William Winter, where he drank from the goblet which his father had used twenty years earlier in toasting his American friends at the farewell party aboard the *Russia*. In all the years since, no lips had dared to profane that glass.[16]

By now the fiasco of Charley's purchase of Gad's Hill, his sale of the chalet, and his harshness as a creditor seemed remote. In spite of her reservations as to his tour, Georgina harboured no personal resentment toward this burdened family man only ten years her junior, who addressed her familiarly as 'Gina' rather than 'Auntie'.[17] He had become to her only an even-tempered, likable contemporary, not steadfast and thoughtful like Harry, to be sure, but yet the object of her good will. The readings, though, were another matter. That anyone, even his father's son, should dare to project those unique Dickens creations, raising the curtain on what had been intended as the final performance in 1870—that came too close to desecration!

With Charley's oldest daughter, Mary Angela, Georgina still acknowledged a special bond. Did not Mekitty recall how her grandfather had spoken with many voices from a lighted London stage? Yet when the girl, stagestruck from childhood, proved herself of Dickens's own blood by taking up a theatrical career, Auntie withheld whole-hearted approval. 'I do *not* think myself she will ever do anything great,' she predicted when Mekitty appeared at the Princess Theatre in a minor role in *The Silver King*. 'She wants physical qualifications, for one thing. She is not *at all* pretty, although she has a pleasant intelligent face.' But the young lady had poise, her great-aunt admitted: 'Although she really *is* nervous, she appears quite at home and perfectly self-possessed on the stage—which is a great point.' And Mekitty was happy to win a measure of success in the career she had chosen. Yet Georgina, for all her connections with theatrical folk, both amateur and professional, regretted her grand-niece's decision. 'I confess I was very sorry, and so were some others of us, when she chose a public life as a profession, but now the thing is *done*, and she is well started, we can do nothing but give her encouragement and cheer her on her way,' she told Annie Fields. For a while Mekitty seemed justified in her choice of vocation. Acting was 'decidedly her "line",' Georgina became convinced, for the girl took her *'tiny* part' in *Claudian,* a new play in 1883, with *'real* success', and all the papers lauded her.[18] Before long, however, Mekitty justified her great aunt's original predictions by abandoning the theatre and taking up a literary career.

* * *

On his return from America in June of 1888 Charley resigned his editorship of *All the Year Round* and became a reader for the Macmillan publishing firm, a happy connection in which he continued until his death. Freed from the harassing details of keeping a weekly journal going, he devoted an increasing amount of his time to writing, some of his articles making valuable contributions by bringing out hitherto unpublished biographical data on his father. For at least one of these pieces, 'Charles Dickens as an Editor', which appeared in the *English Illustrated Magazine* for August of 1889, he had the co-operation of Georgina, who placed a series of letters at his disposal. When Macmillan brought out a new edition of Dickens's works, he prepared the biographical and bibliographical introduction for each volume. And for F. G. Kitton he went through the entire file of *Household Words* from 1850 to 1859, identifying his father's unsigned articles solely on the basis of their individual literary style. (At this time the Office Book, in which Wills had kept the names of all the contributors and their contributions, could not be found.) Productive in the type of work to which his training and temperament suited him, Charley severed all his other connections, dissolving his partnership with Evans in the printing firm and, in 1893, stopping the publication of *All the Year Round.* For the first time in many years he now had the satisfaction of devoting himself solely to congenial occupation without administrative responsibilities.[19]

But past tensions were exacting their toll: Charley was still in poor health; his complaint, a heart condition, was now serious, Georgina informed Annie Fields. With a 'devoted little wife' and affectionate children, however, he was surrounded by every care in his home. 'And beyond our feeling sad at seeing him in such poor health,' Georgina explained, 'we have no need to *trouble* ourselves about him, poor fellow!' Macmillan had made his hours and work as easy and pleasant as possible, and he was highly regarded.[20]

About Mamie there were more serious misgivings. Though at times during the past decade little had been known of her activities, there had always been concern over her health, never robust at best. Now by the winter of 1896 there was real cause for alarm. She had gone into a decline, and though she was in March 'perhaps, a little better', her aunt declared that 'she causes us the greatest anxiety and sadness. Katey and I go to see her [in Manchester] every three weeks—or thereabouts now—and, of course, are always prepared to go oftener, when necessary, or at an hour's notice, at any time.'[21]

It was during these months that Mamie completed a little book entitled *My Father as I Recall Him*, a work which betrayed in every page her worship of the man whom she pronounced 'one apart from all other beings'.[22] Unlike Katey, who also set down her daughterly tribute, then destroyed the manuscript rather than give the world 'only half the truth about my father', Mamie, placing idolatry above understanding, and hiding the darker half of truth even from herself, could hardly have been plagued by such scruples as she prepared her book for the press. But shortly before the proofs were to be sent her for correction, she became too ill for the task. She lingered into July. Then Charley, aged fifty-nine, succumbed to an apoplectic attack similar to his father's. On the day of the funeral Mamie died, her end hastened by the shock of her brother's death. Like her father she had lived to age fifty-eight.

When Mamie's book appeared the following year, Georgina, a double mourner now, could find in it this tribute to herself: 'When I write about my aunt, or "Auntie", as no doubt I may often have occasion to do, it is of the aunt *par excellence*, Georgina Hogarth. She has been to me ever since I can remember anything, and to all of us, the truest, best and dearest friend, companion and counsellor. To quote my father's own words: "The best and truest friend man ever had".'[23]

That Georgina must have written to Annie Fields about Mamie's death is a foregone conclusion; that she also commented on her niece's last years is more than likely. But after a letter reporting Mamie's condition some four months before her end there is a gap in the existing correspondence, as if discretion had prompted the destruction of portions of it. The customary replies to Annie's never-failing June and Christmas letters are missing for 1896, as is that to the February birthday letter for 1897. The answer to Annie's letter for June of 1897 refers to Mamie's death, however, in terms that show it to be no new subject. Katey, her aunt explained, had been rather unwell during the winter: 'It took her a long time to recover from the accumulated sadness of the illness and deaths of Charley and dear Mamie, following so close on each other. And for months she did not seem to rally from the remembrance of it all!'[24]

With Charley's widow, too, Georgina sympathized: 'Poor Bessie Dickens is always brave and good, and her girls work very well. It is hard for them, I always feel. They have so little enjoyment in life! But it is a blessing that they are able to work.' Fortunately, an annual Queen's pension of £100 prevented acute financial distress. They had some assistance from Harry, too, who had turned over to his brother's widow part of his inheritance from Mamie.[25]

Mekitty, since abandoning the stage, had enjoyed some success as a writer of fiction and articles. On her behalf Georgina appealed to Annie Fields. Might it not be possible for this grandniece to contribute a weekly letter to some American newspaper? Or short stories to some of the magazines? Mekitty was grateful for Annie's letter of introduction to Henry James, who had 'received her *most* kindly and promised not to forget her if he should have an opportunity of helping her'.[26]

When Annie suggested the *Youth's Companion*, indicating the sort of contribution that would be acceptable, Georgina passed the word on to Mekitty, who, she declared, would *'most certainly'* investigate this possibility. Since the girl had 'to earn her Bread and Butter! she and all her sisters, except the one who is, happily, married', no opportunity could be neglected. Sydney Margaret, the married one, was now the mother of a little daughter—'My *great* GREAT niece!' marvelled Georgina.[27]

Ten years had passed since the Queen's Golden Jubilee, and now the Diamond Jubilee was in preparation as another 9th June arrived. This time, though, the Abbey was open to the public, and Georgina was gratified to find Dickens's grave laden with more flowers than usual. People were remembering that this year was the diamond jubilee of *Pickwick*, too. She found it 'curious to think that Pickwick *now*—like Scott's Waverley is "Sixty Years Since"!' She reflected, too, on the state of the world, finding 'more difference in *class and manners* in our Country in these last sixty years than in centuries before . . . !' A decade earlier the very word *jubilee* had sickened her; now she shared the elation of 'all London, . . . in a fever' over the celebration. 'It is strange,' she wrote Annie, 'to go along the big thoroughfares. Nothing to be heard but hammering —or to be seen but the enormous stands erected everywhere. Hideous at first, but now beginning to be covered with red cloth.' By mid-June she had caught the contagious excitement of the colourful Colonial troops—Australian, Canadian, Indian—and the babble of foreign tongues as she threaded her way through the crush in the streets. She was going to sleep at Harry's house in Egerton Place the night before the jubilee. Tuesday morning, the 22nd, they would all rise early and leave by eight o'clock to reach St. Martin's Churchyard, where they had seats for the procession. She hoped for 'Queen's weather', fretting that 'everything would be spoiled if it should be a pouring day!' Sympathetically she reflected on the ageing Victoria, who, she was sure, must dread the tiring ordeal and would 'be thankful when the day is over!'[28]

At last the awaited hour arrived and Her Majesty, surmounted by a tiny black parasol, rode through cheering throngs to give thanks at St. Paul's Cathedral. As the royal carriage entered the Strand, the tower of St. Martin's looked down for a moment on two stout little septuagenarians, each ruled by a fanatic fidelity, each a repository of notable memories.

*   *   *

'How the years melt into each other!' Georgina had exclaimed two decades earlier.[29] They seemed to speed even faster now as she watched Harry's children develop. It was indeed 'formidable', as she had once remarked of Charley's flock, how such 'little creatures mark the progress of time!'[30] Already Hal, Harry's oldest son, had left for Cambridge; and the next, Pip, was a midshipman stationed in the East Indies, writing 'delightful letters home *very* constantly'.[31] It was like reliving the days when Harry had been at Cambridge and Sydney at sea. In other ways, too, sharing Harry's family life was like repeating her years in his father's home. Once more she was going on holidays to France and Switzerland, spending part of each summer at the seaside, looking forward to Christmas festivity. Of course, travelling was less easy now, for, with her increased weight, she moved rather slowly. On the Continent she was perpetually in danger of being left behind whenever she alighted from the train during station stops. With the engine puffing and whistling its starting warning, there was general consternation before she got on board. But always she insisted, with irritating deliberateness, 'They won't leave without me'. Then would follow that last-minute struggle to hoist her safely back into her compartment, with one of the party pulling her in, another pushing from behind.[32]

Though Christmas could be cheery once more, Georgina did not forget, of course, to visit the Abbey. 'It will be 28 years since he was taken from us!' she wrote in December of 1897. 'Sometimes it seems to me like yesterday! and sometimes like a whole life time!' On this Christmas Eve she had found the stone brilliant with flowers: 'cheering and hopeful' by contrast with the dark, foggy day, these tokens meant that 'he is not forgotten, thank God!'[33]

Although sharing now so intimately the life of Harry's family, she still preserved her independence by maintaining her own home. Not long after her seventy-first birthday she moved into yet smaller quarters at 31 Egerton Terrace, in a light and airy district where the dwellings had both front and back gardens—almost like the open areas surrounding the houses in a country town. Though she had fewer rooms here than ever before, they were spacious and provided accommodations for Emma and the cook, both ageing noticeably now. Almost no objects of any intrinsic value remained among the furnishings here, but many were the interesting possessions kept for sentiment's sake. There was a veritable picture gallery: portraits of Dickens; of his children at various stages; of the young Mary Hogarth, dead now these sixty years; paintings by Katey. And there were the honours and testimonials given Dickens at Edinburgh and Birmingham. In Georgina's bedroom stood the old-fashioned sofa on which he had died,[34] and somewhere among her private papers were his letters, which she had long ago promised herself to destroy—as soon as she could bear to do so.

But her tranquillity in the new home was soon upset by a sad domestic experience. In January of 1898 her old cook, with her for twenty years, had to give up because of ill health. She was replaced by an acquaintance of Emma's, and for three weeks all went smoothly. Then suddenly the new servant became ill. The doctor whom Georgina called, first diagnosed the woman's complaint as slight bronchitis and indigestion, but the next day pneumonia developed. Thereupon Georgina engaged a nurse and sent for the cook's niece as well. 'And then I felt I had not the individual responsibility,' she explained. But on the third night the woman died, 'quite sensible almost to the last—and perfectly peaceful. . . .' Emma was greatly distressed and her mistress herself 'a good deal "knocked over" by it for some days'. Thereafter Georgina decided to find a younger woman to share the work with Emma, who, after thirty years of service in the same post, was not as active as she used to be.[35]

In the spring Annie Fields came once more to England, accompanied by her most intimate friend, Sarah Orne Jewett. Georgina
had taken care to beg them to visit her before she left for her
summer holidays, but, having absent-mindedly lost the London
address Annie had sent her, could not communicate with them on
their arrival. The Americans surprised her, therefore, when they
drove to Egerton Terrace one warm May afternoon. At the door
Emma, who remembered Annie, welcomed them to the new home,
which charmed them with its bright, clean rooms, cool and comfortable 'even on the hottest of afternoons. . . .' But at the sight
of her hostess Annie was somewhat startled, afterwards making the
diary notation that 'she is growing very old'. The farewell was a sad
one, for Annie 'felt quite sure that [they] were not likely to see each
other again'.[36]

Georgina seems not to have shared her friend's premonition that
there would be no more reunions, for when she answered Annie's
Christmas letter in December of 1900, her wish for the new year was
that it might give 'everything that is good and happy—and healthy!
to you dearest Annie and that you may *turn your steps* to England
and London some time in the course of it!'[37] But the two were not
to meet again.

Given much to reflecting on world events in her later years,
Georgina also commented in her December letter on the Boer War.
Like many moral Englishmen who were deploring the past half
century of hostilities—the Crimean War, the Sepoy Rebellion, con-
flicts in China, New Zealand, Africa—she wished to 'begin the new
century at peace with all the world! But,' she added realistically,
'we are not quite near it yet. However, compared with this time
last year, we have much reason to be *thankful*. . . . But this "Guer-
rilla warfare" going on in S. Africa is very terrible. There is so much
loss of life—on both sides—and *now*, for no result that I can see. I
wish we could take De Wet! then I think there would be an end. He
is a brave man, but one feels that his holding out is only a cruelty
to his own country—as well as to our poor soldiers!'[38]

But the most notable aspect of the letter was an omission. For the
first time there was no mention of a Christmas visit to the Abbey.
Nor was the subject to come up in subsequent Christmas and birthday letters. Even more significant, there was to be no more correspondence concerned with the solemn June anniversary. It was as
if, on the eve of the new century, the two women had agreed that
the grave in Poets' Corner might be allowed to take care of itself.
Perhaps during their brief May visit they had actually made such a
compact. The 'beloved memory' was not receding, however, for

Annie's February letter in 1901 evoked mellow meditations from
Georgina: 'How the years roll away! and *how* strange it seems to
think that he would have been 89!!! an old, *old* man!' As always, she
was thankful that he had not 'outlived Himself and his Faculties'.[39]

Her thoughts then made the natural transition to Queen Victoria,
whose end, at the age of eighty-one, had come on the 22nd January,
Georgina's seventy-fourth birthday. Because, until the very last, the
Queen 'had not become *incapable*', hers had been 'a beautiful Death!
worthy of a splendid *full* life, such as surely no woman ever had before!'
At the time Georgina had been staying in Kent at Foxwold Chase, the
home of her friend Mrs. Horace Pym, but she and her hostess had come
to London especially to see the funeral procession. From their places
close to Victoria Station they had watched the cortege wind slowly
past—a 'deeply touching sight', Georgina recalled. 'The demeanour
of the people was so impressive, *so perfectly still*. The small Coffin
on the gun carriage looked *very* small and lonely amongst the brilliant surroundings of the procession. The King looked very sad,
very *tired* and anxious, but very dignified—and the German Emperor
very fine and soldierly. The Queen and the Princesses were quite
invisible, in closed carriages with their thick black *veils*.' Georgina
expressed complete confidence in Edward VII. Forgotten now was
her disapproval of thirty years earlier when the young Prince had
been involved in the unsavoury Mordaunt divorce scandal. 'Our
Heir Apparent has had to figure in a disgraceful business, has he
not!' she had railed then. 'Hooted up the street' and 'piped at the
Theatre', he had been given a good lesson for the future, she had
hoped. Now she perceived in him 'some fine Royal qualities—and
he certainly inherits much of his Mother's tact and *sympathy*'. But
she could not believe there would ever be 'quite the same intense
feeling of love and loyalty for *any* other Monarch—in our country,
or in any other—as had grown up . . . for Queen Victoria! She was
such a real Woman!'[40]

Chapter Sixteen
'SUFFICIENTLY REWARDED'

PERHAPS the dawn of the twentieth century and the passing of the Queen brought a sharper awareness of the encroaching years. At any rate the winter—'dark and dismal ever since Christmas'—combined with her waning health to keep Georgina in a state of depression. She had a 'constant dull stupid headache—and a general sense of *seediness* and a wish to do nothing and go nowhere!' Even her ideas, she confessed ruefully, appeared 'to be frost bitten and stupefied'. Her doctor had told her that she was suffering from lowered vitality, but she felt certain that sunshine and springtime would work a cure.[1]

The march of the seasons, however, improved her only a little, physically, but when she answered Annie's next Christmas letter she was in better spirits. She was reading Sarah Orne Jewett's only historical novel, *The Tory Lover*, 'with great pleasure and interest'. Unlike Henry James, who had advised Miss Jewett to 'go back to the dear Country of the Pointed Firs',[2] Georgina expressed favourable reactions only, declaring the book to be 'delightfully written' and congratulating the author on the 'excellent notices . . . in many of our best papers'. She was also enjoying the vicarious excitement of her grandniece Enid's wedding preparations. Harry's other two daughters having gone with their father to America that year, the Fields-Dickens ties had been strengthened further, and Georgina could assure Annie that the visitors cherished 'a most vivid and charming remembrance of that "lovely day by the sea" which they spent with you'. There was, moreover, praise for the United States: 'I do congratulate you on your Nation! and I am sure you have every right and reason to be proud of her!' She had been keeping up with political affairs abroad and admired Theordore Roosevelt as 'a man of remarkable *power*—and liberality! two great combinations in a Ruler!'[3]

The next year (1902) brought word of the death of her youngest nephew, Plorn, from whom she had not heard directly since his note of thanks for her wedding gift. His life in Australia had been marked by business failures, gambling losses, and unpaid debts. Eighteen years earlier his frantic appeals had brought a loan of £800 from

Harry, aid which had never been acknowledged. Nor had Plorn ever made any payments on principal and interest. He may have lost the money, it has been conjectured, by gambling in a desperate attempt to bolster up his failing business.[4]

In all this sorry record there is one happy incident worthy of retention, one which Plorn's Aunt Georgy would hardly have known. Sometime between 1889 and 1894, when he was a member of the Australian legislature, Edward Bulwer Lytton Dickens was cheered for his one memorable speech. It came after a colleague, W. N. Willis, had annoyed everyone by his repeated interruptions. 'Mr. Speaker,' said Plorn, taking the floor, 'my late honoured father once wrote "Barkis is willin'." If he had been here tonight, he would have said "Willis is barkin'." '[5]

*   *   *

Early in the century, with the organization of the Dickens Fellowship, Georgina had the gratifying assurance that the 'beloved memory' would go on. A charter member and at one time a vice-president, she continued active in the Fellowship until the year of her death.[6] For several terms she served as president of its Needlework and Charitable Guild, which she supported with annual contributions.[7] At the yearly Dickens birthday celebrations she was always present in her rustling silks and filmy lace fichu. She was especially pleased when, at the 1904 birthday festivity, Harry began the public reading of Dickens's works. That he should do so caused her no misgivings. For his readings, unlike Charley's, were not for private gain; all profits were turned over to public charity. Besides, she thoroughly enjoyed his performances, given without notes and with all his father's dramatic verve. She could close her eyes and almost believe it was dear Charles's voice coming back across the years.[8]

In the Boz Club, an exclusively male body founded in 1900 by Percy Fitzgerald, she was an honorary member. Like the Fellowship, with which it had no connection, it met annually on the novelist's birthday, its celebration taking the form of a gala dinner, to which women were invited in later years.[9] Small wonder if Georgina had discontinued her birthday meditations beside the Abbey grave! 'It was *most* successful,' she wrote Annie Fields after attending the Boz Club dinner in 1907 with Harry, his wife, their daughters Olive and Elaine, and Charley's Mekitty. There had been 'a really *noble* speech! a real tribute to the great memory'. Her Harry, too, had distinguished himself with a 'charming—and very humorous' toast to the speaker.[10]

In the Boz Club, in the Fellowship, in any circle where the novelist was honoured, she was becoming a living legend, old Miss Hogarth, high priestess of the Dickens cult, a link between past and present. She enjoyed the distinction. Forgotten, now, was her once 'anomalous position' which had behoved friends to avoid public mention of her connection with Dickens lest they injure her. And yet the old scandal fires were not altogether quenched. They blazed up briefly in 1908—in India, of all places—when a daring rogue who called himself Hector Charles Bulwer Lytton Dickens applied to the Society for the Protection of Children in Calcutta for assistance in supporting his son. Posing as the child of Charles Dickens and Georgina Hogarth, he told a fantastic story of how, in 1857, he had been brought at the age of three to Gad's Hill. Mrs. Dickens had made a scene on discovering his identity, then left home for ever, to die in 1867. (Here the impostor had not prepared his background facts very carefully.) Before going to America on his reading tour, the statement continued, Dickens had declared his intention of marrying Georgina. As their son, Hector had been amply provided for under her name in the will. But after Dickens's death, according to the melodramatic account, he and his mother had been turned out of Gad's Hill. As a youth he had tried seafaring, then had lived successively in England, India, and Australia, where he had renewed his childhood associations with his half-brother Edward (Plorn), who, Hector alleged, had freely acknowledged the relationship. Now back in India and in financial distress, he appealed for help. With his application he submitted letters from prominent Australians who referred to him as the son of Charles Dickens.[11]

Notified of this amazing claim, Harry wrote to B. W. Matz, the Honorary Secretary of the Dickens Fellowship: 'It makes one's blood boil to think that my dear revered old aunt should be made the subject of such a scandalous story. I sincerely trust that it may never reach her ears.' To Calcutta he immediately sent a denial and supporting evidence.[12]

It transpired that the claimant was actually a Charley Peters, who had lived in North Queensland from 1896 to 1905. Highly imaginative, he had fabricated tales not only about his parentage but also about his supposed service in the Zulu War. At the time of his marriage in Queensland in 1900, he had assumed the name of Dickens, a daring liberty while members of the family were still living to repudiate his falsehoods. It is unlikely that Georgina ever learned of his audacity.

*   *   *

The years had so thinned the ranks of Dickens's friends that

GEORGINA HOGARTH, c. 1912
Dickens House, London

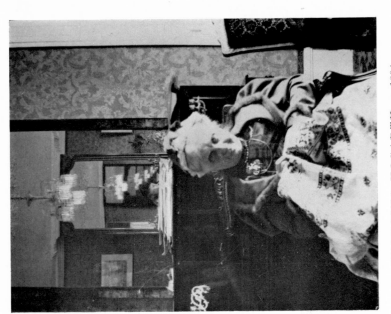

GEORGINA HOGARTH, c. 1894
By courtesy of Mrs. Gladys Reece

almost the only persons with whom the elderly Georgina shared memories were her juniors. Therefore she valued especially her long and happy association with one who was her exact contemporary— Mrs. Cecile Spencer Macready, the actor's widow. Until World War I this old friend called on her almost weekly, often bringing her young granddaughter Lisa, who was entranced by the treasure trove of souvenirs in her hostess's drawing-room and by the reminiscences of the two old ladies. They discussed Dickens frequently, Georgina always insisting that it was the readings which had killed him. Sometimes they spoke of the more remote past: of how the first Mrs. Macready, dead for more than half a century, had, in Georgina's estimation, demanded too much attention, as though she deserved as much recognition as her famous husband; and of how Dickens had seen in the actor's pretty first wife a surface resemblance to Mary Hogarth. According to Georgina, her friend's predecessor had received much of her education from her husband, whose tutelage she had accepted with a degree of reluctance, a matter which prompted some head-shaking over the teacups in the Egerton Terrace drawing-room. If only Macready had married someone like Cecile Spencer early in his career, Georgina assured his granddaughter, he might have had a less bitter outlook on life at times.[13]

Like Macready's granddaughter, all the younger visitors and correspondents were captivated by the stories old Miss Hogarth told about people of her day. Actors, musicians, authors—she had known many and never forgot points of interest she had learned about them, either through personal contacts or hearsay. But she could talk also about figures and events of current importance. As might be expected from her long association with Dickens, she was delighted with the programme of social reform instituted by Asquith's government. But like that Prime Minister, she did not allow liberalism to include the franchise for women. On this subject her views were typically Victorian—and Dickensian. She had no patience with 'the idiotic Suffragettes'.[14] Following a demonstration by the Woman's Movement, she charged that 'women are making themselves odious and intolerable, and are doing their best to destroy the influence which they have, and which they will get more and more by the higher and better education which they are having more and more every year.... Every kind of Employment which is *women's work*, and not man's, I am too thankful they should have— and the education to be the companions and even instructors of men, but I don't see what other *"Rights"* they have a claim to, that they have not got—or nearly all. *I* think ... "Woman's Disability" consists in her own constitution and temperament!' In stating these

s

views to Annie Fields, an advocate of women's rights, she pleaded, 'Don't despise me for this avowal! but I *hate* keeping up any false pretences, and I *must* say what I feel'.[15]

But it was chiefly through her tie with the past that Georgina drew her juniors to her. Sometimes she was sought out to answer puzzling questions or furnish information to assist biographical research. In 1907, for instance, S. M. Ellis, gathering materials for his work on Harrison Ainsworth, appealed to her. Though she was unable to supply Ellis with much of value, the contact brought happy reminiscences of the 1840's, when she and the Dickenses had often joined in the gaieties at Kensal Manor House, the Ainsworth home. 'There were always dinner-parties—succeeded by games and music, and very often winding up with a dance, in which the three young daughters joined,' she recalled.[16] Through Ellis, happily, she and the youngest of the three Ainsworth daughters were brought together again, and a pleasant correspondence ensured. To this friend of early years, Blanche Ainsworth Swanson, she revealed growing infirmities: 'I find great difficulty in getting about—but then, I am very much older than you are! and I have had a great deal of illness of late'. Her next letter to Mrs. Swanson announced that within the week she would be eighty-one: 'That sounds a formidable age! and it seems to me incredible that I shall be so old! I don't feel it—in my *mind* at all!'[17]

Her mental alertness was particularly notable on Dickensian matters: repeatedly she confirmed details referred to her and read manuscripts intended for publication, filling the margins with helpful notes.[18] Only in rare instances was she forced to admit ignorance —as when she was asked to identify the Dickens honeymoon cottage at Chalk. She had been such 'a very small child in those days', she regretted to Mr. William Miller, that she could recall the place only as 'quite an ordinary small house'.[19] Even when they came from strangers, such questions were never too bothersome to command her attention. In the autumn of 1913, in failing health and suffering from a painful eye condition, she received a letter of inquiry signed merely 'Leslie Staples'. 'Dear Miss—(or Mrs.?)—or (Mr.?),' began her answer, 'for I don't know who it is I have to thank for your kind letter.' Then, having explained her eye affliction, she made a cordial suggestion: 'Perhaps . . . you could come and see me, and I could then answer all the questions which you put in your letter to me.'[20] When the inquirer appeared, she found him to be a lad in his teens, a Dickens enthusiast, who had written purely in the hope of getting a note in the hand of the legendary Miss Hogarth. (Twenty-six years later Mr. Staples was to become the Honorary Secretary of the

Dickens Fellowship; thirty-one years later, editor of the *Dickensian*.)

Others, too, were eager to hear from her and meet her. When Katey, as a distinguished matron in her seventies, held her famous 'at homes' for the Fellowship, her guests regarded visiting with Miss Hogarth as a privilege.[21] And Georgina herself never seemed to tire of people who wished to talk about her brother-in-law. Unconsciously, she justified her whole life by maintaining the fidelity of her devotion. Being a repository of Dickensiana was her major excuse for living, her chief boast. 'I suppose I may say I am the "Miss Hogarth",' she had written once in answer to a query. 'There is no other who has the distinction and pride of being the sister-in-law and friend of Charles Dickens.'[22]

*   *   *

By 1910 Harry and his wife were keeping a tender watch over Auntie. Once able to swing along at Dickens's challenging pace, she could no longer walk out alone and, having had a bad fall a year or two earlier, felt nervous about going up and down stairs. When she made her weekly trips to Katey's home in Kensington, she could alight from the cab only by means of a set of steps placed for her descent. And though her hearing was good her eyes troubled her because of incipient cataracts. But these, the doctor had assured her, would not develop at her age.[23] Fortunately, she could still read if she managed the light properly. Not sleeping well, she would on occasion sit over a book half the night when one fascinated her as much as Annie Fields's edition of the letters of Sarah Orne Jewett, who had died in 1909. 'What a delightful creature she was!' Georgina exclaimed to Annie, on receiving the book as a Christmas gift in 1911. 'Reading her letters shows her *nature* so completely—and makes me still more regret that I had not seen more of her. . . .'[24]

In spite of her growing infirmities, Georgina still maintained an independent home. To be near Harry, she had moved again, this time into a small flat at 64 Kenway Road, S.W. Emma being retired at last, there was a helpful new maid who saved her every possible trouble, even answering all but private correspondence. Georgina declared her chief joy in life to be the five little children of her grandniece Enid and the frequent visits from Harry's two younger girls, Olive and Elaine, grown-up women now.[25]

Upon their mother, 'dear Marie', fell most of the responsibility for seeing after the welfare of Aunt Georgy in her decline. For so many years had Harry's devoted wife called forth admiring affection that Georgina might have been altogether incredulous could her first reactions to his marriage have risen to confront her now. Finding in Marie's religion 'the worst drawback', she had confided to Annie in 1877 that the bride, though 'nice and good' and very likable, was 'not *exactly* the girl we would have chosen for our Harry. However when does any one, especially one's *Mankind*, ever marry the person you would have chosen!'[26]

Another of Georgina's 'Mankind', her nephew Alfred, had returned in 1910 from forty-five years in Australia to lecture on his father's life and works. She had not been able to go to hear him, but believed what he had to say 'all very nice'. Unfortunately, like three of his brothers, Alfred had a bad heart, and physicians had predicted that he could not live many months. But his lectures in England had been so successful that 'his head was set on going to America' to continue them in spite of the warning. There he made a good impression and won a number of friends, especially in Boston, from where he wrote in November of 1911, 'No wonder my father liked this city and people so well. It is a most delightful place, and the people themselves are charming.'[27] Among the Bostonians whom Alfred was then still expecting to meet was Mrs. Fields. Georgina had written to brief her on the tragic accident that had robbed him of his first wife many years before, adding, 'I tell you this so that when you do *see* Alfred you will not require him to give you his family History'.[28] (In the forgetfulness of old age she must not have remembered relating this story in detail to Annie back in February of 1879.)

But the tactful caution was unnecessary. On 2 January 1912, three days after she had written her letter, Alfred was suddenly stricken in the lobby of the Astor Hotel at the close of his New York engagements. He died that evening and was buried in the cemetery of Trinity Parish at 155th and Broadway. Among the pall-bearers were Andrew Carnegie and Whitelaw Reid. The chief mourners were a Mr. and Mrs. G. W. Lawrence,[29] whose identity proved a temporary puzzle to Georgina.

When at the end of the month she wrote again to Annie, thanking her for her sympathy and some American newspaper clippings, she could not settle down to a few sober reflections on Alfred, 'poor fellow', until she had protested: 'I have not the slightest idea who Mrs. Lawrence is! Certainly not his *Sister*—he has now only one sister living, Kate Perugini. She told me that a Mrs. Lawrence wrote her about him saying that she was a cousin of theirs, but I don't know *how*.' Recalling the 1868 ado in Chicago over the indigent orphans of Dickens's black-sheep brother Augustus, she likely suspected the mysterious cousin of being a daughter by his common-law wife. But she divulged no such inferences to Annie, remarking only that Mrs. Lawrence 'and her husband seem to have been very kind to Alfred during his short-lived stay in America—and indeed *every one* was'.[30] Later information revealed, however, that Mrs. Lawrence, *née* Emily Barrow, was a connection of Dickens on the maternal side.[31]

Because Alfred's death preceded the centenary of his father's birth by little more than a month, the Boz Club dinner was post-poned until 10th June. When the guests assembled on that date to drink the Bishop of London's toast to 'The Immortal Memory of Charles Dickens', Georgina was, of course, the oldest of the thirteen Dickens relatives present, and in all likelihood, the oldest of the entire distinguished gathering.[32] Of the nine children whom she had watched grow up, she had outlived all but Katey and Harry, the two who, more than any of the others, had transcended or escaped the afflictions and incapacities lingering from a childhood in a divided home. Of George Hogarth's ten, she alone was left, her sister Helen having died in Liverpool in 1890. Only within the last year she had been reminded of her own family and the remote past when Mr. William Miller had sent her a manuscript song composed by her father and set down in his own hand. She had responded promptly with a cheque for one pound, declaring herself 'glad indeed to possess' this family relic.[33] The manuscript was dated January 1846, the month and year of her nineteenth birthday.

During the first decade of the new century her letters to Annie Fields had grown much less frequent and, because of her failing eye-sight, far more brief. But in January of 1913 she roused herself to reply promptly to Annie's Christmas letter, announcing that she had 'returned to Life again thank God!' after 'a very serious surgical operation which removed ALL of one Breast!' Though she would be eighty-six within the week, she had made a remarkable recovery. Writing made her head whirl, she admitted; yet she felt she must tell about her grandniece Olive's coming marriage, 'such an inter-esting event to us all!' Carried away by her enthusiasm, she gave many details of the match, cutting down the account of her own condition to the barest statement of fact.[34]

The previous week she had also demonstrated her recall to life by attending Katey's reception for the Fellowship, an effort that had brought its reward in the performances of four grandnieces: a vocal solo by Harry's Enid; a violin solo by his Elaine, accompanied by her sister Olive; and a piano solo by Alfred's older daughter, Kath-leen.[35] Guests might have observed Auntie in her cap and billowing silks as, ensconced in her place of honour, she beamed and tapped her foot—but a trifle off beat (or so the girls sometimes indulgently noted).

But a month later she was in no mood for a social occasion—not even a Dickensian one. 'What a dismal dripping evening!' she wailed to Sir Nevil Macready. 'And my head aches most desperately! I am going to the Boz Club Dinner, and I wish I wasn't!!'[36]

By this time Annie Fields, though seven years Georgina's junior, was also in failing health. On 13 January 1913 she wrote her last entry in her diary, which she had kept up at intervals during the past decade.[37] If she sent the usual letter the next Christmas, it went unanswered—or she failed to keep the reply in her thick bundle of carefully preserved correspondence. The annual birthday letter seems also to have been discontinued at last, a relaxation of what Annie must long have felt a solemn responsibility: 'I know you never do, and never will, forget' it, Georgina had assured her in 1898. As for Christmas of 1914, it is unlikely that there was any exchange of letters then, for on the eve of the ensuing Twelfth Night Annie Fields died.

Many years before, with the pathetic last days of Poole, Macready, and Landseer fresh in her memory, Georgina had remarked that there were 'so many poor old withered branches left hanging on to the very, very last'. Now she could see herself in the same light.

Because she survived Dickens by forty-seven years, little remained of her legacy toward the end. A series of moves, her medical bills, her maids' wages, and all the expenses of living had largely depleted the eight thousand pounds. But she found another resource. Late in 1906 she had gone one day to the shop of Walter T. Spencer in New Oxford Street to get some Dickens first editions for a bazaar sponsored by the Needlework and Charitable Guild. In time she and this bookseller became 'great cronies' and he began casting an eye over the treasures at her home. He sized up the situation sharply and decided, on slender evidence, that she might be living beyond her means: 'She spent a great deal of money on cut flowers for the decoration of her rooms,' he observed. Reluctantly she began selling off her prized possessions, a few at a time: some of Dickens's less private letters, his New Testament, a lock of his hair, his writing slope, and the speaking tube which had hung beside his chair at the *Household Words* office. She accompanied each item with a note certifying its genuineness. For a while she sent her maid with relics to Spencer's shop once or twice a week, occasionally gleaning as much as £40 from a single week's transactions.[38]

From time to time she dealt also with Maggs of Berkeley Square and others. In this manner such items as a small pearl and rosewood writing-desk, a glass decanter, a Chelsea ornament, and Dickens's carved ivory pipe stop, silver pencil, and rosewood seal left her

hands and eventually found their way into such public repositories
as the Dickens House, London, and the Berg Collection of the New
York Public Library. In her final years, when age had somewhat
clouded her usual shrewdness, dealers less scrupulous than Spencer
and Maggs sometimes came to look over her possessions. Once Harry
arrived just in time to rescue some valuable material that was being
carted off without the family's knowledge.[39]

With no keepsake did Georgina part more painfully—and more
profitably—than the manuscript of *The Cricket on the Hearth*, a gift
from Forster in 1871. Repeatedly she had refused offers for it, once
even denying that she owned it. 'I do not possess *any* manuscripts
of the late Mr. Charles Dickens,' she had vowed to an agent who had
approached her in her late eighties. 'If I did I should certainly NOT
sell them. Still less would I dream of disposing of my private
letters from him.' Nearly a decade later another overture met with
similar resistance: 'I have not the *slightest intention* of EVER parting
with my MS.—and I have settled its disposal, after my Death, also.'[40]
(She had willed it to Harry. Later, at Spencer's suggestion, she
planned to leave it to the British Museum.)

But during the next fifteen years her financial situation altered
and with it, her decision. She recalled how Spencer, seeing the precious manuscript lying open on the edge of her bookcase, had once
offered a thousand pounds for it, should she ever change her mind
about leaving it to the British Museum. The magnitude of the sum
had startled her. Now, needing money to pay her doctor bills, she
sent word to the bookseller, asking whether his offer still held.
Spencer leaped to conclude the transaction that very day. It took
place before family and witnesses, as he had cautiously—and
honourably—suggested.[41]

Although Georgina, like Dickens, was ever pocketbook conscious,
she was also, like him, ever generous. Frequently she gave away
relics that would have commanded a good market price. Chief of
these was the famous sofa on which Dickens had died. After one of
her moves into smaller quarters, she had finally, in 1909, presented
it to the Dickens Museum in Portsmouth.[42] A number of lesser
chattels she gave to persons who would value them as keepsakes. To
Bob Cramp, once the handyman at Tavistock House, she sent a
glazed ware teapot.[43] To her good friend Horace Pym she made a
birthday present of the pewter tankard that Dickens had used during
his last days at Gad's Hill.[44] And there were many others who
received similar tokens.

Until a year or two before her death she spent frequent periods
at the Pym residence in Kent, visiting the son, Major C. E. Pym,

after the passing of the older generation.[45] But finally her infirmities kept her close to home. Yet in 1916 she was still equal to attending a public function. When in February Harry presented a lengthy recital of selections adapted from *Great Expectations,* the subsequent issue of the *Dickensian* noted that 'Miss Hogarth . . . , despite her advancing age, followed the recital with undiminished interest, and undisguised delight as to the humorous passages'.[46] It was her last such appearance.

By this time she was living with Harry once more. The news of World War I enveloped her mind somewhat foggily now; sometimes she stood at the window bowing, thinking she was greeting Field Marshal Lord Kitchener.[47] In this year, which saw Kitchener's death, her grandnephew Major Cedric Charles Dickens, Harry's youngest, was also a war casualty.

But even that autumn she still had periods of unmistakable alertness. In October she received a call from an American book dealer, Charles Sessler, founder of the Philadelphia branch of the Dickens Fellowship. Only the previous May the Anderson Galleries of New York had auctioned off 121 of her letters from Dickens, these having originally been acquired for the library of E. W. Coggeshall. Realizing that any Dickens correspondence still in her hands must soon be scattered, Sessler was in England to buy what he could. Though he knew that she had long refused to part with the last of her letters—they were perhaps some of the more intimate and revealing—he counted on his Fellowship connections and his previous acquaintance with the family to lend him persuasiveness. His scheme succeeded. So brisk-witted could Georgina be in any conversation devoted to Dickens that she impressed Sessler as 'a well-preserved lady with all her faculties unimpaired'. The certificate which she wrote out for him, he remarked admiringly, showed her hand to be 'just as good as it was four years ago'.[48]

Back to Philadelphia Sessler took the ivory field glasses she had given Dickens in 1842 on the eve of his first voyage to America. Better still, he brought with him seventeen valuable letters—sixteen addressed to Georgina, one to Mrs. Hogarth on the death of her son George in 1841. No sooner had Sessler reached the other side of the Atlantic than the Philadelphia *Public Ledger* for Sunday, 19 November 1916, carried an account of the purchase, a photograph of Georgina, the hitherto unpublished letters, and the suppressed portions of some previously printed. These included passages that Georgina would once, probably even yet, have been vexed to see publicized—particularly out of context and assembled into a tell-tale group in the undignified medium of newsprint. Among the long-guarded passages to appear now was one written from Berwick-on-Tweed in 1861: 'O it was a dull Sunday—without a book! ... I took to drinking, so after dark made a jug of whiskey punch and drowned the unlucky Headland's remembrance of his failure.' Another, written a few years after the separation, was the confession: 'I feel that if I had not been reading still, I never could have borne the marriage, and should have excused myself somehow'. Nothing more damaging than these rather mild revelations was to be found in the purchase.

If any of the family heard of the newspaper publication, it is unlikely that they distressed Auntie by mentioning it. Encouraged, perhaps, by the cheque for the sale of the letters, she decided to set up her own establishment again and moved into a tiny cottage in Church Street, Chelsea, her last home. After some difficulties with a maid who took advantage of her helplessness, she settled down to a happy relationship with Polly, the successor, who nursed her devotedly. Most of her time she spent in an invalid chair now. Like Samuel Rogers, whose old age Dickens had described in a letter to Washington Irving, she 'wandered, and lost [herself] like one of the Children in the Wood, grown up there and grown down again'.[49]

Mercifully, she never emerged from that other wood in which she had always wandered somewhat darkly, seeing herself in all ways Charles Dickens's 'best and truest friend'. In stressing only the 'Being full of life, and brightness, and influence over everything and everybody around him',[50] in denying him human frailties, complexities, and all the rich contradictions of his nature, she had ignored the power of *chiaroscuro*. Just as in her own idealized portrait, Agnes Wickfield, Dickens had created a two-dimensional paper doll figure of a woman, so Georgina Hogarth, by her half-century guardianship, had created a hero equally flat. But the facts, contorted and muddied by repression, emerged in her lifetime and after, to the detriment of her hero's reputation. As the pendulum swung from idolatry to detraction, the artist was in danger of being remembered as a roué who had put his middle-aged wife out of her home to carry on with a young actress, a social-climbing Cockney who had driven himself unmercifully for the sake of money when he was already a wealthy man. This distorted picture has been brought into proper focus mainly by a sympathetic study of such letters and passages as the guardian of the beloved memory refused to authorize for publication. From out of her discard rose the vindication of the man she idolized. If the idol, that spirit of Christmas incarnate, commands the world's smiles and tears (a cliché of Dickens comment), the human being at times commands a pathos beyond tears. Having looked into dark corners in his own soul, the artist was able to create a Steerforth, a Rosa Dartle, a Bradley Headstone.

Had the ironic consequences of her devotion been apparent to Georgina, she might have seen fit to leave in delayed trust for the future the complete correspondence and her account of the whole man as she knew him. Yet though she was aware of his 'hope that my books will speak for themselves and me, when I and my faults and virtues, my fortunes and misfortunes are all forgotten',[51] she also knew that as long as he should be remembered for himself, he urgently—and humanly—wished it to be for his 'virtues' and 'fortunes' alone. She remembered also his insistence that a public man's private soul did not belong to the world, even after his death. In acting as she did, she was, in Dickens's judgment and her own, his 'best and truest friend'. She recognized no other judgment.

*   *   *

In her last months Georgina endured not only physical misery but an awareness of her increasing confusion; pathetically, she often realized that she was making the wrong responses. Happily, though, her mental fog may have spared her the knowledge that her little estate was dwindling almost as fast as her strength in that final winter. It was a race that she would barely win.[52] Though for years she had felt dull and depressed with the onset of the dismal English winters, she lived through Christmas 1916, through her ninetieth birthday in January, through one more February anniversary, and on into the season when, all along the pilgrims' road from London past Gad's Hill to Canterbury, the Kentish fields and hedges were rioting with bloom. In April, when 'longen folk to goon on pilgrimages', she slipped into unconsciousness. On the 19th she died—like Dickens, on a Thursday evening.

She was buried in Mortlake Cemetery, near Charley and his wife, in 'a pretty place', wrote Katey the next week, 'which will soon be full of sunshine and flowers'.[53] Her death, remarked the editor of the *Dickensian*, had severed 'a great tie between the present and the past'. Eulogizing her as 'kind-hearted, gentle, amiable and attractive to all with whom she came in contact', he asked in the words of Dickens himself, 'What is prettier than an old lady—except a young lady—when her eyes are bright, when her figure is trim and compact, when her face is cheerful and calm?'[54]

There was another tribute, an *a priori* one in Dickens's own hand. In his memorandum book, along with other jottings and suggestions for stories, is an undated entry sketching the heroine of a projected novel, never written: 'She sacrificed to children, and sufficiently rewarded. From a child herself, always "the children" (of somebody else) to engross her. And so it comes to pass that she never has a child herself—is never married—is always devoted "to the children" (of somebody else), and they love her—and she has always youth dependent on her till her death—and dies quite happily.'[55]

Notes

AN italicized superscript numeral in the text indicates that the note embodies additional information or discussion. References to individual works give the author's surname, the title (shortened wherever feasible), and the page. The following abbreviations have been used throughout:

B H	*Bleak House*
C H E	*A Child's History of England*
D C	*David Copperfield*
Dick.	*The Dickensian*
H. D. *Let.* . . .	*The Letters of Charles Dickens*, ed. Georgina Hogarth and Mary [Mamie] Dickens
Mr. and Mrs. . . .	*Mr. and Mrs. Charles Dickens. His Letters to Her*, ed. Walter Dexter
Nonesuch	*The Letters of Charles Dickens* (Nonesuch Edition), ed. Walter Dexter
T T C	*A Tale of Two Cities*

For an explanation of the symbols used to identify manuscript sources, see the Bibliography. Dates are abbreviated in the following order: day, month, year—27/12/87. For the twentieth century the year is given in full: 23/8/1901.

CHAPTER ONE
[pp. 3-11]

1. According to Henry Burnett, Dickens's brother-in-law, the Hogarth home stood 'opposite orchards and gardens extending as far as the eye could reach'. Cf. Kitton, *Pen and Pencil*, 138.

2. M. Dickens, *My Father*, 30-1.

3. Wright, *Charles Dickens*, 53.

4. *Dick.*, XXII (1926), 221.

5. Ibid., 222.

6. Lockhart, *Life of Scott*, III, 198.

7. *Halifax Courier and Guardian Historical Almanac*, 1924, 149.

8. Information from the Edinburgh Post Office Directories, 1827-1828 and 1828-1829. I am indebted to Mr. J. S. Ritchie of the National Library of Scotland for consulting these directories for me.

9. Nat. Lib. of Scot. MS., George Hogarth to Sir Walter Scott, 30/9/30.

10. Ibid.

11. *Halifax Courier and Guardian Historical Almanac*, 1924, 149. Mr. George W. Almond, who has made an extensive study of Hogarth's association with the *Guardian*, kindly supplied the information about the political issues. Mr. Almond is a resident of Halifax.

12. *Halifax Courier and Guardian Historical Almanac*, 1932, 141.

13. Ibid., 1924, 149.

14. *DNB*, XIX, 722. The Raeburn portrait was hung in Dunheath Castle, Caithness.

15. For these statistics I am indebted to Mr. George W. Almond.

16. For a copy of this advertisement I am indebted to Mr. George W. Almond.

17. *Halifax Courier and Guardian Historical Almanac*, 1924, 151.

18. Nonesuch, I, 40, George Hogarth, 20/1/35.

19. Berg MS., George Hogarth to Dickens, n.d. Hogarth called the operetta to the attention of John Braham, who produced it at his new St. James's Theatre, 6th December, 1836.

20. *Mr. and Mrs.* [1835], 11-12.

21. Nonesuch, I, 68, Thomas Barrow, 31/3/36.

22. *Mr. and Mrs.*, 65 [21/3/36]; 49 [18/12/35]; 60 [6/3/36].

23. Kitton, *Pen and Pencil*, Supp., 10.

24. Ibid., 11.

25. *Halifax Courier and Guardian Historical Almanac*, 1924, 156.

26. Though the number of Hogarth children is sometimes given as fourteen, the records show only ten. Cf. *Dick.*, XIII (1917), 122. According to Mr. George W. Almond of Halifax, part of the discrepancy may be accounted for by the fact that Helen, born in 1833, was listed in the Register of Baptism as Ellen Isabella. Thus she may have figured thrice in the count—as Helen, as Ellen, and as Isabella.

27. In 1911, as Miss Hogarth tried to recall this early period, she wrote Mr. William Miller: 'I was a very small child in those days—under 9 years old—and I was not even present at my sister's wedding. I do remember spending a day at the Chalk House when they were staying there the year after the marriage—but I don't recall much about it.'—Miller MS., Georgina Hogarth to W. Miller, 16/8/1911.

28. *Halifax Courier and Guardian Historical Almanac*, 1924, 153.

29. H. D. *Let.*, III, Diary Fragment for 1838, 8.

30. Nonesuch, I, 107, G. Thomson, 8/5/37.

31. Ibid., I, 113, T. Beard, 16/6/37; 109 [17/5/37].

32. H. D. *Let.*, III, Diary Fragment for 1838, 8.

33. The terms under which Dickens rented the furnished house in Osnaburgh Street are given in a Hunt. MS., Memorandum of Agreement between Charles Dickens and Ann Wheeler, 20/12/41. In later years Georgina Hogarth added the following note to this document: 'This agreement was for the small furnished House which he took for the children and his brother Frederick, for the six months term of his absence, with his wife in America—from January 1842—the Devonshire House being let for the same number of months.'

CHAPTER TWO
[pp. 12-23]

1. C. Dickens, Jr., 'Glimpses of Charles Dickens', 525. The text of 'Guy Fawkes' is given in *Dick.*, VIII (1912), 278-9.

2. Nonesuch, I, 468, C. Sumner, 31/7/42.

3. H. Dickens, *Recollections*, 41-2.

4. M. Dickens, *Charles Dickens*, 86; Hunt. MS., Georgina Hogarth to Mrs. Fields, 29/9/70.

5. For the account of Macready's acting in the dagger scene I am indebted to his granddaughter, Mrs. Lisa Puckle, who had it from Miss Hogarth.

6. Nonesuch, I, 495, T. Beard, 18/12[42].

7. Ibid., 491, T. Hood, 30/11/42.

8. Macready, *Diaries*, II, 179-180, 12/7/42.

9. For a contemporary comment on Georgina Hogarth's attitude toward Dickens's genius, see the Thomson-Stark letter, reproduced in K. J. Fielding's 'Charles Dickens and His Wife', 216. Mr. Fielding has made a convincing case for the authenticity of this letter, hitherto considered by many Dickensians to have been a forgery.

10. Ibid.

11. Forster Collection, V and A MS., Carlyle to Forster, 6/6/44.

12. Nonesuch, I, 487, Miss Coutts, 12/11/42.

13. Ibid., 507, Forster, 12/2/43. The hotel at which Dickens and his 'two petticoats' dined was the Star and Garter. Cf. *Dick.*, VIII (1912), 14-16.

14. Storey, *Dickens and Daughter*, 76.

15. Nonesuch, I, 535, Felton, 1/9/43.

16. Dick. H. MS., Mrs. Dickens to Mrs. Felton, 29/9/43.

17. The field glasses are now on display at the Dickens House. A card in Georgina Hogarth's hand certifies that they were a gift from her to Dickens in 1842.

18. In a letter dated 22 May 1943, Lady Robertson Nicoll wrote the editor of the London *Times*: 'My mother, when a girl, lived in Camden Square, and often used to see the Dickens family, then living in Devonshire Terrace. My grandmother used to relate laughingly that she always knew when a new Dickens baby was coming because Mrs. Dickens would religiously take a walk twice a day, passing her window.'

19. Nonesuch, I, 553, Felton, 2/1/44.

20. Ibid.

21. Ibid., 503, L. Hunt, 3/1/43.

22. Ibid., 564, Jane Carlyle, 27/1/44.

23. Ibid., 519, C. Smithson, 10/5/43.

24. Ibid., 560, Maclise, Stanfield, Forster, 17/1/44.

25. Rosenbach MS., Dickens to Thompson, 15/2/44, as quoted in Johnson, *Charles Dickens*, 494.

26. Nonesuch, I, 519, Mrs. Hogarth, 8/5/43.

27. Ibid., 606, Forster, –/[6]/44.

28. Ibid., 545-6, 1/11/43. Only a friendly loan the previous year had averted an overdrawn account at Coutts's. See ibid., 528-9, Mitton, 22/7/43.

29. C. Dickens, Jr., 'Glimpses of Charles Dickens', 529.

30. Nonesuch, I, 609-10, Forster, 16/7/44; 619 [–/8/44].

31. Ibid., 611-612, Maclise, 22/7/44; 613-14, Forster, 3/8/44.

32. Ibid., 649, Miss Coutts, 8/12/44.

33. Ibid., 626, Forster, 6/10/44; 633, 5/11/44.

34. *Mr. and Mrs.*, 106-9, 8/11/44.

35. Nonesuch, I, 647-8, Mrs. Dickens, 2/12/44.

36. Ibid., 646, 28/11/44.

37. Ibid., 657-8, Georgina Hogarth, 4/2/45.

38. Storey, *Dickens and Daughter*, 71.

39. Nonesuch, I, 646, Mrs. Dickens, 28/11/44.

40. Ibid., 661, Mitton, 22/2/45.

41. Ibid.

42. Ibid., 664, Miss Coutts, 18/3/45; 666, Forster [–/3/45].

43. Una Pope-Hennessy, *Charles Dickens*, 216-17.

44. *Mr. and Mrs.*, 227, 5/12/53.

45. Nonesuch, I, 671-2, Mitton, 14/4/45.
46. C. Dickens, Jr., 'Glimpses of Charles Dickens', 526-7.
47. Nonesuch, I, 711, Stanfield [28/10/45].
48. Ibid., 480, H. Austin, 25/9/42.
49. Ibid., 745, Mme. De la Rue, 17/4/46.
50. Ibid., 773, Forster, 2/8/46.
51. Ibid., 819, T. J. Thompson, 2/12/46.
52. Ibid., 805, Jerrold, 24/10/46.
53. See Carlton, 'Who Was Dickens's French Employer?', for an account of Dickens's connection with the Fillonneaus. For Georgina Hogarth's note on the exchange of manuscripts see Kitton, *Pen and Pencil*, 102, n. 2. Though Miss Hogarth does not specifically mention *The Battle of Life* in this note, it is identified in one of her letters. Cf. Morgan MS., Georgina Hogarth to F. Harvey, 1/6/80. I have not been able to identify the farce whose manuscript Dickens destroyed. Might it have been 'Cross Purposes'? Cf. *Dick.*, XLVI (1950), 94-5.
54. Forster, *Life*, 453.
55. Nonesuch, II, 17, Georgina Hogarth [9/3/47].
56. Forster, *Life*, 453.
57. Morgan MS., Dickens to Macready, 19/4/47. Cited by Johnson, *Charles Dickens*, 614.
58. Nonesuch, II, 64, Georgina Hogarth, 30/12/47.
59. Ibid., 69, A. Dickens, 1/1/48.
60. Ibid., 112, Mrs. Watson, 27/7/48.
61. Ibid., 113, Lytton, 4/8/48; 112, T. Beard and P. Cunningham, 28/7/48.
62. Morgan MS., Mrs. Dickens to Miss Coutts, –/11/48. This occasion was apparently a small family affair, arranged for friends who would not be present at the official dinner on 3rd January to celebrate the publication of *The Haunted Man*. Specifically mentioned in Mrs. Dickens's invitation were the Mittons, Miss Coutts, and the Browns, whose names do not appear in Forster's list of guests attending the 3rd January function. Cf. Forster, *Life*, 527.

CHAPTER THREE

[pp. 24-34]

1. Forster, *Life*, 527; Nonesuch, II, 141, Capt. Marryat, 3/1/49.
2. Morgan MS., Dickens to Macready, 2/2/49 (cited in Johnson, *Charles Dickens*, 662-3).
3. Nonesuch, II, 143, Tagart, 20/1/49.
4. *D C*, Ch. 45. That 'Dora acquires after her marriage more and more of a colouring derived' from Catherine Dickens is convincingly argued by Professor Johnson. See his *Charles Dickens*, 688-9.
5. *D C*, Ch. 18.
6. Ibid., Ch. 34. Recognizing Georgina Hogarth as the inspiration for Agnes Wickfield, Professor Butt suggests that if 'Dora had been allowed to live, Agnes might have maintained her part as "the real heroine", by educating Dora, by superintending the household, and by caring for the children, the very part which Georgina Hogarth was playing in Dickens's own family'. See *Dick.*, XLVI (1950), 129.
7. *D C*, Ch. 19.
8. Nonesuch, II, 195, Cerjat, 29/12/49.

9. Ibid., 113, Lytton, 4/8/48.

10. Cf. Ch. 2, n. 25.

11. Nonesuch, I, 463, Mrs. Colden, 15/7/42.

12. Morgan MS., Carlyle to Mrs. Dickens, 24/4/43.

13. Bliss, *Jane Carlyle*, 188-9, 5/4/49.

14. Ibid., 192, 26/5/49.

15. *The Letters of Thackeray*, II, 569, Mrs. Brookfield, 24/7/49.

16. *Mr. and Mrs.*, 133, 16/6/49.

17. Nonesuch, II, 229, Wills, 29/8/50.

18. *Mr. and Mrs.*, 146, 3/9/50.

19. Hunt. MS., Georgina Hogarth to Mrs. Fields, 18/6/72.

20. Lehmann, *Memories*, 203-4.

21. Ibid., 207.

22. *New Letters of Thomas Carlyle*, I, 188-9; Hewlett, *Chorley*, I, 194.

23. *DNB*; *The Art Journal*, XXV (1863).

24. Nonesuch, II, 242-3, Lytton, 3/11/50.

25. Ibid., 247, Mrs. Watson, 23/11/50.

26. Johnson, *Charles Dickens*, 726.

27. Hunt. MS., Dickens to Mrs. Watson, 9/3/51.

28. Nonesuch, II, 278, Dr. Wilson, 8/3/51; 279, 11/3/51.

29. Hunt. MS., Dickens to Mrs. Watson, 9/3/51.

30. M. Dickens, *My Father*, 62-3.

31. *C H E*, Chs. 28, 35, and 37.

32. Nonesuch, II, 297, Mrs. Dickens, 15/4/51.

33. Ibid., 299, Lytton, 18/4/51; Morgan MS., Dickens to Letitia Austin, 19/4/51.

34. Morgan MS., Dickens to H. Austin, 17/10/51; Hunt. MS., Dickens to Mrs. Watson, 31/10/51 (quoted in *Dick.*, XXXVIII [1924], 162).

35. Hunt. MS., Dickens to Wills, 9/9/51.

36. Kitton, *Pen and Pencil*, 30; Andersen, 'A Visit to Charles Dickens'; Nonesuch, II, 344, B. Smith, 26/9/51; 342, H. Austin, 7/9/51. The bust, executed in 1839 by Angus Fletcher, was presented in 1955 to the Dickens House by Miss J. Jowett. See *Dick.*, LII (1955), 5.

37. Morgan MS., Dickens to H. Austin, 1/10/51.

38. Nonesuch, II, 353-4, Eeles, 22/10/51.

39. *The George Eliot Letters*, II, 17-18, Charles Bray, 17/4/[52].

40. Nonesuch, II, 383, Wills, 13/3/52.

41. Ibid., 383, Howitt, 19/3/52.

42. *B H*, Ch. 23. The theory that Georgina Hogarth may have suggested the character of Esther Summerson has been advanced by Professor Johnson. See his *Charles Dickens*, 766.

43. *B H*, Ch. 3.

44. Ibid., Chs. 8 and 31.

45. Ibid., Ch. 37.

CHAPTER FOUR

[pp. 35-46]

1. Tuke, *A History of Bedford College*, 282.

2. A. T. Dickens, 'My Father and His Friends.'

3. Nonesuch, II, 398, T. Beard, 29/6/52.

4. Ibid., I, 686, Stanfield, 15/7/45.

T

5. Ibid., 705-6, T. Thompson, Leech, Eaton, 1/10/45.
6. Hunt. MS., Dickens to Georgina Hogarth, –/5/48.
7. Nonesuch, II, 412-13, Forster, 29/8/52.
8. C. Dickens, Jr., 'Glimpses of Charles Dickens', 531.
9. Kitton, *Pen and Pencil*, 118.
10. C. Dickens, Jr., 'Glimpses of Charles Dickens', 532.
11. Ritchie, *Some Unwritten Memoirs*, 79.
12. Kitton, *Pen and Pencil*, 115-17.
13. C. Dickens, Jr., 'Glimpses of Charles Dickens', 534.
14. Ibid., 535.
15. Nonesuch, II, 815, Macready, 13/12/56.
16. Budden MS., Georgina Hogarth to Lady Olliffe, 1/12/56.
17. Hunt, MS., Georgina Hogarth to Mrs. Winter, 21/7/57; Johnson, *Heart of Dickens*, 341-2, 20/6/57.
18. Kitton, *Pen and Pencil*, 120, lists only the last two dates. The additional 11th July performance is established from Georgina Hogarth's letter to Mrs. Winter, Hunt. MS., 21/7/57, and a printed programme for that date in the Berg Collection.
19. Nonesuch, II, 303, Lytton, 28/4/51; Adrian MS., Katey Dickens to Miss Wilkins, Monday morning [29/6/57].
20. Hunt. MS., Georgina Hogarth to Mrs. Winter, 21/7/57.
21. Kitton, *Pen and Pencil*, Supp., 17.
22. Nonesuch, II, 521, Georgina Hogarth, 25/11/53.
23. Ibid., 533, Mrs. Watson, 13/1/54.
24. Clark Lib. MS., Georgina Hogarth to C. Felton, 2/6/53.
25. Nonesuch, II, 467-8, Forster, 26/6/53.
26. *Mary Boyle, Her Book*, 237.
27. Nonesuch, II, 584-5, Austin, 6/9/54.
28. Ibid., 692-3, Wills, 23/9/55.
29. Ibid., 697, Collins, 14/10/55.
30. Ibid., 697, Mrs. Dickens, 16/10/55.
31. Hunt. MS., Dickens to Mrs. Watson, 10/11/55 (quoted in *Dick.*, XXVIII [1942], 166); Nonesuch, II, 699, Wills, 21/10/55.
32. Nonesuch, II, 736, M. Boyle, 28/1/56.
33. Ibid., 701, Wills, 24/10/55.
34. Ibid., 681, Gibson, 18/7/55.
35. Johnson, *Heart of Dickens*, 320, 5/7/56.
36. Nonesuch, II, 795, Miss Coutts, 13/8/56.
37. Ibid., 500, Georgina Hogarth, 25/10/53.
38. *Mr. and Mrs.*, 184-5, 16/10/53.
39. Johnson, *Heart of Dickens*, 239, 25/10/53.
40. Ward, *Memories*, 87.
41. *D C*, Ch. LX.
42. Professor Butt has referred to Agnes as 'the Georgina Hogarth of David's household'. See *Dick.*, XLVI (1950), 177.
43. Nonesuch, II, 888, Forster, –/9/57.
44. *D C*, Ch. XLII.
45. Nonesuch, II, 887-8, Forster, –/9/57; Fields Papers, Diary, 24/11/67.
46. Nonesuch, III, 22, A. Smith [Enclosure], 25/5/58; *Mr. and Mrs.*, Appendix II, 273-4.
47. *Mr. and Mrs.*, 245-6, 7/2/56.
48. Nonesuch, II, 740, Georgina Hogarth, 7/2/56; 741, 8/2/56.

49. Hunt. MS., Dickens to Georgina Hogarth, 8/1/62.
50. Nonesuch, II, 569-70, Georgina Hogarth, 22/7/54.
51. *Mr. and Mrs.*, 249, 9/5/56; 239, 16/12/55; Nonesuch, II, 725, Wills, 10/1/56.
52. Nonesuch, II, 764, Wills, 27/4/56; 646, Collins, 24/3/55.
53. Ibid., 769, Georgina Hogarth, 5/5/56; *Mr. and Mrs.*, 249, 9/5/56.
54. Nonesuch, II, 765, Forster, –/4/56.
55. Berg MS., Dickens to De la Rue, 23/10/57 (quoted in Johnson, *Charles Dickens*, 909).
56. Morgan MS., Mary Howitt to Mrs. Dickens, 16/1/[57].
57. Berg MS., Dickens's Memorandum Book. See also Nonesuch, III, 794.
58. Nonesuch, II, 625, Mrs. Winter, 10/2/55; 629, 15/2/55.
59. Ibid., 649, 3/4/55; 739, 5/2/56.
60. Hunt. MS., Georgina Hogarth to Mrs. Winter, 21/7/57.
61. Johnson, *Charles Dickens*, 876.

CHAPTER FIVE
[pp. 47-60]

1. Nonesuch, II, 882, Georgina Hogarth, 12/9/57; 884, 15/9/57.
2. Ibid., Forster, 878, 5/9/57; 887-8, –/9/57.
3. Ibid., 890, Anne Cornelius, 11/10/57.
4. Johnson, *Charles Dickens*, 912.
5. Berg MS., Dickens to De la Rue, 23/10/57 (quoted in Johnson, *Charles Dickens*, 909).
6. Nonesuch, III, 5, Forster, 30/1/58; 14, Collins, 21/3/58.
7. Johnson, *Heart of Dickens*, 353, Editor's summary.
8. Nonesuch, III, 22, Arthur Smith [Enclosure], 25/5/58.
9. Johnson, *Heart of Dickens*, 355, 9/5/58.
10. Fielding, 'Dickens and the Hogarth Scandal', 65, 70.
11. Fielding, 'Dickens to Miss Coutts' (reproduced in Johnson, *Heart of Dickens*, 354-5, 9/5/58).
12. Nonesuch, II, 503, Mrs. Dickens, 28/10/53.
13. Ibid., 358, 13/11/51.
14. Ibid., 605, Hunt, 13/11/54.
15. A case in point was Miss Coutts. Cf. Fielding, 'Dickens to Miss Coutts'.
16. Johnson, *Heart of Dickens*, 352, Mrs. Dickens to Miss Coutts, 1/2/58.
17. Nonesuch, III, 22, A. Smith [Enclosure], 25/5/58.
18. Johnson, *Heart of Dickens*, 355, 9/5/58.
19. See the complete correspondence in *Mr. and Mrs.*, Appendix III, 277-8.
20. *The Letters of Thackeray*, IV, 86-7, 131, Mrs. Carmichael-Smyth, –/5/58, –/2/59.
21. Ouvry Papers, Dickens to Ouvry, 26/5/58 (quoted in Fielding, 'Dickens and the Hogarth Scandal', 67).
22. Ibid., Legal Copy, G. Smith to Ouvry, 27/6/58 (quoted in Fielding, 'Dickens and the Hogarth Scandal', 68).
23. Ibid., Ouvry to G. Smith, 28/5/58 (quoted in Fielding, 'Dickens and the Hogarth Scandal', 69).
24. *Mr. and Mrs.*, Appendix II, 275-6. It is interesting to compare the published statement with the original before Dickens altered it. To the opening sentence of the first draft he added 'and compromising the reputation and good name of others'. In the original the second sentence reads: 'We solemnly

swear that such statements did not originate with, and have not been circulated by either of us'. Most of this was deleted in the final version. As published, the closing sentence is a further modification of the first version:' We know that the statements are wholly repudiated by Mrs. Dickens and we believe them to be entirely destitute of foundation. We pledge ourselves on all occasions to contradict them.' The original draft forms part of the Ouvry Papers.

25. Ouvry Papers, Dickens to Ouvry, 29/5/58 (quoted in Fielding, 'Dickens and the Hogarth Scandal', 70).

26. Ibid., G. Smith to Ouvry, 31/3/58.

27. *Mr. and Mrs.*, 258, 4/6/58.

28. Ibid., Appendix I, 272.

29. *Halifax Guardian*, p. 31, Col. 1, 12/6/58. For this information I am indebted to Mr. George Almond.

30. Fitzgerald, *Memories*, 190.

31. Morgan MS., Dickens to Macready, 7/6/58.

32. Nonesuch, III, 27, Tagart, 14/6/58.

33. Ibid., 29-30, Cerjat, 7/7/58.

34. The complete letter, quoted in part in this paragraph and the four that follow, is reproduced in *Mr. and Mrs.*, Appendix II, 273-4; and in Nonesuch, III, 22-3.

35. Nonesuch, III, 21-2, A. Smith, 25/5/58.

36. Ibid., 54, Georgina Hogarth, 12/9/58.

37. The New York *Tribune*, p. 6, col. 6, 16/8/58.

38. Georgina Hogarth's letter is reproduced in its entirety in *Mr. and Mrs.*, Appendix VII, 290-1. My quotations, in this paragraph and the four that follow, are an exact transcript of the original (Hunt. MS.) and differ in minor details from the printed version. Katey's statement about her mother is recorded in Mrs. Fields's diaries.

39. Nonesuch, III, 25, Leech, 31/5/58. Charley's enclosure is given in a footnote.

40. As quoted in *Dick.*, XXXII (1936), 142-3.

41. Fielding, 'Dickens and Brown', 103-10.

42. Johnson, *Heart of Dickens*, 357, 19/5/58. The wavering hand-writing of this letter, a Morgan MS., suggests agitation.

43. Ibid., 361, 22/8/58.

44. Nonesuch, III, 479, Georgina Hogarth, 1/8/66.

45. Morgan MS., Halliday to Mrs. Dickens, 5/10/69; Mrs. Dickens to Chapman, 15/4/64. William Farren, in the London *Times* for 14/5/1933, reports: 'The last time I met them [Mrs. Dickens and her sister, presumably Helen] was at the production of 'Dombey and Son' at the Old Globe Theatre (1873) in an adaptation of Andrew Halliday called *Heart's Delight*. I sat next to Mrs. Dickens in the stalls, and I remember how moved to tears Mrs. Dickens became. There was no mistaking her feelings'.

46. Johnson, *Heart of Dickens*, 355, 9/5/58.

CHAPTER SIX
[pp. 61–81]

1. Yates, *Memories*, 288.

2. Nonesuch, III, 44-6, Georgina Hogarth, 25/8/58; 47-8, 29/8/58.

3. Ibid., 57, Forster, –/9/58.

4. Ibid., 49, Wills, 2/9/58.

5. Ibid., 40, Georgina Hogarth, 20/8/58; 56, 17/9/58.

6. *Mr. and Mrs.*, 258, 4/6/58.

7. Nonesuch, III, 56, Georgina Hogarth, 17/9/58; 51, 7/9/58.

8. Ouvry Papers, Georgina Hogarth to Ouvry, Thursday afternoon, 1870; Nonesuch, III, 210, Georgina Hogarth, 2/2/61; Hunt. MS., Dickens to Georgina Hogarth, 27/11/61, 3/1/62, 24/1/62.

9. Berg MS., Dickens to Georgina Hogarth, 25/11/53.

10. Nonesuch, III, 53, Georgina Hogarth, 12/9/58.

11. Frith, *My Autobiography*, I, 215-16.

12. Quoted in *Dick.*, XV (1919), 38.

13. Kitton, *Pen and Pencil*, 76, n.

14. Andersen, 'A Visit to Charles Dickens', 185.

15. Nonesuch, II, 828, Cerjat, 17/1/57.

16. Ibid., 751, Georgina Hogarth, 14/3/56.

17. Ibid., 742-3, Miss Coutts, 9/2/56; Morgan MS., Dickens to H. Austin, 12/8/56.

18. Information furnished by Miss W. Stewart Burt, Gad's Hill Place, Kent.

19. Morgan MS., Dickens to H. Austin, 15/2/57.

20. Nonesuch, II, 875, H. C. Andersen, 2/9/57; 862, Macready, 13/7/57.

21. Ibid., 869, Forster, –/8/57; Morgan MS., Dickens to H. Austin, 21/7/57.

22. Nonesuch, III, 30, Cerjat, 7/7/58; Morgan MS., Dickens to Macready, 10/7/57.

23. Nonesuch, III, 59, Georgina Hogarth, 26/9/58.

24. Ibid., 48, 29/8/58. In his 'Table Talk', T. P. O'Connor refers to the gossip about the painted design. Reported in the *Halifax Courier and Guardian Historical Almanack*, 1924, 156.

25. Morgan MS., Dickens to Macready, 27/3/56.

26. Nonesuch, III, 163-4, T. Beard, 12/6/60.

27. Ibid., 167-8, Mrs. A. Dickens, 19/7/60; Storey, *Dickens and Daughter*, 104.

28. Lehmann, *Memories*, 94-5; Storey, *Dickens and Daughter*, 106; Nonesuch, III, 168, Mrs. A. Dickens, 19/7/60.

29. Gissing, *William Holman Hunt*, 157.

30. Storey, *Dickens and Daughter*, 106.

31. Nonesuch, III, 176, Wills, 4/9/60.

32. The description of Gad's Hill, in this and the following paragraphs, is based largely on Dolby, *Charles Dickens*, 49ff.

33. Nonesuch, III, 208, Cerjat, 1/2/61.

34. Ibid., 436, P. Fitzgerald, 23/9/65.

35. Fields Papers, Diary, 15/8/67 (quoted in Howe, *Memories of a Hostess*, 139).

36. Nonesuch, III, 361-2, Bennett, 14/9/63.

37. Ibid., 382, A Chimney-sweep, 15/3/64.

38. Hunt. MS., Dickens to Georgina Hogarth, 24/1/62.

39. Nonesuch, III, 160, Cerjat, 3/5/60; 228, Mrs. Watson, 8/7/61.

40. Forster, *Life*, 654.

41. Dolby, *Charles Dickens*, 423-5.

42. Fitzgerald, *Memories of Charles Dickens*, 16.

43. Kitton, *Pen and Pencil*, Supp., 50.

44. Nonesuch, III, 198, Captain Morgan, –/12/60.

45. Quoted in *Dick.*, XXIX (1933), 100.

46. 'Charles Dickens at Home', 396-7.

47. M. Dickens, *My Father*, 45.
48. Ibid., 40-1; Lucas, *Reading, Writing, and Remembering*, 309.
49. Nonesuch, III, 197, Georgina Hogarth, 28/12/60; 285, T. Beard, 1/2/62.
50. Hunt. MS., Georgina Hogarth to Mrs. Fields, 29/9/70.
51. Nonesuch, III, 160, Cerjat, 3/5/60.
52. Ibid., 230, Georgina Hogarth, 31/7/61; 238, 19/9/61; 197, 28/12/60; 244, 9/10/61; Hunt. MS., Dickens to Georgina Hogarth, 9/1/67.
53. Nonesuch, III, 210, Georgina Hogarth, 2/2/61.
54. Hunt. MS., Dickens to Georgina Hogarth, 18/2/62; 19/2/62.
55. Ibid., 15/4/69.
56. Nonesuch, III, 206, Georgina Hogarth, 17/1/61; Hunt. MS., Dickens to Georgina Hogarth, 18/7/67.
57. Hunt. MS., Georgina Hogarth to Mrs. Fields, 10/10/71.
58. Ibid., Dickens to Georgina Hogarth, 25/11/53.
59. Ibid., Dickens to Georgina Hogarth, 10/1/62, 3/2/64.
60. Ibid., 8/1/62. Incomplete in Nonesuch, III, 277.
61. Ibid., 25/11/53.
62. Nonesuch, III, 251, Georgina Hogarth, 7/11/61; 40, 20/8/58; Hunt. MS., Dickens to Georgina Hogarth, 5/11/53.
63. Nonesuch, III, 203, Georgina Hogarth, 2/1/61, 5/1/61, 7/1/61.
64. Ibid., 197, 28/12/60; 223, 26/5/61.
65. Morgan MS., Dickens to Macready, 2/7/62.
66. Finlay, 'Peeps at Dickens', 100.
67. Morgan MS., Dickens to Overs, 24/8/41 (quoted in Johnson, *Charles Dickens*, 346).
68. Dickens's letter to Baylis (Nonesuch, III, 298) speaks of 'the doctors'; his letter to Macready (Morgan MS.) of the same date speaks of Elliotson. Later Georgina Hogarth was known to be under Beard's care.
69. Morgan MS., Dickens to Macready, 2/7/62; Dickens to Mrs. Austin, 20/6/62, 3/7/62.
70. Nonesuch, III, 301. Collins, 27/7/62; 304-5, 20/9/62.
71. Ibid., 307, Mrs. Austin, 7/10/62.
72. Morgan MS., Dickens to Macready, 2/7/62; Nonesuch, III, 298, Bayliss, 2/7/62; 308, Collins, 8/10/62, 12/10/62.
73. Nonesuch, III, 317, Mrs. Austin, 7/11/62.
74. Six letters in Johnson, *Heart of Dickens*, include Georgina Hogarth's regards, or even 'love', to Miss Coutts: the first is dated 17/11/51; the last, 9/4/57.
75. Nonesuch, III, 317, Mrs. Austin, 7/11/62.
76. Ibid., 316, Forster, *circa* 5/11/62; 318, Wills, 11/11/62.
77. Ibid., 317, Mrs. Austin, 7/11/62.
78. Ibid., 328-9, Mary Boyle, 27/12/62.
79. Morgan MS., Georgina Hogarth to unidentified correspondent, 14/1/63.
80. Nonesuch, III, 338, Mary Dickens, 1/2/63.
81. Hunt. MS., Dickens to Georgina Hogarth, 12/2/63.
82. Nonesuch, III, 348, Carlyle, 13/4/63; 352, Cerjat, 21/5/63.
83. Wright, *Charles Dickens*, 67.
84. Nonesuch, III, 342-3, Macredy, 19/2/63; Hunt. MS., Dickens to Georgina Hogarth, 1/2/63 (quoted in Johnson, *Charles Dickens*, 1008).
85. Nonesuch, III, 359, Collins, 9/8/63.
86. Ibid., 362, Mason, 19/9/63.
87. Ibid., 372, W. Hoskyns, 14/12/63.

CHAPTER SEVEN
[pp. 82-95]

1. Storey, *Dickens and Daughter*, 80.
2. Grubb, 'Dickens and His Brother Fred', 128.
3. Nonesuch, III, 169, Forster, 29/7/60; 170, Parkinson, 9/8/60.
4. Ibid., 173, Mrs. Dickinson, 19/8/60; 174-5, Georgina Hogarth, 21/8/60 (Tuesday evening, Tuesday night).
5. Ibid., 171, Mrs. Parkinson, 9/8/60; Hunt. MS., Dickens to Georgina Hogarth, 24/1/62.
6. Nonesuch, III, 247, Bowring, 31/10/61; 254, Earl of Carlisle, 15/11/61; Morgan MS., Dickens to Mrs. Austin, n.d.
7. Morgan MS., Dickens to Mrs. Austin, 18/7/62.
8. Ibid., 8/10/68.
9. Nonesuch, III, 193, Georgina Hogarth, 27/11/60; 362, Wills, 14/9/63.
10. Ibid., 212, Wills, 11/3/61.
11. Ibid., 243, Forster, –/10/61.
12. Ibid., 349, Collins, 22/4/63.
13. Ibid., 243, Forster, –/10/61; Hunt. MS., Dickens to Georgina Hogarth, 15/10/61.
14. Hunt. MS., Dickens to Georgina Hogarth, 15/10/61.
15. Nonesuch, III, 402, Cerjat, 25/10/64.
16. Ibid., 288, 16/3/62; Johnson, *Heart of Dickens*, 186; 22/8/51; 254, 14/1/54.
17. Nonesuch, III, 402, Cerjat, 25/10/64.
18. Johnson, *Heart of Dickens*, 375, 12/2/64.
19. See the Narrative in the H. D. *Let.*, II, 208.
20. Johnson, *Heart of Dickens*, 376, 12/2/64; Morgan MS., Dickens to Macready 10/2/64.
21. Ouvry Papers, R. N. Carter to Dickens, 4/1/64.
22. *Dick.*, XLIX (1953), 100.
23. Johnson, *Heart of Dickens*, 376, 12/2/64.
24. Hunt MS., Dickens to Georgina Hogarth, 12/10/64.
25. Ouvry Papers, Col. Priestly to Dickens, 16/7/64.
26. Ibid., Capt. George Cockburn to Maj. Moffatt, 14/1/64.
27. Ibid., Native Merchant to C. O., 27/12/63.
28. Nonesuch, III, 104, Mrs. Watson, 31/5/59; 160, Cerjat, 3/5/60; 209, 1/2/61; 378, Collins, 24/1/64.
29. Ibid., 288, Cerjat, 16/3/62; Johnson, *Charles Dickens*, 995.
30. Nonesuch, III, 421, Layard, 17/5/65.
31. Alfred Dickens's itemized bills form part of the Ouvry Papers.
32. Nonesuch, III, 160, Cerjat, 3/5/60; 178, Mrs. Watson, 14/9/60.
33. Ibid., 180-1, Georgina Hogarth, 24/9/60; 183, Forster, 4/10/60.
34. Ibid., 288, Cerjat, 16/3/62.
35. Cellier and Bridgeman, *Gilbert and Sullivan*, 250-1.
36. Hunt. MS., Dickens to Georgina Hogarth, 12/10/64.
37. A. Dickens, 'My Father and His Friends', 641.
38. Nonesuch, III, 449, Rusden, 27/12/65.
39. It should be emphasized that the decisions affecting his sons were Dickens's own and not the result of any sly suggestions from Georgina Hogarth, as has sometimes been charged by her detractors. The assumption that her

influence prompted him to get them out of her way is invalidated by irrefutable evidence of her affection for them. Besides, her brother-in-law knew her too well not to see through any such covert scheme, detecting which, he would hardly have held his high opinion of her until the end.

40. Nonesuch, III, 153, Bewsher, 14/3/60.

41. Ibid., 249, Georgina Hogarth, 1/11/61.

42. Ibid., 350, Brookfield, 17/5/63; 370-1, Sawyer, 6/11/63.

43. H. F. Dickens, 'The History of the Gad's Hill Gazette', 256. Professor Johnson has suggested July 1863 as the probable date for the first issue. Cf. his *Charles Dickens*, 1063, n. 102.

44. H. F. Dickens, 'The History of the Gad's Hill Gazette', 255-9; *Recollections*, 22.

45. Kitton, *Pen and Pencil*, 187.

46. H. F. Dickens, *Recollections*, 23-4.

47. Nonesuch, III, 160, Cerjat, 3/5/60.

48. Ibid., 478, Lytton, 16/7/66.

49. Ibid., 298, Baylis, 2/7/62.

50. Ibid., 209, Cerjat, 1/2/61; 288, 16/3/62; 348, Muspratt, 13/4/63.

51. Ibid., 402, Cerjat, 25/10/64.

52. Forster, *Life*, 654; M. Dickens, *My Father*, 37.

53. Nonesuch, III, 411, Forster, 7/1/65.

54. M. A. Dickens, 'A Child's Recollections of Gad's Hill'.

55. Nonesuch, III, 650, Mrs. Fields, 25/5/68. Mention of the telescope appears in a letter from Charles Dickens, Jr., to Georgina Hogarth, Ouvry Papers, 19/7/70: 'I am writing to Layard. The telescope out of the chalet isn't it you have kept for him? Let me know at Henley.'

56. Nonesuch, III, 416, Forster, 3/3/65.

57. Forster, *Life*, 700.

58. T. W. Hill, 'The Staplehurst Railway Accident', 149-50.

59. Nonesuch, III, 423, F. Beard, 10/6/65; 425-7, Mitton, 13/6/65.

60. Hunt, MS., Dickens to Wills, 25/10/58; Nonesuch, III, 235, Webster, 9/9/61.

61. Storey, *Dickens and Daughter*, 128.

62. Nonesuch, III, 429, J. Thompson, 25/6/65.

63. Ibid., 424, Lever, 12/6/65; 425, Headland, 12/6/65.

64. Hunt. MS., Dickens to Mrs. Winter, 14/6/65. Incorrectly addressed to Louis Winter in Nonesuch, III, 427.

65. *Mr. and Mrs.*, 264, 11/6/65.

66. Nonesuch, III, 431, F. Lehmann, 13/7/65; Lytton, 20/7/65.

CHAPTER EIGHT
[pp. 96-115]

1. Nonesuch, III, 429, Forster, -/[6]/65.

2. Ibid., 459-460, Georgina Hogarth, 9/2/66.

3. Ibid., 460, F. Beard, 16/2/66.

4. Hunt, MS., Dickens to Ouvry, 8/3/66.

5. Nonesuch, III, 487, W. Collins, 4/10/66.

6. Ibid., 467, Georgina Hogarth, 17/4/66.

7. Hunt. MS., Dickens to Georgina Hogarth, 6/3/67 (Wednesday night).

8. Nonesuch, III, 468, Georgina Hogarth, 19/4/66.

9. Morgan MS., Dickens to A. Smith, 26/1/59 (incomplete in Nonesuch, III, 89; quoted in Nisbet, *Dickens and Ellen Ternan*, 54).

10. Hunt. MS., Dickens to Georgina Hogarth, 24/5/66.

11. Nonesuch, III, 477-8, Lytton, 16/7/66.

12. Ibid., 479, Georgina Hogarth, 1/8/66.

13. Ibid., 526, Rev. J. Taylor, 4/5/67; 537, 15/7/67.

14. Hunt. MS., Dickens to Georgina Hogarth, 3/11/66.

15. Ibid.

16. Ibid., 5/11/66.

17. Ibid.

18. Ibid., 7/11/66.

19. Nonesuch, III, 513, Mrs. Elliot, 4/3/67.

20. Ibid., 502, Georgina Hogarth, 21/1/67; 508, 15/2/67.

21. Hunt, MS., Dickens to Georgina Hogarth, 2/3/67.

22. Ibid., 4/3/67; 6/3/67.

23. Berg MS., Dickens to Georgina Hogarth, 15/3/67 (incomplete in Nonesuch, III, 515-6).

24. Hunt. MS., Charles Dickens to Georgina Hogarth, 16/3/67; Nonesuch, III, 516, M. Dickens, 16/3/67.

25. Hunt. MS., Dickens to Georgina Hogarth, 7/3/67; 16/3/67.

26. Ibid., 20/3/67; 26/4/67; 4/3/67.

27. Nonesuch III, 527, Georgina Hogarth, 10/5/67.

28. Ibid., 526, Rev. J. Taylor, 4/5/67.

29. Hunt. MS., Dickens to Wills, 6/6/67 (incomplete in Nonesuch, III, 530).

30. Ibid.

31. Wright, *Charles Dickens*, 307. For further discussion of Dickens's relations with Ellen Ternan see Nisbet, *Dickens and Ellen Ternan*, and Johnson, *Charles Dickens*, 1005-8.

32. Berg MS., Diary of Charles Dickens for the Year 1867.

33. Nonesuch, III, 476, Mrs. Elliot, 5/7/66.

34. Ibid., 555, Georgina Hogarth, 30/9/67.

35. Hunt. MS., Dickens to Georgina Hogarth, 1/8/67; Nonesuch, III, 540, Georgina Hogarth, 2/8/67.

36. Nonesuch, III, 540, Forster, 6/8/67.

37. Ibid., 544, Fields, 3/9/67; 544, Finlay, 3/9/67.

38. Hunt. MS., Georgina Hogarth to Mrs. Fields, 5/8/72.

39. Ibid., Mary Dickens to Charles Kent, 27/10/67.

40. Ibid., Carlyle to Charles Kent, 20/10/67; Ruskin to Charles Kent, 1/11/67.

41. Yates, *Memories*, 298; Ellis, *The Hardman Papers*, 288.

42. *The Charles Dickens Farewell Dinner*.

43. Hunt. MS., Dickens to Georgina Hogarth, 10/8/67. According to his pocket diary, Dickens was alone on 9 August 1867: 'Ride alone. Olympic', reads the entry for that day. On 10th August, however, he was cheered by seeing Nelly, according to his diary entry: 'To P at 11 (N)'.

44. Berg MS., Memoranda to Wills (quoted in Nisbet, *Dickens and Ellen Ternan*, 53).

45. Berg MS., Diary of Charles Dickens for the Year 1876 (quoted in Nisbet, *Dickens and Ellen Ternan*, 54; and in Johnson, *Charles Dickens*, 1006). For another interpretation of the code see G. G. Grubb's review of Miss Nisbet's

Dickens and Ellen Ternan in *Dick.*, XLIX (June, 1933), 121-9. Also see Felix Aylmer's refutation of Grubb's thesis, *Dick.*, LI (March, 1955), 85-6.

46. Hunt. MS., T. A. Trollope to J. T. Fields, 18/4/73; Nisbet, *Dickens and Ellen Ternan*, 88, n. 6.

47. Hotten, *Charles Dickens*, 89.

48. Nonesuch, III, 566, Mary Dickens, 10/11/67; Georgina Hogarth, 13/11/67; 567, 16/11/67.

49. Ibid., 572, Georgina Hogarth, 25/11/67.

50. Ibid., 581, Mary Dickens, 11/12/67.

51. Ibid., 595, Georgina Hogarth, 3/1/68.

52. Walker MS., Georgina Hogarth to Mary Howitt, 25/12/67.

53. Nonesuch, III, 583, Georgina Hogarth, 16/12/67.

54. Ibid., 584, 22/12/67.

55. Ibid., 588-9, Mary Dickens, 26/12/67.

56. Ibid., 590, Mary Dickens, 30/12/67; 606, Georgina Hogarth, 21/1/68.

57. Ibid., 601, Georgina Hogarth, 12/1/68.

58. Hunt. MS., Dickens to Georgina Hogarth, 6/12/67 (incomplete in Nonesuch, III, 597, which is misdated 4/1/68).

59. Nonesuch, III, 595, Georgina Hogarth, 3/1/68; 607, Mary Dickens, 23/1/68; 633-4, 3/16/68.

60. T T C, Bk. III, Ch. 5.

61. Hunt. MS., Dickens to Georgina Hogarth, 10/1/68.

62. Ibid., 27/2/68.

63. Ibid., Dickens to Wills, 21/10/66 (incomplete in Nonesuch, III, 488).

64. Ouvry Papers, *Re* Augustus Dickens, 17/10/67.

65. Hunt. MS., Dickens to Georgina Hogarth, 8/3/68 (incomplete in Nonesuch, III, 629).

66. See *Dick.*, XXXV (1939), 145.

67. Nonesuch, III, 617, Georgina Hogarth, 7/2/68.

68. Fields Papers, Diary, 7/2/68.

69. Ibid., 2/12/67 (quoted in Howe, *Memories*, 144).

70. Ibid., 24/11/67.

71. Ibid., 8/1/68 (incomplete in Howe, *Memories*, 155).

72. Ibid., undated entry, early in 1868.

73. Ibid., 3/3/68; –/4/68; 8/1/68 (quoted in Howe, *Memories*, 155).

74. Hunt. MS., Dickens to Georgina Hogarth, 29/1/68.

75. Nonesuch, III, 628, Mary Dickens, 2/3/68.

76. Fields Papers, Diary, –/4/68.

77. Hunt. MS., Dickens to Georgina Hogarth, 1 & 2/4/68 (incomplete in Nonesuch, III, 641).

78. Ibid.

79. Fields Papers, Diary, 2/4/68 (quoted in Howe, *Memories*, 171).

80. Nonesuch, III, 642-3, Mary Dickens, 7/4/68.

81. Fields Papers, Diary, 19/4/68 (quoted in Howe, *Memories*, 184).

82. Ibid., 22/4/68; 24/4/68.

83. Ibid., 24/4/68.

84. Ibid., 2/5/68.

85. Ibid., 24/4/68.

86. Ibid., 3/5/68.

87. Ibid., 6/12/71.

88. Nonesuch, III, 650, Mrs. Fields, 25/5/68.

89. Ibid.

CHAPTER NINE

[pp. 116-139]

1. Nonesuch, III, 654, Macready, 10/6/68; 648, Fitzgerald, 18/5/68; 647, Fields, 15/5/68.
2. Hunt. MS., Dickens to Georgina Hogarth, 25/6/68.
3. Ibid., Dickens to Mrs. Wills, 26/6/68 (incomplete in Nonesuch, III, 655); Nonesuch, III, 669, Wills, 27/9/68.
4. Nonesuch, III, 646, Mrs. Weston, 11/5/68; 647, Beard, 14/5/68; 654, Macready, 10/6/68; 664, Ouvry, 23/8/68.
5. Ibid., 664, Ouvry, 23/8/68.
6. Dana, 'Longfellow and Dickens', quoted in Johnson, *Charles Dickens*, 1099.
7. Nonesuch, III, 657, Fields, 7/7/68.
8. H. D. *Let.*, II, Narrative for 1868, 326.
9. Nonesuch, III, 667-8, E. Dickens [26/9/68].
10. Ibid., 669, Mary Dickens, 26/9/68; H. F. Dickens, *Memories of My Father*, 23.
11. Hunt. MS., Dickens to Dolby, 29/9/68; Dickens to Georgina Hogarth, 11/10/68.
12. Nonesuch, III, 620, H. F. Dickens, 11/2/68.
13. Ibid., 673, 15/10/68.
14. Ibid., 677, Forster, –/10/68.
15. Ouvry Papers, H. F. Dickens to Ouvry, 25/4/71.
16. Hunt. MS., Dickens to Georgina Hogarth, 12/12/68.
17. Nonesuch, III, 568, Forster, 18/11/67.
18. Ibid., 676, Georgina Hogarth, 29/10/68.
19. Hunt. MS., Dickens to Georgina Hogarth, 16/10/68.
20. I am indebted to Mr. H. S. Johnston of the Public Record Office and to Mr. R. Eldridge of the Society for Army Historical Research for helping me identify Lynch, an officer at Chatham from 1866 to 1870.
21. Hunt, MS., Dickens to Georgina Hogarth, 25/10/68; Nonesuch, III, 676, Georgina Hogarth, 29/10/68.
22. Nonesuch, III, 688, Georgina Hogarth, 18/12/68.
23. Hunt. MS., Dickens to Georgina Hogarth, 16/12/68.
24. Nonesuch, III, 686, Mary Dickens, 15/12/68.
25. Ibid., 691, Lady Molesworth, 25/12/68.
26. Ibid., 692, Dolby, 26/12/68.
27. Charles Dickens, Jr., 'Glimpses of Charles Dickens', 680-1.
28. Ibid., 681.
29. Hunt. MS., Dickens to Georgina Hogarth, 21/1/69, 24/1/69.
30. Dolby, *Charles Dickens*, 362.
31. Hunt. MS., Dickens to Georgina Hogarth, 4/2/69.
32. Nonesuch, III, 705, Fields, 15/2/69.
33. Ibid., 708, Georgina Hogarth, 26/2/69.
34. Hunt. MS., Dickens to Georgina Hogarth, 8/4/69.
35. Nonesuch, III, 721, Georgina Hogarth, 21/4/69.
36. Ibid., 722, Mary Dickens, 22/4/69.
37. Ibid., 722, Georgina Hogarth, 1/5/69.
38. Hunt. MS., Dickens to Georgina Hogarth, 5/3/69, 7/3/69.

39. Ouvry Papers, S. Dickens to Dickens, 19/3/69.
40. Among the Ouvry Papers are five such statements for the short period of 4 May to 7 June 1869.
41. Hunt. MS., Georgina Hogarth to Mrs. Fields, 18/6/72.
42. Nonesuch, III, 725-6, G. W. Rusden, 18/5/69.
43. Forster, *Life*, 804-5; Nonesuch, III, 724, Wills and Fitzgerald, 3/5/69; Mrs. F. Lehmann, 9/5/69.
44. H. D. *Let.*, II, 405, Narrative for 1869; Nonesuch, III, 719, Childs, 10/4/69.
45. Nonesuch, III, 727, Fields, 19/5/69, 25/5/69; 725, Sol Eytinge, 15/5/69.
46. Howe, *Memories of a Hostess*, 7.
47. Fields Papers, Mrs. Fields to Mother and Sarah, –/6/69; to Louisa, 23/5/69.
48. Ibid.
49. Ibid., Diary, 2/6/69; Mrs. Fields to Mother, 4/6/69.
50. Ibid., Mrs. Fields to Mother, 4/6/69; Diary, –/6/69.
51. Ibid., Diary, –/6/69; Mrs. Fields to Mother, 4/6/69.
52. T. P. O'Connor, 'Table Talk', quoted in the *Halifax Courier and Guardian Historical Almanack* (1924), 155-6.
53. Fields, 'Our Whispering Gallery', –/11/71, 632.
54. Hunt. MS., Georgina Hogarth to Mrs. Fields, 15/6/69.
55. Fields Papers, Diary, –/6/71.
56. Nonesuch, III, 177, Wills, 4/9/60; Storey, *Dickens and Daughter*, 107.
57. Nonesuch, III, 416, Macready, 1/3/65.
58. Lytton MS., Georgina Hogarth to Lady Lytton, 20/3/1900.
59. Hunt. MS., Dickens to Georgina Hogarth, 12/11/69, 5/11/69.
60. Ibid., Georgina Hogarth to Mrs. Fields, 12/11/69.
61. Ibid.
62. Ibid., Dickens to Georgina Hogarth, 20/12/69.
63. Ibid., Georgina Hogarth to Mrs. Fields, 28/12/69.
64. Ouvry Papers, Fechter to Dickens, 12/11/69.
65. Hunt. MS., Dickens to Georgina Hogarth, 12/11/69.
66. Ibid., Georgina Hogarth to Mrs. Fields, 21/11/70.
67. H. F. Dickens, *Memories of My Father*, 23-4.
68. Nonesuch, III, 755, Mrs. F. Elliot, 28/12/69.
69. Hunt. MS., Georgina Hogarth to Mrs. Fields, 28/12/69.
70. Ibid.
71. Ibid.
72. Fields Papers, Diary, 30/8/70. For additional details of the estrangement between Dickens and Collins see my note in the *Huntington Library Quarterly*, XVI (February 1953), 211-13.
73. Hunt. MS., Georgina Hogarth to Mrs. Fields, 25/2/70.
74. *Halifax Courier and Guardian Historical Almanack* (1924), 155.
75. W. Rossetti, *Reminiscences*, I, 100.
76. Hunt. MS., Georgina Hogarth to Mrs. Fields, 25/2/70.
77. Ibid.
78. Ibid.
79. Ibid.
80. Fields Papers, Diary, 25/2/70.
81. Hunt. MS., Georgina Hogarth to Mrs. Fields, 25/2/70.
82. Dolby, *Charles Dickens*, 447; Hotten, *Charles Dickens*, 95.
83. Hunt. MS., Georgina Hogarth to Mrs. Fields, 4/5/70.

84. Mary Angela Dickens, 'My Grandfather', 110.
85. Charles Dickens, Jr., 'Glimpses of Charles Dickens', 683.
86. Hunt. MS., Georgina Hogarth to Mrs. Fields, 4/5/70.
87. Ibid.
88. Ibid. The donor was George Holme, Cavendish House, Prince's Park, Liverpool, as is revealed by two letters which Dickens addressed to him on the subject of the ornaments (Victoria and Albert Museum MS., 14/3/70, 1/4/70). For this information I am indebted to Mrs. Humphry House and Mr. William J. Carlton. Miss Gladys Storey informs me that Mrs. Perugini had the silver basket in her possession at one time.
89. Nonesuch, III, 779, Rusden, 20/5/70.
90. Ibid., 780, A. Dickens, 20/5/70.
91. Ibid.
92. Hunt. MS., Georgina Hogarth to Mrs. Fields, 4/5/70.
93. Nonesuch, III, 776, Brunt, 13/5/70.
94. Ibid., Mrs. Ward, 11/5/70.
95. Forster, *Life*, 656.
96. Storey, *Dickens and Daughter*, 133-4; M. Dickens, *My Father*, 118; K. Perugini, *'Edwin Drood* and the Last Days', 652; Johnson, *Heart of Dickens*, 370, 8/4/60.
97. K. Perugini, *'Edwin Drood* and the Last Days', 654.
98. *Pall Mall Magazine*, XXXVII (June, 1906), 654.
99. M. Dickens, *My Father*, 119-20.
100. Storey, *Dickens and Daughter*, 139-40; The London *Times*, 11/6/70.
101. M. Dickens, *My Father*, 123; The London *Times*, 11/6/70.
102. M. A. Dickens, 'A Child's Recollections', 70-71.
103. *Mary Boyle, Her Book*, 242-3.
104. Storey, *Dickens and Daughter*, 137.
105. Ibid.
106. Hunt. MS., Georgina Hogarth to Mrs. Fields, 4/7/70.
107. *Dick.*, IV (1908), 290; Millais, *Life and Letters*, 31, 33.
108. H. D. *Let.*, II, 448.
109. West. A. MS., Dean Stanley's Recollections. The material for this paragraph and the two that follow has been adapted largely from these recollections; from Locker-Lampson's *My Confidences*, 328-9; and from Hotten, *Charles Dickens*, 331-3. For further details on Dean Stanley's recollections see my article, 'Charles Dickens and Dean Stanley', *Dick.*, LII (1956), 152-6.
110. Nonesuch, III, 733, E. Ollier, 3/8/69.
111. Hunt. MS., Georgina Hogarth to Mrs. Fields, 18/8/71, 18/6/72.

CHAPTER TEN

[pp. 143-161]

1. My account of the funeral sermon has been adapted from Dean Stanley's Recollections, West. A. MS.; Hotten, *Charles Dickens*, 334-9; and the London *Illustrated News*, Supp., 25/6/70.
2. Walker MS., Georgina Hogarth to Mary Howitt, 27/9/70.
3. Ibid.
4. Hunt. MS., Georgina Hogarth to Mrs. Fields, 5/8/72.
5. Walker M.S., Georgina Hogarth to Mary Howitt, 27/9/70.
6. The *Athenaeum*, 694, 29/11/79.

7. Miller MS.
8. Hunt. MS., Georgina Hogarth to Mrs. Fields, 4/7/70.
9. Ibid., Leslie Stephen to Fields, 31/7/70.
10. Fields Papers, Diary, 30/8/70.
11. Ouvry Papers, Georgina Hogarth to Ouvry, 8/7/70; Hunt. MS., Georgina Hogarth to Mrs. Fields, 4/7/70; Forster, *Life*, 655, n.
12. Dick. H. MS., Georgina Hogarth to Jane, 15/8/70.
13. Nonesuch, III, 797, 798-9.
14. Fields Papers, Diary, 30/8/70.
15. Bigelow, *Retrospections*, IV, 383.
16. Ouvry Papers, Georgina Hogarth to Ouvry, [12/6/70].
17. Ibid.
18. Ibid., [18/6/70].
19. Ibid., [13/7/70].
20. Dick. H. MS., The Estate of Charles Dickens, Executors' Account, 1/8/70.
21. Ouvry Papers, Georgina Hogarth to Ouvry, 19/9/70.
22. Ibid., [30/7/70, 31/7/70].
23. Ibid., Barnett to Ouvry, 6/1/68; Lewis & Lewis to Fechter, 21/3/68; Fechter to Dickens, 19/5/68; Fechter to Ouvry, n.d.
24. Ibid., Georgina Hogarth to Ouvry, 1/7/70.
25. Hunt. MS., Georgina Hogarth to Mrs. Fields, 4/7/70.
26. Ibid., 15/8/70. The MS. of *Our Mutual Friend* is now owned by the Pierpont Morgan Library.
27. Ibid., Dickens to Ouvry, 12/2/70.
28. Quoted in M. Harrison, *Charles Dickens*, 251.
29. Ouvry Papers, Georgina Hogarth to Ouvry, 1/11/70.
30. Ibid., 14/8/70.
31. Ibid., Thursday afternoon.
32. Ibid., [10/8/70]; Hunt. MS., Dickens to Wills, 8/10/59; Ouvry Papers, Georgina Hogarth to Ouvry, 6/9/70.
33. Ouvry Papers, Georgina Hogarth to Ouvry, 3/9/70, 30/10/70, 6/12/70, 8/12/70.
34. Ibid., 8/12/70, 3/12/70, 6/12/70, Thursday.
35. Ibid., [30/6/70], 2/7/70.
36. Ibid., 17/9/70, 19/9/70.
37. Ibid., 5/10/70.
38. Ibid., [18/6/70].
39. Dick. H. MS., Georgina Hogarth to F. Beard, 22/6/70.
40. Wright, *Charles Dickens*, 66.
41. Berg MS., Georgina Hogarth to Carlyle, 27/6/70.
42. Hunt. MS., Georgina Hogarth to Mrs. Fields, 15/8/70.
43. Quoted in C. L. Reade, *Charles Reade*, 391.
44. 'At Dickens's Sale', 502-4.
45. Ouvry Papers, Georgina Hogarth to Ouvry, 6/7/70.
46. Ibid., [10/7/70].
47. Harlan MS., Forster to Carlyle, 11/7/70.
48. Ouvry Papers, Georgina Hogarth to Ouvry, 16/7/70, 25/6/70.
49. Hunt. MS., Georgina Hogarth to Mrs. Fields, 15/8/70.
50. 'Announcements of Gadshill Place Sale', Victoria and Albert Museum.
51. Ouvry Papers, Georgina Hogarth to Ouvry, [30/7/70, 31/7/70].
52. Ibid., 1/8/70.

53. Ibid.
54. Hunt. MS., Georgina Hogarth to Mrs. Fields, 15/8/70; M. Dickens to Mrs. Fields, 1/9/70.
55. Ouvry Papers, Georgina Hogarth to F. Ouvry, 23/7/70.
56. Hunt. MS., Georgina Hogarth to Mrs. Fields, 15/8/70, 29/9/70.
57. Dick. H. MS., Georgina Hogarth to Jane, 15/8/70.
58. Ouvry Papers, Georgina Hogarth to Ouvry, 30/8/70, 3/9/70.
59. Dick. H. MS., Georgina Hogarth to Mrs. Armitage, 5/8/70.
60. Storey, *Dickens and Daughter*, 149.
61. Ouvry Papers, Georgina Hogarth to Ouvry, 12/8/70.
62. Hunt. MS., Georgina Hogarth to Mrs. Fields, 15/8/70.
63. Ibid., M. Dickens to Mrs. Fields, 1/9/70.
64. Harlan MS., Forster to Carlyle, 9/8/70.
65. Hunt. MS., Georgina Hogarth to Mrs. Fields, 15/8/70; Ouvry Papers, Georgina Hogarth to Ouvry, 10/8/70, 12/8/70, 16/8/70, 1/9/70.
66. Harlan MS., Forster to Carlyle, 29/8/70; Ouvry Papers, Georgina Hogarth to Ouvry, [19/8/70].
67. Ouvry Papers, Georgina Hogarth to Ouvry, 16/8/70.
68. Ibid., 24/8/70, 25/8/70, 16/9/70.
69. Ibid., 30/8/70.
70. Hunt. MS., Georgina Hogarth to Mrs. Fields, 29/9/70 (partially reproduced in Howe, *Memories of a Hostess*, 193-5).
71. Ibid.; Walker MS., Georgina Hogarth to Mary Howitt, 27/9/70.
72. Hunt. MS., Georgina Hogarth to Mrs. Fields, 15/8/70.
73. Ibid., 29/9/70.

CHAPTER ELEVEN
[pp. 162-187]

1. Ouvry Papers, Georgina Hogarth to Ouvry, 30/10/70.
2. Hunt. MS., Georgina Hogarth to Mrs. Fields, 21/11/70.
3. Ibid.
4. Ibid., 21/11/70, 23/12/70.
5. Ibid., 21/11/70.
6. Ouvry Papers, Georgina Hogarth to Ouvry, n.d. (Friday).
7. Hunt. MS., Georgina Hogarth to Mrs. Fields, 17/3/75.
8. Ibid., 23/12/70.
9. Nonesuch, III, 384, Mrs. Mary Nichols, 1/4/64.
10. Ouvry Papers, S. Dickens to Ouvry, 22/11/70.
11. Ibid., Georgina Hogarth to Ouvry, n.d., 3/12/70.
12. Ibid., n.d. (Wednesday).
13. Ibid., 25/3/70, 12/4/71, 21/9/71, 2/10/71, n.d. (Thursday evening).
14. Hunt. MS., Georgina Hogarth to Mrs. Fields, 17/3/71, 20/4/71.
15. Ouvry Papers, Georgina Hogarth to Ouvry, 25/3/71.
16. Ibid., −/3/71; Hunt. MS., Georgina Hogarth to Mrs. Fields, 1/3/71.
17. Ouvry Papers, Georgina Hogarth to Ouvry, n.d. (Sunday evening), n.d. (Saturday evening).
18. Ibid., Richardson & Sadler to Ouvry, 15/3/71; Georgina Hogarth to Ouvry, 17/3/71.
19. Ibid., 20/3/71, n.d. (Wednesday morning).

20. Hunt. MS., Georgina Hogarth to Mrs. Fields, 20/4/71; Ouvry Papers, Georgina Hogarth to Ouvry, 4/5/71.
21. Hunt. MS., Georgina Hogarth to Mrs. Fields, 20/4/71.
22. Ibid., 10/10/71.
23. Ouvry Papers, Georgina Hogarth to Ouvry, 4/10/71, n.d.
24. Harlan MS., Forster to Carlyle, 29/8/70.
25. Ouvry Papers, C. Dickens, Jr., to Wills, 3/1/71; Wills to C. Dickens. Jr., 4/1/71.
26. Ibid., Georgina Hogarth to Ouvry, n.d. (Thursday morning), 7/3/71.
27. Ibid., 3/3/71, 7/3/71, n.d. (Saturday morning).
28. Ibid., Richardson & Sadler to Ouvry, 3/5/71; Georginia Hogarth to Ouvry, 9/5/71; M. Dickens to Ouvry, 9/5/71; Mr. and Mrs. C. Collins to Ouvry, 11/5/71.
29. Hunt. MS., Georgina Hogarth to Mrs. Fields, 18/6/72.
30. Ibid., Dickens to Dallas, 12/11/64.
31. Ibid., Georgina Hogarth to Mrs. Fields, 18/6/72.
32. Ibid., 5/8/72.
33. Ibid., 20/4/71, 10/10/71.
34. Ibid., 29/1/72, 16/2/72.
35. Ibid., 29/1/72.
36. Ibid., 20/4/71, 5/8/72, 31/12/72.
37. Ibid., 12/5/73.
38. Ibid.
39. Ouvry Papers, Georgina Hogarth to Ouvry, 12/10/71.
40. Hunt. MS., Georgina Hogarth to Mrs. Fields, 28/2/73, 30/8/73.
41. Ibid., 5/6/71, 18/8/71, 2/2/74.
42. Ouvry Papers. Georgina Hogarth to Ouvry, 3/8/72.
43. Ibid., 17/10/73.
44. Ibid., 13/5/74.
45. For this information I am indebted to Miss Gladys Storey.
46. Hunt. MS., Georgina Hogarth to Mrs. Fields, 13/5/74, 9/6/74.
47. Storey, *Dickens and Daughter*, 158.
48. Hunt. MS., Georgina Hogarth to Mrs. Fields, 9/6/74.
49. Ibid., 15/6/74, 18/7/74, 24/10/74.
50. Ibid., 5/6/71, 18/7/74.
51. Ibid., 24/10/74.
52. Ibid.
53. Quoted in M. Dickens, *My Father*, following 86.
54. Hunt. MS., Georgina Hogarth to Mrs. Fields, 24/10/74; Ouvry Papers, Georgina Hogarth to Ouvry, n.d. (Friday).
55. Hunt. MS., Georgina Hogarth to Mrs. Fields, 24/10/74; Morgan MS., M. Dickens to Childs, 6/2/74.
56. Hunt. MS., Georgina Hogarth to Mrs. Fields, 24/10/74.
57. Georgina Hogarth's letter of 13/11/72 is the first without the border.
58. Hunt. MS., Georgina Hogarth to Mrs. Fields, 1/3/71, 20/2/74.
59. Ibid., 5/6/71.
60. Ibid., 20/4/71, 18/6/72, 18/6/73, 9/6/74, 18/7/74, 15/6/75.
61. Ibid., 31/12/72.
62. Ibid., 29/1/72, 16/2/72, 31/12/72.
63. Ibid., 30/8/74.
64. Ibid., 20/2/74, 28/3/74, 13/5/74.
65. Fields Papers, Diary, –/11/72.

66. Bigelow, *Retrospections*, V, 130.
67. Hunt. MS., Georgina Hogarth to Mrs. Fields, 10/10/71.
68. Ibid., 17/3/75.
69. Ibid., 30/12/75, 15/5/76.
70. Ibid., 31/7/76.
71. Ibid., 23/6/77.
72. Ibid., 24/11/73, 24/11/74, 1/10/75.
73. Ibid., 16/1/77.
74. Ibid.

CHAPTER TWELVE
[pp. 188-205]

1. Hunt. MS., Georgina Hogarth to Mrs. Fields, 23/5/77.
2. Ouvry Papers, Georgina Hogarth to Ouvry, 6/5/77.
3. Hunt, MS., Georgina Hogarth to Mrs. Fields, 25/6/77.
4. Ibid., 30/10/77, 22/5/77.
5. Ibid., 23/6/77.
6. Ibid., 30/10/77.
7. Ibid., 15/1/78.
8. Ibid., 23/2/78.
9. Nonesuch, III, 715, Wills, 30/3/69.
10. Ouvry Papers, Georgina Hogarth to Ouvry, 2/10/70.
11. Ibid., n.d. (Sunday afternoon), 1/8/72.
12. Hewlett, *Henry Fothergill Chorley*, 273-4.
13. Hunt. MS., Georgina Hogarth to Mrs. Fields, 3/5/72.
14. Ibid.
15. Nonesuch, II, 271, Lytton, 10/2/51.
16. Hunt. MS., Georgina Hogarth to Mrs. Fields, 5/8/72, 21/2/73.
17. Ibid., Dickens to Georgina Hogarth, 3/1/62.
18. For this information I am indebted to Mrs. Lisa Puckle, Macready's granddaughter.
19. Hunt. MS., Georgina Hogarth to Mrs. Fields, 22/11/71.
20. Ibid., 22/11/71, 12/5/73, 15/6/75, 1/11/75.
21. Ibid., 15/6/75, 1/10/75.
22. Ibid., 17/10/73.
23. Ibid., 17/3/75.
24. Ouvry Papers, Georgina Hogarth to Ouvry, 24/8/70.
25. Hunt. MS., Georgina Hogarth to Mrs. Fields, 21/2/73, 12/5/73, 5/8/72, and elsewhere.
26. Ibid., 23/6/77.
27. Harlan MS., Forster to Carlyle, 25/7/70.
28. Hunt. MS., Georgina Hogarth to Mrs. Fields, 7/1/74, 15/5/76.
29. Nat. Lib. of Scot. MS., Georgina Hogarth to Carlyle, 26/3/78, 1/1/80.
30. Ouvry Papers, Georgina Hogarth to Ouvry, 29/9/70.
31. Hunt. MS., Georgina Hogarth to Mrs. Fields, 29/9/70.
32. Ibid., 1/3/71, 3/4/72.
33. Ibid., 2/4/73.
34. Ibid., 29/9/70, 3/5/72.
35. Ibid., 17/3/75.
36. Ibid., 13/11/72, 2/4/73.
37. Ibid., 11/11/78.

U

38. Upon the publication of *Hide and Seek* in 1854 Georgina Hogarth had apparently remonstrated that the story was an imitation of Dickens. Cf. Nonesuch, II, 570, Georgina Hogarth, 22/7/54.

39. Hunt. MS., Georgina Hogarth to Mrs. Fields, 10/10/71, 30/8/73.

40. Ibid., Fields to Longfellow, 1/1/73.

41. Fields Papers, Diary, 6/11/73.

42. Hunt. MS., Georgina Hogarth to Mrs. Fields, 24/11/73, 29/2/74.

43. Robinson, *Wilkie Collins*, 273.

44. Hunt. MS., Georgina Hogarth to Mrs. Fields, 31/12/72, 21/2/73. The inkstand given by Georgina Hogarth to Grace Norton was presented to the Dickens House in 1929. See *Dick.*, XXV (1929), 141.

45. Hunt. MS., Georgina Hogarth to Mrs. Fields, 12/5/73.

46. Dick. H. MS., M. Dickens to Norton, 9/5/73.

47. Hunt. MS., Georgina Hogarth to Mrs. Fields, 24/9/73.

48. Ibid., 19/6/79.

49. Ibid., 24/10/74.

50. Ibid.

51. Bigelow, *Retrospections*, IV, 368.

52. Hunt. MS., Georgina Hogarth to Mrs. Fields, 30/10/77.

53. Ibid., 22/5/80

54. Ibid., 14/12/83.

55. Nonesuch, III, 780, Rusden, 20/5/70; Forster, *Life*, 829-30.

56. Berg MS., Dickens to Mrs. Gore, 31/5/58.

57. Hunt. MS., Georgina Hogarth to Mrs. Fields, 10/10/71.

58. Ibid., 5/8/72.

59. Ibid.

60. Ouvry Papers, Georgina Hogarth to Ouvry, n.d.

61. Morgan MS., Georgina Hogarth to Harvey, 1/6/80, 3/6/80.

62. Ibid., 13/12/80; Berg MS., Georgina Hogarth to Childs, 14/12/80.

63. Information supplied by the Pierpont Morgan Library.

64. Morgan MS., Georgina Hogarth to Harvey, 15/12/80.

65. Sotheran MS., Georgina Hogarth to Ella Winter, 6/4/87. This letter forms part of the 'Dora' Collection owned by Henry Sotheran, Ltd., by whose kind permission this excerpt is quoted.

66. Hunt. MS., Georgina Hogarth to Mrs. Fields, 22/5/80.

67. *Dick.*, XXXI (1935), 239. In Georgina Hogarth's letters to Mrs. Fields there are occasional references to visits in Margate.

68. Mrs. Gladys Reece, Ellen Ternan Robinson's daughter, responded generously to my request for her childhood recollections of Georgina Hogarth. She also gave me a prized photograph and an autograph of Miss Hogarth.

69. The quoted portion of the closing sentence is taken from a letter which Georgina Hogarth wrote to Thomas Carlyle, 27/6/70, Berg MS.

CHAPTER THIRTEEN
[pp. 206-227]

1. Hunt. MS., 22/3/78, 10/10/71, 18/8/71, 22/3/78.

2. Ibid., 22/3/78.

3. Morgan MS., Georgina Hogarth to Charles Reade, 22/6/78.

4. Hunt. MS., Georgina Hogarth to Mrs. Fields, 26/6/78.

5. Ibid., 26/6/78, 11/8/78.

6. Ibid., 11/8/78.

7. Ibid., 13/10/78, 19/9/78.

8. Adrian MS., Mrs. C. Dickens to Robert Hogarth, 26/9/78.

9. Hunt. MS., Georgina Hogarth to Mrs. Fields, 11/11/78.

10. Storey, *Dickens and Daughter*, 163.

11. Hunt. MS., Georgina Hogarth to Mrs. Fields, 11/11/78, 27/2/79.

12. Storey, *Dickens and Daughter*, 165. According to G. B. Shaw, at one time Katey considered burning the letters. Asked for his opinion, he told her 'that the sentimental sympathy of the nineteenth century with the man of genius tied to a commonplace wife had been rudely upset by a man named Ibsen, and that posterity might sympathize much more with the woman who was sacrificed to the genius's uxoriousness to the appalling extent of having had to bear ten children in sixteen years than with a grievance which, after all, amounted only to the fact that she was not a female Charles Dickens'. Shaw urged Katey to give the letters to the British Museum, 'there to abide the judgment of the future'.—*Time and Tide*, 27/7/1935, 1111-12.

13. Storey, *Dickens and Daughter*, 131.

14. Ibid.

15. Hunt. MS., Georgina Hogarth to Mrs. Fields, 27/2/79, 23/12/74.

16. Ibid., 13/10/78, 19/9/78.

17. Ibid., 11/11/78.

18. Ibid., 22/5/80. Gad's Hill was sold to Major Budden, who lived there from 1879 to 1891.

19. Ibid., 27/2/79. Alfred's daughters were reared by a sister of his wife and eventually came to England.

20. Ibid., 19/6/79.

21. Ibid.

22. Ibid., 13/10/78.

23. Ibid., 19/9/78.

24. Ibid., 19/6/79.

25. Ouvry Papers, F. Chapman to Georgina Hogarth, 13/1/79; Georgina Hogarth to Ouvry, 17/7/79.

26. Ibid., 1/8/79, 2/8/79, 3/8/79.

27. H. C. Dickens MS., G. Bentley to W. Collins, 28/7/79; W. Collins to Georgina Hogarth, 25/7/79.

28. Ouvry Papers, Georgina Hogarth to Ouvry, 17/11/79; C. Dickens, Jr., to Georgina Hogarth, 29/1/79.

29. Ibid., Georgina Hogarth to Ouvry, 31/1/79.

30. Ibid., 13/11/79, 14/11/79.

31. Ibid., 14/11/79, 16/11/79.

32. Storey, *Dickens and Daughter*, 164.

33. Hunt. MS., Georgina Hogarth to Mrs. Fields, 18/12/81. A one-volume edition of the letters was published in 1893.

34. Ibid., 25/12/82.

35. St. Pan. Pub. Lib. MS., Georgina Hogarth to Mrs. G. L. Banks, 11/2/80, 20/3/80.

36. Hunt. MS., Georgina Hogarth to Mrs. Fields, 20/2/74.

37. Cf. ibid., Dickens to Georgina Hogarth, 19/2/67, and H. D. *Let.*, II , 279,

38. Cf. Berg MS., Dickens to Georgina Hogarth, 25/11/53, and H. D. *Let.*, I, 337.

39. H. D. *Let.*, I, 99, Macready, 3/1/44.

40. Ibid., 350, Rev. James White, 7/3/54.

41. Ibid., 268, Mrs. Charles Dickens, 13/11/51.
42. Ibid., 123, 8/11/44; II, 258, Georgina Hogarth, 11/5/66.
43. Cf. *Mr. and Mrs.*, 121, 19/12/46, and H. D. *Let.*, I, 165.
44. Cf. Hunt. MS., Dickens to Georgina Hogarth, 3/1/62, and H. D. *Let.*, II, 172.
45. H. D. *Let.*, I, 422, W. Collins, 19/1/56.
46. Cf. Hunt. MS., Dickens to Georgina Hogarth, 8/1/62, and H. D. *Let.*, II, 173.
47. Cf. Nonesuch, III, 123, W. Collins, 16/9/59, and H. D. *Let.*, II, 101. See also Robinson, *Wilkie Collins*, 132-3. Robinson dates this letter 30/10/59.
48. Hunt. MS., Dickens to Wills, 6/6/67.
49. Sermon of the Reverend Justin D. Fulton, the Boston *Herald*, 4/7/70.
50. Hunt. MS., Georgina Hogarth to Mrs. Fields, 18/8/71.
51. H. D. *Let.*, I, 352-3, Wills, 12/4/54.
52. Ibid., II, 130, Collins, 24/10/60.
53. Ibid., I, 19-20, Mitton, 6/3/39.
54. Ibid., 135, Georgina Hogarth, 4/2/45.
55. Cf. Nonesuch, III, 779, Rusden, 20/5/70, and H. D. *Let.*, III, 297.
56. H. D. *Let.*, III, 297-8, Rusden, 20/5/70.
57. Cf. Hunt. MS., Dickens to Wills, 6/6/67, and H. D. *Let.*, II, 290-1.
58. H. D. *Let.*, III, 106, Mrs. C. Clarke, 22/7/48.
59. Hunt. MS., Georgina Hogarth to Ouvry, 5/5/79.
60. Professor Gerald G. Grubb first suggested to me the strong probability of Wilkie Collins's responsibility for some of the obliterations. A subsequent examination of Dickens MSS. in the Huntington Library has lent support to Professor Grubb's theory.
61. Hunt. MS., Dickens to Georgina Hogarth, 24/1/69.
62. *Mr. and Mrs.*, 59-60 [?6/3/36].
63. H. D. *Let.*, I, 14, Mrs. C. Dickens, 1/11/38.
64. Ibid., III, 149, 25/10/53.
65. Cf. *Mr. and Mrs.*, 208, 14/11/23, and H. D. *Let.*, I, 330.
66. H. D. *Let.*, I, 139 and 141, Mitton, 17/2/45.
67. Cf. Nonesuch, II, 570, Georgina Hogarth, 22/7/54, and H. D. *Let.*, I, 359-60.
68. Cf. Hunt. MS., Dickens to Georgina Hogarth, 19/4/66, and H. D. *Let.*, II, 255.
69. Cf. Hunt. MS., Dickens to Wills, 2/1/62, 5/4/62, and H. D. *Let.*, II, 171.
70. The published letter dated 16/11/64 includes one paragraph written 2/4/64; that for 30/6/67 takes its last paragraphs from one not written until 3/8/69. Similarly, two letters, 13/6/67 and 3/8/69, have been combined under the earlier date.
71. Cf. Nonesuch, II, 880-1, Georgina Hogarth, 9/9/57, and H. D. *Let.*, II, 28.
72. *Westminster Review*, –/4/80, 205-16.
73. The *Athenaeum*, 29/11/79, 687-8.
74. The *Saturday Review*, 6/12/79, 694.
75. The *Fortnightly Review*, 1/12/79, 845-63.
76. Ouvry Papers, Georgina Hogarth to Ouvry, 12/12/79.
77. The London *Times*, 27/12/79, 9.
78. The *Atlantic Monthly*, –/2/80, 280-2.
79. The *Contemporary Review*, –/1/80, 77-85.
80. *Dick.*, XLV (1940), 199.
81. Hunt. MS., Georgina Hogarth to Mrs. Fields, 26/6/80.

82. Ibid., Storey, *Dickens and Daughter*, 166-7.
83. Hunt. MS., Georgina Hogarth to Mrs. Fields, 23/6/81, 18/12/81.
84. Ibid., 2/5/82, 20/6/82, 27/2/83.
85. Ibid., 18/10/82, 31/10/82.
86. Ibid., 25/12/82.

CHAPTER FOURTEEN
[pp. 228-240]

1. Hunt. MS., Georgina Hogarth to Mrs. Fields, 17/3/75, 15/1/78, 17/8/83.
2. *Nash's Magazine*, –/9/1911.
3. Hunt. MS., Georgina Hogarth to Mrs. Fields, 10/10/71.
4. Ibid., 20/11/73.
5. *The Atlantic Monthly*, –/2/73, 237-9.
6. Hunt. MS., Georgina Hogarth to Mrs. Fields, 20/2/74.
7. Nonesuch, I, 548, R. H. Horne, 13/11/43.
8. Ouvry Papers, Nation to Forster, 20/11/73.
9. Ibid., Forster to Ouvry, 20/11/73.
10. Ibid., Georgina Hogarth to Ouvry, 23/11/73.
11. Ibid., Forster to Ouvey, 22/11/73.
12. Ibid., Nation to Ouvry, 23/11/73.
13. Except for minor modifications, this discussion of Nation's attempt to revive *The Strange Gentleman* has followed my article in *Dick.*, LI (1955), 158-60.
14. Hunt. MS., Georgina Hogarth to Mrs. Fields, 15/5/76.
15. Ibid.
16. Ibid.
17. Ibid., 17/8/83. Georgina Hogarth's letter does not identify the author of the article nor the newspaper in which it appeared.
18. Ibid., Georgina Hogarth to Ouvry, 15/5/79.
19. Information concerning the disposition of the Ouvry Letters, as summarized in these paragraphs, is given in a handmade book in the Victoria and Albert Museum: *Charles Dickens's Birthplace and Unpublished Letters*, by Thomas William Newton, 1844, II, 27ff. I am indebted to Professor Gerald G. Grubb for calling this item to my attention.
20. Hunt. MS., Georgina Hogarth to Mrs. Fields, 16/2/84.
21. Ibid.
22. East. H. MS., Georgina Hogarth to P. Fitzgerald, 3/31/93. I am indebted to Mr. W. J. Carlton for the transcript of this letter, as well as the identification of the John Dickens letter referred to.
23. East. H. MS., Georgina Hogarth to P. Fitzgerald, 19/12/87, 11/12/90, 6/3/81, 24/3/1911.
24. Kitton, *Pen and Pencil*, 'Introductory', vi.
25. Ibid., 61.
26. Hunt. MS., Georgina Hogarth to Mrs. Fields, 28/12/1900.
27. Kitton, *Pen and Pencil*, 169.
28. Ibid., 128.
29. Forster, *Life*, 69, n. 74.
30. Kitton, *Pen and Pencil*, 173.
31. Berg MS., Georgina Hogarth to [Sabin, Dexter], 3/3/91.
32. Kitton, *Pen and Pencil*, 82.

33. Wright, *Charles Dickens*, 283.

34. My summary of the Druce case is based on Besterman, *The Druce-Portland Case*.

35. Anstey, *A Long Retrospect*, 291.

36. Adrian MS., Georgina Hogarth to Blanche Swanson, 17/1/1908.

CHAPTER FIFTEEN

[pp. 241-253]

1. Hunt. MS., Georgina Hogarth to Mrs. Fields, 18/7/74, 27/2/83.

2. Ibid., 27/2/83.

3. Ibid.

4. Ibid., 14/12/83, 19/1/88.

5. Ibid., 16/2/84.

6. *Letters of Henry James*, I, 16, Alice James, 10/3/[69].

7. Storey, *Dickens and Daughter*, 177.

8. This paragraph and the one following are a summary of Austerlund, 'The Visit to Moline Illinois of Capt. Francis Jeffrey Dickens'.

9. Hunt. MS., Georgina Hogarth to Mrs. Fields, 13/6/87.

10. For these details I am indebted to Mrs. Robert Shuckburgh (Olive Dickens) and Mrs. Alec Waley (Elaine Dickens).

11. Hunt. MS., Georgina Hogarth to Mrs. Fields, 27/2/83.

12. Ibid., 13/6/87.

13. Ibid., 13/8/87.

14. 'The First Reading of Charles Dickens', New York *Daily Tribune*, 28/10/87.

15. Hunt. MS., Georgina Hogarth to Mrs. Fields, 19/1/88.

16. Winter, *Old Friends*, 188.

17. Ouvry Papers, Charles Dickens, Jr., to Georgina Hogarth, 19/7/70.

18. Hunt. MS., Georgina Hogarth to Mrs. Fields, 27/2/83, 14/12/83.

19. Hill MS.

20. Hunt. MS., Georgina Hogarth to Mrs. Fields, 20/3/96.

21. Ibid., 20/3/96.

22. M. Dickens, *My Father*, 8.

23. Ibid., 15.

24. Hunt. MS., Georgina Hogarth to Mrs. Fields, 17/6/97.

25. Ibid., 17/6/97, 27/12/97; Ouvry Papers, Henry F. Dickens to Jarrett, 4/8/96. Only the previous year Charley, needing money to pay his creditors, had sold his reversing interest in the Dickens estate to Harry. When Mamie's assets were divided among the heirs, Charley's share fell to Harry, who was happy 'to make some provision for [his] poor brother's widow out of this', there being a substantial balance after he had repaid himself the amount given originally for the reversible interest.

26. Hunt. MS., Georgina Hogarth to Mrs. Fields, 27/12/97, 15/2/98. Mary Angela Dickens (Mekitty) was the author of *Dickens's Dream Children* (illustrated by Harold Copping), several magazine articles on her father, and popular novels: *Cross Currents*, 1891; *A Mere Cypher*, 1893; *A Valiant Ignorance*, 1894; *Prisoners of Silence*, 1895; *Against the Tide*, 1897; *On the Edge of a Precipice*, 1899; *The Wastrel*, 1901; *Unveiled*, 1907; *The Debtor*, 1912.

27. Hunt. MS., Georgina Hogarth to Mrs. Fields, 15/2/98.

28. Ibid., 17/6/97.
29. Ibid., 22/5/77.
30. Ibid., 16/1/77.
31. Ibid., 17/6/97.
32. For these details I am indebted to Mr. Henry Charles Dickens, O.B.E., Georgina Hogarth's nephew.
33. Hunt. MS., Georgina Hogarth to Mrs. Fields, 27/12/97.
34. Fields Papers, Diary, –/5/98.
35. Hunt. MS., Georgina Hogarth to Mrs. Fields, 15/2/98.
36. Fields Papers, Diary, –/5/98.
37. Hunt. MS., Georgina Hogarth to Mrs. Fields, 28/12/1900.
38. Ibid.
39. Ibid., 23/2/1901.
40. Ibid., 25/2/70, 23/2/1901.

CHAPTER SIXTEEN
[pp. 254-267]

1. Hunt. MS., Georgina Hogarth to Mrs. Fields, 23/2/1901.
2. Cf. Bishop, 'Henry James Criticizes *The Tory Lover*'.
3. Hunt. MS., Georgina Hogarth to Mrs. Fields, 27/12/1901.
4. Storey, *Dickens and Daughter*, 166-74.
5. E. H. Collin, *Lost Years, a Backward Glance at Australian Life and Manners* (quoted in *Dick.*, XLV [1949], 219).
6. Matz, 'Miss Georgina Hogarth', 122-3.
7. Mr. William Miller has a note addressed by Georgina Hogarth to Emilie M. Miniken, Honorary Secretary of the Needlework and Charitable Guild, 12/11/1906: 'I enclose my annual small contribution to your guild of needlework'.
8. Information concerning Miss Hogarth's reactions to Henry F. Dickens's readings was given me by Mrs. Shuckburgh (Olive Dickens) and Mrs. Waley (Elaine Dickens).
9. For this information I am indebted to Mr. Leslie Staples.
10. Hunt. MS., Georgina Hogarth to Mrs. Fields, 11/2/1907.
11. Dick. H. MS., 'Copy of the Statement of Charley Peters'.
12. Ibid., H. F. Dickens to B. W. Matz, 1907.
13. Mrs. Lisa Puckle, Macready's granddaughter, generously provided the information introduced in this paragraph.
14. Adrian MS., Georgina Hogarth to Sir Nevil Macready, 6/2/1913.
15. Hunt. MS., Georgina Hogarth to Mrs. Fields, 26/6/78.
16. Ellis, *Ainsworth*, II, 37.
17. Adrian MS., Georgina Hogarth to Mrs. Swanson, 8/1/1908, 17/1/1908.
18. Matz, 'Miss Georgina Hogarth', 122-3.
19. Miller MS., Georgina Hogarth to W. Miller, 16/8/1911.
20. Dick. H. MS., Georgina Hogarth to L. Staples, 12/9/1913.
21. *Dick.*, IX (1913), 312.
22. East. H. MS., Georgina Hogarth to Cattermole (son of G. C. Cattermole), 8/6/78.
23. Storey, *Dickens and Daughter*, 188; Adrian MS., Georgina Hogarth to Mrs. Swanson, 17/1/1908.
24. Hunt. MS., Georgina Hogarth to Mrs. Fields, 30/12/1911.

296 *Georgina Hogarth and the Dickens Circle*

25. Ibid.

26. Ibid., 16/1/77.

27. Quoted in *Dick.*, VII (1911), 283.

28. Hunt. MS., Georgina Hogarth to Mrs. Fields, 30/12/1911.

29. *Dick.*, VIII (1912), 41.

30. Hunt. MS., Georgina Hogarth to Mrs. Fields, 31/1/1912.

31. *Dick.*, VIII (1912), 41.

32. Ibid., 191.

33. Miller MS., Georgina Hogarth to W. Miller, 15/4/1911.

34. Hunt. MS., Georgina Hogarth to Mrs. Fields, 17/1/1913.

35. *Dick.*, IX (1913), 46.

36. Adrian MS., Georgina Hogarth to Sir Nevil Macready, 7/2/1913.

37. Howe, *Memories*, 304-5.

38. Spencer, *Forty Years*, 98-100. Though Spencer does not give the exact year in which he met Miss Hogarth for the first time, all the evidence points to 1906. On 5th December of that year Miss Hogarth opened the bazaar of the Needlework and Charitable Guild, for which she had sought the Dickens first editions. See *Dick.*, III (1907), 21.

39. For this information I am indebted to Mr. Henry Charles Dickens, O.B.E.

40. Morgan MS., Georgina Hogarth to an unnamed addressee, n.d. The letter was sent from 70 Wynnstay Gardens, where Miss Hogarth lived in the late 80's.—Ibid., Georgina Hogarth to C. E. Shepherd, 23/6/99.

41. Spencer, *Forty Years*, 98-102. To E. D. Brooks of Minneapolis Spencer sold the manuscript for just double what he had paid. In 1919 it was purchased for the Pierpont Morgan Libary, where two other manuscripts had preceded it—*The Battle of Life* and *Our Mutual Friend*.

42. *Dick.*, V (1909), 172.

43. Ibid., XIV (1918), 67.

44. Information furnished by Major C. E. Pym, Brasted, Westerham, Kent.

45. Ibid.

46. *Dick.*, XII (1916), 80.

47. Information supplied by Mr. Henry Charles Dickens, O.B.E.

48. Philadelphia *Public Ledger*, 19/11/1916.

49. Nonesuch, II, 784, Washington Irving, 5/7/56.

50. Hunt. MS., Georgina Hogarth to Mrs. Fields, 26/6/80.

51. Nonesuch, III, 29, Cerjat, 7/7/78.

52. After her death Georgina Hogarth's effects realized £317. 6s. 3d. Storey, *Dickens and Daughter*, 191.

53. Miller MS., Mrs. Perugini to W. Miller, 25/4/1917.

54. Matz, 'Miss Georgina Hogarth', 122.

55. Berg MS., Dickens's Memorandum Book. This passage has been reproduced in published sources, one of the more readily accessible being *The Recollections of Sir Henry Dickens*, 20.

Bibliography

I. *Unpublished Sources*

(Manuscript sources are referred to in the Notes by the identifying symbols given in parentheses below.)

Letters in the author's possession (Adrian MS.).

Letters and other documents in the Berg Collection of the New York Public Library (Berg MS.).

Letter owned by Mr. E. S. Budden, Reading, England (Budden MS.).

Letter in the William Andrews Clark Memorial Library, Los Angeles, California (Clark MS.).

Letters owned by Mr. Henry Charles Dickens, O.B.E., London (H. C. Dickens MS.).

Letters and other documents in the Dickens House, London (Dick. H. MS.).

Letters in the Percy Fitzgerald Collection, Eastgate House, Rochester, England (East. H. MS.).

Letters and diaries of Mrs. James T. Fields in the Massachusetts Historical Society Library, Boston (Fields Papers).

Letters owned by Professor J. Lee Harlan, Fort Collins, Colorado (Harlan MS.).

A handwritten manuscript by the late T. W. Hill, *Charles Dickens, the Younger*, owned by Mr. Leslie Staples, London (Hill MS.).

Letters and other documents in the Henry E. Huntington Library and Art Gallery, San Marino, California (Hunt. MS.).

Letters owned by Lady Hermione Cobbold, Knebworth, Hertfordshire, England (Lytton MS.).

Letters owned by Mr. William Miller, Brighton, England (Miller MS.).

Letters and other documents in the Pierpont Morgan Library, New York (Morgan MS.).

Letters in the National Library of Scotland, Edinburgh (Nat. Lib. Scot. MS.).

Letters and other documents relating to Frederic Ouvry's association with members of the Dickens family; owned by Sir Leslie Farrer, K.C.V.O., London (Ouvry Papers).

Letters in the Borough of Saint Pancras Public Libraries, London (St. Pan. Pub. Lib. MS.).

Letters in the 'Dora' Collection; owned by Henry Sotheran, Ltd., London (Sotheran MS.).

Letters and other documents in the Victoria and Albert Museum, London (V. and A. MS.).

Letters owned by Mrs. Mary Walker, Traralgon, Victoria, Australia (Walker MS.).

A handwritten manuscript in the Westminster Abbey Library, *Recollections of Events Connected with Westminster Abbey*, by Dean A. P. Stanley (West. A. MS.).

II. Published Sources

[Ainger, Alfred.] 'Mr. Dickens' Amateur Theatricals'. *Macmillan's Magazine* (January 1871), 206-15.

Andersen, Hans Christian. 'A Visit to Charles Dickens.' *Eclectic Magazine*, N.S., XIII (1871), 183-96.

Anstey, Frank [Thomas Anstey Guthrie]. *A Long Retrospect*. London, 1936.

Asterlund, Mrs. Louise Jamieson. 'The Visit to Moline, Illinois, of Capt. Francis Jeffrey Dickens, Son of Charles Dickens, the English Novelist.' *Journal of the Illinois State Historical Society*, XVIII (1925), 386-89.

Aylmer, Felix. 'Dickens and Ellen Ternan.' *The Dickensian*, LI (1955), 85-6.

Besterman, Theodore. *The Druce-Portland Case*. London, 1935.

Bigelow, John. *Retrospections of an Active Life*. New York, 1913.

Bishop, Ferman. 'Henry James Criticizes *The Tory Lover*.' *American Literature*, XXVII (1955), 262-4.

Bliss, Trudy, ed. *Jane Welsh Carlyle. A New Selection of Her Letters*. New York, 1950.

Boyle, Mary. *Mary Boyle, Her Book*. New York, 1902.

Butt, John. 'The Composition of *David Copperfield*.' *The Dickensian*, XLVI (1950), 90-4, and in subsequent issues.

Carlton, William J. 'Who Was Dickens's French Employer?' *The Dickensian*, LI (1955), 149-54.

Carlyle, Alexander, ed. *Letters of Thomas Carlyle*. New York, 1923. *New Letters of Thomas Carlyle*. London, 1904.

Cellier, Francois, and Cunningham Bridgeman. *Gilbert and Sullivan and Their Operas*. Boston, 1914.

The Charles Dickens Dinner: An Authentic Record of the Public Dinner Given to Mr. Charles Dickens, at the Freemasons' Hall, London, on Sunday, November 2, 1867, Prior to His Departure for the United States. London, 1867.

'Charles Dickens at Home.' *Every Saturday* (6 October 1866), 396-8.

Dana, H. W. L. 'Longfellow and Dickens: The Story of a Trans-Atlantic Friendship.' *Cambridge Historical Society*, XXVIII (1942).

'Devonshire House Theatricals.' *Bentley's Miscellany* (June 1851), 660-7.

Dexter, Walter, ed. *The Letters of Charles Dickens*. London, 1938. *The Love Romance of Charles Dickens*. London, 1936. *Mr. and Mrs. Charles Dickens. His Letters to Her*. London, 1935.

Dickens, Alfred T. 'My Father and His Friends.' *Nash's Magazine* (September 1911), 627-42.

Dickens, Charles, Jr. 'Glimpses of Charles Dickens.' *North American Review*, CXVI (1895), 525-37, and subsequent issue. 'Reminiscences of My Father.' *Windsor Magazine*. Supplement (December 1934), 1-46.

Dickens, Sir Henry F. 'The History of the Gad's Hill Gazette.' *The Dickensian*, XXV (1929), 255-9.

Memories of My Father. New York, 1929.

The Recollections of Sir Henry Dickens, K.C. London, 1934.

Dickens, Mary [Mamie]. *Charles Dickens*. London, 1885.

My Father as I Recall Him. London, 1897.

Dickens, Mary Angela. 'My Grandfather as I Knew Him'. *Nash's Magazine* (October 1911).

'A Child's Recollections of Gad's Hill.' *Strand Magazine* (January 1897), 67-74.

Dictionary of American Biography.

Dictionary of National Biography.

Dolby, George. *Charles Dickens as I Knew Him*. London, 1885.

Duffy, Sir Charles Gavan. *Conversations with Carlyle*. London, 1892.

Ellis, S. M., ed. *The Letters and Memoirs of Sir William Hardman*. Second Series: 1863-1865. London, 1925.

William Harrison Ainsworth and His Friends. London, 1911.

Fielding, K. J. 'Charles Dickens and Colin Rae Brown.' *Nineteenth-Century Fiction*, VII (1952), 103-10.

'Charles Dickens and His Wife. Fact or Forgery?' *Etudes Anglaises*, VIII (1955), 212-22.

'Dickens and the Hogarth Scandal.' *Nineteenth-Century Fiction*, X (1955), 64-74.

'Dickens to Miss Burdett Coutts.' London *Times Literary Supplement* (2, 9 March 1951).

Fields, James T. 'Our Whispering Gallery.' *Atlantic Monthly*, XXVIII (August-November 1871).

Finlay, Francis D. 'Peeps at Dickens.' *The Dickensian*, XXIX (1933), 99-100.

'The First Reading by Charles Dickens.' New York *Daily Tribune* (28 October 1887), 4.

Fitzgerald, Percy. *Memories of Charles Dickens*. Bristol, 1913.

Fitz-Gerald, S. J. Adair. *Dickens and the Drama*. London, 1910.

Ford, George H. *Dickens and His Readers*. Princeton, New Jersey, 1955.

Forster, John. *The Life of Charles Dickens*, ed. J. W. T. Ley. London, 1928.

Francis, John. *A Literary Chronicle of Half a Century*. London, 1888.

Frith, W. P. *My Autobiography and Reminiscences*. London, 1887.

Gissing, Alfred Charles. *William Holman Hunt, a Biography*. London, 1936.

Gray, W. Forbes. 'The Edinburgh Relatives and Friends of Dickens.' *The Dickensian*, XXII (1926), 218-26, and in successive issues.

Greville, Charles C. F. *The Greville Diary*, ed. Philip W. Wilson. Garden City, 1927.

Grubb, Gerald G. 'Charles Dickens and His Brother Fred.' *The Dickensian*, L (1954), 123-31.

    'Dickens and Ellen Ternan.' *The Dickensian*, XLIX (1953), 121-8.

    'An Unknown Play by Dickens?' *The Dickensian*, XLVI (1950), 94-5.

Haight, Gordon S., ed. *The George Eliot Letters*. New Haven, 1954-5.

The Halifax Courier and Guardian Historical Almanack for 1924 and 1932.

Harris, Edwin. *Gad's Hill Place and Charles Dickens*. London, 1910.

Harrison, Michael. *Charles Dickens*. London, 1953.

Hewlett, Henry G., ed. *Henry Fothergill Chorley: Autobiography*. London, 1873.

Hill, T. W. 'The Staplehurst Railway Accident.' *The Dickensian*, XXXVIII (1942), 147-52.

[Hogarth, Georgina, and Mary Dickens, eds.]. *The Letters of Charles Dickens*. London, 1880-1882.

Hotten, John Camden. *Charles Dickens. The Story of His Life*. London, 1870.

House, Humphry. *All in Due Time*. London, 1955.

Howe, M. A. DeWolfe. *Memories of a Hostess*. Boston, 1922.

Hutton, Laurence, ed. *Letters of Charles Dickens to Wilkie Collins, 1851-1870*. Selected by Georgina Hogarth. London, 1892.

Johnson, Edgar. *Charles Dickens. His Tragedy and Triumph*. New York, 1952.

    The Heart of Charles Dickens. New York, 1952.

Kitton, Frederic G. *Charles Dickens by Pen and Pencil*. London, 1889-1890.

La Chance, Vernon, ed. 'The Diary of Francis Dickens.' *Bulletin of the Department of History and Political and Economic Science* in Queen's University, Kingston, Ontario, Canada (May 1930).

Latimer, Elizabeth W. 'A Girl's Recollections of Charles Dickens.' *Lippincott's Magazine* (September 1893).

Lehmann, Rudolph C. *Memories of Half a Century*. London, 1908.

Locker-Lampson, Frederick. *My Confidences*. London, 1896.

Lockhart, J. G. *Memoirs of Sir Walter Scott*. London, 1900, 1914.

Lubbock, Percy, ed. *The Letters of Henry James*. New York, 1920.

Lucas, E. V. *Reading, Writing, and Remembering*. London, 1932.

Macready, William Charles. *The Diaries of William Charles Macready*, ed. William Toynbee. London, 1912.

Matz, B. W. 'Miss Georgina Hogarth." *The Dickensian*, XIII (1917), 122-3.

    'A New Portrait of Dickens.' *The Dickensian*, XV (1919), 37-40.

Millais, John G. *The Life and Letters of Sir John Everett Millais*. New York, 1899.

Miller, William. *The Dickens Student and Collector*. Cambridge, U.S.A., 1946.

Moran, Benjamin. *The Journal of Benjamin Moran, 1857-1865*, ed. Sarah Agnes Wallace and Frances Elma Gillespie. Chicago, 1948-1949.

Nisbet, Ada. *Dickens and Ellen Ternan*. Berkeley, California, 1952.

Perugini, Kate Dickens. 'Edwin Drood and the Last Days of Charles Dickens.' *Pall Mall Magazine* (June 1906), 643-54.

Ray, Gordon N. *The Letters and Private Papers of William Makepeace Thackeray*. Cambridge, U.S.A., 1945-1946.

Thackeray. New York, 1955.

Reade, C. L., and Compton Reade. *Charles Reade, a Memoir*. New York, 1887.

Ritchie, Anne Thackeray. *Letters of Anne Thackeray Ritchie*. London, 1924.

Chapters from Some Unwritten Memoirs. New York, 1895.

Robinson, Kenneth. *Wilkie Collins*. New York, 1952.

Rolfe, Franklin P. 'More Letters to the Watsons.' *The Dickensian*, XXXVIII (1942), 113-23, and successive issues.

Rossetti, William Michael. *Some Reminiscences of William Michael Rossetti*. New York, 1906.

Shaplen, Robert. *Free Love and Heavenly Sinners*. New York, 1954.

Spencer, Walter T. *Forty Years in My Bookshop*. Boston, 1923.

Storey, Gladys. *Dickens and Daughter*. London, 1939.

Tuke, (Dame) Margaret Janson. *A History of Bedford College for Women, 1849-1937*. London, 1939.

Van Amerongen, J. B. *The Actor in Dickens*. New York, 1927.

Ward, Henrietta [Mrs. E. M. Ward]. *Memories of Ninety Years*, ed. Isabel G. McAllister. London, 1924.

Winter, William. *Old Friends*. New York, 1909.

Woodring, Carl R. *Victorian Samplers: William and Mary Howitt*. Lawrence, Kansas, 1952.

Wright, Thomas. *The Life of Charles Dickens*. New York, 1936.

Yates, Edmund. *Fifty Years of London Life. Memories of a Man of the World*. New York, 1885.

Index

The following title abbreviations are used in parentheses to identify characters in Dickens's works:

BH *Bleak House*
CC *A Christmas Carol*
DC *David Copperfield*
GE *Great Expectations*

OCS *The Old Curiosity Shop*
OMF *Our Mutual Friend*
OT *Oliver Twist*
TTC *A Tale of Two Cities*

ADELAIDE, QUEEN, 5
Adelphi Theatre, 77
Ainsworth, Harrison, 258
Albany, N.Y., 109
Albany Street, No. 19, Edinburgh, 4
Albaro, 17
Albert, Prince Consort of England, 38; visits Boulogne, 39
All the Year Round, launched, 63; 66, 87, 90, 97, 104, 107; Charley sub-editor of, 116, 119, 122; Dickens's share left Charley, 147; Charley buys Wills's share, 170; 213; Charley resigns editorship of, 247; discontinued, 247
Amateur theatricals, *Animal Magnetism*, 29, 37; *Every Man in His Humour*, 20, 28, 29; *The Frozen Deep*, 37, 46; *The Lighthouse*, 36; *The Merry Wives of Windsor*, 35; *Mr. Nightingale's Diary*, 36; *Not So Bad as We Seem*, 36; *Uncle John*, 37; *Used Up*, 29
Andersen, Hans Christian, visits Gad's Hill, 63; his opinion of Catherine, 63; 65
Anderson Galleries, New York, 264
Animal Magnetism (Inchbald), Georgina's roles in, 29, 37
Appleton, Tom, 116, 165
Armadale (W. Collins), 221
Armitage, Isaac, legacy of, 157; Georgina's houseboy, 158
Armitage, Mrs., 158
Ashburton, Lady Harriet, 27
Asquith, Herbert Henry, 257
Athenaeum, 191, 224
Atkins, Susan, 18
Atlantic Monthly, 206, 218, 225; review of Forster's *Life*, 228-9

Austin, Henry, 21; inspects Tavistock House, 31, and Gad's Hill, 64; death, 83; funeral, 84; 203
Austin, Letitia (Mrs. Henry Austin), 21, 31, 77; pensioned, 83; 84, 139, 148; Georgina's plan for, 170-1
Avenue des Champs Elysées, No. 49, 39

BAKER STREET BAZAAR, 239
Ballantyne, James, 4
Baltimore, Maryland, 109
Baring's Bank, 39
Barnett, H., 149
Barrow, Emily, *see* Lawrence, Mrs. G. W.
Barrow, Robert, 83
Barrow, Thomas, 7
Battle of Life, The (MS.), presented to Mme. Fillonneau, 21; sale of, 203-4; 217, 236
Baylis, Thomas, 91
Beadnell, Maria, 3, 7, 24; publication of Dickens's letters to, 238-9; *see also* Winter, Maria Beadnell
Beard, Dr. Francis Carr, 76; diagnoses Georgina's illness, 77; 79, 94, 96, 116, 120, 121, 123; at Dickens's farewell readings, 132; 139, 148, 150; receives a Dickens keepsake, 153; 216
Beard, Thomas, 8, 10
Bedford College, 35
Beecher, Henry Ward, 108, 200
Belfast, 66, 121
Bengal Mounted Police, 87
Benham, Canon, 239
Bentley, George, 213

w

Fields, Mrs. James T.—*cont.*
flowers for Dickens's birthday, 110;
reflects on him in diary, 111; notes
his dependence on Georgina, 111,
and his dark mood on wedding
anniversary, 113; reflects on Dickens's return to England, 114, and
his strange lot, 114, and his reunion with loved ones, 114; possible knowledge of Ellen, 114; 121,
122; visits England, begins friendship with Georgina, 124-6; impression of Gad's Hill, 125-6;
reports sleepless night in Dickens's
room, 126; impression of Georgina,
126; conscious of shadow over Gad's
Hill, 127; on Dickens-Collins estrangement, 130; feels Georgina's
anomalous position, 131; 132, 133,
134, 137; 146-61 *passim*, 162-89
passim; on Forster's *Life*, 184; 189-
202 *passim*; impression of W. Collins, 198; 206-27 *passim*; death of
Fields, 226; visits Georgina, 227,
252; 228-35 *passim*, 241-52 *passim*,
255-62 *passim*; death, 262
Fillonneau, Amelia, 21, 203-4
Finlay, Francis, 71
Fitzgerald, Percy, 71; Dickens's
interest in, 91; 94; his family, 100;
119; tribute to Mrs. Bouncer, 179-
80; 187; rebuked by Georgina and
Harry, 235-6; Georgina's later
relations with, 236-7; founds Boz
Club, 255
Five Bells Inn, 102
'Flaster Floby', *see* Dickens, Charles,
Jr.
Florence, Italy, 104
Folkestone, Kent, 78, 93
Forster, John, 15, 17; annoys Dickens, 28; 47; represents Dickens in
the separation, 49-52; 56, 66, 67;
opposes American reading tour,
101; 102, 105, 113, 118, 121, 129;
arranges for Dickens's burial,
138-9; co-executor of Dickens's
will, 147; 149, 153; comments on
sale at Christie's, 155, and Charley's
purchase of Gad's Hill, 158-9;
165, 166, 171, 177; works on the
Life, 182-4; 188, 190, 192; death,
194; exhibit of his collection, 194-5;
201, 206, 215, 217; *Atlantic
Monthly* review of the *Life*, 228-9;
opposes unauthorized performance
of *The Strange Gentleman*, 229-31;
sketch of in *Temple Bar*, 231-2;
233, 236

Forster, Mrs. John, 66, 121, 195
Fort House, Broadstairs, not original
of Bleak House, 237
Fort Pitt, 243
Fortnightly Review, 225
*Fortunio and His Seven Gifted Ser-
vants* (Planché), 36
Foxwold Chase, Kent, 253
Franco-Prussian War, 163
Freemasons' Hall, 103
Frith, William Powell, paints por-
trait of Dickens, 62; 154, 194
Frozen Deep, The (Collins), Georgina's
role in, 37; played for Jerrold
benefits, 37, and before Queen,
37-8; 46, 67, 94
Fulham Road, Chelsea, 3
Furnival's Inn, 9

GAD'S HILL, 47, 61, 63; negotiations
for, 64; improvements at, 64-5;
setting and appearance, 66; interior arrangement, 67-8; reception
of guests at, 70-72; wine-cellar
thefts at, 74-5; 79-95 *passim*, 96-
112 *passim*; Dickens returns to
from America, 114-15; 119-39
passim, 145-58 *passim*; Charley's
purchase of, 158-9; 162; desolate
look of, 164; 179, 180, 182, 191,
195; Charley's sale of, 210; 211,
219, 238, 240, 242, 243, 246, 256,
266
Gad's Hill Gazette, The, 89-91
Gallery of Illustration, Regent Street,
38
Garrick, David, 143
Garrick Club, 53, 172
Garrick Club affair, 197
Gaskell, Mrs. Elizabeth, 26
Genoa, 17, 18, 21
Gibbs, Mrs. Charles, 50
Girl at the Waterfall, The (Maclise),
13
Gladstone, William E., 103
Glasgow Athenaeum, 22
Glasgow *Daily Bulletin*, 58
Gloucester Crescent, No. 70, Cath-
erine's home after the separation,
59, 209
Gloucester Terrace, No. 81, first
residence of Georgina and Mamie,
160, 162, 164, 177, 187, 188, 215
Godfrey, Dan, 103
Gordon, Andrew, 62
Gordon, Sheriff, 62
Grace (*The Battle of Life*), 217
Graves, Caroline, 217

316 *Georgina Hogarth and the Dickens Circle*

Lytton, Edward Bulwer (Lord Lytton), 22; amateur theatricals at Knebworth, 28-9; resemblances to Dickens, 28; fondness for Georgina, 79, 95; 103; proposes toast at farewell dinner, 104; gets Dickens keepsakes, 154; death, 191-2; Georgina's affection for, 192; 194, 214

MACAULAY, THOMAS B., 143
Macbeth, 13
Maclise, Daniel, paints Georgina, 13; 31, 194, 195
Macmillan, Alexander, 212, 247, 248
Macready, Benevenuta, 192
Macready, Cecile Spencer, Dickens's opinion of, 192; Georgina's friendship with, 192; devotion to husband, 192; 217; Georgina's later visits with, 257
Macready, Katie, 122
Macready, Lisa, later Mrs. Puckle, 257
Macready, Sir Nevil, 262
Macready, William, 10; Georgina sees him in *Macbeth*, 13; resists hypnotism, 14; 65; reaction to Dickens's reading, 75-6; 77, 86, 116, 127; old age and death, 192-3; publication of reminiscences, 193; 216, 262
Macready, Mrs. William, 10
Macrone, John, 8
Maggs Brothers, Berkeley Square, 262
Maidenhead, Berkshire, 176
Malta, S.S., 171
Malvern, *see* Great Malvern
Manchester, 35, 47
Manchester Free Trade Hall, 46
Manette, Lucie (*TTC*), 109
Marble Arch, 129
Margate, Kent, 205, 290 *n*.67
Marguerite (*Faust*), 80, 131
Mary (*Used Up*), 220
Marryat, Captain Frederick, 24
Marsh, a stableman, 77-8
Marshalsea Prison, 8
Martineau, Harriet, 217
Mason, R. H., 81
Matz, B. W., 238, 256
Melbourne, Australia, 175
Memorandum Book (Dickens), 44, 266-7
Mendelssohn, Felix, 71
Merry Wives of Windsor, The, 35, 220
Meyerbeer, Giacomo, 103

Micawber, John Dickens as, 235
Midlothian, Sheriff of, *see* Gordon, Sheriff
Milan, Italy, 18
'Mild Glo'ster', *see* Dickens, Mary
Millais, John E., 103, 128; sketches head of Dickens, 137; 173; at Perugini wedding, 177
Miller, William, 258, 261
Minto, William, 225
Mitton, Thomas, 22, 221, 223; publication of Dickens's letters to, 233-5
Moline, Illinois, 243, 244
Monument House, Weybridge, 157
Mordaunt divorce scandal, 253
Morning Chronicle, 6
Mortlake Cemetery, 266
Moscheles, Ignaz, 187
Mozart, Wolfgang, 71, 103
Mr. Nightingale's Diary (Lemon), 36
Mrs. Bouncer, a dog, 69, 78, 79, 115, 131, 157; death of, 178-80
Mulready, William, 41
My Father as I Recall Him (Mamie Dickens), 248
Mystery of Edwin Drood, The, 127, 129, 132, 135, 136, 137, 145, 153, 163

NANCY (*OT*), 120
Naples, Italy, 18
Nash, Mrs., owner of honeymoon cottage, 9
Nash's Magazine, 228
Nation, W. H. C., 230
National Portrait Gallery, Edinburgh, 5
National Portrait Gallery, London, 194
Needlework and Charitable Guild, 255, 262
Nelson Street, No. 2, Edinburgh, 4
Newcastle-on-Tyne, Northumberland, 100
Newman Noggs, a pony, 66, 122
Newton, Thomas, 235
New York, 107, 109, 260
New York Press Dinner, 113
New York *Tribune*, 57, 234
Niece Hawk (*Uncle John*), 37
No Name (W. Collins), 77
Northern Whig, 71
Northwest Mounted Police, 180-1, 243
Norton, Charles E., 117; bereavement of, 198; residence in London, 199; return to America, 199; 243
Norton, Mrs. Charles E., 198, 243
Norton, Grace, 198, 199, 200

Tavistock House, inspection and purchase of, 31; remodelling of, 31-2; theatricals at, 36-7; 39, 43, 48, 49, 50, 58, 62, 65, 70, 82, 127, 154, 200, 209

Taylor, Bayard, 117

Tedworth, Square, No. 15, 244

Temple Bar, 231

Tennyson, Alfred, 20, 103, 127, 143, 201

Ternan, Ellen Lawless, later Mrs. George W. Robinson, hired for performance of *The Frozen Deep*, 46; 48, 53, 54, 56; her unsatisfactory relationship with Dickens, 80; in Staplehurst accident, 94; increasing friendship with Dickens and Georgina, 94; a deterrent to Dickens's American tour, 97, 101; arrangements for during tour, 104-5; in Italy, 106; not to follow Dickens, 106; Mrs. Fields's possible knowledge of, 114; at Gad's Hill during Dickens's last hours, 137; provisions for in will, 147; receives Dickens relic, 153; marriage, 205; friendship with Georgina and Mamie, 205; death, 205; 218, 220, 238-9

Ternan, Frances Eleanor, 94, 104

Ternan, Maria, 46

Ternan, Mrs. Frances Eleanor Jarman, 46

Thackeray, Anne, 36; *see also* Ritchie, Anne Thackeray

Thackeray, William Makepeace, 27, 53, 127, 197

Thomson, George, friend of Robert Burns, 4, 5

Thomson-Stark Letter, 271 *n*.9

Thompson, Sir Henry, 102

Thompson, John, a servant, 64, 94; dismissed for theft, 98-9

Tib (*Every Man in His Humour*), 29

Ticknor and Fields, 125

Tilton *v.* Beecher, 200

Timber, a spaniel, 12, 17, 21, 35

Tiny Tim (*CC*), 104

Titian, 19

Tom Thumb (Fielding), 36

Topping, a groom, 12

Torquay, Devonshire, 75

Tory Lover, The (Sarah Orne Jewett), 254

Tottenham Court Road, London, 239

Traddles, Tommy (*DC*), 25

Tremont Temple, Boston, 218

Trinity Hall, Cambridge, 118, 173

Trinity Parish, New York, 260

Tristram, 80

Trois Frères, The, 219

Trollope, Anthony, 103

Trollope, Thomas, 104

Tuke, Harrison, 75

Tunbridge Wells, Kent, 89

Turk, a dog, 69. 90

Turning the Tables (Poole), 29

Twelfth Night Parties, 16, 24, 36

UNCLE JOHN (Buckstone), 37

Used Up (Mathews), 29, 32, 220

VANCOUVER ISLAND, 123

Vatican, 19, 20

Verdi, Giuseppe, 103

Vesuvius, Mount, 19, 223

Victoria, Queen, 3, 12; sees performance of *The Frozen Deep*, 37-8; Dickens's audience with, 133; sends condolences to Catherine, 145; 201; special copy of *Letters* for, 214; Golden Jubilee, 245; Diamond Jubilee, 249-50; death, 253-4

Victoria and Albert Museum, 194

Victoria Hotel, Naples, 18

Village Coquettes, The, 6, 270 *n*.19

'Violated Letter, The', 56-7

WARREN'S BLACKING, 30 Strand, 129

Warwick, George, 237

Washington, D.C., 109, 110

Water Colour Dudley Gallery, 173

Watson, Hon. Mr. Richard, 29

Watson, Hon. Mrs. Richard, 29, 66, 70, 116

Watson, Sir Thomas, 123

Watson, W. S., 5

Waverley (Scott), 249

Welbeck Abbey, 239, 240

Wellington House Academy, 237

Wellington Street, No. 16, headquarters for *Household Words*, 27

West Indies, 162

Westminster Abbey, Dickens buried in, 139; funeral sermon in, 143-5; 165, 177, 182, 211, 240, 241, 245, 251, 252

Westminster Hotel, New York, 113

Westminster Review, 224

Weybridge, Surrey, 157

What Shall We Have for Dinner? (Catherine Dickens), 32-3

White, Rev. James, 27

White, Mrs. James, 236, 241

White, Lotty, 66

White Rose of York, The, 5

Printed in Great Britain by
The Camelot Press Ltd., London and Southampton

15 Christmas carol
19 climbing Vesuvius
37 The Queen.
47 Gads Hill
65 Gads Hill

74
82
117
118
136-139 Death & funeral
253 Divorce scandal
255 Barkis is willin'